1 MONTH OF
FREE
READING

at

www.ForgottenBooks.com

By purchasing this book you are eligible for one month membership to ForgottenBooks.com, giving you unlimited access to our entire collection of over 1,000,000 titles via our web site and mobile apps.

To claim your free month visit: www.forgottenbooks.com/free133553

ISBN 978-0-428-98337-6
PIBN 10133553

This book is a reproduction of an important historical work. Forgotten Books uses
state-of-the-art technology to digitally reconstruct the work, preserving the original format
whilst repairing imperfections present in the aged copy. In rare cases, an imperfection in
the original, such as a blemish or missing page, may be replicated in our edition. We do,
however, repair the vast majority of imperfections successfully; any imperfections that
remain are intentionally left to preserve the state of such historical works.

THE GREAT REBELLION:

ITS SECRET HISTORY, RISE, PROGRESS, AND DISASTROUS FAILURE.

BY

JOHN MINOR BOTTS, OF VIRGINIA.

𝕿𝖍𝖊 𝕻𝖔𝖑𝖎𝖙𝖎𝖈𝖆𝖑 𝕷𝖎𝖋𝖊 𝖔𝖋 𝖙𝖍𝖊 𝕬𝖚𝖙𝖍𝖔𝖗 𝖁𝖎𝖓𝖉𝖎𝖈𝖆𝖙𝖊𝖉.

"I know no North, no South, no East, no West; I only know my country, my

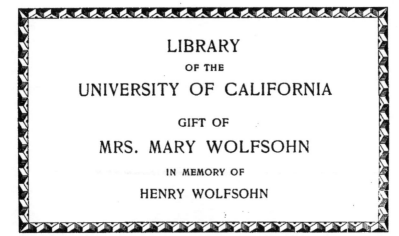

THE GREAT REBELLION:

ITS SECRET HISTORY, RISE, PROGRESS, AND DISASTROUS FAILURE.

BY

JOHN MINOR BOTTS, OF VIRGINIA.

𝕿𝖍𝖊 𝕻𝖔𝖑𝖎𝖙𝖎𝖈𝖆𝖑 𝕷𝖎𝖋𝖊 𝖔𝖋 𝖙𝖍𝖊 𝕬𝖚𝖙𝖍𝖔𝖗 𝖁𝖎𝖓𝖉𝖎𝖈𝖆𝖙𝖊𝖉.

"I know no North, no South, no East, no West: I only know my country, my whole country, and nothing but my country."—JOHN M. BOTTS.

NEW YORK:

HARPER & BROTHERS, PUBLISHERS,

FRANKLIN SQUARE.

1866.

Dedication.

PREFACE.

In presenting this work to the public, I do not *invite* criticism, but, of course, do not expect it will escape either that of the press or others. If it is not harshly and bitterly denounced by the Democratic press, it will fare better than any thing I have said, written, or done since my first entrance upon the political stage.

I have been told that there was an art to be studied in writing a book, different from all other arts and all other writings, without which no one was likely to be successful. If this be true, then this, my first effort at book-writing *for publication*, must prove a sad failure, for the only art I have studied has been the art of telling the truth in a *plain, simple* style that every reader can readily comprehend, and I think there will not be found a passage in the book that it will be necessary for any child to read twice to catch its meaning.

The chief merit I claim for the work is its strict fidelity to historical facts, which will be recognized by every intelligent and impartial reader as he proceeds. The truth is, that in this extraordinary age of rapid progress, one striking political event succeeds another with such remarkable rapidity that the occurrences of yesterday are obliterated from the mind by those of to-day, and thus there is hardly one man in a million who keeps up a connected chain of events in his memory, as my position in public life and other circumstances have enabled me to do.

This Rebellion is, in point of fact, a key to my whole political life. There has been no question of public interest for the last thirty-five years or more in which I have not taken an active part; while my personal associations with many of the leading Democrats enabled me to know much that did not appear upon the surface or to the public, and I had been but a short time in Congress before I was satisfied that there was a most active and persevering party in the South laboring with indefatigable zeal to prepare the people for an ultimate dissolution of the Union, and against this party and their objects I have been warring all the time. I need hardly say that I have made but few speeches for the last twenty-five years that did not contain an admonition to the country on this subject; and it was perhaps owing to this fact, more than any other, that I have been enabled to keep constantly in mind so minute a record of facts as they have occurred.

This work treats of a period and of a history that no other writer, I believe, has undertaken; and without arrogance or presumption, I think I may say that I doubt if there is another person in the country who *could* write it (without *extraordinary labor and research*) that *would*, for those who are most familiar with the facts would rather desire to cover up and conceal what it has been my purpose to expose and lay bare before the world.

When I made up my mind to write this history of the antecedents of the Rebellion, it was with no view to make a dollar by the work: it was to enlighten the public mind, of the South particularly, as to the great impositions that had been for a long succession of years designedly practiced on their credulity by those in whom they had trusted as their leaders, with what disastrous consequences to the fortunes, the happiness, and lives of every household, in every gradation of life, all are now but too familiar.

I have often had occasion to say that no man alive knew more of this war than I did, and if the people knew as much about it as I knew, or if I knew as little as they did, we should probably all have been together in our sympathies.

I find it extremely difficult to blame any man for rushing to arms in defense of his wife and his children, his property, his liberty, and his honor, who could believe they were all invaded and endangered by a government that they had been educated to look upon as their natural and constitutional protector; and all this was whispered and *hissed* into their ears by profligate politicians, stupid and abandoned public presses, who, in most cases, had not the nerve or the will, when the danger arrived, to fight for their own wives and daughters, their own property, their own liberty or honor, but who made every manner of excuse for shirking the dangers and hardships of a war of their own creation; *but the responsibility they can not escape.* For such men the English language is too poor to enable me to express the utter loathing and contempt I feel toward them.

Early in the war I characterized it as "*the rich man's war and the poor man's fight.*" Whether I was right or wrong in this, those who did the hard fighting can best determine.

One thing, at least, all who read this book can tell—now that the war is over and the result ascertained—and that is, whether I would have been more or less worthy of their confidence and regard by advising them to *go into it* or to *stay out of it;* and none will hereafter be surprised, when they have learned the true nature and design of the Rebellion, that from first to last I resolved that no earthly power should induce me to lend it either my co-operation, my respect, or my sympathy.

With these prefatory remarks, this work is respectfully submitted to the candid judgment of an enlightened country by THE AUTHOR.

EDITOR'S PREFACE.

It is a well-known maxim that "a good cause makes a stout heart and a strong arm," and never was the truth of the adage more strikingly illustrated than in the political career of the Hon. John Minor Botts, of Virginia, than whom no man in the United States at this day stands more prominent before the people as a consistent and patriotic advocate and supporter of "THE UNION, THE CONSTITUTION, AND THE ENFORCEMENT OF THE LAWS."

An intimate friend of the illustrious Henry Clay, and a compeer of statesmen and legislators during the most important political eras of the last thirty years, the leading actions of Mr. Botts's life, and his speeches and writings, form as interesting and instructive a portion of the story of the progress of our great Republic from youth to manhood as any part of American history. Especially interesting, however, is the record of the manly and fearless stand made by Mr. Botts in support of the Union cause during the inauguration and progress of the late great conspiracy against the life of the nation, the culmination of which will ever form an eventful era in the world's history. His intimacy with the prominent actors in the great tragedy, and the privilege which he possessed of having the *entree* behind the scenes in the

theatre of the rebellion, placed him in a position "to un-
fold a tale," and "to reveal the secrets of his prison-
house," which, if it does not "harrow up the soul" or
make "the hair stand on end," will assuredly excite to
the utmost the just indignation of every honest man in
the country, and rouse up to action every lover of the
nation in the land.

The circumstances under which this work was written
are as follows:

In October, 1861, the French consul in Richmond
applied to his friend, Mr. Charles Palmer, for all the information he could furnish him upon the question of
secession and the rebellion, the merits or demerits of
which he did not understand. Upon this request being made, Mr. Palmer applied to Mr. Botts, who he was
well aware was far more competent to enlighten his
friend upon the subject than himself, or, indeed, any other
gentleman in the South. Thereupon the information desired was furnished in a letter, which contained, in a con-
cise form, the important history constituting the basis of
the present work. Since 1861, time and circumstances
have led to an enlargement of the history, and the views
it presents have been enforced by additional arguments,
and the facts related substantiated by incontrovertible
testimony.

Shortly after this letter was sent to the French consul,
it became rumored about Richmond that Mr. Botts was
engaged in writing a secret history of the rebellion, and,
as a matter of course, the Confederate authorities were
soon trying to ferret out the truth of the matter. For
some time nothing of any importance in relation to the

subject transpired. On the first day of March, 1862, however, the Confederate Congress passed an act suspending the writ of Habeas Corpus, and declaring martial law. The next morning, which was Sunday, about an hour before daybreak, the late General—then Captain—Godwyn, assistant provost-marshal under General Winder (of Andersonville memory), with a hundred armed men, surrounded Mr. Botts's house, obtained admission, arrested him in bed, and carried him off to a filthy negro jail, where he was lodged, and kept in solitary confinement for eight weeks, his house and family in the mean time being placed in custody of two of General Winder's satellites. After his arrest, his trunks, writing-desk, and every receptacle for private papers were closely searched, and his private letters and papers taken possession of and carried to the provost-marshal's office, where they were examined. Mr. Botts, knowing how obnoxious he had made himself to the Confederate authorities by his bold, outspoken hostility to the doctrine of secession, and also to all engaged in inaugurating the wicked and atrocious rebellion, had concluded—as soon as he heard of martial law having been declared—that he would probably be among the first victims of their vengeance, and he had taken the precaution to conceal the historical sketch in question in a place where the rebels would not be likely to find it, and through the medium of a friend it was privately conveyed to the office of one of the foreign consuls for safe keeping until called for.

Two days after the imprisonment of Mr. Botts, Captain Godwyn, who was acting as his jailer, presented himself in his cell, and the following conversation occurred.

After interchanging the ordinary salutations, Captain Godwyn remarked to Mr. Botts that he thought they did not get hold of all his papers in their search.

Mr. Botts. Ah! perhaps not. Did you miss any particular paper, captain, that you had reason to expect was there?

Captain Godwyn. Yes, there was one we did not find that we were led to believe was there.

Mr. Botts. Indeed! and what paper was that, captain?

Captain Godwyn. Well, I don't know exactly how to describe it.

Mr. Botts. I expect I could tell you, captain, what it was. Are you really anxious to get possession of it?

Captain Godwyn. Well, yes; I should like to get it. Where is it?

Mr. Botts. Ah! that you must find out for yourself, captain. You had no difficulty in finding me *at midnight*, and you will have to find that for yourself. But, if you are very anxious to get it, you shall have it, but only on my terms, and upon none other can you get it.

Captain Godwyn. What are your terms?

Mr. Botts. My terms are that you shall bring me the affidavit of Jeff. Davis, sworn to before Judge Haliburton, that, upon my delivery of that paper to you or to him, it shall be transferred, without alteration or mutilation, to the editors of the Enquirer and Examiner for publication, just as it came from my hand; and, to show you that I am not afraid or ashamed to let your government or the world know what I have written, I will accompany the document with five hundred or a thousand dollars to pay for the expense of the publication.

Captain Godwyn. It must be a very important paper that you will give so much to have made public. What is it?

Mr. Botts. I presume you know what it is you are in search of, but if not you shall know. It is the secret history of this rebellion for thirty years before it broke out.

Captain Godwyn. Why are you so anxious to have it published?

" Because," replied Mr. Botts, rising from his seat and advancing toward the captain, at the same time shaking his huge fist within a few inches of his face, and speaking with great vehemence in voice and manner, " because, by Heaven, sir, if the people could read it and learn the truth, it would lead to a revolution *within a revolution* in which I could take active part!"

Upon this the committee rose, and the captain departed to report progress and ask leave to sit again.

During Mr. Botts's imprisonment, the French minister, Count Mercier, visited Richmond, and expressed to the friends of Mr. Botts great anxiety to see him and converse with him on the subject of the war, as he had great reliance on his views. But this he was not permitted to do. From this fact it may be justly inferred that the French consul had previously communicated some of Mr. Botts's views upon this subject to the embassador at Washington; at all events, a copy of the letter was placed in Count Mercier's hands during his visit to Richmond, and that the document made an important impression in that quarter is not at all improbable.

Suffice it to say, in conclusion, that the lucid explanations made; the statesmanlike views expressed; the
startling facts presented; the hidden plots disclosed; and
the vital importance of the subject altogether, certainly
makes this secret history of the rebellion one of the most
valuable and interesting contributions to American historical literature ever presented to the public.

CONTENTS.

CONTENTS OF THE APPENDIX.

THE GREAT REBELLION.

ORIGIN OF THE BOOK.

To Charles Palmer, Esq.:

Home, near Richmond, October, 1861.

MY DEAR SIR,—By your letter of yesterday, I am informed that the French consul has applied to you for such information as you can furnish or obtain for him respecting the origin and progress of the doctrine of Secession, together with whatever else may be deemed important or interesting, as connected with the purposes and designs of the authors of this great Southern Rebellion; and, as one more familiar with the subject than yourself, you appeal to me for the information required, to which I answer.

It has generally been supposed that this doctrine of Secession had its origin with the famous "Hartford" Convention that was held in Hartford, Connecticut, in the year 1814, during the last war with Great Britain; but, with all the research I have been able to make, I have not succeeded in tracing this wild and pernicious assumption to that body. That it embraced a large degree of disaffected and disloyal spirit to the government of the United States, is undoubtedly true; that the authors of its creation were *suspected* and *charged* with entertaining such a design, is also beyond question; but it does not appear, by its published proceedings, to have claimed such right, or to have resorted to such a remedy for the evils of which they complained. They certainly manifested a deep hostility to the war then existing, and a great want of respect for the Constitution, and of good feeling for the government; and to the former they proposed certain amendments, which received the sanction of two only of those States that were represented in the Convention, to wit, Massachusetts and Connecticut.

It is not at all improbable, that in the outset, the members of that Convention did contemplate a resort to some such Quixotic scheme, and that they were driven from their purpose by the universal condemnation of every patriotic voice and pen that could be raised or wielded in the land; for such was the odium and the infamy that attached to that body, from the bare suspicion of its disloyalty and treasonable design of originating separate action for the States, as sovereign powers independent of their obligations to the Constitution and their allegiance to the national government, that it was quite enough to damn the fame of any man in the nation, and to hold him up to public obloquy and contempt, if upon him could be fastened the stain of being a "Hartford Conventionist" either in fact or in sympathy of feeling; and it is not less remarkable than true, that no *New England man,* from that day to this, no matter what the extent of his capacity, integrity, or patriotism, has been able to achieve for himself a great national popularity and strength, because of the odium that stuck, like the shirt of Nessus, to those States for having been held to entertain such unpatriotic and unconstitutional sentiments, and for having permitted such a Convention to have been held within their limits; and every man at all familiar with the history of the country will recognize the truth of the assertion, that for more than twenty years after that Convention was held, whenever the Southern Democracy determined to hunt an adversary down by blackening his reputation, or destroying his claims to public confidence, he was assailed as being a "*Hartford Conventionist;*" while in later years, when, in order to retain their power, they contemplated an ultimate resort to the same infamous and treasonable expedient of separation from the Union, they have *singly*, in *pairs* and in packs, hunted down and defamed the character of every antagonist by substituting the charge of being an *Abolitionist* in lieu of their famous cry of "*Hartford Conventionist.*"

SECESSION ODIOUS IN THE SOUTH PRIOR TO 1832.

I will take it upon myself to say here, that at the time this charge of " secession" was made upon that Convention, there was not one man in any party in the Southern States that did not hold the doctrine in utter abomination, and did not openly proclaim it to be *treason* against the government; and if there were any who thought differently, they did not dare to give public utterance to the sentiment. Mr. Jefferson, Mr. Madison, and Judge Spencer Roane, were all open and loud in their denunciation of the "*treason*" on the part of those who were supposed to claim such right; while now we find, that what was imperishable dishonor and infamy at that day, is regarded as the highest test of patriotism at this; and it is almost as much as a man's life is worth to be found in opposition to this odious doctrine and to its practical application. At that time there was another gentleman who exerted a great influence over the minds of the Democracy of the state, who is now no more —I mean Thomas Ritchie, of the Richmond *Enquirer*. The *Enquirer* of that day—then under the control of the party headed by Mr. Jefferson, and with the whole body of the ablest men of the Democracy in the Union as its contributors and advisers, and when no step was taken by that paper that was not approved by the "*Junto*"—said,

"No man, no association of men, no state or set of states, has a right to withdraw itself from the Union of its own accord. The same power which knit us together can alone unknit. The same formality which formed the links of the Union is necessary to dissolve it. The majority of states which formed the Union must consent to the withdrawal of any one branch of it. Until that consent has been obtained, any attempt to dissolve the Union or obstruct the efficacy of its constitutional laws is TREASON—TREASON, TO ALL INTENTS AND PURPOSES."

THE AUTHOR OF SECESSION.

No, sir! The unfading honor, and the crowning glory of originating a measure for the practical destruction of this government, and for the annihilation of the liberties of mankind, were reserved for a disappointed aspirant for the Presidency, who, Lucifer-like, preferred to "*reign in hell rather than serve in heaven.*" The name of Erostratus has been handed down to posterity for centuries past as the destroyer of the Ephesian Temple; in like manner will the name of John C. Calhoun be handed down, for ages to come, as the destroyer of the last great temple of liberty left standing on the globe, provided this rebellion should prove successful.

Mr. Calhoun, who was a most plausible and ambitious, but extremely metaphysical yet popular politician in his own state, disappointed in his reckless cravings for the Presidency, first conceived, in the year 1832, the idea of establishing a separate independence for South Carolina, over which state he held omnipotent sway, and in the control of which none could compete with him for supremacy.

While he proposed this separate action for that state, it was not without hope that other Southern States would come to its aid in the event of an attempt on the part of the general government to enforce obedience to its laws in the revolted state. The pretext then set up for this absurd claim was, the oppression under which it was pretended they were suffering through the practical operation of the protective system, of which Mr. Calhoun himself had been an earnest advocate and efficient champion at an earlier period of his life.

SECESSION IN 1832.

At that day South Carolina had few sympathizers any where, and a very small number only in the South who professed to believe in the right of a state to secede from the Union. But to such an extent had this fever raged in that unfortunate and discontented state, where Mr. Calhoun was idolized, that they proceeded to call a Convention, and actually passed an ordinance declaring their connection with the government of the United States dissolved, unless the tariff was adjusted to suit their views. General Jackson was then President of the United States, *and also a native of South Carolina;* and whatever may be said in disparagement of this old chief, it can not be denied that he possessed many very strong and estimable traits of character, among the most prominent of which were a stern, unflinching devotion to the Union, a resolute purpose to prosecute vigorously whatever he undertook, and an iron will that was not to be controlled when his mind was once made up.

GENERAL JACKSON'S PROCLAMATION.

Upon the passage of this Ordinance of Secession, General Jackson issued his celebrated proclamation, calling upon the

B 2

people to retrace their steps, to repudiate the action of their leading men, and return to their allegiance to the government established by their fathers. One passage from this proclamation is here inserted, and is worthy of being stamped indelibly upon the mind and heart of every true friend of his country. General Jackson said,

"No act of violent opposition to the laws has yet been committed, but such a state of things is hourly apprehended; and it is the intent of this instrument to proclaim not only that the duty imposed upon me by the Constitution to take care that the laws be faithfully executed, shall be performed to the extent of the powers already vested in me by law, or of such other as the wisdom of Congress shall desire and intrust to me for that purpose, but to warn the citizens of South Carolina, who have been deluded into an opposition to the laws, of the danger they will incur by obedience to the illegal and disorganizing ordinance of the Convention. . . . . The laws of the United States must be executed. I have no discretionary power on the subject. My duty is emphatically pronounced in the Constitution. Those who told you that you might peaceably prevent their execution deceived you. They could not have been deceived themselves; they know that a forcible opposition could alone prevent the execution of the laws, and they know that such opposition must be repelled. Their object is disunion. But be not deceived by names. Disunion by armed force is TREASON. Are you ready to incur its guilt? If you are, on the heads of the instigators of the act be the dreadful consequences; on their heads be the dishonor, but on yours may fall the punishment. On your unhappy state will inevitably fall all the evils of the conflict you force upon the government of your country. It can not accede to the mad project of disunion, of which you would be the

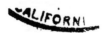

first victims. Its first magistrate can not, if he would, avoid the performance of his duty. The consequence must be fearful for you, distressing to your fellow-citizens here, and to the friends of good government throughout the world. . . . . Snatch from the archives of your state the disorganizing edict of its Convention; bid the members to reassemble and promulgate the decided expressions of your will to remain in the faith which alone can conduct you to safety, prosperity, and honor. Tell them that, compared to disunion, all other evils are light, because that brings with it an accumulation of ills. Declare that you will never take the field unless the star-spangled banner of your country shall float over you; that you will not be stigmatized when dead, and dishonored and scorned while you live, as the authors of the first attack on the Constitution of your country. Its *destroyers* you can not be. You may disturb its peace; you may interrupt the course of its prosperity; you may cloud its reputation for stability, but its tranquillity will be restored, its prosperity will return, and the stain upon its national character will be transferred, and remain an eternal blot on the memory of those who caused the disorder."

This was the language held by this *son of South Carolina* when his own state was in a condition of revolt against the Union. By the masses of unselfish, honest, patriotic people every where, this proclamation was received with enthusiastic shouts of admiration, while by the *selfish, profligate*, and *corrupt politicians*, it was received with murmurs of discontent; yet none ventured or dared to stigmatize Jackson as a traitor. The harshest term any Democratic orator or writer applied to him was that he was an "old Federalist." Yet Jackson, twelve years after, went down to his grave the idol of his party. Now contrast all this with the disgusting and nauseating denunciations we daily read of General Scott for not binding himself to the treasonable designs of the reckless and profligate politicians of this his native state.

General Jackson at the same time appealed to Congress to confer upon him additional powers to crush this rebellious movement on the part of South Carolina; whereupon Congress, without hesitation or delay, passed what has been known as the *"Force Bill,"* by which his power over the whole land and naval forces of the United States was greatly enlarged; and this bill was passed by such overwhelming majorities in both branches of Congress, as to furnish, in the most unmistakable manner, the conclusive fact that the public sentiment was every where in vehement opposition to the ridiculous pretension that the Union, as formed by our fathers, was constructed on the principle of a *bombshell* (as is this Southern Confederacy), containing the elements of its own destruction in its midst, which would sooner or later explode and leave a wreck behind, by recognizing the right of any one or more states, in a fit of passion, excitement, interest, or caprice, to retire from the obligations they had voluntarily entered into, one with the other, and each with all the rest, for their common welfare and general security; but that it was, as it was intended to be, and was declared in express terms by the old Articles of Confederation to be, a *permanent* and " perpetual Union." The good sense of the country at that day laughed to scorn the preposterous idea that when the framers of the Constitution declared that the object of that instrument was to form "a *more perfect Union*" than that which was already declared to be "*perpetual*," they were actually engaged in a work the object of which was to pull down and destroy the fruits of their own labor, instead of fortifying and strengthening what was then universally cherished as an imperishable monument of greatness, achieved by the wisdom and patriotism, the toil and suffering of our never-to-be-forgotten Revolutionary sires.

AN ARGUMENT AGAINST DISUNION.

And, in this connection, you will excuse me for giving a short extract from my own speech delivered in Lynchburg in the campaign of 1860. I then said, if all other authority should prove inconclusive, " I still appeal to the Constitution of my country to show that there is no such right as the right of secession. This Constitution declares that

" ' This Constitution, and the laws of the United States which shall be made in pursuance thereof, shall be the supreme law of the land, and the judges in every state shall be bound thereby, *any thing in the Constitution or laws of any state to the contrary notwithstanding.*'

" Who adopted this Constitution of the United States? We, the people of Virginia, through our representatives in Convention, are just as much parties to the Constitution of the United States as to our own State Constitution. But let us go back a little. Let us go back to the Articles of Confederation under which we lived before the Constitution was adopted, and see what we did there.

" My purpose is to show you that this is a *perpetual Union*, which there is no power to destroy. Under the old Articles of Confederation it is provided ' that no two states shall enter into any alliance whatever between them *without the consent of Congress*, specifying accurately the purpose for which the same is to be entered into, and how long it shall continue.' Again, Article 13th :

" ' Every state shall abide by the determination of the

United States, in Congress assembled, on all questions which by this Confederation are submitted to them: and the Articles of this Confederation *shall be inviolably observed by every state,* AND THE UNION SHALL BE PERPETUAL.'

"And the concluding Article reads:

"'And we do farther solemnly plight and engage the faith of our respective constituents, that they shall abide by the determination of the United States, in Congress assembled, on all questions which by the said Confederation are submitted to them. And that the Articles thereof shall be *inviolably observed* by the states we respectively represent, and that the UNION SHALL BE PERPETUAL.'

"There was the compact between the states—there was the marriage ceremony solemnly performed in the face of the world, by which we bound ourselves together for better or for worse, for richer, for poorer, in sickness and in health, in prosperity and in adversity, through good and evil report, till death do us part. And under this Constitution of the United States it is declared that ' we the people of the United States, in order to form A MORE PERFECT UNION, establish justice, INSURE DOMESTIC TRANQUILLITY, etc., etc., etc., do ordain and establish this Constitution for the United States of America.'

"'To make this a more perfect Union.' And in what respect did they make it more perfect? They provided for its perpetuity by giving to the government the power to enforce its laws and protect its own existence.

"Yes, but gentlemen say it is *a reserved right!* *How* was it reserved? *When* was it reserved? *Where* was it reserved? It is a reserved right in their own imaginations, and theirs only. What a calumny and libel upon the name and fame of the great and good men who made the Constitution to say, that when they declared that the Constitution of the United States, and all laws made under it, should be the supreme law of the land, and that the judges of the courts in the several states should be bound thereby; when they prohibited you from the right, even in your organic law, in the adoption of your state Constitution, to say or do any thing that would, to *any* extent, conflict with *any* law made under it, that they reserved the right to permit the destruction of the CONSTITUTION and *all* law at any moment it suited their pleasure to do so!   Why, when did that right begin?   Here I have shown you it was a perpetual contract, that it was never intended to be dissolved; and yet, after they had done their work, one state, on the very next day, had the right to withdraw and break up the whole! with or without cause — they being made judges of the cause."

The tenth Article of the Amendment to the Constitution reads, "The powers not delegated to the United States by the Constitution, nor prohibited by it to the states, are reserved to the states respectively, or to the people."   It is under this *reservation* that the secession leaders claim the constitutional right to break up the government at their pleasure; and it will be perceived that the article contains two provisions; one relating to the *prohibitions* to the states, and the other *reservations* to the states.   It is well, then, to inquire, what are the powers reserved, and what prohibited?   The power reserved is to legislate on all legitimate subjects of state legislation with which there can be no interference; such, for example, as our own domestic institutions — slavery, for one; the solemnization of marriages; the laws of descent; the regulation of suffrage; the duties and powers to be assigned to the executive, legislative, and judicial departments of the government, and all municipal or state affairs; these powers are reserved to the states respectively, and there can be no legitimate interference by Congress, or by any other state or power whatever, provided they in no manner conflict with that clause in the Constitution of the United States quoted above declaring "this Constitution, and all laws made in pursuance thereof, shall be the supreme law of the land."

Having ascertained what are the powers reserved, let us next see what it is that is prohibited to the states. First, then, every state is prohibited from passing any constitutional, legal, or conventional enactment that shall in any degree conflict with the Constitution or laws of the United States. It is furthermore prohibited, in express terms, that any state "shall enter into any treaty, alliance, or confederation; grant letters of marque and reprisal; coin money; emit bills of credit; make any thing but gold and silver coin a legal tender in payment of debts; pass any bill of attainder, *expost facto* law, or law impairing the obligation of contracts, or grant any title of nobility; lay any impost or duties on imports or exports, except such as may be necessary for executing its inspection laws, and *they* shall be for the *use of the Treasury of the United States;* and *no state* shall, WITHOUT THE CONSENT OF CONGRESS, KEEP TROOPS or SHIPS OF WAR in *time of peace*, ENTER INTO ANY AGREEMENT OR COMPACT WITH ANOTHER STATE, or WITH A FOREIGN POWER, or engage in war, unless actually invaded, or in such imminent danger as will not admit of delay.

Such, then, are the reservations and prohibitions contained in the Constitution, under which it is claimed that the power was reserved to each state to *annihilate* the Constitution of the United States, and all law *made under it;* to enter into treaties, alliances, and confederation; grant letters of marque and reprisal; and enter into agreements and compacts with other states; engage in war with the United States, and smash all things up generally, and the government of the United States in particular; such are the nonsensical and absurd pretensions of the disciples and followers of their great, *impracticable, selfish, ambitious, and mischievous* leader, John C. Calhoun.

I am aware that a good many honest, well-meaning persons have been cheated into the belief that in this state the right to withdraw from the Union at pleasure was expressly reserved at the time of the adoption of the Constitution; than which nothing could be more fallacious or unfounded.

Upon this point it can only be necessary to quote the letter of Mr. Madison to Mr. Hamilton in 1787. The State of New York had proposed to adopt the Constitution, and thereby become a member of the Union, but upon the conditions of certain amendments to the Constitution; and Mr. Hamilton addressed a letter to Mr. Madison, asking his opinion whether New York could come in on the conditions stipulated, to which Mr. Madison replied,

"My opinion is, that a reservation of a right to withdraw, if amendments be not decided on under the form of the Constitution within a certain time, is a conditional ratification; that it does not make New York a member of the new Union, and, consequently, that she could not be received on that plan. Compacts must be reciprocal: this principle would not in such a case be preserved. The Constitution requires an adoption IN TOTO, AND FOREVER. *It has been so adopted by the other states.* An adoption for a limited time would be as defective as an adoption of some of the articles only. The idea of reserving a right to withdraw was started at Richmond, and considered as a conditional ratification, which was itself abandoned as worse than a rejection."

In a letter written to Mr. Webster in 1833, Mr. Madison says,

"I return you my thanks for your late very powerful speech in the Senate of the United States. It crushes nullification, *and must hasten an abandonment of secession.*"

Speaking in the same letter of the Constitution, he says,

"It makes the government, like other governments, to operate directly on the people, places at its command the needful physical means of executing its powers, and, finally, proclaims its supremacy, and that of the laws made in pursuance of it, over the Constitutions and laws of the states; the powers of the government being exercised, as in other elective and responsible governments, under the control of its constituents, the people, and the Legislatures of the states, and subject TO THE REVOLUTIONARY rights of the people *in extreme cases.*"

By reference to the proceedings of the Virginia Convention of 1787, it will be seen from what this dangerous and most unfounded pretense has been derived. A preamble was then and there adopted, containing the following language:

"We, the delegates of the people of Virginia, elected . . . . . do, in the name and on the behalf of the people of Virginia, declare and make known that the powers granted under the Constitution, being derived *from the people of the United States,* may be *resumed by them*" (the people of the United States) "whenever the same shall be perverted to *their* injury or oppression; and that every power not granted thereby remains with them, and at their will," etc.

This, it will be perceived, is a mere declaration of a philosophical opinion expressed in a preamble, and which, whether true or false, can not modify or change the effect of the resolution following it. In this case, however, it happens to be a truism founded upon a universally recognized principle, to wit, that the powers of the government are derived from the *people of the United States*, and *may be resumed by them—the people of the United States*—whenever these powers are perverted to the injury or oppression of the people *of the United States*.

When it can be shown that the people of South Carolina, or Virginia, or even of all the Southern States combined, constitute the *people of the United States*, it will be time enough to waste time and breath, or ink and paper, for the discussion of this proposition.

But when you arrive at the resolution adopting the Constitution, it will be found *absolute* and *unconditional*, and containing no reservation whatever. The resolution is as follows:

"We, the said delegates, in the name and in behalf of the people of Virginia, do, by these presents, assent to and ratify the Constitution recommended on the 17th day of September, 1787, by the Federal Convention for the government of the United States, hereby announcing to all those whom it may concern that the said Constitution is binding upon the said people, according to an authentic copy hereto annexed."

In like manner, we hear a great deal said about the "sovereignty" of the states. Now what is the sovereignty of the states? That the states are *supreme*, and—if you choose to misapply the term—are "sovereign," in the exercise of all their legitimate powers, is true; but no more so than is a county court, or a grand or petit jury, with whose functions no other power can interfere. What are the functions and powers of sovereignty? I presume it will not be denied that the power to declare war; make peace; regulate commerce; impose duties, imposts, and excises;

prepare for the common defense; to coin money and regulate its value; to establish post-offices and post-roads; to grant letters of marque and reprisal; to provide and maintain a navy; to make treaties; enter into alliances, etc., etc., are all sovereign powers, *each one of which* can be exercised by the government of the United States; *and not one of which* can be exercised by any state in the Union, and *there never has been a moment of time when they could.*

What an anomaly it would be to see thirty-six *sovereignties,* not one of which could have a civil officer in its service, from a constable up to the governor, without his taking an oath to support the Constitution of another government which was not sovereign; and that which is not sovereign having the service of all its officers, domestic as well as foreign, in every state, not one of whom was required to swear to support one of the sovereignties!

It is an entire misapplication of the term to apply "*sovereignty*" to a state. There is no state in the Union that ever could exercise a sovereign power, unless *Texas* (though never a government *de jure*) might constitute an exception. It will not be questioned that what are now the States were originally the *colonies of Great Britain,* and it will not be claimed that *while colonies* they set up any pretensions to *sovereignty.* In 1776 the then thirteen colonies entered into a Declaration of Independence and common compact, under the designation of the "*United States,*" and declared themselves free, and, as a *united* body, claiming the right *of the whole united, not of each one,* to levy war, conclude peace, contract alliances, establish commerce, and do all other acts and things which independent states may of right do; but it never was pretended that any one of these states could of itself exercise any one of these powers of sovereignty.

In 1778, these colonies, while engaged in a common struggle for independence, and five years before their independence, or claim to the character of states, was *established*, entered into "*Articles of Confederation and* PERPETUAL UNION" under the "*style*" of the United States, and from these "Articles of Confederation and perpetual Union" they went into their present form of government, which was adopted, to make *that* which was already declared *to be "perpetual"* a "*more* perfect Union."

The argument used, that the mother country, by the treaty of peace in 1783, which recognized each state *of the United States by name*, thereby established their sovereignty and separate existence, is of no more weight than it would be to claim the same sovereignty for each of the counties of what now constitutes West Virginia, because the act creating the state mentioned by name the counties which composed the state.

When, where, and how, then, did any state forming the Union now or originally ever exercise, or claim the right to exercise, a sovereign power? Mr. Calhoun himself, the great leader of this states-sovereignty party, which claims every thing to suit itself, utterly repudiated the idea that there could be sovereignty in the *government*, and broadly asserted that all sovereignty was in the *people of the states, united in their federal Union*, and not a particle in the government. In 1833 he said, "No one will pretend that sovereignty is in the *government*. To make that assertion would be to go back to the *Asiatic idea of government*. It is scarcely *European*, as the most intelligent writers of the globe have *long since* traced sovereignty to a higher source. No, the sovereignty is not in the government, *it is in the people*. Any other conception is utterly abhorrent to the ideas of every American. There is not a particle of sovereignty in the *government*.   The sovereignty, then, is in the people of the *several states, united in their federal Union*. It is not only in them, but in them unimpaired.   *Not a particle resides in the government*."

Without assenting to this doctrine of Mr. Calhoun's, it utterly annihilates, as far as his authority goes, all idea of sovereignty in the state government, for he embraces *all governments—federal, state, European,* and *Asiatic*.

Much, too, has been said about the "*coercion of a state.*" No such thing is known to the theory of our government as the "coercion" of a state.   Under the Constitution, the government does not operate on states but upon the people.   Under the old Articles of Confederation, the government operated upon states, and derived their revenue from the states, which was found not to answer a good purpose; and one of the distinctive features of the present form of government from the Confederation is that it operates on each individual citizen, and requires each and every citizen to obey the law; and if they resist, the law is *enforced*, or they are "coerced" to obedience by the magisterial power of the government; and if they resist by force of arms, or by combinations too powerful to be controlled by the magisterial or judicial powers, such resistance becomes *treason*, and must be suppressed by the military powers of the country.   It would be about as difficult to "coerce" a state as it would be to try and *hang* a *state* for treason; while it is quite within the powers of the government to compel any citizen to obey the laws, as it would be first to try and then to hang him for the treason, in taking up arms to resist the authority and overthrow the government of the United States.

AN IMPORTANT NOTE.

July 1, 1864. I have just read in the Richmond *Sentinel* of the 18th of June the "manifesto" of the Confederate Congress, which that paper announces to be from the pen of the Hon. William C. Rives, and that, by joint resolution, is to be sent to "our commissioners abroad, to the end that the same may be laid before foreign governments."

This extraordinary document, coming from so distinguished a source, I think should be given entire, and therefore it is inserted here without mutilation or curtailment.

How far its assertions in reference to the origin of the war can be sustained by undeniable historical facts, each one can determine for himself; *my impression* is, that they are about as well founded as the predictions made as to the final result which will ere long be made manifest to all the world. Here is the MANIFESTO.

"*Manifesto of the Congress of the Confederate States of America relative to the existing war with the United States.*

"The Congress of the Confederate States of America, acknowledging their responsibility to the opinion of the civilized world, to the great law of Christian philanthropy, and to the Supreme Ruler of the universe, for the part they have been compelled to bear in the sad spectacle of war and carnage which this continent has, for the last three years, exhibited to the eyes of afflicted humanity, deems the present a fitting occasion to declare the principles, the sentiments, and the purposes by which they have been and are still actuated.

"They have ever deeply deplored the necessity which constrained them to take up arms in defense of their rights and of the free institutions derived from their ancestors; and there is nothing they more ardently desire than peace, whensoever their enemy, by ceasing from the unhallowed war waged upon them, shall permit them to enjoy in peace the sheltering protection of those hereditary rights and of those cherished institutions. The series of successes with which it has pleased Almighty God, in so signal a manner, to bless our arms on almost every point of our invaded borders since the opening of the present campaign, enables us to profess this desire of peace in the interests of civilization and humanity, without danger of having our motives misinterpreted, or of the declaration being ascribed to any unmanly sentiment, or any distrust of our ability fully to maintain our cause. The repeated and disastrous checks, foreshadowing ultimate discomfiture, which their gigantic army, directed against the capital of the Confederacy, has already met with, are but a continuation of the same Providential successes for us. We do not refer to these successes in any spirit of vain boasting, but in humble acknowledgment of that Almighty protection which has vouchsafed and granted them.

"The world must now see that *eight* millions of people, inhabiting so extensive a territory, with such varied resources and such numerous facilities for defense as the benignant bounty of Nature has bestowed upon us, and animated with one spirit to encounter every privation and sacrifice of ease, of health, of property, of life itself, rather than be degraded from the condition of free and independent states into which they were born, can never be conquered. Will not our adversaries themselves begin to feel that humanity has bled long enough; that tears, and blood, and treasure enough have been expended in a bootless undertaking, covering their own land, no less than ours, with a

pall of mourning, and exposing them far more than ourselves to the catastrophe of financial exhaustion and bankruptcy, not to speak of the loss of their liberties by the despotism engendered in an aggressive warfare upon the liberties of another and kindred people? Will they be willing,
by a longer perseverance in a wanton and hopeless contest,
to make this continent, which they so long boasted to be
the chosen abode of liberty and self-government, of peace
and a higher civilization, the theatre of the most causeless
and prodigal effusion of blood which the world has ever
seen, of a virtual relapse into the barbarism of the ruder
ages, and of the destruction of constitutional freedom by
the lawlessness of usurped power?

"These are questions which our adversaries will decide
for themselves. We desire to stand acquitted before the
tribunal of the world, as well as in the eyes of omniscient
justice, of any responsibility for the origin or prolongation
of a war as contrary to the spirit of the age as to the tradi-
tions and acknowledged maxims of the political system of
America.

"On this continent, whatever opinions may have prevailed elsewhere, it has ever been held and acknowledged
by all parties that government, to be lawful, must be founded on the consent of the governed. *We were forced to dissolve our federal connection with our former associates by
their aggressions on the fundamental principles of our compact of union with them; and in doing so, we exercised a
right consecrated in the great charter of American liberty*
—the right of a free people, when a government proves destructive of the ends for which it was established, to recur
to original principles, and to institute new-guards for their
security. *The separate independence of the states, as sovereign and co-equal members of the federal Union, had never*

C

been surrendered; and the pretension of applying to independent communities so constituted and organized the ordinary rules for coercing and reducing rebellious subjects to obedience, was a solecism in terms as well as an outrage on the principles of public law.

"The war made upon the Confederate States was, therefore, wholly one of aggression. On our side it has been strictly defensive. Born freemen, and the descendants of a gallant ancestry, we had no option but to stand up in defense of our invaded firesides, of our desecrated altars, of our violated liberties and birthright, and of the prescriptive institutions which guard and protect them. We have not interfered, nor do we wish, in any manner whatever, to interfere with the internal peace and prosperity of the states arrayed in hostility against us, or with the freest development of their destinies in any form of action or line of policy they may think proper to adopt for themselves. All we ask is a like immunity for ourselves, and to be left in the undisturbed enjoyment of those inalienable rights of 'life, liberty, and the pursuit of happiness' which our common ancestors declared to be the equal heritage of all the parties to the social compact.

"Let them forbear aggressions upon us, and the war is at an end. If there be questions which require adjustment by negotiation, we have ever been willing, and are still willing to enter into communication with our adversaries in a spirit of peace, of equity, and manly frankness. Strong in the persuasion of the justice of our cause, in the gallant devotion of our citizen soldiers, and of the whole body of our people, and, above all, in the gracious protection of Heaven, we are not afraid to avow a sincere desire for peace on terms consistent with our honor and the permanent security of our rights, and an earnest aspiration to see the world once more restored to the beneficent pursuits of industry and of mutual intercourse and exchanges, so essential to its well-being, and which have been so gravely interrupted by the existence of this unnatural war in America.

"But, if our adversaries, or those whom they have placed in authority, deaf to the voice of reason and justice, steeled against the dictates of both prudence and humanity by a presumptuous and delusive confidence in their own numbers, or those of their black and foreign mercenaries, shall determine upon an indefinite prolongation of the contest, upon them be the responsibility of a decision so ruinous to themselves, and so injurious to the interests and repose of mankind.

"For ourselves we have no fear of the result. The wildest picture ever drawn of a disordered imagination comes short of the extravagance which could dream of the conquest of eight millions of people resolved with one mind 'to die freemen rather than live slaves,' and forewarned by the savage and exterminating spirit in which this war has been waged upon them, and by the mad avowals of its patrons and supporters of the worse than Egyptian bondage that awaits them in the event of their subjugation.

"With these declarations of our dispositions, our principles, and our purposes, we commit our cause to the enlightened judgment of the world, to the sober reflection of our adversaries themselves, and to the solemn and righteous arbitrament of Heaven."

If this most extraordinary document had emanated from any other source in either branch of the Confederate Congress, it would not have attracted my attention, nor would any other notice have been taken of it than of a thousand gasconading, braggadocio speeches delivered in that body,

or thrown off to the world in the form of editorials or communications through the public press.   But, coming from so
distinguished a statesman as Mr. Rives, whose name is associated with the history of this country not only as a senator
of the United States but as a foreign representative to one
of the first courts of Europe, it is entitled to something
more than a passing notice.

It is with the fifth paragraph of this *"manifesto,"* beginning with the words *"On this continent, whatever opinions
may have prevailed elsewhere,"* etc., etc, that I propose to
deal.

If it be true that the right of secession, as exercised by
Virginia and other Southern States, was *"a right consecrated in the great charter of American liberty,"* and if it
be true that the separate independence of the states, as sovereign and coequal members of the federal Union, had never
been surrendered, and the pretension of applying to independent communities so constituted and organized the ordinary rules for coercing and reducing rebellious subjects
to obedience, was a solecism in terms as well as an outrage
on the principles of public law," I say, if there is truth in
these declarations, then I can not stand acquitted to myself
or before any enlightened community for the position I occupy, or for the course I have pursued, or for the grounds
I have taken in this work.

Feeling this, and knowing that by far the ablest production of Mr. Rives's life was to be found in his earnest and
able defense of the proclamation of General Jackson and of
the *Force Bill* in 1833, I lost no time in turning to that very
lucid, logical, and conclusive argument for comfort and relief from the unenviable position in which his manifesto had
placed me as well as others who occupied the same grounds;
and the honorable gentleman must bear with me while, in

my own defense, I avail myself somewhat freely of the co-
gent arguments used by him on that memorable occasion.

On the 14th of February, 1833, on a bill then pending
before the Senate of the United States commonly known as
the "*Force Bill*," Mr. Rives said,

"Most of the questions involved in the discussion of the
bill now under consideration have sprung up during the period of my absence from the country; and the short period
which has elapsed since my return has afforded me neither
time nor opportunity for a detailed examination of them.
I bring to them, therefore, no other resources of argument
or illustration than those settled principles and fundamental notions which are rooted in the mind of every American citizen in regard to the Constitution of his country.
. . . . In this state of things we are called upon to say
if the government of the United States shall acquiesce in
this open defiance and violation of the laws of the Union,
without taking any step whatever for their enforcement.
For myself, I am free to say that I do not thus read my
oath to support the Constitution of the United States. I do
not thus understand my duty to my country, or the interest and honor of my own state. . . . . The example
would inflict a mortal wound on the Constitution. The
government would be thenceforward virtually dissolved,
and we should inevitably fall backward into anarchy and
confusion of the 'Articles of Confederation,' if, indeed,
after such an example of weakness, the states should continue connected by any tie whatever. For one, therefore,
I feel myself constrained, by the highest considerations of
duty, to give my assent to such measures as may be necessary and proper to provide for the execution of the laws
while they remain unrepealed. . . . . Whatever may be
the true doctrine in regard to the sovereignty of the states

individually, it is unquestionably clear that, while the government of the Union is vested in its legislative, executive, and political departments, the actual sovereign power resides in the several states, who created it in their separate and distinct political character. But, by an express provision of the Constitution, it may be amended or changed by three fourths of the states; and each state, by assenting to the Constitution with this provision, *has surrendered its original rights as a sovereign,* which made its individual consent necessary to any change in its political condition, and has placed this important power in the hands of *three fourths of the States,* in which the *sovereignty of the Union,* under the Constitution, does now actually reside." . . . . The plain result is that the paramount or sovereign power is not *in the people of any one state,* but in three fourths of all the states. . . . . It has become fashionable of late to deny that there is any sovereignty in the United States (I speak, of course, of the United States as a political community, and not of the *government* of the United States), and to claim for the states separately an absolute, complete, and unqualified sovereignty, to all intents and purposes whatever. Sir, this is a novelty unknown to the founders of the Constitution, and has sprung up in the hot-bed of excited local politics. At the period of the adoption of the Constitution, it was distinctly made known and universally understood, that to the extent to which *sovereignty* was vested in the Union that of the states severally was relinquished and diminished. . . . . Now, sir, let us see in what light it was presented to the people in reference to this question of state sovereignty by its distinguished advocates and expounders, the writers of the '*Federalist.*' Nothing would have been better calculated to procure its ready adoption by the states than to have told them that it left their sovereignty entirely

unimpaired. But, sir, its honest and enlightened advocates,
the writers of the '*Federalist,*' attempted no such imposi-
tion on the good sense of the people. They told them distinctly that 'sovereignty in the Union, and complete independence in the members, are things repugnant and irreconcilable.'—*Federalist, No.* 15. . . . . In rapidly glanc-
ing over this celebrated collection, I find the expression,
'residuary sovereignty of the states,' as distinguished from
a complete and undiminished sovereignty, used in three
several numbers (Nos. 39, 43, and 62), all written by Mr.
Madison, whose guidance, I confess, I always follow with
peculiar confidence, for no man, from the relation in which
he stands to the Constitution, can be supposed to be more
thoroughly imbued with its true philosophy. It is a remarkable circumstance, as evincing the unvarying fidelity
of Mr. Madison's mind to this fundamental truth of a partial
surrender of sovereignty by the states, that, at the distance
of more than ten years from the publication of the '*Federalist,*' in his celebrated report of the Virginia Legislature of
1799, he again uses the same form of expression—'the residuary sovereignty of the states.' Sir, that report, in recognizing, as it does, in express terms, '*the sovereignty of
the United States,*' as well as in attributing to the several
states a *residuary* sovereignty only, shows that the idea of
an absolute and undiminished sovereignty still remaining
in the states was as little entertained by the fathers of the
political church, from which the senator from South Carolina
professes to derive his tenets, as by the founders and original advocates of the Constitution. . . . . The Republicans
of '98 and '99, Mr. President, never contended that the states
retained, under the Constitution, an *absolute* and undiminished sovereignty; that they still possessed what they had
given up; that the whole was not diminished by the sub-

traction of a part. But they contended that all the sovereignty which had not been voluntarily surrendered to the
Union was inviolably reserved to the states; that the states
are sovereign within their several spheres as the Union is
in the sphere marked out to it, and that the harmony of the
whole system is only to be preserved by each power revolv-
ing in its proper orbit. It was reserved for modern times
to assert that *eccentric* and lawless state sovereignty which
'shoots madly from its sphere' to arrest the movements
and to *nullify* the acts of the federal authority. . . . . Sir,
this argument is plainly founded on a total misconception
of the nature of our present political system, and of the
characteristic differences between it and the Articles of Confederation. From the moment of the adoption of the present Constitution, a direct relation is created between the
government of the United States and the citizen. The authorities of the Union no longer act through the states by
requisition, as under the Articles of Confederation, but *directly*, on persons and things, by its own laws. The great
object of the change of system was to render the government of the Union entirely independent of the action of
states in the performance of its high constitutional functions.
For this purpose it was not only invested with the power
of making *laws*, but of *executing* them by regular, judicial,
and executive organs, and by the physical force of the country also, if need be; for it will not be forgotten that among
the powers vested in Congress is that of 'providing for calling forth the *militia* to execute the laws of the Union.' To
mark still more unequivocally the intention of the new Constitution to place the government of the Union, in the exercise of its powers, above the control of individual states, it
is expressly declared that the 'Constitution and law of the
United States, which shall be made in pursuance thereof,

etc., shall be the supreme law of the land, *any thing in the Constitution* or laws of any state to the contrary nothwith-standing.' . . . . That the interposition of a state acting in her sovereign capacity through a convention of the people, as in the case of South Carolina, is of no more avail to arrest the execution of the laws of the United States than an interposition in her ordinary political capacity, is apparent from the language of that clause of the Constitution which asserts the supremacy of the Constitution and laws of the United States, 'any thing in the *Constitution* or laws of any state to the contrary notwithstanding.' The *Constitution* of a state is always the act of a state in her highest sovereign capacity; and if it can oppose no obstacle to the laws of the Union, as is here declared, it follows that neither the sovereign nor the legislative interposition of a state is sufficient, under the Constitution, to defeat a law of the United States. If any thing farther were wanting to show that the interposition of a state can not, under the Constitution, absolve the citizen from his obligations to the Union, conclusive proof is furnished by the rejection of the amendment proposed in the Convention by Mr. Luther Martin, which was brought to the view of the Senate a few days since by the honorable senator from Delaware (Mr. Clayton). Mr. Martin, with the express view, as he told us, of securing the citizens of the respective states against the effects of their responsibility to the United States, where, in obedience to the authority of their own state, they should oppose the laws of the Union, submitted a proposition in the following words, as an amendment to the article in the Constitution concerning treason: 'Provided that no act or acts done by one or more of the states against the United States, or by any citizen of any one of the United States, *under the authority of any one or more of the said states,* shall be deemed treason, or punished as such, etc.' This proposition, sir, was rejected; and the inference drawn from the fact by Mr. Martin is irresistible, that it was intended to preserve the constitutional authority of the Union over the citizens of the United States in full force and effect, whatever might be done or enjoined by a state to the contrary. . . . . Sir, proud as I am of the title of citizen of Virginia, grateful as I am for the unmerited favor which that honored mother has shown to me, I yet feel, with the Father of the country, that 'the just pride of patriotism is exalted' by the more comprehensive title of citizen of the United States; that title which gives me a share in the common inheritance of glory which has descended to us from our revolutionary sages, patriots, and heroes; that title which enables me to claim the names of the Rutledges, the Pinckneys, and the Sumters of South Carolina, and the Hancocks, the Adams's, and Otis's of Massachusetts, and all the other proud names which have illustrated the annals of each and all of these states as compatriot with my own. I have thus, Mr. President, reviewed the fundamental tenets of that new school of constitutional law which has sprung up within the last four or five eventful years of our political history. I have endeavored to show that they have no foundation whatever in any just view of the Constitution, that they are directly at war with contemporary understanding and expositions of its founders, and that they derive no countenance whatever from the principles of that genuine republican school which re-established the Constitution in its purity after the temporary perversion to which it had been subjected. These *modern* doctrines, I do firmly believe, are in their tendency utterly subversive of that happy system of government, the preservation of which is not only the sole security for liberty with us, but the last hope of freedom throughout the world. . . . . But one thing is certain, *a state can never, as South Carolina has done, directly and formally annul a law of the United States, without an open departure from the Constitution and a total renunciation of all its obligations.* . . . . What, then, was the conduct of Virginia in the memorable era of '98 and '99 ? She solemnly *protested* against the Alien and Sedition Acts as 'palpable and alarming infractions of the Constitution;' she communicated that protest to the other states of the Union, and earnestly appealed to them to unite with her in a like declaration that this deliberate and solemn expression of the opinions of the states, as parties to the constitutional compact, should have its proper effect upon the councils of the nation in procuring a revision and repeal of the obnoxious act. This was 'the head and front of her offending, nothing more.' The whole object of the proceeding was, by the peaceful force of public opinion, embodied through the organ of the state Legislatures, to obtain a repeal of the laws in question, not to oppose or arrest their execution while they remained unrepealed. That this was the true spirit and real purpose of the proceeding is abundantly manifested by the whole of the able debate which took place in the Legislature of the state on the occasion. All the speakers who advocated the resolutions, which were finally adopted, distinctly placed them on that legitimate constitutional ground. I need only refer to the emphatic declaration of John Taylor, of Caroline, the distinguished mover and able champion of the resolutions. He said, 'the appeal was to *public opinion*—if that is against us we must yield.' The same sentiment was avowed and maintained by every friend of the resolutions throughout the debate. . . . . There is no proceeding whatever, in any part of this affair, against *South Carolina.* The government of the United States, in the execution of the laws, can have no proper reference to states. It acts upon individuals, not upon states, as I have already had occasion abundantly to show; and the Constitution of the United States, when it declared that nothing in the *Constitution or laws of a particular state* should control the laws·of the United States, has not permitted the government of the Union, in executing the laws of the United States, to inquire if opposition to them is or is not authorized by a particular state. If the laws be opposed by ' combinations too powerful to be overcome in the ordinary course of judicial proceedings,' there is the same *right*, under the Constitution, to *execute the laws* by calling in the aid of the military power, whether such combinations be authorized by a law of a state (which the Constitution has declared in such a case to be a *nullity*), or whether they be purely voluntary. I have not, then, the slightest difficulty then in regard to the right and power of the government to employ the *physical force of the country*, in a case like the present, if it should be necessary. . . . . I would make no new provision of this sort (the Force Bill) until an *overt act* had been committed; and then I verily believe, with Mr. Jefferson, that a republican government would show itself as *strong*, in a good cause, as any on earth. ' At the call of the law every good citizen would fly to the standard of the law, and the defense of public order would be considered by every citizen as his individual concern.' . . . . I do, in my conscience, believe that the preservation of the Union is our only security. If we are to be broken into separate confederacies, constant wars and collisions with each other must ensue, out of which will grow up large military establishments, perpetual and burdensome taxes, and an overshadowing executive power; and, amid these deleterious influences, what hope can there be that liberty would survive? It is here, I confess, that I see the danger of military despotism, and not where the imagination of the senator from South Carolina (Mr. Calhoun) has found it. Is not the actual condition of South Carolina in this respect an impressive admonition to us on the subject—the whole state converted into a camp, the executive and other authorities armed with dictatorial powers, the rights of conscience set at naught, and an unsparing proscription ready to disfranchise one half of her population? Sir, this is but a prefiguration of the evils and calamities to which every portion of this country would be destined if the Union should be dissolved. *Let us, then, rally around that sacred Union, fixing it anew, and establishing it forever on the immutable basis of equal justice, of mutual amity and kindness, and an administration at once firm and paternal. Let us do this, and we shall carry back peace to our distracted country, happiness to the affrighted fireside, restore stability to our threatened institutions, and give hope and confidence once more to the friends of liberty throughout the world.* Let us do this, and we shall be, in short, what a bountiful Providence has heretofore made us, and designed us ever to remain, the freest and happiest people under the sun."

Such were the opinions, and such the principles of the honorable and distinguished gentleman (Mr. Rives) in 1833, as the representative of Virginia democracy, in the Senate of the United States, when enforcing the proclamation of General Jackson and the passage of the "*Force Bill*," which placed the whole military and naval power of the United States at the disposal of the President for the suppression of the rebellion in South Carolina, and for enforcing the laws of the United States on the citizens of that state, who were by an *ordinance of convention* resisting their execution. Such were also the principles then indorsed and sustained by the Democracy of this state. Such were the principles that *I* too then sustained, in common with the Democracy (which were the only measures of General Jackson's whole administration, as far as I recollect, that I did support, but from which I could not withhold my judgment or my assent). Such were the principles by which I have lived, and by which I expect to die; and if I do not stand *vindicated* and *justified* for the part I have taken during the progress of this rebellion by the recognized congressional champion of secession, and author of the Confederate "*Manifesto*," designed as a justification of the rebellion before the foreign powers of the globe, then should I stand rebuked, "*though Moses and the prophets were to rise from the dead*" for my vindication.

But again, Mr. Rives, in his congressional " Manifesto," uses this most extraordinary language:

"The war *made* upon the Confederate States was, therefore, *wholly one of aggression.* On our side it has been strictly defensive. . . . . We had no option but to stand in defense of our invaded firesides, of our devastated altars, of our violated liberties and birthright, and of the prescriptive institutions which guard and protect them."

When Mr. Rives penned and made himself responsible to the world for this extraordinary statement, had he forgotten that he was one of five commissioners appointed by the state to represent her in the Peace Congress that met in Washington, and that that Congress of the nation offered to the South terms of compromise and conciliation, with which he himself was satisfied, and recommended for adoption to the Convention then in session, but which every Democrat in that body refused to accept? Had he forgotten the bombardment of Fort Sumter, and its seizure, together with all the arms, ammunition, and other property of the United States that had been forcibly taken possession of by the Confederate government, before the authorities of the United States had raised a hand in its own defense? or does Mr. Rives regard these acts of aggression and war as "strictly defensive" on the part of the South, and as unjustifiably aggressive and hostile on the part of the United States?

But it is not my purpose here to give you a treatise on this fruitful theme, but to point out the manner by and purpose *for* which the country has been rashly, inconsiderately, and wickedly plunged into this horrible civil war, by the short-sighted, blundering, and stupid action of the demons of Democracy, who have miscalculated in this the operations and effects of their own work, as they have in all else they have undertaken.

The Force Bill was passed in the House of Representatives by a vote of 149 to 48; and in the Senate by 32 to 1 only.

CALHOUN BARELY ESCAPES HANGING.

General Jackson was in earnest, and honest in his threat at that day to have Mr. Calhoun, who was then a senator of the United States, immediately arrested, and "hung in chains" for treason; and he would, no doubt, through the intervention of the law, have seen this most anxious and patriotic desire of his executed, but that Mr. Clay, who, although a violent opponent of Jackson's administration, yet a patriotic supporter of his measures in this momentous question of secession — even on the very day that Mr. Calhoun had been notified by Mr. Benton that he was to be arrested—in an unfortunate moment of generosity and magnanimity, and in a rather too earnest desire for pacification, staved off a resort to steps of violence by bringing forward his celebrated measures of compromise, called and ever since known as "the Compromise of 1832," which served as a *pretext* for Calhoun and his state to back down from the difficulties in which they had entangled themselves and outraged the country; and thus the question was for the time settled.

I say it was an unfortunate moment at which Mr. Clay interposed, for, but for this compromise, an example would at that day have been made by General Jackson which would have crushed secession, with all its advocates, into the earth; and all the consequences of this rebellion, the end of which is not yet, nor its calamities in the future yet appreciated, would have been spared not only to the present generation, but it could never again have raised its horrid head on this continent, no matter who had been constitutionally chosen by the people to preside over their destinies.

But South Carolina, from that day to the present, has never ceased to feel her degradation, and never ceased to be a discontented, querulous disturber of the public peace. She has been at all times ready for a revolt whenever she felt that the time had arrived when any portion of the South would step in to fight her battles, shield her from danger, and protect her against the enforcement of the law by the general government; and from that time the politicians of that state, as a general thing, have differed only in degree, the larger portion, led on by Mr. Calhoun, being in favor of immediate dissolution, the rest waiting only for "co-operation" by other Southern States, and they were, therefore, themselves divided and classed as "secessionists" and "co-operationists."

SECESSION NOT KILLED.

But although such a decisive death-blow was given in 1833 to the right of a state or states to withdraw from the Union, yet the fire was only smothered, the embers still burned; and her leading men have been *quietly*, but *constantly* and *actively*, engaged from that day, now nearly thirty years since, in sowing seeds of discontent throughout the Southern States.

For the accomplishment of this end, it became necessary to hit upon some expedient, or to select some more exciting subject upon which the South could be brought to act as a unit, and not as a divided section as on the tariff question, and by that means combine the entire Southern States in one harmonious whole; and as the Democracy was largely in the ascendant throughout the South, it became necessary that the whole South should become democratized. This being the first great object in view, it required no great sagacity or foresight to see that there was but one question, or one subject, on which common interest would beget community of feeling in every Southern State, and that was the question of *slavery*, and this could only be used for that purpose by exciting the apprehensions of the slaveholder as to the security of his property; and how could this alarm be kept up otherwise than by adopting such a course as would unavoidably excite and increase the hostility of the anti-slavery interest of the South, and, by constant agitation, keep the political caldron ever at fever heat? The argument was this: By keeping up a constant agitation of the slavery question, we can sooner or later force the Whig party in the South to co-operate with the Democracy on all sectional issues, of which we will take care to have an abundant supply on hand, and thus in time the whole South will become democratized. Accordingly we find that, in an address of Mr. Calhoun's to the people of South Carolina in 1835, he recommends a change of issue from the tariff to the slavery question, and that that question must be driven home upon the people of the North; in what manner they did drive this question home upon the people of the North will be seen in the sequel.

By the more rapid increase of population in the North, the power is gradually fading away from the South; and when the time shall arrive that the Democracy can no longer hold their power under the national government, it will require but little art or persuasion addressed to the selfishness of the leaders of the opposition to join in breaking up the old government, and perpetuating *their* power and *our own* under a Southern Confederacy; how well they have succeeded in the scheme, at least so far as the effort is concerned, we all too well know and too painfully feel.

THE DISUNION SCHEME OF THE DEMOCRACY.

I set up no pretensions to superior sagacity, but I had been but a short time in Congress, mixing freely with the public men of the country, before I saw the whole scheme as plainly as it may be seen by others now; and from the first I set myself against it, and resolved to resist them at every step of their unhallowed proceedings, and make a willing sacrifice of myself, if, by so doing, I could save the Union and rescue my country from ruin; and therefore it was that I have been found uniformly, on every sectional issue raised by the Democracy, *not against the South,* but in opposition to the measures of the Democratic party, until I brought upon myself the unlimited denunciation of the Democratic press and politicians, and not unfrequently the suspicion of some of my own party of a want of fidelity to

Southern interests. And I may here ask emphatically, on what occasion have I failed to raise my voice to its utmost pitch in warning the people that the object of each successive issue was the ultimate dissolution of the Union? This solemn conviction, so deeply impressed upon my mind, will furnish the key to my whole public course. It was to *protect*, as far as I could, and *save* the Union; to prevent a civil war of an exterminating character, which I saw and knew must attend any effort at dissolution. Others there were who looked at these issues only to ascertain how far it would affect their personal popularity at home—whether it would retain this one in the Legislature, or that one in Congress, or secure a nomination for this or that political preferment; while I claim to have paid no regard to the fact whether it kept either them or myself in place. The Union was the god of my idolatry on earth; and from its preservation I never permitted my eye to be turned for a moment. You will excuse me for this brief episode in regard to myself, as it affords a defense and justification of my past course which none may make for me hereafter; and as I have quitted public life forever, I may have no other opportunity of making for myself.

Slavery, then, was to be the pretext, the perpetuation of power the real object of every movement that was made on the political chess-board by Mr. Calhoun and his followers from the year 1833 down to the fatal day when South Carolina, on the 20th of December, 1860, during the Democratic administration of Mr. Buchanan, and nearly three months before the inauguration of Mr. Lincoln, rushed headlong into secession, denied the authority and defied the power of the United States, and commenced hostilities by firing upon the steamer "Star of the West," bearing the flag of the United States, and repeating these hostilities by again attacking the United States troops in Fort Sumter, which precipitated the whole South into this fatal rebellion.

THE SECESSION PROGRAMME.

The first steps taken for the accomplishment of the end in view, that is to say, in getting up *excitement* and *agitation* on slavery, was by the adoption of what is so well known through the country as the 21st rule; by which the sacred and inalienable right of petition was denied to the North on all questions connected with slavery, which at once produced, as was clearly foreseen it would, a perfect *furor* throughout the North, and this it was that gave the first impetus toward the regular organization of a formidable Abolition party in all the Northern States. This is just what the leaders desired, for as long as that rule remained in force, thousands of petitions were poured into Congress in the very wantonness of excitement that was created; and upon the presentation of every such petition the South was warned, with solemn voice, of the danger to slavery, and the determination of the North to destroy it—by legislation if possible, but by force if necessary.

During the long protracted struggle that ensued, every rash and intemperate speech that was made in Congress or out of it upon the subject of slavery by the Northern representatives was sent all over the South, while others equally rash and intemperate, and made for the occasion and the purpose in the South, were hurried off to the North; and each successive year saw additional exasperation and bitterness mixed up with the never-ending discussions that were studiously encouraged, until the simple-minded people on either side really felt that these artful and designing politicians gave utterance to the general sentiment of the section they represented; and many honest, well-meaning, and patriotic men persuaded themselves that if a peaceful separation could be effected, it would be to the advantage of both parties that it should be brought about; hence the laborious effort that was made in this state to persuade the people that secession was a measure of peace, and that the only way by which it was possible to insure peace was for Virginia to follow in the wake of South Carolina. What a wicked and willful perversion of truth! for the parties that so represented knew it was false. What fatal credulity and misplaced confidence on the part of the people, *their condition*, before this war terminates, will illustrate.

But what measure of execration is in store for those who practiced the deception when the war fever subsides? At present the nervous system of all men, and women too, is alike stretched to its utmost tension, and none stop to count the cost; but when the war is over, and the raging fever subsides, and men look aghast at children, brothers, and fathers slain; mothers, wives, and sisters left broken-hearted; fortunes sacrificed; homes abandoned or destroyed; the country every where, that the tread of either army has been felt, presenting one general scene of devastation and ruin; the slave property that has either made its escape or been carried off, with no labor left to carry on the ordinary pursuits of agriculture; with the country groaning under a weight of debt heretofore unknown to our people; with a system of taxation twice tenfold greater than ever before, while the means of paying them are diminished in the same proportion, it can not be, in the nature of things and in the nature of man, but that the inquiry will be universal, *Why is this?* For what good purpose have I and my country been thus reduced to ruin? What was I suffering from before the war? and if at all, how have those sufferings been re-

lieved? Who are the authors of all this mischief and misery? and what did they propose or hope to accomplish by
their folly and madness? And when it is seen that the
whole and sole object was the perpetuation of power for a
party under a Southern Confederacy, when they found
they could no longer retain it under a national Confederacy, what measure of indignation, I may ask, is in store for
them? Now, my dear sir, I beg you to mark well one prediction that I here venture to make, and that is, that more
especially and in particular will this be the case, if the
Southern States should ultimately succeed in separating
themselves from all connection with the United States,
which will then become a deadly hostile and extremely an-
noying and dangerous neighbor; and when the Border
States will necessarily have large standing armies constantly quartered on their people, to protect their frontiers from
the continual John Brown raids that will be made upon
them, while it would require a navy equal to that of the
British Empire to protect their commerce on the seas.

The war itself has been calamitous enough, but believe
me, when I will tell you a separation of the South from the
United States, with their independence recognized, would
be far more disastrous to their interests, and future prosperity and happiness, than the war itself *has been* or *will be*,
bad as it surely must and will be in the end.

But to return to the action of the Democratic party on
the subject of slavery. This letter is written at your urgent solicitation; and as I have undertaken the task of en-
lightening you on the subject (as one who has been as fully
identified with all the movements of parties in this country
for the last thirty years as any other one man now alive),
you will excuse me if I tax your patience by calling your
attention to the following extracts taken from my letter of

January, 1859, addressed to certain leading members of our State Legislature, who did me the honor to seek my views on the then existing affairs of the country. The extract is lengthy, but if you want to understand the history of this war thoroughly, its perusal will be worth the time it will take you to read it. This was one of the late warnings I gave the people of the designs of the Democracy for retaining the money-places and power of the government in their own hands, and the uses they had made of the institution of slavery for that purpose.

THE DEMOCRACY REVIEWED.

The following are the extracts referred to:

It may not be either uninteresting or uninstructive to review briefly the history of the past, as far as the slavery question is connected with the politics of the country; and here, once for all, I wish to say that, whenever I use the term "Democracy," I mean to apply it only to the leading politicians or *bossmen* of that party, who cut out the work for the masses to execute. Occasionally it happens that a head journeyman is permitted to come into their councils, but the apprentices are never consulted, and they, at last, have more at stake, have more honesty, patriotism, and good common sense than the men by whom they suffer themselves to be misled.

For the first twelve years after the formation of our government, its administration was in the hands of the Father of his Country and John Adams, the elder. In the year 1800 a revolution in the politics of the country occurred, chiefly through the activity and energy of Aaron Burr, who was the legitimate father of Democracy, and not Mr. Jefferson, who was only the beneficiary of Burr's work, as all will admit who will read Parton's life of Burr; and whether the disunion portion of the Democratic party have inherited their treasonable principles from their distinguished progenitor will be left for each one to determine for himself. The Washingtonian party were called Federalists, because they, originally favored the adoption of the Constitution under which the present federal government was formed; and those unfriendly to the Constitution and to its adoption were then called Republicans, and are now called Democrats. But, from the time of this revolution—which was inaugurated on the 4th of March, 1801—down to the 4th of March, 1841, a period of forty years, the Republican or Democratic party held undisputed sway and almost unrestrained control over the destinies of the country, with the single interruption of four years, from 1825 to 1829—during which time it was in the hands of John Quincy Adams.

Those who recollect the violent and stormy passion exhibited at that day at the loss of their long-enjoyed power, with the fierce and bitter denunciation and invective that characterized the opposition to the administration of Mr. Adams (which was one of the most able, conservative, prosperous, and economical that the country has ever enjoyed from its earliest foundation), and of those flagitious charges of "*bargain and corruption*" against one of the purest and most unselfish patriots (as all of every party now admit) that the nation has boasted since the days of Washington, together with the desperation and unscrupulous means resorted to for the recovery of power that marked the period referred to, will admit that nothing has since occurred that will serve as an analogy. The Democracy succeeded, and General Jackson was inaugurated in March, 1829; and then began the reign of terror—then commenced for the first time that universal system of proscription under which devotion to Democracy and partisan services in elections were held to be the only passports to power, and the only tests of fitness for office, from the highest to the most humble in the government; then the system was inaugurated by which every opponent to Democracy was to be annihilated, and every man's character was to be assailed and blackened who did not bow down and worship at the shrine of Jacksonism, which was another term for Democracy. And for eight years—ay, even long after his retirement from public life, a "*hurrah for Jackson*" was the only answer deemed necessary to the most potent arguments against the most lawless and unconstitutional acts of aggression and usurpation of power. During all this time the numerical strength of the country had been gradually but rapidly increasing in the North and diminishing in the South, and yet, for thirty-six years, the Southern Democracy had steadily persisted in putting none other than Southern men in the presidency. Under this state of things Northern politicians were becoming restive. The policy of the North and the South essentially differed at this time on the subject of protection to domestic manufactures and the currency; and to counteract this increasing influence on the part of the North, and the popularity of those questions, certain leading politicians, of whom Mr. Calhoun was at the head, felt the necessity of adopting some new device for the preservation and perpetuation of Southern Democratic ascendency, and that device was, to use the question of slavery as a great political engine, by which the South was to be kept united, and by the divisions which the distribution of spoils and power among the Northern Democrats would create, the power would be retained in the hands of Democracy, as they supposed, for long years to come; and the first scene in this new drama opened with a denial of the right of petition on the subject of slavery, which was the laying of the corner-stone of the

D

foundation on which the present Abolition party has been erected. This was the first step toward strengthening Democracy, by uniting the South and dividing the North, and most fatally has it worked in the end. But, in the mean time, how many in the South have been cajoled or driven into their ranks by the eternal cry that slavery was in danger, and that the Democracy was the only national party that could save it, and from an apprehension that they might be regarded as disloyal to the South, it would be difficult to enumerate.

Mr. Van Buren being the special pet of General Jackson, the Democracy dared not oppose his will, and in 1836, for the first time, they yielded to the necessity of conferring the high distinction of a nomination on a " *Northern man with Southern principles ;*" and but for the shameful waste and extravagance, the enormous peculations and corrupt practices that prevailed and were connived at, and rather rewarded than rebuked during his administration, the slavery question and its consequent agitation might have prolonged their power to an indefinite period. But this it was that led to the policy of denouncing every man in the South as an Abolitionist, no matter what his interest in slave property, no matter what the evidence of his patriotism or fidelity to the Constitution, no matter what the extent of his services to the public, who did not bend the knee to the god of their idolatry, which was *brazen-faced* Democracy. And this policy, then established, it is that has induced those who have no interest in the institution themselves, and who are in very many cases not likely to have such an interest at any future day, and who care nothing for it farther than that it will contribute to the success of Democracy, to take upon themselves the prerogative of assuming the lead in its defense over every slaveholder of the South, and of branding every man of mark or note opposed to their misrule as unfaithful to the South, and a sympathizer, an aider and abettor of the Abolition party, unworthy the confidence and support of a Southern state.

In 1840, General Harrison, an upright, honest, patriotic man, a native of Virginia, was nominated by the Whigs. He was at once branded throughout the state of his nativity and the South as an Abolitionist, while his competitor, Mr. Van Buren, was held up as a patron saint of the "peculiar institution." But the charge against General Harrison proved to be of no avail; the disreputable device failed to accomplish its end; the indignation of the country had been aroused against the administration of Mr. Van Buren, and he was swept with the force of a tornado from power. This was the second time that in forty-four years the Democracy had been overthrown. They stood aghast and dismayed at the result; they felt that every hope was gone; the last and strongest card had been played, and the game had been lost. In thirty days from his inauguration General Harrison suddenly died, and the estate fell to the heir apparent, the Vice-president, a man whose vanity and ambition being readily approached and easily excited, was in an incredibly short time won over to those who had but a few months before been his bitterest revilers, and he turned his back on the friends who had elevated him to power and to fame. At once the hopes of the Democracy revived. By an unlooked-for act of Providence on the one hand, and an act of unparalleled treachery on the other, they found themselves again in possession of the government; but how to retain it was the point. Agitation of the slavery question must be kept up in some form, and they struck upon the expedient of annexing a foreign government to the United States; not for the purpose of extending and strengthening the institution of slavery, but of extending and strengthening the institution of Democracy; for in the late election General Harrison had carried eight Southern States and seventy-eight Southern electoral votes, which must be recovered, or their power was gone forever. Slavery could not be *strengthened* by its extension into new territory, but Democracy might, by increasing the political power of the South, which was under the absolute control of Democracy. As an army of one hundred thousand men in a compact body is stronger and more capable of defending and protecting itself than if divided into a hundred parts of one thousand each, which may by an inferior force be cut up in detail, so is slavery, when confined to the fifteen states in which it exists by the Constitution and local law of the states, far stronger than if it were scattered over all the territory of the United States, when it too would be cut up in detail, and no vestige of it would be left in twenty years.

Upon this issue of the annexation of Texas and the agitation of the question of slavery, they not only cheated Mr. Van Buren out of his nomination that the people desired, but they again succeeded in placing a *Southern* Democrat in the chair over Mr. Clay, another native son of Virginia, and a citizen of Kentucky, who was the owner of a large body of slaves, but who was nevertheless bitterly denounced as an Abolitionist. So flushed were they with the unexpected victory they had achieved over the foremost man of all the land, and so elated at the success of this new issue, that they were determined to press the matter of acquisition still farther in time for the campaign of 1848; and, utterly regardless of all precedent or constitutional restraint, they acquired and admitted Texas as one of the states of this Union by a joint resolution of Congress, which, as a mere act of ordinary legislation, is liable at any time to be repealed; for in law it was null and void from the beginning, for the reason that the Constitution gave no power to the Legislature to enter into a contract with a foreign government for the purchase, sale, or surrender of its territory. In truth, the power did not exist any where; but there was a precedent in the acquisition of Louisiana for acquiring territory by the *treaty-making power*, for which Mr. Jefferson subsequently suggested the propriety of an amendment of the Constitution; so that, if that joint resolution should be repealed to-morrow, Texas would no longer *legally* be a member of this confederacy, although *practically* it would have no effect on her *status* as a state. I only refer to this question to show to what extremities the Democracy resorted for slavery issues to control presidential elections.

But Texas answered the purposes of 1844. Having dodged the *two-third vote* required for its admission *by treaty*, they were in hot haste to get up a new issue for the campaign of 1848, and they struck upon the expedient of having a war with Mexico "to conquer a peace," and "for indemnity for the past and security for the future," which would inevitably lead to the acquisition of additional territory, and necessarily to the question of the extension of slavery into it, which would as infallibly be resisted by the North as it would be claimed and insisted on by the South. And this it was that led to the introduction of the Wilmot Proviso, to be applied to any territory that might be acquired from Mexico; but they were quite as artful in dodging the war-making power as they had been before in dodging the treaty-making power; for they knew the war-making power could not be induced to make a declaration of war, for the reason that we had no cause of complaint against Mexico, while she had ground of complaint against us for annexing a territory the title to which she had never relinquished, but always claimed, and whose independence had been asserted only, but never fully established; so they managed through Mr. Polk, just elected, to send a fleet of observation to the coast of Mexico and an army to Corpus Christi, which was acknowledged to be "*the most western point now (then) occupied by Texas*," a distance of one hundred and eighty miles from the Rio Grande—all of which intermediate territory was then acknowledged by the President, Secretary of War, and our Minister to Mexico, Mr. Donaldson, to belong to Mexico. After waiting at Corpus Christi long enough to see that Mexico did not mean to make war upon us, this little army was marched across to the banks of the Rio Grande, a fort erected, and our guns were pointed upon the Mexican town of Matamoros; and thus was the war commenced without the authority or knowledge of the war-making power, to prepare the way for the slavery issue in the campaign of 1848.

      *   *   *   *   *   *   *   *   *

      *   *   *   *   *   *   *   *   *

General Taylor was elected as the candidate in opposition to General Cass, and although he was said to have been the owner of some two or three hundred slaves, he too, in turn, was vehemently denounced as an Abolitionist not fit to be trusted by the South; nor is it probable he would have been trusted, but for the division of a portion of the Northern Democracy in favor of Mr. Van Buren, who, to resent his defeat in the Convention of 1844, had by this time made an exhibition of his "Southern principles" not very much to the taste of his former admirers in the South, and ran as a Free-soil candidate. Here, then, all their issues had thus failed in 1848; the twenty-first rule, the cry of abolition, the annexation of Texas, the Mexican War, had all availed them nothing, and for the third time the "sceptre had departed from Judah." This they could no longer stand, and what was their next resort? Why, nothing short of a dissolution of the Union and the organization of a Southern confederacy, in which their title to power would be perpetual and omnipotent, and we poor devils of the Whig party were to be made the hewers of wood and drawers of water for our hard task-masters except on the condition of bending the knee to Baal; this cry of disunion was hushed and trodden under foot by the happy influence of the compromises of 1850, which they sternly resisted to the end, and rather than submit to which they called a convention at Nashville for the purpose of initiating a movement in favor of dissolution; that failing, and finding these measures were overwhelmingly popular with the people, they wheeled to the right about, claimed the compromises as their own sacred work, put up their candidate from New Hampshire on the platform of the Compromise Measures, swore he was a better Southern man, and more to be relied on for his devotion and faithful adherence to those compromises as a final settlement of the question than General Scott, another native of Virginia, whom they denounced also as a radical Abolitionist, and subject to the influence and control of Abolitionists, and they carried every Southern state against him except three—Maryland, Tennessee, and Kentucky.

It was by these means, and by a resort to such expedients, that they were enabled, by making a foot-ball for party of the slavery issue and turning it into a sectional party question, to succeed at all—always expressing doubt and distrust of every Southern man who did not agree with their general policy of government, and confiding in, trusting to, and coalescing with every man of the North whose natural and educational instincts were opposed to slavery, if they would only do the one needful thing, and that was, to help them to *money, place,* and *power.*

Seeing the success with which this sectional pro-slavery party had played their game, by keeping the South general-ly united upon the slavery question as a political issue for retaining power, it was not unnatural that the Northern politicians, having a large majority of the electoral vote in the Northern States, and which had been steadily increas-ing, should have made a political hobby of the anti-slavery side of the question, and have used *their* exertions to unite the North in opposition to the extension of slavery for the purpose of acquiring power. How far, or how soon they would have succeeded in obtaining an ascendancy over the Southern Democracy, is questionable, if Democracy had been gifted with common prudence or common honesty; but the supreme folly of that party in 1854, in order to make anoth-er new slavery issue for the election of 1856, in breaking down the Missouri Compromise, in order to force slavery into territory devoted to freedom, and which had been hal-lowed by time, and recognized by the whole country as a bargain and compact sacred and inviolate as the Constitu-tion itself, was the last grain that broke the camel's back. It aroused the indignation of the whole North; it opened their eyes to the aggressions of the Democratic party in the South; Northern politicians seized upon the occasion, and using with adroitness the instruments thus placed in their hands, have at last succeeded in beating down South-ern Democracy with their own weapons and at their own game; and thus the whole story respecting the slavery is-sue is plainly and fairly told. It has been used by both parties for political purposes; by one, for the purpose of retaining, the other, for acquiring money, place, and power; and while the leaders on both sides have excited their followers to a condition of unreasonable pretension and demand, they are sitting hob-nob at Washington, dining, drinking wine, cracking nuts, and cracking jokes together, as familiarly and unconcerned, and as careless and indifferent about results growing out of the agitation they have created, beyond its immediate effect upon parties, as if never a slave had been heard of in the country. Thus has Southern Democracy lost the game and the stakes played for; and now they call upon us, the conservative Whigs of the South, whom they have treated as worse than aliens, whose counsels they have spurned, whose fidelity they have derided, whose remonstrances against making a party and sectional issue of slavery they have contemned, whose patriotism they laughed at, and whose loyalty they have denounced; after all this, in the hour of their humility and defeat, they call upon us for aid which, in the hour of their triumph and pride, they scoffed at and rejected with disdain; failing in which, they threaten to tear down the fairest fabric of government ever erected by human hands. I can only say, if they get no aid until they get it from me, their patience will be exhausted, unless they have an interminable supply; for doomsday might crack, and they would still be found without it. It has been under their control that the country has been brought to its present deplorable and disgraceful condition in every aspect in which it can be viewed. They have shown themselves to be utterly unworthy and incompetent to manage the affairs of the nation, because each one has been managing for himself. Let them be set aside, and let some other party be called to the helm of State, and let them howl, and rave, and "tear their passions to tatters" at the loss of money, place, and power, which they have so long enjoyed and so wildly abused.

Is there any truth or sincerity in the declarations made on the floor of Congress and in the public presses by the Democracy that the institution of slavery is in danger? Let us look for one moment at their declarations, and then at their actions, and every man, *with brains* or *without* them, must at once become satisfied that it is the merest hypocrisy, trickery, and jugglery for political effect, for *money, place, and power*, that was ever played off on the credulity of sensible men.

THE REBELLION FORESHADOWED.

By the foregoing extracts I have shown you how and for what purpose the subject of slavery was kept in constant agitation and in increased peril by those who professed to be its most devoted champions, and the only true friends of the South. They have shown you, too, *how* and for what purpose Texas was hurried into the Union, in outrageous violation of every constitutional impediment and without a precedent for its justification. I was one of those who made strenuous opposition to the annexation of Texas, and this was *another* occasion on which I raised a voice of warning to the people. I was the first man in the United States who made public opposition to it at the time, to the manner it was acquired. I had learned through a private source that a treaty was then being negotiated by Mr. Tyler and his prime minister (Mr. Upshur), by which Texas was to be annexed to the United States. I immediately left Washington, came home to Richmond, and in a speech delivered at the African Church disclosed the fact, and took strong grounds against it. I then went on to New York, and there at the Tabernacle also was the first to inform the people of that city of the design of the administration of Mr. Tyler, and *then* and *there* foretold the danger to which the Union would be exposed by the ratification of such a treaty at that time, and in the condition that Texas then occupied. Allow me to give you an extract or two from my New York speech, delivered on the 12th of April, 1844, and from a letter written subsequently to one of my former constituents (Mr. Hackett, of Louisa), which letter was published in the papers of that day through the country. In the speech I said, as taken from the New York papers of that day, "And now, fellow-citizens, I approach a graver and more serious question; one which strikes at the very root of the government, and can not fail to stir up from its utmost depths the very foundations of society. I mean this secret and clandestine attempt to annex Texas to the United States, or, more properly speaking, to annex the United States to Texas — a question, in my judgment, the magnitude of which no man can over-estimate. If accomplished, that it will lead to the disturbance of our harmony, the distraction of our people, and, sooner or later, to the dismemberment of this government, I have no shadow of doubt. That the Union of these States will be hazarded by its success, is enough to deter me from giving it my sanction or approval. I am a Union man! I am no *Southern* man with *Northern* principles. I am a Southern man with national principles; and if it ever falls to my lot to be sacrificed for any political act of my life, God grant it may be in the defense of the Union of these States." This prayer has been vouchsafed to me; upon this question I have made a willing sacrifice of myself, and I rejoice that I have done so. . . . . .

"Mr. Tyler has made up the issue for Congress whether *we* or England shall have Texas. For my own part, I do not choose that Mr. Tyler or his minister shall make up any such issue for me. Neither his opinions, nor the ends and aims of the disunionists, nor the co-operation of Texas land speculators, nor of the holders of Texas scrip or bonds, shall induce me to credit for an instant the absurd idea that England would be willing to take Texas, with her slave population, as a province, if it were offered to her to-morrow. . . . But what are the terms of this treaty? Who yet knows? But let them be what they may, I for one, if I stand alone, will never accede to the annexation of that country as long as I believe there is any chance thereby of shaking the stability of this Union. I am for this country, this country as it is, and this Union as it is, and I will never agree to dissolve it for the formation of any new one."

The above speech was made in New York in the month of April; the correspondence which follows took place in December following. In the mean time Mr. Upshur had been killed, and Mr. Calhoun had succeeded him as Secretary of State. I give more of this letter than I should otherwise have done, because this Texas annexation was the starting-point, or first *entering* wedge of disunion, and gave to the secessionists the first symptoms of encouragement they had met with in the incipient labor of twelve years, which had been devoted to the object of disunion. The following is a letter to me from one of my then constituents:

Green Springs, Louisa, December 19, 1844.

DEAR SIR,—Taking great interest in your political weal and prosperity, as well as feeling a lively solicitude in your re-election to the Congress of the United States, as also from personal respect, I am induced to make this communication.

As there exists a considerable division in the ranks of the Whig party in relation to the subject of the annexation of Texas, I would respectfully ask if you are unconditionally opposed to this measure?

There is a large and respectable portion of the Whig party (much larger than is generally supposed, I am, from indubitable evidence, induced to believe), not only in this county, but in Goochland and Hanover, who consider this question of paramount importance, so much so as to induce them to hesitate in casting their vote for a candidate unconditionally and "unqualifiedly" opposed to them on this important measure. Indeed I have, on several occasions, heard gentlemen of considerable influence, who have uniformly co-operated zealously with the Whig party, and who consistently advocate and support its *prominent* measures, declare that the vital importance of this subject to the particular interests of the Southern portion of this Confederacy, and the dependence arising from our *peculiar* institutions, under the present aspect of political affairs, for support and balance of power, has induced them to waver in their allegiance to their party, and produced in their minds a condition of doubt and uncertainty as favorable to the success of the opposite party as injurious to the prospects and organization of our own. This is the prolific source of the numerous calls for a convention for the purpose of selecting a suitable candidate to represent this congressional district, and not "*individual attachments*," as represented by the Whig. I believe that an answer favorable to the views of those gentlemen will insure your re-election without the least difficulty, and an adverse one will detach a "segment of a larger vote" than the nomination of either Rhodes, Daniel, Lyons, or Fleming, with you in the field.

For myself, individually, though ardently in favor of this measure, I shall unhesitatingly yield a cheerful vote to the man who has battled so gloriously in defense of our cause; who has stood forth the fearless champion of our invaded rights; who, alike unseduced by the blandishments of power as unappalled by its frowns, has ever exposed its corruptions; who has, with chivalrous courage, unheeding the siren songs of place or office, lifted the veil that concealed the traitor, and exposed him in all his hideous deformity to the astonished gaze of a deluded people, and defied his impotent rage, be the response what it may.

But why may not a Whig, without divesting himself of his party allegiance, without worshiping Baal, without being expelled from his political church, without yielding the cherished opinions of a lifetime on those subjects so dear to his heart, which he has ever been and will ever be proud to maintain—yes, why may he not favor the annexation of Texas to this Union? The fact of the purchase of Louisiana by Mr. Jefferson did not detract from his republicanism. May we not have a national bank and a tariff as well with Texas as without it? But *verbum sap.* Excuse the liberty I have taken, for I can assure you that nothing but an earnest zeal in your behalf, and a deep interest in the ensuing contest, would have induced me thus to trespass on your time and patience.

Very respectfully, your obedient servant,

WM. R. HACKETT.

Half Sink, December 23, 1844.

MY DEAR SIR,—Your letter of the 19th instant has remained unanswered until this time, first, because my mind and time since I received it have both been closely occupied in private matters which could not be neglected, and secondly, because, when I did answer it, I desired to do so at some length, not only that my views on that subject might not be misunderstood by any one voter of the district, but because my vanity (it may be) induced me to indulge the hope that when I presented all my objections to the scheme of the political, as well as the land and scrip stock-jobbers, for the annexation of Texas to the United States, they might not be without their influence in bringing your own mind to a different conclusion from that to which it seems to have arrived.

In anticipation of presenting myself once again as a candidate for Congress, I not only recognize your right, but the right of every (even the humblest) voter in the district to know my opinions on this as on all other subjects upon which, as their representative, I might be called on to act; and, although the opinions I entertain relative to the Texas question might endanger my election, I can with conscientious truth declare that, if I were now a candidate for the highest office known to our institutions, and the result turned upon that question alone, I would not withhold my opposition to the measure to insure my success. I believe, not only as a matter of honesty, but of policy, that there is but one path for a public as well as a private man to tread, and that is, one of straightforward integrity and independence; for if he be honest in his views, however mistaken they may be, he can at least, at all times, give such reasons for his course as will satisfy all who are interested of the purity of his purpose; which, with a generous constituency, will cover a multitude of errors in which the heart does not participate. I have no prejudices and no interests to consult, and no feeling other than that derived from a desire to discharge my duty faithfully to my country; but I believe the success of that measure would prove ruinous to the best interests of the present states, particularly the Southern States, hazardous to the Union, and dangerous as a precedent, without one single benefit resulting from it.

With these preliminary remarks, I proceed, then, to answer your inquiry, by declaring myself unconditionally, un-

qualifiedly, and unalterably opposed, not only to the Texas
treaty, but to Mr. Benton's bill, Mr. M'Duffie's joint resolution, or any other scheme of annexation of the United States
with Texas or any other foreign power that has been or
can be devised; and I rejoice to have been the first in the
United States, in public discussion, to have taken a decided
stand against it, even before the treaty was concluded, my
reasons for which I will endeavor to give as briefly as possible, so as to make myself intelligible.

It must be admitted by all to be a question of the most
delicate, interesting, and important nature, differing from all
others that can arise during the term for which the coming-
in administration will be in power—not only involving the
honor of the nation and the integrity of the Union, but, un-
like the questions of Tariff, Distribution, or Currency, which
may be settled to-day and unsettled to-morrow, as they may
prove pernicious or beneficial, it is perpetual and unalterable
when it is once settled.   It becomes us, therefore, as a people (I will not say as a Southern people, because as yet we
are, as I hope we shall ever continue to be one people, and
as we *must be*, when wise counsels prevail and wicked men
no longer bear swáy), to look to this question in all its aspects and bearings before we conclude hastily upon it; and,
while it is by no means my strongest objection, yet I take
up first the question of expediency.

In the first place, I prefer this Union as it is, and as it has
been handed down to us, and as we were expected to hand
it down " as a rich legacy unto our issue," to any other and
all others that can be formed; and it is enough for me to
know that, if the Texas scheme did not have its origin with,
it has found in its negotiators and chief advocates only the
interested land and scrip holders and political tradesmen,
who have avowed, and daily do avow their anxious desire

for a dissolution of our glorious Union, and to believe at the same time, as I do, that a dissolution would prove the first fruit of annexation.

Can any observing or reflecting man have read the correspondence of the negotiator of the treaty, Mr. John Catiline Calhoun—as he was once characterized by the *Globe* and *Inquirer* for his supposed dark designs upon the Union, a suspicion from which he has to this very day never relieved himself, and which his State of South Carolina openly boasts —without being inevitably led to this conclusion?

Look to his correspondence during the last spring with Mr. Pakenham, the British minister, the representative of a government known to be hostile to *black* slavery in all its aspects (I use the term black slavery, because I think there is less freedom, comfort, and happiness among their white laborers or operatives than among our slaves, for whom they manifest so much sympathy), in which he opens, and thereby invites a correspondence on that delicate subject, which he has been clamorous in claiming to be purely a domestic question with which we could allow no interference. He not only opens a correspondence with Mr. Pakenham, which, to his credit be it said, he had the good sense and wisdom to decline, but in it he based the whole object of the treaty upon the ground of the extension and perpetuation of slavery; and while in one breath he declared that Texas was a sovereign and independent power over which Mexico had no claim and could exert no authority, either *de facto* or *de jure*, he in the next, even on the day after the negotiation of the treaty, dispatched a special envoy to Mexico to purchase her claims on Texas, and at the same instant of time the Executive threatened Mexico with vengeance and war if she should dare to attempt, during the pendency of the treaty, the recovery of her acknowledged claim to a "revolted province," for the relinquishment of which a representative or agent of the United States was sent, as I have just said, to offer millions of gold, while the western division of the army of the United States was actually marched to the confines of Texas, and confidentially made subject to the Texan government, and a portion of the United States Navy was sent to cruise in the Gulf of Mexico, with orders to show themselves occasionally before Vera Cruz.

What was this but a covert declaration of war, made by the executive branch of the government on a weak and resistless power, and that, too, in the presence of and during the session of Congress, which a majority of that body winked at? What was it but such a war as the Texas schemers knew the Northern States would not embark in—an unjust, unrighteous, unprovoked, and ungodly war with Mexico to rob her of her revolted province, and, as Mr. Calhoun says, for the extension and perpetuation of slavery?

Now, whatever may be my feelings on the subject of slavery, I make bold, as a Southern man, to declare that in my judgment these are very insufficient causes for a national robbery or for war with a friendly power making no effort and entertaining no design to interfere with that or any other of our concerns.

It was a South Carolina movement, first, to create dissension, heart-burnings, and division between the North and the South, and, if war should be the result, then to drive the North from its support, and, in the accomplishment of their heart's most earnest desire—one that is daily avowed by their most prominent public men, to wit, the dissolution of the Union—throw the odium and responsibility from their own shoulders upon the North for refusing to participate in a war for any such purpose. There are thousands and millions at the North who believe this institution guaranteed by the Constitution to the South, and will adhere to the South on this question; but there are none, I believe, who desire its extension and perpetuation—they rather deplore its existence; but the North might as soon expect the South to back her in a war for its extermination as for the South to ask the North to go to war to extend and perpetuate it; and this no man knew better than the Secretary of State, the negotiator of the treaty.

Look, too, to the bold, open, and treasonable proceedings of the friends and followers of the negotiator in South Carolina during the last summer and fall, and you find nothing but Disunion, Disunion! Texas, Texas! Disunion without Texas, and Texas *and* Disunion!

To ascertain their views fully, it were as well to look to the declarations of one of Mr. Calhoun's friends from South Carolina, made about the time of the Texas treaty, in the House of Representatives. I mean Mr. Rhett, who declared he would scorn himself if he were capable of singing hosannas to this *Union;* while another of his faithful followers, even to the abandonment of all his former cherished principles (I mean Mr. M'Duffie), entered into a calculation in the Senate Chamber upon the value of the Union, and undertook to show the advantages of three separate confederacies formed out of the United States, declaring upon his soul that, for a quarter of a century, he had not known this government but for its most iniquitous oppressions; and, when charged by Mr. Benton to his face with treasonable designs in the Texas movement, blanched and quailed, and could not utter a word in his defense; even this Mr. M'Duffie, who, in his message to the South Carolina Legislature in 1836, when speaking of the application of Texas for admission into the Union, said: "In my opinion, Congress ought

not even to entertain such a proposition in the present state
of the controversy. If we admit Texas into our Union
while Mexico is still waging war against that province with
a view to re-establish her supremacy over it, we shall, by
the very act itself, make ourselves a party to the war; nor
can we take this step without incurring this heavy responsibility *until Mexico herself shall recognize the independence
of her revolted province*." And now, disunion being at the
bottom, this gentleman is the first to step forth, in the absence of that recognition on the part of Mexico, and while
our Executive is complaining in his annual messages of the
savage and inhuman war carried on by that power against
Texas, which he thinks we ought to put a stop to, he steps
forward and proposes to take it, *nolens volens*, by the simple adoption of a joint resolution, as if it were a matter of
no more moment than the payment of a messenger's wages.
It serves well to show the degeneracy of the times and of
our people. A few years back, and such a proposition
would have aroused the indignation of all men of all parties; and he who would have presented it would have been
regarded as little short of a madman, and the party that
would have entertained it would have been overwhelmed
with popular resentment. Well might Mr. Gallatin have
expressed his surprise that such a mode of acquiring Texas
could have entered into the imagination of man.

But again, at a more recent period, you find this able and
most skillful and accomplished negotiator and diplomatist,
who has done nothing but blunder and stumble on like a
blind horse over plowed ground ever since he has been in
the department, whose sensibilities have been so much
shocked at the bare presentation of abolition petitions from
members of this confederacy as to propose at one time to
the whole Southern delegation in Congress to retire from

the halls of Congress, and thus by violence dismember the government, you find him throwing wide the whole question of domestic slavery, and not only authorizing but inviting the interference and co-operation of the French government in the treaty or other new-fangled mode of annexation, for the purpose of perpetuating the blessings and advantages of slavery. Now, if it be conceded by our government that France may rightfully interfere, I pray to know upon what principle of civil or international law the same right can be denied to Great Britain, whose pretended designs upon this question were made the first pretext for immediate, *instantaneous* annexation, or slavery was to be abolished and Southern interests destroyed? And why is this interference on the part of France with our peculiar fireside domestic rights courted and entreated, but that it may lead to an interference on the part of Great Britain for its destruction; and which may lead, by their natural sympathies and affinities, to a co-operation between the Abolitionists of the North and that government that would tend to unite more closely the sympathies and interests of the South, lead to a division of the empire, and annexation with Texas? This I believe to be the design, and this, I fear, will be the result, if this Texas humbug is not speedily and decisively settled by the good sense of our countrymen. Upon no other view of the subject can the weakness and puerility — I should say madness — of his diplomatic correspondence be accounted for.

But apart from all this, apart from Mexican rights, the national honor, the integrity of the Union, what are the advantages that we are to derive from the annexation of Texas? We already see that our negotiator and his confederates have placed us in a position toward Mexico that we can not escape a war without dishonor to the executive branch of the government, and we can not get into one without disgrace to the nation. But let that terminate as it may, what, I ask, are the advantages to be derived from such annexation, even with the assent of Mexico? Is not our territory already sufficiently capacious to contain our' population? Are our millions of unsold public lands, which must sooner or later inure to the benefit of the states, to whom it belongs, to be surrendered or rendered valueless in order to satisfy the demands of speculators in Texas lands or Texas scrip, or to favor the views of political tradesmen? Are we to depreciate the land of the old states (in Virginia, for example) and depopulate our state to people Texas? Are we to despoil it of the most active, industrious, and useful portion of its population, by holding out an invitation and inducement to the energetic and enterprising young men of the state to seek adventures and fortunes in a new country? Are we to plunder our treasury to pay the debts of Texas—at a time, too, when the credit of our states is dishonored? Are we so harmonious in our councils now as to make occasion for new difficulties and new strife? Is our legislation so satisfactory to all parts of the present Union that we should desire to extend its influence, diversify still more the interests to be cared for, and introduce among us an additional number of disaffected disorganizers and repudiationists? Are we to open still wider the door to fraud and corruption, not by the introduction of individual foreigners, but of a foreign nation? When it has become an interesting and a prominent question whether we shall restrict or prohibit entirely all future naturalization, is it expedient to naturalize two hundred thousand at a batch—seven tenths of whom, no doubt, have the same leveling and destructive propensities common to too many of our own people? Have we not, as a nation, deteriorated in morality sufficiently in the last sixteen years, without the introduction of Texas adventurers among us?

EFFORTS TO EXTEND SLAVERY.

Up to this period secession had made but little perceptible progress. But the archfiend of secession, Mr. Tyler's Secretary of State (Mr. Calhoun), took good care, as you will perceive, to see that the extension of slavery should constitute a prominent feature in the foreground of the negotiation, as a great and momentous issue, upon the result of which the safety and existence of Southern institutions was to depend. He openly proclaimed that the great object of the annexation was for the expansion of slave territory, and consequent increase and continuance of power to the *Democracy* of the South, and this it was, *as I had it from his own lips*, that first drove John Quincy Adams into the ranks of the Abolition party. I was at that time in Washington, contesting the seat of the late John W. Jones. Mr. Adams had made a speech, in which he had given utterance to sentiments on the subject of slavery which did not correspond with the views he had been supposed to entertain; for up to that time he had made himself obnoxious to the Abolition party in his district, and they had on several occasions brought forward an Abolition candidate against him.

Upon the adjournment of the House we walked down together, and I took occasion to refer to his remarks (which I do not now precisely recollect), and said I thought he did not mean to say all that his language could imply. "Yes," he replied, "I said it deliberately and purposely." "But," said I, "Mr. Adams, you are not an Abolitionist." "Yes, I am," said he; "I never have been one until now; but when I see the Constitution of my country struck down by the South for such purposes as are openly avowed, no alternative is left me; I must oppose them with all the means within my reach; I must fight the devil with his own fire; and, to do this effectually, I am obliged to co-operate with the Abolition party, who have been hateful to me heretofore. If the South," he continued, "had consulted her true interests, and followed your counsels on the 21st rule and on this Texas question, their institutions would never have been endangered by the North; but if matters are to take the shape foreshadowed by Mr. Calhoun and others of the Democratic party, then no one can foretell what may be the consequences."

Much more conversation of a similar nature passed between us before we separated; but this is enough to show what influences operated on him, and, *through him*, on a large portion of the North, over which he exercised more influence than any other living man.

In this connection, and as farther proof, I attach an extract from an editorial of the Charleston *Courier* (at a later period), the mouth-piece and organ of the whole secession school of politicians, which of itself plainly shows that the purposes and ends of this war was to perpetuate the power of Southern Democracy: "Every battle fought in Mexico, and every dollar spent there, but insures the acquisition of territory which must widen the field of Southern enterprise and *power* in future. And the final result will be to re-adjust the balance of power in the confederacy so as to give us control over the operations of government in all time to come." This was the only kind of "balance of power" they ever sought—a *balance* all on one side.

Such a declaration Mr. Calhoun well knew would unavoidably engender an embittered sectional contest, which would necessarily, as it did, more and more unite and cement the South into one common brotherhood of Democracy. He also knew full well that the annexation of Texas, whose independence had not been recognized by Mexico, would necessarily lead to a war with Mexico, provided she felt herself in a condition to resent the outrage upon her well-known right to Texas as a revolted province, and through his instruments at home he raised the cry of "*Texas without the Union, rather than the Union without Texas,*" which soon became the rallying-cry of the Democratic party throughout the Southern States; and it was upon this issue, thus adroitly but mischievously made, that thousands of the Whig party, of easy virtue and shallow brains, were democratized, and through their instrumentality, to the infinite surprise of the nation and the world, Mr. James K. Polk beat Mr. Clay for the Presidency in 1844.

THE STRICT DISCIPLINE IN THE DEMOCRATIC RANKS.

Thus you have seen, though not exactly in chronological order, *how* and *for what purpose* Texas was annexed, and how and for what purpose the war with Mexico was made by the Democratic party through their agent and representative, Mr. Polk, and without the sanction of Congress, though then in session. This was made, not because war in itself was at all more desirable to Democracy than to any other people, but because it would lead to acquisition of territory, and to long and angry sectional disputes, and ultimately either to the security of their power under the national government or to a dissolution of the Union, all of which followed as had been anticipated; for whatever else may be said of the Democratic party, it can not be denied that it was the best-organized and the best-drilled party that the world has produced in any age or country; and it never lacked the boldness to do any thing, however mon-

E

strous and violent, or unconstitutional, to accomplish the object of its leaders. One of the distinguishing features that has always marked the difference between the Democratic and Whig parties in this country has been, that the former was never afraid to do what they knew to be wrong to accomplish an end, while the latter was always afraid to do what they knew to be right for the same end.

No army under the lead of the great Napoleon was ever more under his control, or more obedient to his orders, than were the masses of the Democracy to the demands made upon them by the hungry and greedy set of demagogues, their leaders, after the spoils of office, the dispensation of patronage, and the exercise and perpetuation of power; and so far did this well-digested plan succeed that the safety of the Union was then greatly imperiled by the result. I repeat here what I said in my Academy of Music speech in New York in 1859:

"I do not mean to say, because I do not believe that vice and corruption pervade the entire body of Democratic politicians, although there is far too much of it in politicians of all parties, and none are too good to bear watching; but it is the nature and character of their organization, which is the most perfect, compact, and formidable that ever controlled a party, that leads to all these mischiefs; it is the system and policy they pursue, and to which few of them do not subscribe; and when they do not they are excluded from the fleshpots, which is the severest punishment known to their codes—that policy is to make all things bend to success, to sacrifice all things human and holy to the ascendency of party and the perpetuation of power; neither the lights of experience, the peace of the country, the harmony of sections, the preservation of the Constitution, the safety of the Union, the prosperity of the nation, the purity of the bench, the sanctity of the church, neither one nor all these combined are allowed to break through the serried ranks of their political organization, which has no principle for its basis, and no manly incentive for its conduct."

THE WILMOT PROVISO.

So alarming were the threats of dissolution occasioned by the application of the Wilmot Proviso (which was nothing but the revival of the provisions of the Ordinance of 1787, and for which this same Southern Democracy had themselves just before voted—I believe unanimously or nearly so —when applied to the Territory of Oregon) to all territory acquired from Mexico, of which full notice had been given during the war, and before the territory was acquired, that Mr. Clay, who had resigned his seat in the Senate and retired to private life with a determination never again to engage in the turmoil of political strife, was induced by a lofty spirit of patriotism to leave the comforts of home, which at his advanced age had become essential to his health and repose, to return again to the Senate, once more to still the elements of an approaching political hurricane that threatened to sweep every thing of value in our institutions before it. The result you well know to have been the adoption of the Compromise Measures of 1850.

The adoption of these measures of compromise was hardly a less staggering blow struck at the wicked aims of this reckless and disloyal party than that struck by General Jackson in 1833, even at the moment that they had indulged in the insane fancy that the time had arrived for a bold outbreak into open revolution. But discomforted and disheartened as they were, the leaders did not lose their courage, for they were always a bold, daring, and desperate set of men, who had set their hearts on the destruction of a government that they saw must soon pass from under their control. The standard of rebellion was raised, and they called a Southern Convention, to be held at Nashville, for the purpose of resisting by force the measures which had been adopted; but the loyalty of the people had not then been sufficiently corrupted to encourage an open outbreak. Nevertheless, the secession flag was raised in most of the Cotton States. In Mississippi, General Quitman was the secession candidate for governor, and the Mr. Henry S. Foote now a member of the Confederate Congress, and the constant eulogist of his then opponent, and as active a champion of secession as is to be found in all the South, was the Union candidate. He boldly repudiated and denied the right of a state to secede, denounced it as treason, and in a short time Davis was driven from the field. Jeff. Davis supplied his place, but the people of Mississippi triumphantly sustained Foote, and he was elected governor by a large majority. The same flag was also raised in Georgia under the lead of the then Governor M'Donough. Howell Cobb, late Secretary of the Treasury of the United States, and now a general of the Confederate Army, was the Union candidate; he also denounced secession as treason, and was likewise triumphantly sustained by the people of Georgia.

The party seeing these overwhelming indications of determined hostility to the doctrine of secession, and of the popularity of the measures they had so persistently opposed, wheeled to the right about, claimed the compromises as their own, went into convention to nominate a candidate for the Presidency, and adopted a platform, pledging themselves unequivocally to a faithful support of the measures they had thus resisted.

This it was necessary they should do to give them a ghost of a chance to elect a Democratic President; and for that end they were prepared, as they always had been, to do any thing deemed requisite to their success. This was their solemn pledge to the people of the United States; how far they adhered to this pledge, after they had deluded and cheated the people into a trust to their sincerity and honesty, will be seen in the sequel. But upon this pledge to the nation they set up Mr. Franklin Pierce, of New Hampshire, a man unknown to fame, a man, for *such a position*, of absolute obscurity, a man without talents, without firmness, without reputation, without popularity or influence, as the Democratic candidate for the Presidency against General Scott, whom they charged with being unsafe, and unsound, and not to be trusted on the measures of compromise; and, by hard swearing, they succeeded in persuading the great masses of the Southern people that this New England pettifogger was more to be relied on for the protection of Southern rights and Southern institutions than General Scott, a native born Virginian, who was not only born and raised in the midst of slavery, but whose whole property and interests were located here in Virginia, and who had a most enlarged national reputation—one, indeed, that extended throughout the world, and who was known to have been extremely active and efficient in Washington in procuring the passage of the Compromises of 1850.

THE EXTREMISTS OF BOTH SECTIONS UNITED IN ACTION.

It is a circumstance not to be overlooked here, that throughout the period that these measures were before Congress, the extreme men of both sections, to wit, the Northern Abolitionists and the Southern Seceders and "Fire-eaters," as they were called, uniformly and invariably acted and voted together. In illustration of this, I will mention an amusing incident that occurred at the Exchange Hotel in Richmond. Shortly after the passage of these measures, the celebrated John P. Hale, senator from New Hampshire, came to Richmond. I happened to be present with the late Caleb Jones — a near neighbor and friend, although a violent Democrat, with whom I had walked to the Exchange—when the Northern cars arrived, and Mr. Hale entered the room. After the usual salutations, Jones said, "Why, *Hale*, ain't you afraid to come to Richmond?" Hale, who affected surprise and uneasiness, looking around the room, in which there were quite a number of persons, replied, "Well, I don't know; is there any danger in my coming here? Don't Mason come to Richmond? Don't Hunter come to Richmond? Don't Seddon come to Richmond? And if they can come, can't I come also, for I voted with *them* all the winter? If they gave Southern votes, so did I; and if I gave Northern votes, so did they; and don't you think what is sauce for the goose should also be sauce for the gander?" This happy retort on the part of Hale not only discomfited poor Jones (who was a warm political friend and supporter of these three gentlemen), but completely turned the laugh of the whole company, Whigs and Democrats, who recognized the truth of what he had said, upon Jones, who joined in the laugh, but, as he told me afterward, he never enjoyed one so little, for there was more truth than poetry in the answer.

AGITATION THE OBJECT IN VIEW.

It is curious to inquire how and why it happened that for so long a time these two extremes were thus found in active co-operation, voting side by side with each other, and on that particular subject upon which the greatest antagonism existed. The solution is simple: these two parties were always alike in favor of constant and eternal agitation, and alike opposed to all compromise or settlement of the questions arising out of the slavery issue. The Abolitionists relied on agitation and excitement to make proselytes to their cause, while the Secessionists thought that, by keeping this subject alive in Congress, and wherever else it could be introduced, the fears of our people would become the more susceptible, and their passions more easily aroused, and the way be thus paved for ultimate disunion. These Southern men never cared for disunion, nor desired it, except as a necessary means of retaining power in the government; nor would they have tolerated it as long as they could hold that power in their own hands; and after all the New England States became anti-Democratic, thus presenting an insuperable barrier to the permanency of their power, a new idea presented itself to their imaginations, which was a *partial* disunion, and that was to be effected by sloughing off the New England States, not because they were more thoroughly imbued with Abolition than Ohio and other Western States, but that they were more certainly anti-Democratic in their proclivities.

In like manner the extreme Abolitionists were anxious for a *partial* dissolution; their object was to get rid of the institution of slavery, and they were willing to do any thing that would drive the Cotton States off, into which all the slaves of the Border States, as they thought, would soon find their way. Thus, and for these objects, the question of slavery was used as a foot-ball, or, rather, as a shuttle-cock, with which the political game of battle-door was played by these two extremes—extreme in their folly and fanaticism; extreme in their disregard of all other views than their own; extreme in their utter disregard of all constitutional obligations; extreme in their disloyalty to the government; extreme in their general disturbance of the public tranquillity and safety; extreme in their extravagance and. violence, and extreme in their hatred and contempt of each other. And now, I will venture on one other prediction, and that is, that if a proposition shall ever be made by the South for a restoration of peace, it will be *one* based, if not in *direct terms*, at least upon the *idea* of a restoration of power to the Democratic party by throwing off the New England States, or something else that will insure their future triumph.

SECESSIONISTS BECOME FILIBUSTERS.

It was during the progress of the events I have here related as part and parcel of the designs entertained by the Democracy, that the various expeditions for the violent seizure of Cuba were gotten up, which at last terminated so fatally for both leader and men in the memorable landing of Lopez upon that island. That expedition was to have been led on by the late General Quitman, a violent secessionist, although a man of *Northern birth*, but for some reason he declined it, and the command fell upon the unfortunate Lopez, who lost his life in the cause of Southern Democracy. So, too, was the repeated defiance and utter contempt of all law and treaty obligations for the suppression of the African slave-trade, which was but part and parcel of the same scheme for agitation and excitement, and for creating a still deeper feeling of opposition and hostility on the part of the North toward the South. Nobody at the present day can believe for a moment that these secessionists ever desired the revival of the African slave-trade, for the purpose of introducing a set of naked, worthless, and degraded kidnapped barbarians on their plantations, and at the moment, too, when they affected to believe that the safety of the South required an outlet through Texas, and

at a later day through Kansas, for an overgrown and re-
dundant slave population, except for the object of agitation
and excitement on the negro question that was to set the
North and South farther and farther apart.

In like manner, and for the same purpose, were all those
expeditions on the part of General William Walker to Nic-
aragua gotten up, in defiance of all the laws and obligations
of neutrality, amity, and good neighborhood, and which excited the indignation of all conservative men at home, and
the hostility and disquiet of all abroad.

THE SOUTHERN COMMERCIAL CONVENTIONS.

Then, too, came the Southern Commercial Conventions,
composed *chiefly*, though not entirely, of Southern secessionists (for their objects were not universally known),
which conventions never did, and never were designed to
do any thing more than bring together every year such a
body of politicians and secessionists as would enable them
to make their organization more complete and more perfect
for dissolution, whenever the proper time arrived that it
was necessary for the perpetuation of their power. To be
sure, in their open, daily meetings, they would make gran-
diloquent speeches for the Southern papers on Southern
commerce, direct trade, and commercial independence, what
a great country the South would make, etc., etc.; but that
was the last you would hear of Southern direct commerce
until the year rolled on, and another meeting was held,
when the same old formula was gone through with. In
confirmation of what I say on this subject, let me call your
attention to what the Richmond *Examiner*, one of the leading organs of that party, said but a few days ago, to wit, on
the 27th of this month (October 27, 1861). In comment-
ing on the proceedings of the late meeting of the Southern

E 2

Commercial Convention in Macon, the editor said, "We had supposed that the mission of this and other kindred political conventicles would be fulfilled by the '*fait accompli*' (accomplished fact) of secession," etc. — thus showing that secession was, at least in the opinion of that editor, who was thoroughly in the confidence of the party, and cognizant of all their proceedings and actions, the only object that they had met to consider and digest. I myself attended one or two of these conventions as a delegate from the city of Richmond—one especially at Memphis, at which I satisfied myself thoroughly of the disorganizing and dangerous character of these meetings, and came home with a determination never to attend another.

THE CALM BEFORE THE STORM.

But to come back to the more regular, open, and distinct proceedings of the party. I had brought you down to 1852, and the platform of that year. At this time every question of difficulty between the North and the South had been adjusted; there was not left one inch of territory about which a dispute could arise; harmony was happily and rapidly being restored to the country; the Northern party, it is true, every where complained of the rigor and harshness of some of the features of the Fugitive Slave Law, such as that which authorized the marshal of the district to call to his aid any citizen or citizens to assist him, *not* in vindicating the offended law, which was about to be resisted by a mob in an attempt to rescue a slave already in his custody, but to enable him *to catch* a runaway slave, which they said, and said truly, was the exaction of a distasteful and degrading duty to which no Southern man was subjected at home. Such a provision should never have been there. It ought to have been, and, under the bitter state of feeling daily growing up between the masses of the two sections, would have been modified. It was·put there at the instance of a senator from this state, Mr. James M. Mason, one of the principal of the secession party in Congress; whether for the purpose of forcing the North to defeat the passage of the bill, and thereby getting up additional excitement on that subject in the South, or of defeating the whole batch of compromises, or of inviting resistance to the execution of the law, is a secret confined, perhaps, to his own breast.

DEATH OF JOHN C. CALHOUN.

Shortly after the passage of the Compromise Measures Mr. Calhoun died, leaving as a legacy to his Southern friends, in a speech carefully prepared, which he was too feeble to deliver, but which was read to the Senate at his request by this same Mr. James M. Mason, of Virginia, containing a recommendation for the establishment of two republics, or else a " dual government," with *two Presidents*— one for the South and the other for the North, under the same republic: a speech so filled with gall and treason toward his government that it was a matter of astonishment to many that the Senate should have permitted it·to have been read in their presence, and in the halls of legislation. Mr. Clay and Mr. Webster, the two great leaders of the Union party, soon followed Mr. Calhoun to the grave; so that when Mr. Pierce succeeded to power; and was inaugurated in March, 1853, the Union party in the South was without a head or acknowledged leader in their ranks. Jealousy and distrust of each other rendered the efforts of all who were fit to lead inoperative and useless; there was no concert of action, no harmony, and no confidence; and any political party without a leader will as certainly become disorganized and demoralized, as will an army in the field without commanders. The Whig party thus situated, without a head, soon became thoroughly demoralized, and, consequently, many of its prominent politicians thoroughly democratized. It would be useless here to enumerate those who, at this period, went over to the strong party, or the party in power, to look for a softer place on which to rest than they had been able to find in the ranks of their old associates. Some pretended that it was because General Scott *was* nominated, others because Mr. Fillmore—who had made a "model President," as all parties in the South, secessionists included, represented him to be, because he sent Federal troops to Boston to enforce the law upon the people of Massachusetts—was *not* nominated. But there is not wanting a *pretext* when a politician resolves upon a change; a reason is one thing which it is sometimes difficult to furnish, but none of that class are ever at a loss for an excuse. With them it may truly be said, *Where there's a will there's always a way.* Now, as I approach the most important period in the progress of secession, allow me to go back a little, and indulge in a slight repetition of what I have already gone over. You will not have forgotten the platform of the party to which I have already referred, and upon which Mr. Pierce was elected, by which they pledged themselves "to adhere to a faithful execution of the acts known as the Compromise Measures, settled by the Congress of 1850," and declaring "that all efforts of the Abolitionists *or others* to induce Congress to interfere with the question of slavery, or to take incipient steps in relation thereto, were calculated to lead to the most alarming and dangerous consequences; and that all such efforts have an inevitable tendency to diminish the happiness of the people, and *endanger the stability* and permanency of the Union, and ought not to be countenanced by any friend of our political institutions!"

The Whig party, in their platform, declared as follows: "We deprecate all farther agitation of the question thus settled as dangerous to our peace, and will discountenance all efforts to continue or renew such agitation whenever, wherever, or however the attempt may be made; and we will maintain this system as essential to the nationality of the Whig party and the integrity of the Union." These were portions and the principal features in the platform of the two parties upon which they went before the country, both pledged in the most unequivocal and solemn manner against taking any incipient steps in relation to the farther agitation of the slavery question. Mr. Pierce was elected by a most overwhelming majority; General Scott got only eight electoral votes. The Whig party, who had lent their aid in breaking down the Missouri Compromise, exhibited such a want of strength in this election that many of weak knees, weaker nerves, and still weaker principles and softer brains, grew tired of working in a minority, and, like rats in a sinking ship, began at once to look about for better quarters.

UNION WHIGS TURN DEMOCRATIC SECESSIONISTS.

With the great triumph they had just achieved in the election of Mr. Pierce, and the great accession to their ranks from their old opponents, the Toombs's, Stephens's, Faulkners, and many others of less prominence and weight, the Democratic party ran wild and riotous in the exuberance of their overgrown power, and yet, with all their strength, they knew that, without some new issue on the slavery question, the continuance of their power was of great uncertainty.

Now I beg you to recollect what I have already said, that at this time there was no territory within the jurisdiction of the United States over which it was possible to get up a quarrel or excitement. All the territory acquired by the treaty for Louisiana had been settled by the Compromise of 1820, which had stood undisturbed for thirty odd years, until it had become as sacred in the eyes of the whole nation as a part of the Constitution itself. The Legislature of this state had in 1847 declared, by a vote of 117 to 13, that "any attempt to interfere with that Compromise would be just cause for a dissolution of the Union, and would be resisted at all hazards, and to the last extremity;" and the feeling in this state was no stronger in favor of that healing measure of peace than in other portions of the country North and South; and all the territory acquired by the war with Mexico, extending from the Louisiana purchase to the Pacific Ocean, was provided for and settled by the Compromises of 1850.

THE FUGITIVE SLAVE LAW.

Thus you will see that all causes of dissension had been removed; old sores were fast healing up; the occasional resistance to the Fugitive Slave Law alone furnishing ground of complaint. The constitutionality of that law was tested before the proper tribunals in several of the states, and in every instance judgment was pronounced in favor of the law; the people of the North were fast becoming reconciled to it, or at least opposition to its execution was on the decline, and with a modification of the obnoxious features to which I have already adverted, and which did not add at all to its efficiency, would in another year have ceased altogether, except with a handful of the most violent and mischievous of the Abolitionists, who could of themselves have offered no serious obstacle to its faithful execution.

Every thing had so far quieted down that John P. Hale, senator from New Hampshire, declared "*Othello's occupation's gone;*" he retired from the Senate and set up a law office in Wall Street, New York, and every patriot in the land rejoiced at the prospect of peace between the different sections of the country, and at the final settlement of this disturbing question of slavery that had been a source of constant irritation and excitement in the public councils for thirty years.

But this was just precisely the state of things that did not suit the Democracy. They did not want quiet; they wanted *excitement.* They did not want the question of slavery to sleep; they wanted *agitation.* They did not want peace; they wanted *war.* They did not want Union, unaccompanied with the power of the government in their own hands; they wanted secession and Southern independence, where their power would be perpetual. Therefore it was again necessary to elect a Democratic President in '56, or the Union must be dissolved. Do you doubt this? Call them to the bar, and let them testify on oath whether this was their deliberate, determined purpose or not; let them answer to an injured and deeply-wronged people, whether the perpetuation of power in their own hands has not been the whole and sole cause of this infernal war, which will cost the Southern people, *every thing* included, not less than from six to ten thousand millions of dollars before they get through with it, to say nothing of four or five hundred thousand lives that will be lost; and how much more, the Lord only knows, if the principles of Democracy, as applied to poor, feeble Mexico, should be extended to them, of "indemnity for the past and security for the future," to cover the whole expenses of the war on the part of the United States. What have they themselves told us for the last twenty years? Has there been a Democratic paper published in the South—has there been a Democratic speaker on the stump within that period that has not wrung it into our ears over and over again, "THAT IT WAS NECESSARY TO ELECT A DEMOCRAT TO SAVE THE UNION?" which it is now manifest meant nothing more nor less, in plain English, than this, "that whenever the *ballot-box* fails to secure us our accustomed triumph, we will resort to the *cartridge*-box for our deliverance; and that secession, rebellion, and treason will all be encountered, rather than surrender the power we have so long enjoyed and abused."

THE DEMOCRACY TO RULE, OR DISUNION TO FOLLOW.

The people could not be made to believe it. Nobody took it for any thing else than an attempt to frighten the weak-minded and timid into their support; they did not believe any party base enough, bad as they knew this party to be, to commit such a deed for such a purpose, nor did they believe that they had the power, if they had the will; they did not believe that that old Whig conservative Union element in the South, and in this state particularly, could either be seduced or driven into such a measure at the dictation of a mob as we have since seen it done with our own eyes. There has been no time within the last twelve years that the *leaders* have not been prepared for it on a failure to elect their candidate. They dared not try it with General Taylor, for he was a Southern man, and a large slaveholder, although every where denounced as an Abolitionist, nor had they any confidence in his Whiggery. They would not have dared to try the experiment if General Scott had been elected, because he too was a Southern man of known conservative views. But the leaders were not only rife for it in '56, if Fremont had been elected, but I see no reason to doubt that the same course of events might not have been carried out then as now.

DEVELOPMENT OF THE CONSPIRACY.

They all say they were Union men until Lincoln issued his proclamation, but this I have shown to be false. This proclamation was for the protection of the Capitol at Washington and of his own life, which they would have taken in three weeks if he had not made the call, the design being to employ a body of men collected from New York, Newark, Philadelphia, Baltimore, Washington, Alexandria, Richmond, Petersburg, and Norfolk; headed by two leading men of the South—one from Texas, who has since been slain in battle, and the other from Virginia, who has never taken the chances of being slain. I *knew* at least that this was the opinion of Mr. Lincoln when he issued his proclamation, for I was cognizant of the communication that was made to him on this subject; for when I left the city of Washington on the day the proclamation was issued, the windows of a portion of the Treasury building had already been barricaded. Of these facts, no doubt, abundant proof will be found hereafter.*

* Nov. 5, 1863.—Such proof now begins to leak out; and in confirmation of what I have said, I take the following editorial paragraph from the Richmond *Sentinel* (the recognized organ of the administration) of Nov. 2, 1863, edited by a Mr. Smith, who in 1860, '61, conducted a secession journal in Alexandria, and may well be supposed to have been in the secrets of the plot. The *Sentinel* says, "Indeed a formidable organization existed all the winter in Baltimore and the counties adjacent to Washington, having for its object the capture of that city, the seizure of the government officers, and the inauguration of a provisional government in the interests of the South. Such a step would have given the South the

But this was not all.   Mr. Jefferson Davis had boastfully threatened "that the North should smell Southern powder,

command of the United States Army and Navy; it would have consigned the North to anarchy, at least for a while—perhaps to a civil war at their own doors; but wise and politic as was this measure in the eyes of those who saw the value of striking the first blow, it was too rash to be hazarded until the support of Virginia could be secured, and for that there was no chance."

Here, then, is a precious confession by a precious rebel of a concerted scheme, not to protect or "defend the South from a ruthless, heartless, savage invasion by the North," as has since been pretended; not to throw off the yoke "of an intolerably oppressive government," and to set up an independent government for themselves simply, as the people have been made to believe, but here it is openly avowed that there was a formidable organization to capture the Capitol of the nation, to depose the lawfully-elected President of the country, and inaugurate a provisional government in the interests of the South, by which they were to have secured the army and navy of the United States, and to have involved the North in a civil war at home among themselves, while Southern Democracy reveled in the enjoyment of the spoils derived from their own hellish treason, from the consequences of which they now shrink, and piteously whine that "*all they ask is to be let alone.*"

Now I may as well say here that this whole scheme was fully developed to me on the 8th of April, 1861, by General James Wilson, with whom I had formerly served in Congress—a gentleman of the highest respectability, to whom it had been disclosed by one of the parties implicated, as being a part of the plan of operations contemplated by the outside Convention which met in the city of Richmond on the 16th of April, '61.   General Wilson, who now resides in California, mentioned these facts to me that I might communicate them to the government, which I did without loss of time; I went at once to Mr. Lincoln, to whom I made the communication, and, at his request, I rode immediately to the residence of General Scott, who was then engaged in planning defenses for the city, and laid all the facts before him.   When, therefore, upon the fall of Sumter (which it might well be supposed would precipitate the contemplated attack on Washington), I saw the proclamation of Mr. Lincoln calling for the seventy-five thousand troops, it was not unnatural to con-

and feel Southern steel." Mr. Walker, the Secretary of War, at Montgomery, on the night of the fall of Fort Sumter, had declared in a public speech that the Confederate flag should float over the walls of the Capitol in Washington in less than thirty days. Mr. Robert Toombs had but recently before the breaking out of the rebellion declared in the Senate of the United States that the day was not distant when he would be able to call the roll of his slaves at the foot of Bunker Hill Monument. Mr. Henry A. Wise had, over and over again, insisted upon fighting for "OUR RIGHTS" *in the Union*, which every body seemed puzzled to comprehend; and it was to this plan that the South was committed by their leaders, to possess themselves of Washington, seize upon the archives of the nation, get control of the army, navy, and treasury, and spread Democracy and slavery all over the United States in the event of their success. Mr. Lincoln would have been assassinated in 1861 instead of 1865; and to this plan of operations many of the leading Northern Democrats had pledged their support (see the speeches of *General Gantt*), which would have developed itself at that day but for the rashness and impetuosity of

clude that they were designed to repel this lawless and treasonable invasion of the Capitol of the nation.

The overthrow of the government of the United States, the subjugation of the North, and the usurpation of the powers of the government by the leaders of the Southern Democracy, is the war which from the first I have condemned, and which to the last I shall continue to denounce; and for which I have incurred the loss of my personal liberty, and the odium and opprobrium of the *once Union men* of the South. Let them who are satisfied with the results up to this time and with the prospects for the future continue to lavish their epithets against me; but let all others (if *they dare* not approve) at least be silent. Thanks, many thanks to the *Sentinel* for this open avowal of the purposes of this rebellion. Upon whom does it establish the crime of treason?

the Southern leaders, who precipitated the attack upon Fort Sumter, by a declaration made to the people of Charleston through their agent and representative, Mr. Roger A. Pryor, on the 10th of April, that upon the firing of the first gun Virginia would go out; but so startling was the result upon the popular mind of the North, that it was more than their lives would have been worth for one of these Northern sympathizers and coadjutors at that time to have lent such aid or have expressed such sympathy, which has been so freely and fully developed since that time.

Only a few days after the proclamation, when Mr. Alexander H. Stephens came on to Richmond to receive this once proud and grand old commonwealth, bound hand and foot like a sheep in shambles, to be transferred to the slaughter-house of the Montgomery government, wherever he stopped on the cars to wood, water, or eat, he addressed the people, and his whole address consisted of "On to Washington," "On to Washington," "On to Washington." Yet they were all friends to the Union until a fatal stab was made at the *vitals* "of the Union;" they were all friends to "the Constitution" until the Constitution was trampled down and spit upon; they were all friends to "the execution of the laws" until it became necessary to execute them. I know of nothing that could afford a stronger illustration of this than may be found in a speech delivered by Alexander H. Stephens, of Georgia, in the city of Richmond, on the 22d of April last (1861), when contrasted with what this gentleman had said only a few weeks before in his discussion with Mr. Toombs, and again repeated shortly after, with still more force, before the Georgia Convention. This Richmond speech I append:

SPEECH OF ALEXANDER H. STEPHENS AT RICHMOND IN 1861.

The following is from the Richmond *Dispatch* of April 23, 1861:

Serenade to Vice-president Stephens.—Last night, at the hour of 9 o'clock, a large number of citizens congregated in front of the Exchange Hotel, with the First Regiment band, and serenaded the Hon. Alexander H. Stephens, Vice-president of the Confederate States of America. The distinguished gentleman was introduced to the throng by Mayor Mayo, and received with hearty cheers. In response, Mr. Stephens returned his acknowledgments for the warmth of the personal greeting, and his most profound thanks for it as the representative of the Confederate States. He spoke of the rejoicing the secession of Virginia had caused among her Southern sisters. Her people would feel justified if they could hear it as he had. He would not speak of the states who were out, but those who were in. North Carolina was out, and did not know exactly how she got out. The fires that were blazing here he had seen all along his track from Montgomery to Richmond. At Wilmington, North Carolina, he had counted on one street twenty flags of the Confederate States.

The news from Tennessee was equally cheering; there the mountains were on fire. Some of the states still hesitated, but soon all would be in. Tennessee was no longer in the late Union. She was out by resolutions of her popular assemblies in Memphis and other cities. Kentucky would soon be out. Her people were moving. Missouri—who could doubt the stand she would take when her governor, in reply to Lincoln's insolent proclamation, had said, "You shall have no troops for the furtherance of your illegal, unchristian, and diabolical schemes?" Missouri will soon add another star to the Southern galaxy. Where Maryland is you all know. The first Southern blood had been shed on her soil, and Virginia would never stand idly by and see her citizens shot down. The cause of Baltimore was the cause of the whole South. He said the cause we were engaged in was that which attached people to the old Constitution of the late United States—it was the cause of civil, religious, and constitutional liberty. Many of us looked at that Constitution as the anchor of safety. In Georgia the people had been attached to the previous Union, but the Constitution which governed it was framed by Southern talent and understanding. Assaults had been made on it ever since it was established; lately a latitudinous construction had been made by the North, while we of the South sought to interpret it as it was—advocating strict construction, state rights, the right of the people to rule, etc. He spoke of all the fifteen Southern States as advocating this construction. To violate the principles of the Constitution was to initiate revolution, and the Northern States had done this.

The Constitution framed at Montgomery discarded the obsolete ideas of the old Constitution, but had preserved its better portion, with some modifications suggested by the experience of the past, and it had been adopted by the Confederate States, who would stand to it. The old Constitution had been made an engine of power to crush out liberty, that of the Confederate States to preserve it. The old Constitution was improved in our hands, and those living under it had, like the phœnix, risen from the ashes. The revolution lately begun did not affect alone property, but liberty. He alluded to Lincoln's call for seventy-five thousand volunteers, and said he could find no authority in the old Constitution for such a flagrant abuse of power. His second proclamation had stigmatized as pirates all who sailed in letters of marque; this was also in violation of the Constitution, which alone gave Congress that power. What had the friends of liberty to hope for? Beginning in usurpation, where would he end? You were, however, said he, no longer under the rule of this tyrant. With strong arms and stout hearts, you have now resolved to stand in defense of liberty. The Confederate States had but asserted their rights. They believed that their rulers derived their just powers from the consent of the governed. No one had a right to deny the existence of the sovereign right of secession. Our people did not want to meddle with the Northern States — only wanted the latter to let them alone. When did Virginia ever ask the assistance of the general government?

If there is sin in our institutions, we bear the blame, and will stand acquitted by natural law and the higher law of the Creator. We stand upon the law of God and nature. The Southern States did not wish a resort to arms after secession. Mr. Stephens alluded to the negotiations between Major Anderson and the authorities of the Confederate States to demonstrate the proposition. History, he said, if rightly written, would acquit us of a desire to shed our brothers' blood.

The law of necessity and of right compelled us to act as we did. He had reason to believe that the Creator smiled on it. The Federal flag was taken down without the loss of a single life. He believed that Providence would be with us and bless us to the end. We had appealed to the God of battles for the justness of our cause. Madness and folly ruled at Washington. Had it not have been so, several of the states would have been in the old Union for a year to come.   The gods first made mad those they would destroy.   Maryland would join us, and maybe, ere long, the principles that Washington-fought for might be again administered in the city that bore his name.   Every son of the South, from the Potomac to the Rio Grande, should rally to the support of Maryland.   If Lincoln quits Washington as ignominiously as he entered it, God's will will have been accomplished.   The argument was now exhausted. Be prepared; stand to your arms; defend your wives and firesides.   He alluded to the momentous consequences of the issue involved.   Rather than be conquered, let every second man rally to drive back the invader.   The conflict may be terrible, but the victory will be ours.   Virginians, said he, you fight for the preservation of your sacred rights —the land of Patrick Henry—to keep from desecration the tomb of Washington, the graves of Madison, Jefferson, and all you hold most dear.

Why did not Virginia fly to arms and seize on all the United States property within her reach on the proclamation of Jackson?   Lincoln had more cause than Jackson to issue a proclamation, for no one threatened to march on Washington in Jackson's day.   No one had fired into a vessel sailing under the flag of the United States, as was the Star of the West; no one had seized upon all the arsenals, arms, ammunition, mints, custom-houses, post-offices, and revenue cutters within their reach; no one had forced one of the forts of the United States to lower and dishonor its flag; and yet the calling of seventy-five thousand men for the immediate protection of the puplic property and public men in Washington furnished a *ready excuse* for all those to jump into rebellion who had not the courage or manliness to stay out of it, when they were threatened to be turned out of doors by a lawless mob if they did not go in for it. As the President of the Convention, John Janney, Esq., said to a friend of mine, as he left the Convention on the day the ordinance was passed, " The proclamation was not the *cause* of *secession*, it only served as a bridge for the Convention to pass over on."*

* For the following important statistics I am indebted to M'Pherson's History of the Rebellion, first edition.

In the year 1860, Mr. Floyd, then Secretary of War, sold and transferred from Northern to Southern arsenals the following arms:

Sold, 31,610 muskets, at $2 50 each; 25,000 do., do., to Belknap, of Texas; and 250,000, at $2 15 each, which Secretary Holt refused to confirm. Of arms transferred from Northern to Southern arsenals and states, there were, of percussion muskets, 105,000; rifles, 10,000; columbiads ordered, 110; and of thirty-two pounders, 11.

Of property seized by Southern States prior to March 4, 1861, there was in *South Carolina*, Fort Moultrie, Castle Pinckney, the United States Arsenal, with 70,000 stand of arms, with other stores; post-offices and custom-houses, with their contents; light-house tender, schooner William Aiken, steamer Marion, etc. The United States steamer was fired into, and Fort Sumter taken, before Mr. Lincoln issued his proclamation for 75,000 men.

Georgia had seized Forts Pulaski and Jackson, arsenal at Augusta, containing two twelve-pound howitzers, two cannon, and 22,000 muskets and rifles, large stores of powder, balls, grape, etc. They also seized the United States steamer Ida, brig N. R. Kilby, and seven other New York vessels, together with the Custom-house, with all the money therein.

Florida seized the navy yard, Forts Barrancas and M'Rae, Fort Mason, and arsenal at St. Augustine; the Chattahoochee Arsenal, containing 500,000 musket-cartridges and 300,000 rifle do.; 50,000 pounds of powder, besides coast survey-steamer, etc.

Alabama had taken Fort Morgan, with 5000 shot and shell; Mount Vernon Arsenal, with 120,000 stand of arms, 150,000 pounds of powder, and a large amount of other munitions of war, and revenue cutter *Lewis Cass*.

Mississippi had taken the fort on Ship Island and United States hospital on the Mississippi River.

F

A RETROSPECTIVE GLANCE.

But this theme is so fruitful that I find it difficult to confine myself to proper limits. Let me get back to Washing-

Louisiana had taken Forts Jackson and St. Philip, on the Mississippi, and Fort Pike, on Pontchartrain; arsenal at Baton Rouge, with 50,000 small-arms, four howitzers, twenty heavy pieces of ordinance, two batteries, and 300 barrels of powder, hospital, etc. ; at New Orleans, the Mint and Custom-house, containing $599,303 in gold and silver, which was transferred to the Confederate government; the armament of the revenue cutter at Belleville, iron-works, quartermaster's and commissary's stores to a very large amount, and the revenue cutter M'Clellan.

Texas had taken the United States government stores on board steamer Texas, Forts Chadbourne and Belknap, Fort Brown, revenue cutter Dodge, $55,000 in specie, 35,000 stand of arms, twenty-six pieces of mounted artillery, forty-four dismounted do.; munitions, horses, wagons, forage, etc., amounting to about $1,300,000.

Arkansas had seized the arsenal at Little Rock, with 9000 stand of arms, forty cannon, and large quantities of ammunition.

On the 29th of February, 1861, four days before the inauguration of Mr. Lincoln, by act of the Confederate government, Mr. President Davis was directed to assume control of all military operations in the several states in rebellion, and was authorized to receive into government service such forces of these states as may be tendered for any time not less than twelve months, and on the 6th of March was authorized to employ the military and naval forces of the Confederate government to the extent of 100,000 men for twelve months.

In the spring of 1861, the Mobile *Advertiser* said, "During the past year 135,430 muskets have been quietly transferred from the Northern Arsenal at Springfield *alone* to those in the Southern States. We are much obliged to Secretary Floyd for the foresight he has thus displayed in disarming the North and equipping the South for this emergency. There is no telling the amount of arms and munitions which were sent South from Northern arsenals. There is no doubt that every man in the South who can carry a gun can be supplied from private or public sources. The Springfield supply *alone* would supply all the militia-men in Alabama and Mississippi."

ton in 1854, when, as I said, every patriotic heart was rejoicing at the prospect of harmony between North and South, because there was nothing for them to quarrel about. Yet in the first year of Mr. Pierce's administration the party began to quarrel among themselves over the spoils, and the appointments in New York had split the Democracy into the "Hard and Soft Shells," as they were called, and they were actually in that short time themselves demoralized and fearfully divided. It became necessary, therefore, to get up another exciting slavery issue for the canvass of '56. For a long time it puzzled their wits to find one, but one must be manufactured, and it was done.

Accordingly, on a certain Sabbath morning, some five or six leading secessionists met, whether accidentally or not I am not informed, and came to the conclusion that the most efficient and only means left of creating excitement and agitation, and of stirring up the worst passions of the multitude in sectional controversy, and of preparing an en-

On the 13th of April, 1861, on the day of the fall of Fort Sumter, and two days before the proclamation of Mr. Lincoln, the Richmond *Inquirer* published the following article, "Attention, Volunteers! Nothing is more probable than that President Davis will soon march an army through North Carolina and Virginia to Washington; those of our volunteers who desire to join the Southern Army, as it shall pass through our borders, had better organize at once for that purpose, and keep their army accoutrements, uniforms, ammunition, and knapsacks in constant readiness."

And it was after these most extensive robberies of public property, and still more extensive preparations for invading the Capitol at Washington —of taking possession of the archives of the government, and spreading Democracy and slavery over the whole country—that the most extraordinary consternation was produced on the public mind, and which ran every body crazy, when Mr. Lincoln called for seventy-five thousand men for his own protection, and the safety of the Capitol and all its archives.

tering wedge which would sooner or later enable them to split the Union in twain, would be the repeal of the Missouri Compromise, the first in the long series of compromises which had been received throughout the South at the time of its adoption as a great Southern triumph, which had become sanctified by the lapse of a third of a century, and had become consecrated in the hearts of the people. The result has shown that they calculated wisely as to the effect to be produced; for out of this iniquitous step has grown all our troubles, and the universal ruin that awaits us; and few gave more efficient aid to this outrage than the two senators Messrs. Mason and Hunter, whose state had just before declared that "such an act" would be just cause for a dissolution of the Union, and would be resisted "at all hazards, and to the last extremity."

Let it be borne in mind that, out of thirty millions of people; not one human being outside of the political circles in Washington had murmured or complained; not a single application from any quarter had arisen to justify this most unwarrantable and flagitious movement.

THE REPEAL OF THE MISSOURI COMPROMISE.

In the afternoon of that same Sabbath, these half dozen gentlemen waited on Mr. Pierce to communicate the result of their deliberations, and to represent to him the importance of the measure as a means of securing a Democratic triumph in '56. He declined to receive them, alleging that he did not transact political business on the Sabbath—so at least ran the gossip of Washington at that day, which also gave assurance that there were other "potent influences" besides those of a devotional nature that forbade the interview. Be this as it may, great, but temporary offense only, it was said, was given by this procrastination of a day; and when the visit was repeated on the next day, and the subject was broached, Mr. Pierce was said to have been very decided in his opposition; his organ, the *Union*, certainly took very strong ground against it, but, of course, when it was made clear to his mind that this measure of abomination was indispensable to the success of the Democratic nomination in '56, which he hoped, and, perhaps, did not doubt would fall on his own shoulders, at least as a reward for his acquiescence, it did not require much time or labor to remove his objections; the temptation was too strong; he could wait no longer; he acquiesced, and took the matter under his own especial charge and management. At the same time, it was necessary to win over the "Little Giant of the West," the late Stephen A. Douglas, without whose co-operation, not only as Chairman of the Committee on Territories, but as the leader of a very formidable wing of the Democracy, there was no hope of its passage. To him, also, was the glittering prize of a nomination held up as a reward for any disinterested sacrifice he might make in the premises; the temptation was too strong for him too; *he* could resist no longer, and swallowed at one gulp all that he had so often committed himself to in the most unequivocal terms on the subject of this compromise; he became a competitor with Mr. Pierce, and it was from that time a struggle between the two which should play the most prominent part in the great drama that was to result in the bloodiest, most destructive, and costly civil war known to ancient or modern times.

There is much of this that, in the nature of things, there is no record proof to be found, but I give you what was generally spoken of in the political circles of Washington at that time—every where received as true and authentic, and which has never, to my knowledge, been denied, and which after circumstances fully sustained. The occasion was too important, the opportunity too favorable for the selfishness of the greedy and hungry leaders of the old Whig party, now thoroughly demoralized in every sense, not to make themselves acceptable to the Democracy. In a body as one man, or like automatons moved by machinery, they *all* fell into line, and went to work with all their might and main, in season and out of season, to aid in this mischievous, wicked, nefarious work.

JOHN BELL, OF TENNESSEE.

There was one man who has the credit of having resisted it, but it is not so; and that was John Bell, of Tennessee. The running debate between himself and Mr. Toombs in the Senate will show that he attended their secret caucuses, and gave them all the aid and comfort he could impart. He had the will, but not the courage to face the storm that was rising up not only in the North, but in his own State of Tennessee, through the combined efforts of those of his colleagues in the House, Etheridge, Cullom, and Bung.

"He was prepared to vote with his friends on the repeal of the Missouri Compromise on the ground of its unconstitutionality, but was not exactly prepared to vote for that bill because it violated our treaty obligations with the Indians;" this was repeated several times in my hearing during his speech on the bill, though possibly not to be found in his published speech, which did not appear for some five or six weeks after its delivery, when the Northern storm had nearly reached its height, and it was found to be a dangerous experiment for any aspiring politician to face it; and for this, as well as for his unsuccessful efforts to dodge the final vote, this gentleman was afterward honored with a nomination for the Presidency upon the platform of "The

Union, the Constitution, and the Enforcement-of the Laws."
The nomination he accepted, the platform he adopted, and
stood firmly upon it while there was a hope that it would
lead him into office; but the moment it failed to do that, he
kicked the platform from under his feet, and was among
the first to join in breaking down the Union, trampling
upon the Constitution, and resisting, by a resort to civil
war, the enforcement of the laws; and for this man I was
fool enough to vote (for which God forgive me), and I labored for his success day and night, because I thought if he
was unselfish in nothing else, and was *politically* to be relied on for nothing else, he was to be trusted for his devotion to the Union; and I owe an apology now, which is
here tendered to all those whom I may have misled on this
subject as I was misled myself.

But I was misled by Mr. Bell himself, who, in a speech
delivered in Memphis in August, 1859, had said, "I am willing to co-operate with the Black Republicans of the North
for the sake of preserving this government and perpetuating the American Union. I am willing to co-operate with
the corrupt and profligate leaders of the Democracy to accomplish the same desirable object." It was such language
as this that secured him the confidence of the friends of the
Union. It was such sentiments as these that secured him
the nomination and support of the Union party of the
United States; and yet, in less than one year from the time
he made that speech, he was found actively co-operating
with these same corrupt and profligate leaders of Democracy to destroy the Union.

HISTORY OF THE MISSOURI COMPROMISE.

As several generations have passed away, and others
sprung up to supply their places, and millions of the foreign

population have sought a home upon our shores since the adoption of the Missouri Compromise in 1820, it is not unreasonable to suppose that the number of our people who understand the nature of this memorable compact between the North and the South is quite limited, and in this view it is deemed important that the history of this Compromise, and its repeal as the proximate cause of the war, should be given in this letter; and I know of no more convenient form in which it can be given than by copying here what I said in what is known as my African Church speech, delivered in 1856. The present is a propitious time for its close study. Speaking of the Democrats, I said,

."They have made the issue for themselves, and I stand here to-night ready to address an argument to you, the people of Richmond, and through you to the people of the state, including persons of all parties whose minds are open to conviction, and who are unprejudiced and impartial—to those who are anxious, at least willing to ascertain the true condition of things in this country, and to be governed by their convictions.

" All arguments are thrown away upon those benighted, ignorant, and besotted partisans who prefer party to country; but if there are any here of the Democratic party, or of any other party, whose minds are open to conviction, and who prefer their country to their party, I think I may say, that before I have concluded, if they will give me their patient attention, I will show them that, instead of coming forward with a boldness and audacity, defying all shame, singing that sweet siren song which we have heard periodically for the last twenty years of ' *help us to save the Union*,' this Democratic party would bow their heads in shame, and ask forgiveness for the past, and more especially would they ask forgiveness of the South, and, like honest men and patriots, if there was patriotism among them, they would acknowledge their incapacity to administer the government with credit to themselves or advantage to the country, and ask to be relieved of the responsibilities resting upon them.

"They have said that the great issue in this contest was, and should be, the repeal of the Missouri Compromise. I permit the party to make their own issue, and I meet them. Let us see how that issue stands. I am gratified that the opportunity is at length afforded me of addressing an argument on this subject to all true friends of the South, for the public press has been closed to all arguments except upon one side, and that the wrong side; and it would be strange indeed if the people were not misled under such circumstances.

"Now let me ask you, first, what was this Missouri Compromise? What were the circumstances under which it was adopted? What were its fruits? By whom were they enjoyed? And what has been the effect of its repeal?

"I set out with the declaration, as being the most conscientious conviction of my best judgment, feeble and imperfect as I acknowledge and know it to be, but I set out with the declaration that, according to the best convictions of my judgment, *that* Missouri Compromise, at the time and under the circumstances it was adopted, was for the peace of the country, for the interests of the South, and for the perpetuity of the Union—*beyond all question*, the best and wisest measure that ever obtained the sanction of an American Congress; and that, consequently, its repeal, with the consequences and circumstances that have grown out of it, was the most wanton, the most mischievous, the most suicidal, and the most unpardonable act that ever was committed by the representatives of the people.

"In tracing the history of this Missouri Compromise, it

F 2

will be necessary that I shall go back to the time of the adoption of the Constitution, and even a little beyond that. At the time of the formation of the Constitution, and of the United States government under it, there was a large territory lying northwest of the Ohio River, known as the .Northwestern Territory. This was provided for by those who participated in the Revolution, and in the formation of the Constitution, by the application of what has since been known as the Wilmot Proviso—that is to say, that slavery in all the territory then belonging to the United States should be prohibited. That law has been recognized, and has been in practical operation, with no attempt to interfere with it, from that time to this—that is, from 1787 down to 1856. In the year 1803, by a treaty that was negotiated during the administration of Mr. Jefferson, we acquired from the government of France what was known as the Louisiana Territory. This territory constituting no part of the Northwestern Territory, which had been provided for by the Ordinance of 1787, gave rise to extreme difficulties between the North and the South in reference to this question of slavery. Out of a portion of that territory acquired from Louisiana the State of Missouri was formed, and she asked for admission into the Union. The Northern States having at that time acquired a superiority in numbers, had it in their power to refuse the admission of Missouri, except upon the condition that slavery should be excluded, or, in other words, that the Ordinance of 1787 should be applied also to that territory. It was necessary to settle the question in some form. It was obliged to be settled, either by the minority or by the majority, in Congress, and we of the South unfortunately constituted the minority. At length this far-famed Missouri Compromise was introduced, not by the North, but by the South, pretty much under the same circumstances, however, that the repeal of the Missouri Compromise was introduced in 1854; they selected a Northern man to introduce it, but it was first agreed upon as a Southern measure, and it was passed by Southern votes.

"And what was it that was thus agreed to by the South and passed by the South? It was not, as has been commonly said, a measure imposed upon the South by the North. It was proposed on the part of the South to the North, 'that if you will allow us—you being in the majority and having the control—if you will permit us to carry slavery up to the line of 36° 30′, we will pledge ourselves not to attempt to carry slavery beyond 36° 30′.' They said, 'We will allow every state south of 36° 30′ that chooses to adopt slavery or reject it, as they please; but if they make an application to Congress, as the people of Missouri have done, for admission into the Union as slave states, then you shall make no objection to their admission on the ground that they recognize slavery;' and the South, with the aid of a few of the Northern votes, was able to carry the measure. We find that this measure was voted for in the Senate of the United States by 'twenty' out of the 'twenty-two' Southern senators—only two Southern senators voting against it, and only four Northern senators voting for it. And those who voted for it were, Barbour and Pleasants, of Virginia, Brown and Johnson, of Louisiana, Eaton and Williams, of Tennessee, Elliott and Walker, of Georgia, Galliard, of South Carolina, Johnson and Logan, of Kentucky, Loyd and Pinckney, of Maryland, King (the late William R.) and Walker, of Alabama, Leake and Williams, of Mississippi, Van Dyke and Horner, of Delaware, and Stokes, of North Carolina, making twenty Southern senators, and four from the North. Mr. Macon, of North Carolina, and Mr. Smith, of South Carolina, were the only

two Southern senators that voted against it, while only four
Northern senators voted for it, and eighteen against it.   It
went to the House of Representatives, and it passed that
body by a vote of 134 to 42—forty Southern representatives
voting for it, and thirty-seven against it.   Thus was the
Compromise of 1820 brought about.   And the history of
that day will show that. it was regarded (as it really was)
as a great Southern triumph, in which the North reluctant-
ly acquiesced.   The most distinguished Southern men, including Mr. Clay, Mr. Lowndes, Mr. William Smith, Louis
M'Lane, and others being its chief advocates.   And upon
its final passage it was submitted to Mr. Monroe for his
signature; and there being some wiseacres at that day, as
there are at all times, who set up the pretension that it was
a violation of the Constitution for us to agree *not to do*
what it was contended we had a *right to do* for the sake of
the peace, the harmony, and the prosperity of the country,
Mr. Monroe submitted the constitutionality of that measure
to his Cabinet — of which John C. Calhoun was one, Mr.
Crawford another, and Mr. Wirt, of Virginia, a third — and
he required a written opinion of each member of his Cabinet
upon the constitutionality of this Missouri Compromise.
The Cabinet were unanimous in the opinion that the law
was in strict and perfect conformity with the Constitution
of the United States.   It must be admitted that these were
mere pigmies in comparison with the giants and the dwarfs
of the present day.   But when the bill became a law, it
was received throughout the South with the ringing of bells
and the firing of cannon, with illuminations and shouts of
joy and gladness, and heralded every where as a great
Southern victory.

   " Under the operation of that law to which the integrity
and the honor of the South was pledged, the South obtained

the admission of Missouri and Arkansas as slave states when it was in the power of the North to have rejected them. They also obtained the admission of Florida as a slave state, Texas as a slave state, and never — never while there was an opportunity to make a slave state out of Southern territory—did they dream that it was proper to repeal that law. But when they had populated all their own territories, and obtained the admission of all their slave states, when there was no necessity for it whatever, they attempted to rob the North of its just due, and thereby dishonestly sacrificed the integrity and honor of the South, that were pledged to carry out in good faith the bargain entered into. But I will show before I get through that it was never the object of this Democratic party to sanction any thing that would produce peace and harmony in the country; that their object was to keep up agitation on the slavery question, and that it was their purpose that the Missouri Compromise should be disturbed in order to agitate the question of slavery, and provoke resistance to the Fugitive Slave Law in order to agitate.

REPEAL OF THE 21ST RULE.

"Things went on in this way pretty satisfactorily for some fifteen or sixteen years, when Mr. Calhoun, the great leader of the Southern States'-rights party, set himself to work, as seemed to be his object to the last moment of his life, to excite the apprehension and alarm of the Southern people upon the question of slavery, in order, as he said, to unite the South—to unite us, the Whigs of the South, with the Democrats — upon the subject of slavery; and every man of the Whig party, every politician of the Whig party, every press in the Whig or American interests that has aided in keeping up this agitation have only added strength to the Democratic party, and aided them to rivet a chain on their necks that they will wear as long as they live, or until the people become better informed as to their objects. It was for these reasons, because there was too much peace in the country, that they could not remain satisfied; and there being a contemptible handful in the North at that time who were not of sufficient consequence to disturb any body or any body's property, we were daily warned to fortify ourselves upon the subject of slavery. Then it was that the famous 'twenty-first rule' was gotten up for the purpose of exciting the Abolitionists into an issue with us, whereby the great constitutional right of petition was denied to the people. Men in the South who claimed the right of the constituent body to instruct their representatives, were guilty of the supreme folly of denying to the same body their right to petition. As a matter of course, these things produced a very angry state of feeling in the North. The right of petition was blended with the question of slavery, and it fell to my lot upon that occasion to stand in the minority of one or two in the whole Southern country until parties of every complexion came up to my position; and at last the Democratic party themselves, seeing the incalculable mischief which was likely to grow out of it, repealed the 'twenty-first rule,' and from that day to this the question has remained settled as far as abolition petitions are concerned; for while there were upward of six thousand abolition petitions presented to Congress during the session preceding that in which the 'twenty-first rule' was repealed, there were only about *six* in all presented at the session following that repeal—thus showing how infinitely the practical operation of that famous 'twenty-first rule,' which Mr. Calhoun had a large share in getting up, had weakened the South and strengthened the Abolition party at the North, which had by this time become a formidable power by this false issue presented by the peculiar champions of Southern rights. Still, it accomplished the great object had in view by the leaders of Democracy. It kept alive agitation, and there were continual appeals to Southern men of every political shade and complexion to unite for the safety of the South on the slavery question, and form a sectional party that would present a united front, of which Mr. Calhoun was to be the leader, and which was to inure to his benefit by bringing him into power, or of accomplishing his next most ardent wish, that of dissolving the Union, and having a Northern and Southern republic, at the head of the latter of which he never dreamed that any other could be placed than himself.

"Well, we will proceed now to the consideration of the question of the annexation of Texas, which is next in order. Texas was annexed to the Union, and it became necessary to adopt .this now unconstitutional Missouri Compromise line and apply that to Texas also. Mark you now that, by the Ordinance of 1787, all of the Northwestern Territory belonging to the United States was provided for; the Missouri Compromise line was applied to the territory acquired by the Louisiana Treaty, and thus that was settled. There could then be no farther controversy upon this question, but when we acquired Texas, it became necessary to make some farther provision in regard to that territory.

"A Southern gentleman, Mr: Brown, of Tennessee, proposed the extension of the Missouri Compromise line to the State of Texas. Judge Douglas, of Illinois, then a member of the House of Representatives, and now Chairman of the Committee on Territories in the Senate, submitted a modification in the following words by way of amendment:

"'And in such *states* as shall be formed out of said territory.

tory north of said Missouri Compromise line, slavery or involuntary servitude, except for crime, shall be prohibited'
—thus applying the Wilmot Proviso to the states as well
as to the territories north of 36° 30'.

"This is the 'Little Giant,' the great Southern champion.
Mr. Brown accepted the modification, and it was agreed to
by a vote of ayes 120, noes 98 — every Southern Democrat
in the House, without exception, voting for it; so that, by
the resolution annexing Texas and adopting the Missouri
Compromise line as applicable to it, the question was settled
permanently in reference to the territory acquired from
Texas.

"I am tracing this matter on step by step, to show you the
wisdom of those who went before us in providing against
all this agitation, by a settlement of this question between
North and South as we acquired additional territory.

"Shortly after this, however, we became possessed of a
very large territory by purchase and by the war with Mexico, including California and the Territories of Utah and
New Mexico. During the administration of Mr. Polk, a
Southern Democratic President, a bill organizing a territorial government for Oregon was presented to him for his
signature after having passed the two branches of Congress.
That bill contained, not the Missouri Compromise clause,
but the Wilmot Proviso. It was passed by a Democratic
majority in the House and in the Senate, and was then sent
to Mr. Polk for his signature, while Mr. James Buchanan
was a member of his Cabinet and Secretary of State, and he
(Mr. Polk) of course put his signature to the Oregon Bill,
with the Wilmot Proviso attached to it. And what was
the ground of excuse made by the Southern Democrats for
their votes upon this bill, and what did they say in justification of their Democratic President, Mr. Polk, who signed it?

Why, that it was all right, because it was in conformity with the principles of the Missouri Compromise, although that Compromise did not extend to this territory; and now they have the bold effrontery to pretend that the Missouri Compromise was itself an unconstitutional measure, thus justifying what they maintain was an unconstitutional act by the exercise of another equally unconstitutional. Have they lost all sense of reason, or have they lost all conscience and regard for consistency, truth, and honor?

"At a subsequent period, to wit, in 1848, having settled the Oregon difficulty in the manner I have shown, it became necessary to do something in reference to the Territory of California, and the following proposition was before the Senate:

"'That the line of 36° 30' of north latitude, known as the Missouri Compromise line, as defined by the eighth section of an act entitled an act, etc., approved March 6, 1820, be, and the same is hereby declared to extend to the Pacific Ocean; and the said eighth section, together with the compromise effected, is hereby revived, and declared to be in full force and binding for the organization of the territories of the United States, in the same sense, and with the same understanding with which it was originally adopted.' And the vote in the affirmative stood—Atchison, Badger, Bell, Berrien, Benton, Borland, Bright, Butler, Calhoun, Cameron, Davis, of Mississippi, Dickinson, Douglas, Downs, Fitzgerald, Foote, Hannegan, Houston, Hunter, Johnson, of Maryland, Johnson, of Georgia, Johnson, of Louisiana, King, Lewis, Mangum, Mason, Metcalf, Pearce, Sebastian, Sherman, Sturgeon, Turney, and Underwood—every Southern senator voting for it. And now it is insisted by some of these same gentlemen that the Missouri Compromise, thus voted for and passed by the Senate, was an unconstitutional meas-

ure forced upon them originally by the North. I have only
to ask, in what position do they place themselves by now
asserting that they voted for a measure in violation of that
Constitution which they had sworn not to violate?

THE COMPROMISE OF 1850.

"Well, gentlemen, we next come to the Compromise
Measures of 1850. There was still territory acquired from
Mexico which had not been provided for. Serious difficulty
and danger was apprehended in regard to it, unless some
amicable adjustment or compromise could be effected on
the subject of slavery in that territory.

"And I know the fact personally, from correspondence
held with him at the time, that no other consideration than
that of the loftiest patriotism that ever animated the bosom
of man induced the venerable Sage of Ashland to quit his
home of retirement and peace, to come back into the Senate
of the United States in the hope of being able to compromise this question between the North and South. No man
—I say it in no vainglorious spirit—but no man out of the
halls of Congress had more, I believe, to do with that Missouri Compromise than the humble individual who is now
addressing you.

"I was in the city of New Orleans in February, 1849, and
I received a telegraphic dispatch from Mr. Clay requesting
me most strenuously to come forthwith to Washington, as
he required my services. He did not state what those services were. I dispatched what little business I had remaining in New Orleans and hurried on to my home, where I remained only twenty-four hours to see my family before I
went on to Washington; and when I got there, he (Mr.
Clay) disclosed to me the purposes and object he had in
view, stating that he wanted me to lend him whatever influ-

ence I could exert to aid him in the accomplishment of his work.

"You may remember that Foote, of Mississippi, had proposed that a committee be appointed, and Mr. Clay strongly resisted it. Mr. Foote (then of Mississippi, now of California) called upon me one Sunday morning and invited me to walk. As we went along, he told me that his great object in getting that Committee of Thirteen appointed to take this subject under consideration was, that their report would be more likely to be adopted, and the question more easily settled through them than in any other form. I concurred with him in that opinion. He asked me to see Mr. Clay upon the subject. I repaired immediately to his room and broached the subject to him. He was in the habit frequently of taking a great many liberties with me and saying what he pleased. He did not receive my remarks very kindly. I was very much in the habit of taking many liberties with him, and saying to him very much what I pleased, just as he was accustomed to do in reference to me, and so we had quite a rough roll-and-tumble dispute for a considerable time upon this subject. Mr. Clay was of opinion that if they got the committee, they would put on a majority of Democrats, and his proposition would be smothered by the committee. I reasoned with him to show that, if that was the case, it would be as well to defeat it there as in the open Senate, and that it would be more likely to carry in a committee fairly organized, and with the best men of the Senate upon it, than if left to an open Senate, where the Democratic majority would be so much larger than in committee; that I felt entirely assured that Foote was actuated by honest and patriotic motives in his suggestion; and that if a favorable report could be had from the committee, it would insure or greatly increase the chances of its passage through

the Senate. I did not leave him until he had yielded his
assent to the appointment of the committee, which led to
the final settlement of the question.   The Compromise Measures were passed.   They brought the healing intelligence
upon their wings which restored peace, and harmony, and
brotherly feeling between the different sections of the Union.
The illustrious patriot had accomplished his work.   He folded his arms and surrendered his spirit to his God, under the
firm persuasion that he had accomplished the last good that
Providence designed him to perform upon earth—that of
giving tranquillity to the nation.

"From what quarter did these Compromise Measures
meet with opposition?   From those who upheld the 'twenty-first rule' to get up agitation in the South—the extremes
of the South and the North—the Abolitionists of the North,
the Seceders of South Carolina, with those of the same school
in Virginia and elsewhere, united in opposition to the Compromise ; and you will not have forgotten that, so strong
was their hostility to those measures, because they quieted
agitation, they called a convention at Nashville, as was plainly proved by Foote and others at the time, to bring about a
dissolution of the Union by resistance to the Compromise.
Harmony was not what they wanted.   Harmony did not
suit their purposes or their interests.   Agitation, agitation,
agitation and excitement, apprehension and alarm among
the Southern people on the subject of slavery was what they
wanted, because by it they had *obtained* power, and by it,
and by it alone, they would have been enabled to *retain* it.

"Go with me a little farther, and see how the Calhoun
wing of the Democracy, which has now the absolute control over the other wing in this state, continued to vote with
the Free-soilers for farther agitation and excitement.   In
the House of Representatives, Colonel Jackson, of Georgia,

offered the following resolution early in the session that followed the adoption of the Compromise.

"'*Resolved*, That we recognize the binding efficacy of the compromises of the Constitution, and believe it to be the intention of the people generally, as we hereby declare it to be ours individually, to abide such compromises, and to sustain the laws necessary to carry them out, the provision for the delivery of fugitive slaves and the act of the last Congress for that purpose included, and that we deprecate all farther agitation of questions growing out of that provision of all the questions embraced in the acts of the last Congress known as the Compromise, and of questions generally connected with the institution of slavery, as unnecessary, useless, and dangerous.'

"Now, scan this resolution closely, examine it with all possible care, and tell me what there is in it to which a Southern man desiring peace between the two sections of the country and a settlement of the slavery question could make an objection? Yet there were sixty-four votes against it, and the Baltimore *Sun* of that day, from which I now read, says: 'WE NOTICE THAT THE ULTRA SOUTHERN MEMBERS FROM SOUTH CAROLINA VOTED WITH THE FREE-SOILERS.' This is Democratic authority! The Baltimore *Sun* continues: 'Mr. Hillyer offered the following addition to the above resolution, being the same as that which was offered by Colonel Polk, and voted down by the Democratic caucuses of the House at the beginning of the session.

"'"*Resolved*, That the series of acts passed during the first session of the Thirty-first Congress, known as the Compromise, are regarded as a final adjustment, and a permanent settlement of the questions therein embraced, and should be regarded, maintained, and executed as such."'

"Take a calm and clear view of *this* resolution, and tell

me why a party desirous of settling the slavery question and arresting agitation should oppose it. . Yet it was opposed, and by the same combination of Free-soilers and Southern Calhoun nullifiers — sixty-five voting in the negative. And upon this resolution the ayes and noes are given, and I will read the names of those who voted in the negative; they are Messrs. Aiken, Allison, Ashe, Averett, Baily, of Georgia; Barrere, Bartlett, Bocock, Bragg, Brenton, Buel, Cable, Campbell, of Ohio; Campbell, of Illinois; Caskie, Chapman, Clingman, Congar, Daniel, Doty, Durkee, Eastman, Edgerton, Floyd, Fowler, Gaylord, Goodenow, Goodrich, Grow, Harper, Holliday, Horsford, T. M. Howe, Ives, Jenkins, Johnson, of Ohio; Jones, of New York; King, of New York; Mann, McQueen, Meachem, Meade, Millson, Minor, Moloney, Newton, Orr, Penniman, Perkins, Powell, Rantoul, Sackett, Schoolcraft, Scudder, Smart, Stanton, of Ohio; Stratton, Sweetzer, Thompson, of Massachusetts; Tuck, Venable, Walbridge, Wallace, Washburn, Wells, and Woodward.

"These were the Southern men (*all Democrats*) who voted with the Free-soilers North against these resolutions, deprecating agitation, and pledging themselves to those measures that had put down agitation.

"But I am far from being done with these gentlemen yet. The contest of 1852 had come on, and those measures had, in the mean time, become so popular with the people that the Democratic party found it necessary to take the lead of us, the conservative party of the country, who had given them from the first an honest, earnest, and cordial support. But they shot far ahead of us in '52, seized upon these measures as their own property, claimed all the credit for their own party, and made them the prominent question in the Presidential election of that year.

"Both parties met in convention, and each pledged itself to resist all attempts, no matter when, where, or how, or by whom made, in Congress or out of it, to reopen or agitate the slavery question, and farther pledged themselves to abide by the Compromise as a final settlement of the whole question; and you will all recollect that the chief issue, and almost the only one raised in that contest, was whether Scott or Pierce was most unqualifiedly pledged, and which was most to be relied on, to look upon the settlement that had been made as a finality of the whole question of slavery.

"The pretension set up by the friends of Mr. Pierce, and insisted on with so much apparent earnestness of superior fidelity to the South, and the bold declarations of his sincerity and devotion to the Compromise of 1850, seduced a portion of the sappy-headed Whigs from the support of Scott, and they voted for Pierce. The country, most unfortunately for itself and for all parties, unwisely concluded that Pierce was the most reliable man, and he was elected; and so vehement were the assurances of his friends, and so constant their promises and pledges of his good faith and honor, that we all felt disposed to give him a fair trial, and judge the tree by its fruits. Of one thing none could well entertain a doubt, and that was that public opinion had been so unmistakably expressed in favor of adhering faithfully to all the compromises on the question of slavery that no man would have the hardihood to advance a step toward the farther discussion of that question. The 4th of March arrived, and with it the inaugural address, full of promises, and pledges, and declarations that made assurance doubly sure, and all were satisfied and happy.

"Mr. Pierce was inaugurated and installed into office, and then came the selection of his Cabinet; but we find

that instead of calling to his aid as his constitutional advisers those identified with the main principles upon which he
was elected, he confided chiefly in those men who were
most bitter in their opposition to.the.measures of 1850:
Davis, M'Clelland, and Cushing.   Now I wish you to observe this point that, when Mr. Pierce came into power, all
the territory that originally belonged to, and that has since
been acquired by the United States government up to that
time, had been provided for, and all was sunshine, peace, and
concord.   Every question of sectional difficulty was harmoniously settled, and there was nothing in the world to quarrel about.   The Fugitive Slave Law was the only issue,
and the people of the North were well reconciled, at least
the great majority of them, to the execution of that law. ·
In some instances it was opposed by a few, for the purpose
rather of creating disturbance than of offering any organized opposition to its execution; so that there would not
have been, in a short time, even that bone of contention between the North and the South.   Well, that was the condition of the country when Mr. Fillmore left the Presidential chair—that was the condition of the country when Mr.
Pierce took possession of it.   What—what, let me ask you,
is its present condition?   I charge upon the Democratic
party that, by the disturbance of the Missouri Compromise,
they have not only sacrificed the integrity and honor of the
South, pledged in good faith to the Missouri Compromise,
but which pledge they violated after they had received
from it all the benefits they could derive.   I charge upon
the Democratic party that they have violated every pledge
that was made in the Convention that nominated Mr.
Pierce to resist any and all efforts, no matter when, where,
or by whom made, in Congress or out of it, to reopen the
agitation of the slavery question.   I charge upon them that ·

they have built up the Black Republican party from the ground, which had no existence prior to the disturbance of the Missouri Compromise. I charge upon them that they have brought civil war upon the country. I charge upon them that they have sacrificed every acre, every foot, and every inch of territory now belonging to the United States, or that may hereafter be acquired, to the cause of the Free-soilers. I charge upon them that, if they have not involved us in a foreign war, it is only because there has been more discretion, forbearance, and wisdom in British statesmen than there has been exhibited by the Cabinet in Washington. And I charge them with exciting a revolutionary and rebellious spirit throughout the limits of this broad land, and that, having taken possession of the government when all was peace, they have brought us to that point when threats of dissolution are heard in every quarter of the land. And now they come, as I said before, with that old deceptive siren song of 'Help us to save the Union. The Union can not be saved except by the Democratic party.'

"They have had a convention at Cincinnati, and they have fully indorsed the policy and measures of Mr. Pierce's administration, that has produced civil war, that has sacrificed all the territory of the United States to the cause of the Free-soilers, and that has brought about a condition of things in which disunion is openly threatened, in a greater or less degree, in every congressional district throughout the United States. They have indorsed all these measures, and they have put their candidate, Mr. Buchanan, upon the platform, and he tells you that he stands not only upon that platform, but that he is no longer James Buchanan, but merely the candidate of the Democratic party.

" Well, now, I want to know if the Democratic party can accomplish all this from the 4th of March, 1853, to the 4th of March, 1856, how much longer it would take them to bring about an actual dissolution of the Union? They have accomplished more than three fourths of their task already. Let this policy be pursued but little longer and the Union is gone; and if any thing can dissolve the bond of this con-federacy, it will be another administration of the Democrat-ic party.

"You have been told by Mr. Seward that the day for com-promises has passed away. Mr. Seward is right; blame him who may, Seward is right. The day for compromises has passed away, and has passed by the fiat of Southern Democ-racy. They have told you they would have no more com-promises. They, in the minority, without the power to con-trol, have said to the North, in the majority, 'We will have no more compromises; compromises are unconstitutional; either you or we must control this territory.' The North said to them, 'Gentlemen, we have the power'—I mean they said it substantially—'we have the power to control, but we have no disposition to control. This question has been harmoniously settled for thirty odd years—all these disputed questions have been harmoniously settled; let them remain settled according to the compromises that have been adopted.' 'No,' said the South, 'we will stand by no such compromises; compromises are unconstitutional; you must have your way, or we must have ours.' 'Very well, said the North, 'if you are resolved upon that, and to present to us the broad issue of whether you, the minority, or we, the ma-jority, shall control, no alternative is left. We must fight the question out.' I say the Southern Democracy has raised the whirlwind; let them direct the storm. I say Southern Democracy has raised the whirlwind; they have raised up that Black Republican party in the North that is likely to overwhelm the country. Let them see to it; let them make such atonement to the South as they can. I say, as I said before, that if it was not for the boldest audacity that ever controlled a party bloated with spoils, they would bow their heads in shame and ask forgiveness of the country. Instead of asking us to support their candidate, they would be inviting us to release them from the burdens of government, which they are incompetent to conduct.

"Suppose Texas were now to be annexed as a slave state or territory, with the Missouri Compromise line repealed, does any man in his proper senses believe that the North would consent to it? If so, let me tell him that he knows little of the feeling pervading all ranks and all parties among the people throughout that entire region of the country. You might find a politician here and there who would betray the confidence of his constituents for the hope of reward, but among the masses of the people you would find none that would listen to it for a moment, and for this the Democracy are responsible, to the South especially and to the country generally.

THE KANSAS-NEBRASKA BILL.

"But that Kansas-Nebraska Bill is now objected to, upon the ground that it contains the squatter sovereignty principle, and you find the public press throughout the South ready to resort to arms to bring about a dissolution of the Union rather than submit to squatter sovereignty. I tell them it is too late to play that game. Who adopted the feature of squatter sovereignty? The South. Who sustained it? The Whig and Democratic press of the South. Who passed it into a law? I say that they, the Southern representatives of the people, have established squatter sovereignty, and did it knowingly; they did it willfully and deliberately, if they knew the meaning of English terms. They advocated the passage of the bill expressly upon the ground of 'non-intervention.' Was not that so? And what is that but squatter sovereignty—that there should be no interference on the part of the government or of Congress with the alien squatters to regulate their own domestic affairs? And now they pretend that they do not know what that means. They ought to know; if not, they ought to go to school again and learn. Why, did they not know that upon the passage of this bill General Cass congratulated the country upon the recognition of his favorite but, as he said, much-abused doctrine of 1848, called squatter sovereignty, which was subsequently denied by the Democracy, and for which denial he complimented them by saying that none but fools could put such an interpretation upon his letter as they sought to represent?

"When Judge Douglas, who was the ostensible author of the bill, went to New York during its pendency, and was serenaded at the St. Nicholas, they knew that he made a speech which was republished in the Southern country, and in which he took the ground that the leading feature of the bill and that which laid at the foundation of it was the right of the people of Kansas, aliens and all, to regulate their own affairs, and that he asked the pertinent question, 'If you, the people of New York, are competent to regulate your own affairs, would you be less competent if you were inhabitants of Kansas? We of Illinois have a right to regulate our affairs, and if we went to Kansas we would expect to exercise the same powers as residents of the territory.' But they have found out that this principle did not work so well, and now they take the back track. And for what object have they done so? They have met in convention at Cincinnati, and we find this one of the leading principles of the platform there adopted. They, in fact, either shortened

Mr. Buchanan or stretched him out so as to suit the plat-form exactly, and he indorses that feature of it especially; and immediately after he indorses it, the Senate of the United States, alarmed at the consequences likely to result from the repeal of the Missouri Compromise, admitted it was all a humbug and cheat in the commencement, condemned the laws of Kansas by a vote of forty to three (on Geyer's amendment), and passed a new law providing for a new government for Kansas.

"Gentlemen, I am repeating historical truths. I am indulging in no idle declamation or vain speculation. I am telling you historical facts.

"But they tell you, also, that the Compromise Measures of 1850 repealed the Compromise Measures of 1820. In the first place, I would like to ask who said so then? Next, I would like to ask who thought so? Nobody!—nobody thought so, and nobody said so; and the man who would have said so would have been regarded as a fit subject for a lunatic asylum. For how could any thing be more stupid than to have settled one question by unsettling another question? If by the terms of the act of 1850 you repeal the act of 1820, you are settling the difficulty in regard to the territory acquired from Mexico, and unsettling the difficulty in regard to the territory acquired from France.

"On this point only hear what Mr. Douglas, as Chairman of the Committee on Territories, reported from that committee so late as January 4, 1854. That report says: 'Your committee do not feel themselves called upon to enter into the discussion of these controverted questions' (whether the Constitution secures the right to Southern citizens of carrying their slaves into the territories). 'They involve the same issues which produced the agitation, the sectional strife, and the fearful struggle of 1850. As Congress deemed it wise and prudent *to refrain from deciding* the matters in controversy then, either by affirming or repealing the Mexican laws, or by an act declaratory of the true intent of the Constitution, and the extent of the protection afforded by it to slave property in the territories, *so your committee are not prepared now to recommend a departure from the course pursued on that memorable occasion, either by affirming or repealing the eighth section of the Missouri act*, or by an act declaratory of the meaning of the Constitution in respect to the legal points in dispute.'

"Thus it appears that, in January, 1854, the Territorial Committee of the Senate had no idea that the Missouri Compromise was disturbed by the Compromise of 1850, but expressly disclaimed it; yet now it is hypocritically and falsely pretended that it did.

"Now, where are those men who voted for the repeal of the Missouri Compromise? Where is Jones, of Tennessee, Benjamin, Dixon, Toombs and Geyer, Pratt, and Pearce, of Maryland? Just precisely where they ought to be when they placed themselves under the lead of the Little Giant, Douglas, and the great dwarf, Pierce. Seven out of ten of the Whig senators who voted for the repeal of the Missouri Compromise have gone where they ought to have gone long since—they have gone home to roost, not in the bosom of Abraham, but in the bosom of Buchanan. And lo! they make it a pretext—I am speaking now of some of my personal friends, but that has nothing to do with my public duties—they have made it a pretext for voting for Buchanan that they did not think Fillmore would be elected. Well, it is quite certain he can not be if his friends do not vote for him. But I apprehend it will be with them as it was with those who left us in 1852 because Fillmore was *not* nominated. They now go for Buchanan because Fillmore *is* nominated.

"But they say that the Missouri Compromise was unconstitutional. Well, gentlemen, I only ask you to take the subject into consideration for yourselves; just weigh the authority that I have adduced upon this subject: one hundred and thirty-four to forty-two in the House of Representatives; twenty out of twenty-two senators in 1820; Monroe, the Southern President, and all his Cabinet, with John C. Calhoun among them; the whole body of Democrats in the Senate of 1845; Polk and his party in 1847, upon the admission of Oregon; and then take the pigmies, and the butterflies, and the grasshoppers of the present day, who are croaking in every corner of the street about the unconstitutionality of the Missouri Compromise, and tell me, then, where is the authority for its unconstitutionality?

"But, admit it to have been unconstitutional, what was the object in disturbing it? What practical injury did it inflict? You are obliged to have free and slave states, and dividing-lines between them. Is it not as well to have a straight line as a crooked one? and was it not as well to have let alone the straight line established by our forefathers, which had become sanctified by time, and was held for years almost as sacred as the Constitution under which we live? It was as well for us, but it was not as well for the Democratic party. And why? Because they were without food to live upon; they were without the elements of combination that gave them strength; they had nothing upon which they could unite their party. Pierce, by his Cabinet appointments, his appointments in New York, by his turning out Bronson because he would not turn out the Hard-shells and put in the Soft-shells, had broken down the Democratic party. It was a rickety-rackety concern, a sort of broken-down monster that could not stand the test of public scrutiny and observation. And it was necessary to repeal the Missouri Compromise to get up agitation upon the question of slavery, in order to delude weak-minded, sappy-headed, tender-footed, faint-hearted Whigs and Americans to vote for the Democratic nominee upon the plea that the South was in danger, that slavery was in danger.

"Gentlemen, I can truly say that there is nothing that I predicted in 1854, as the result of the repeal of the Missouri Compromise, that has not happened. I said at the time, 'You gentlemen of the South regard Mr. Seward as your greatest enemy. I tell you that every man in the South who votes for the repeal of the Missouri Compromise is unwittingly engaged in the service of Mr. Seward. After you have repealed this Missouri Compromise you will have no more national Democracy and no more national Whiggery; you will have in the North no more Hunkers, Hard-shells, or Adamantines; they will all become Soft-shells, Barn-burners, and Free-soilers.' And so they are; all are now united under the cognomen of Republicans, and I added, he that does not see the dark spirit of disunion lurking around this bill is a short-sighted man.

"Now, gentlemen, I part with this subject by saying that those men who take the ground that the Missouri Compromise was unconstitutional, or that the Compromise Measures of 1850 repealed the Compromise Measures of 1820, perpetrate a libel upon the living and a calumny upon the dead. I am here, gentlemen, not only to tell you what I think, but to tell you all I think as far as time will allow me to do it. I am not speaking for the South or for the North. I am neither a Southern man nor a Northern man, but I am a National Union man.

"My position on the question of slavery is this, and, so far from wishing to conceal it, I desire it should be known to all. Muzzles were made for dogs, and not for men, and no press and no party can put a muzzle on my mouth so long as I value my freedom. I make bold, then, to proclaim that I am no slavery propagandist. I will resort to all proper remedies to protect and defend slavery where it exists,.but I will neither assist in nor encourage any attempt to force it upon a reluctant people any where, and still less will I justify the use of the military power of the country to establish it in any of the territories. If it finds its way there by legitimate means it is all well, but never by force through any instrumentality of mine. I am myself a slaveholder, and all the property my children have in the world is slave property, inherited from their mother; and he who undertakes to connect my name or my opinions with Abolitionism is either a knave or a fool, and sometimes both. And this is the only answer I have to make to them. I have not connected myself with any sectional party or sectional question, and, so help me God, I never will.

"I lay claim here to a sentiment of which I have been to some extent robbed. It has been appropriated by Mr. Clay, but he did not need any emanation from any mind to bolster up his reputation, and therefore I will not allow him to have the credit of it. But I claim to be the first man that said 'I know no North, no South, no East, no West.' I used it upon this stand in 1844, at the time of the annexation of Texas. I know I was rebuked by the Democratic party for not knowing the South. Since that time these have become talismanic words, and now every man who is a candidate for office is required to say that he knows 'no North, no South, no East, no West;' and the Democrats may say with truth they know no North, no South, no East no West; for they know nothing but the cohesive power of public plunder, as Mr. Calhoun said of them, and that is all they know, and all they care for."

THE MISSOURI COMPROMISE AGAIN.

The repeal of this time-honored measure, which had given satisfaction and peace for so many years, and the subsequent efforts to force slavery into territory from which by that compromise it had been forever excluded, and with which they stood pledged in *honor* and in *law* never to interfere, and that, too, against the known and expressed will of the people inhabiting the territory, produced the effect foreseen and mainly desired, viz., that of stirring up discord and sectional animosities such as had no previous parallel; and this repeal it was that gave *rise to the Republican organization*, which increased in numbers and influence with such rapidity as to render it plainly manifest that they would soon attain the ascendency in the Union.

Do you recollect when I found every Southern senator, and almost every Southern press in favor of the repeal of that sacred compromise, in absolute defiance of their solemn pledges to the country, how I threw myself alone into the breach, and implored the South to listen to my appeals and to strangle the proposition in its birth? Do you recollect, for this self-sacrificing act, which should have entitled me to the confidence and gratitude, not only of my own party, but of all peace and Union loving men, how I was assailed by the presses of both parties as no public man was ever assailed before or since? These assaults were not confined to my political character, they extended to my personal honor and to the honesty of my motives. Enough was said against me to have justified me, if any thing could, in shooting down in the public streets a score of editors in a day. There was fighting matter enough in these assaults, God knows. But who was I to fight? If I had called one to the field I had to call all in turn, for all were alike abusive; and as I was not disposed to do this, I resolved to pursue the even tenor of my way, unawed and uninfluenced by the storm that was raging around me on every side; and, though I stood alone, yet I was not to be deterred from the faithful discharge of what I conceived to be a public duty, and I did not shrink from the discharge of that duty or from the position I had taken. I chose to await the result of time, which I knew would bring all things right. If never before, that time has now arrived, and I can with confidence appeal to honest men of all parties for the rectitude of my position and the truth of my predictions.

The occasion was one of sufficient importance to justify me in encumbering this document with a few extracts taken from my letters on that subject, as published at the time. They are as follows:

I said, "It is my misfortune once again to find myself in a situation that obliges me to take part against many of my best personal and political friends upon a subject and under circumstances that, feeling and believing as I do, it would be criminal on my part to be silent; and, however much I may regret the occasion and the necessity, I must appeal to you, as national men and the conductors of a truly national paper (the *National Intelligencer*), to allow me the privilege of addressing a few reflections to the people of the South through your columns on a subject of the gravest consequence to their interests—I mean the Nebraska Bill, now pending before the Senate, which, from all we can now see, is likely to become a law without a word against it from the South, and by which it is proposed to repeal or declare inoperative the Missouri Compromise of thirty-four years' standing, and acquiesced in by all parties of the country.

"It is true, I have little now to do with politics, and I am not in a position to give influence and currency to what I may say. I have no congressional seat from which I can speak 'by authority,' but my interest in the settlement of this question, and my regard for the welfare of the country is none the less on that account.

"After the most careful examination of this portentous question, I am satisfied it is the most mischievous and pernicious measure that has ever been introduced into the halls of Congress.

"With the institution of slavery acknowledged in a sounder and better condition than it has ever before been; with the public mind gradually subsiding and acquiescing in the peaceful and healthy measures of 1850; in the absence of any public necessity or demand from any party or section of the country; with an application from no human being outside of the political circles of Washington; without the question ever having been presented for the consideration of the public, who are the only proper parties to be consulted; with solemn pledges from both parties and both sections to resist all future efforts at agitation, it is proposed to throw wide open the whole question of slavery, to unsettle all that has been done to produce harmony between the North and the South for the last thirty years by those who were quite as wise and patriotic as the men of the present day, and to revive sectional animosities and feuds in the most aggravated and embittered form, the end whereof no man can foresee. Is it not, then, legitimate for any citizen, however humble, feeling an interest in his country's welfare, to ask emphatically, Why is this to be done?

"Is this last and only chance for reconstructing the disordered and scattered fragments of a dissevered party with any intelligent mind held to be a sufficient reason for so much mischief? Are the grasping and reckless aspirations of ambitious men, who seek their own advancement by a spirit of turbulence and discord throughout the land, a sufficient justification for the wholesale scene of riot and disorder that is to follow?

"As a *Southern* man I raise my voice against it. I oppose it, because it involves a breach of faith on the part of the South, who have for thirty odd years enjoyed the advantages obtained by them in the formation and admission of the States of Missouri and Arkansas. I oppose it, because it necessarily and unavoidably begets another angry sectional controversy, which there are none left among us strong enough in the confidence of the people to allay. I oppose it, because it uproots and destroys the Compromise Measures of 1850, to which the North is no more pledged than the South to the compromise now proposed to be abrogated. I oppose it, because it would be an act of infatuated madness on the part of the South to accept it. I oppose it, because it will be impossible ever again to obtain as favorable terms from the North, with their seven millions majority of white population, as we obtained when that population more nearly approximated equally. I oppose it, on the ground that it places a barren privilege in the hands of the South, for which not only no equivalent is offered, but by which she must be an ultimate and great loser. I oppose it, because I do not like the source from which it comes, nor the power by which it is represented. '*Timeo Danaos et dona ferentes.*' It is proposed by a Northern aspirant for the Presidency, and is supported by a Northern administration, surrounded by the enemies of peace, harmony, and union, whose Free-soil proclivities have been manifested from the first moment they set their feet upon the footstool of power. I oppose it, because I see Tammany Hall, Free-soil, and Adamantine political associations and committees uniting in its support.

"By almost superhuman efforts, such as went far to carry the most distinguished man of the age to his grave, we have just extinguished a conflagration that threatened the destruction of the noblest ship of state that was ever launched upon the waters; and we have scarcely had time to realize the result and exchange congratulations on our safety, when *one* more rash, and wild, and frantic than the rest seizes a blazing torch in each hand, rushes madly into the magazine of powder, flourishes his firebrands aloft, and, bidding defiance to all consequences, calls upon us to imitate his example. Those may follow him who choose; but, for my own part, on all such occasions I prefer the hose to the flambeau. I beg the South to listen and reflect while yet the opportunity is offered.

"I know that the champions of slavery in the South have made every concession to Free-soilism since it came in conflict with Mr. Pierce and the spoils. . . . . . . But let them not venture to sacrifice the sacred and solemnly-secured rights of the South to promote the ambitious designs of selfish aspirants to power, nor yet with the vain hope of building up the fallen fortunes of their party.

"As a *Southern* man, and as a national man, I should like to see this misshapen and ill-begotten monster killed. I should rejoice to see this Pandora's box of evils forever buried, and I would resort to any fair and legitimate means to accomplish so desirable an end; and, as I stand in the presence of my Maker, I will do what I can to defeat it; and I say to my friends, in the South particularly, and to the people of the country every where, that their cry should be, 'Let the demon of discord be strangled in its birth. Let it have no resting-place for its disturbed repose. Let it be hooted, scouted, and driven from door to door like a worthless, penniless, beggarly thief. Let no man give it a shelter from the pitiless storm. Let it die and rot upon the dung-hill. Let every lover of his country, and of its peace, and harmony, and good-will, and honor, and good faith, and durability, turn from it with loathsome and shuddering disgust, as they would avoid a pestilence or a plague. Let him treat it as a disturber of his country's peace, honor, welfare, and perpetuity.'

"The South professes to despise Mr. Seward as its worst enemy. I tell the South that every man who helps to destroy the Compromise of 1820 is unwittingly engaged in the service of Mr. Seward. He is uniting the North as one man on a sectional issue, in which their pride and principle are as much involved as ours, and which will throw them all into the ranks of Mr. Seward. You will have no more national Whiggery, no more national Democracy, no more 'Hard-shells,' nor 'Hunkers,' nor 'Adamantines.' You make them all Free-soilers, Soft-shells, and Barn-burners; and he who can not see the dark spirit of disunion lurking around this bill is not a far-sighted man. In my opinion, no sectional strife we have ever had will begin to compare with it, either in intensity or duration."

These are a few brief extracts from the appeals I addressed to the South in 1854, and it was for the utterance of such sentiments as those that I was bespattered with the most filthy abuse by all the leading papers of both parties, Whig and Democratic; but, I am proud to say, never an inch did I give way to them.

The immediate result of all this most unjustifiable and dishonorable conduct in violating a compact from which the South had derived all the benefit she could claim by the admission of every territory lying south of the line of 36° 30' as slave states, including Missouri, Arkansas, Florida, and Texas, and providing for four more slave states out of the

Territory of Texas—I say the immediate effect of it was to give form, and substance, and organization to the party ever since known as the Republican party, in which was combined all the anti-slavery men of every degree, most of the old-line Whigs, and a very large portion of the Democracy, all of whom were shocked and indignant at the effort on the part of the South to appropriate to themselves a territory to which they claimed a title-deed, with uninterrupted possession for thirty-four years.

In my African Church speech of 1856, as has been already seen, I said, "Under the operation of that law, to which the integrity and the honor of the South was pledged, the South obtained the admission of Missouri and Arkansas as slave states when it was in the power of the North to have rejected them. They also obtained the admission of Florida as a slave state, Texas as a slave state, and never—never while there was an opportunity to make a slave state out of Southern territory did they dream that it was proper to repeal that law. But when they had populated all their own territories, and obtained the admission of all their slave states, when there was no necessity for it whatever, they attempted to rob the North of its just due, and thereby dishonestly sacrificed the integrity and honor of the South, that were pledged to carry out in good faith the bargain entered into."

The utterance of this unwholesome and, as they thought, most untimely truth, created intense excitement in the Democratic ranks. It was isolated from the rest of my speech by Mr. Robert G. Scott at Corinthian Hall, and commented on with much sourness of temper. But it can not be forgotten with what a spirit of demoniac bitterness and venom it was assailed by Governor Wise, who followed Mr. Scott, nor the severity with which I answered these two gentlemen the next night at the African Church, and again at Petersburg. After characterizing me as an agitator and disturber of the public peace, a demon who had furnished arguments to the *Herald* and *Tribune* for Fremont, as an incendiary that ought to be arrested and indicted, he says: "An offense like this cries to Heaven against one who ought to have let his right hand forget its cunning, and his tongue cleave to the roof of his mouth before he uttered treason to the hearth and home of the mother '*who*' bore him." Now let us see what this same Governor Wise himself said a short time after, in one of the numerous letters he was daily throwing off to the North and South to bolster up his pretensions to the Presidency. He said:

"I would protect her (the South) from the authors of the Kansas-Nebraska Bills, from the wickedness, and the fraud, and the folly of a minority attempting to establish a rule of '*fas aut nefas*' in the face of an unscrupulous majority. We were strong on the moral ground of equality; we relinquished that when we attempted to assume more than equality, and we lost all character for justice. We were wise men in demanding no more than our due, and we have been foolish since and of late in trying to deprive others of their due. We have challenged a competition of settlement with a then slaveholding agricultural population, on our part against a majority host of commercial-trading, free white, free-soil people, who have *not* all houses, and who are keeping a sharp look-out for them, and who can use Sharp's rifles, put into their hands by fanaticism, to acquire them.

"If I am to be driven out as a dreamer, I will at least preserve mine integrity, and time and the day of famine will show whose counsel and whose course will have saved the household." Now if this is not a plagiarism from my

my own speeches, it can not be denied that it is nearly allied
to one, and I leave it to time and the present day to show
whose counsel and whose course would have "saved the
household."

But what am I to think of the man who would publicly
and semi-officially denounce me for what I had said, and, before the words were cold that fell from his lips, borrow my
views, and, as nearly as possible, my language on this very
point, in one of his written communications, where possibly
it might help him to use it, but which at a later day found
its way to the public press? This I leave to the better
judgment of an impartial public. But to return from this
digression.

THE PRESIDENTIAL QUESTIONS OF 1856.

The time for the nomination in 1856 rolled on, the Democratic Convention met in Cincinnati, the two great actors
in the Nebraska swindle were set aside—Pierce and Douglas were both defeated; they had only served, like poor
puss, to pull the chestnuts out of the fire for the monkey
to eat. Mr. Buchanan, who was understood to have been
opposed to the disturbance of the Missouri Compromise
(though then abroad), was nominated; and thus was a
triple swindle perpetrated by the Democracy: they first
cheated the country, and then cheated both of the principal
instruments they had employed for cheating the people.
Poor Douglas made all the amends he could for his folly,
and struggled hard to get out of the meshes into which his
Southern friends and allies had entangled him, but if he had
lived to the age of Methusaleh, he could not have recovered
his former position.

The more miserable Pierce was left, as it were, to rot
upon his own dunghill in New Hampshire; his name has

scarcely ever been called in the South since, and he has no place in the confidence, the affections, or respect of the North. So much for politicians suffering themselves to be seduced from the path of rectitude by an overweening ambition. Mr. Fillmore, the "model President," as he had been almost universally termed by the Democracy, after his defeat for the nomination in 1852 by General Scott was nominated by the American party, but was nowhere in the race.

The Republican party nominated John C. Fremont as their standard-bearer. During the progress of the campaign, the prospects of his election were so encouraging as to render his success next akin to certainty, and it was thought the last Presidential card of Democracy had been played, and the trick, as they thought, would be trumped by this newly-organized party of Republicans; and at once the cry went up with much more than its usual force "*that it was necessary to elect a Democrat to save the Union.*"

The Richmond *Inquirer* put forth an editorial, from which the following is an extract: "Let the South present a compact and undivided front. Let her show to the barbarians that her sparse population offers little hopes of plunder; her military and self-reliant habits, and her mountain retreats little prospect of victory; and her firm union and devoted resolution no chances of conquest. *Let her, if possible, detach Pennsylvania and Southern Ohio, Southern Indiana, and Southern Illinois from the North, and make the highlands between the Ohio and the Lakes the dividing line. Let the South treat with California, and, if necessary, ally herself with Russia, with Cuba, and Brazil.*"

Mr. Preston Brooks, the nephew of Senator Butler, upon whom, as his colleague, the mantle of Calhoun seemed to have fallen loosely for the moment, in a speech made to the people of South Carolina, said, "As to his own position, *he was now, as he was in* 1851, *a co-operation disunionist.* He thought it best to dissolve the government under which we now live; but, in doing this, there was a difference of opin-ion as to the means to be employed. He believed that something was due to our sister Southern States, who had the same interest at stake as we — that we should be pre-pared to act with them and to wait on them. . . . . . The great question of the Presidency would be settled, and if on the second Monday of November next it shall be found that Fremont is elected, he thought our course was plain. It is his deliberate opinion that *we should then, on the* 4*th of March next, march to Washington, seize the archives and the Treasury of the government, and leave the conse-quences to God.*"

The then governor of this state (the Unwise Henry A.), maddened by an insane and devouring ambition to be do-ing something that would keep his name in all men's mouths, seized upon these indications of what he considered to be the public feeling, and, perhaps, what he knew to be the general sentiment of the leaders of the party to which, in the premature decline of his manhood, he had allied him-self, and was disposed to make himself superserviceable in any capacity, set himself to work to organize and officer the militia of the state, and called a meeting of all the govern-ors of the Southern States to meet him at Raleigh, for the purpose of organizing a force to march to Washington, seize upon the archives and the Treasury of the government, and "leave the consequences to God" or the devil, as it is clear he was the master in whose service they were em-ployed. Governor Adams, of South Carolina, was the only one who met him, and thus this scheme was at once played out. The sensible and reflecting leaders had concluded that the time was not yet, or that it was better to wait the result of the election, as there might still be time enough to prevent the inauguration of Fremont in the event of his election.

To all this, which I cited in a note to my African Church speech in 1856, I called the attention of the people in the following language:

"Let what may happen after this to involve us in civil commotion and disunion, no man of the Democratic party can plead as an excuse his ignorance of the mischief he was perpetrating by acting with a party whose objects are thus plainly disclosed, not by their enemies, but by themselves.

"Let the people read and reflect before they vote.

"If any public press had dared to utter such sentiments as these at any time before the Calhoun party obtained a foothold in the South, the walls of his building would have been torn down, his type thrown into the river, and the author himself would have received a coat of tar and feathers, and have been driven beyond the pale of civilized society; and now they are permitted to cast the odium from themselves by the silly and childish attempt to fasten Black Republicanism and Abolitionism on all who do not foster and encourage their infamous doctrines."

Here, then, was another warning that I gave the people as to the designs of their leaders, and I was again denounced for that.

But this threat to break up the government so far operated on the timid men of Pennsylvania, together with the use of money freely contributed in New York and expended in the Keystone State, secured the election of Mr. Buchanan, and thus was the revolution staved off four years, which it is now manifest they were then earnestly bent on bringing about, rather than surrender their power and submit to a full investigation and exposure of all the atrocities they had committed in the last five-and-twenty years. True, the people were not prepared for such an issue, nor were they in 1861; yet, if they suffered themselves to be bullied into it now as they did, why would not the same routine of operations have served the purpose then?

But "*the handwriting was on the wall,*" and it was clearly foreseen that this was the last expiring effort of Democracy, and that this was the last Democratic President to be elected; and they at once went to work and cleared the deck for action, and from that time to the day of secession the country has been kept in a constant state of turmoil and commotion. It was expedient, if not necessary, to familiarize the public mind to the idea of disunion, as they thought, and it was still more necessary to keep the mind of the South in a frenzied state of excitement on the subject of slavery, and of the injustice, inequality, and wrong of not being permitted to extend it to the territories, from which it had been expressly excluded by the founders of the government in 1787, and, still more recently, actually excluded by their own legislation in 1820.

THE ATTEMPT TO MAKE KANSAS A SLAVE STATE.

The next step taken by the Southern Democracy was the attempt to force slavery into the Territory of Kansas — for what purpose? it may be asked. It was considerably beyond the slaveholding region of the United States, where neither the soil nor climate were adapted to slave labor, and where the insecurity of the property would have deterred any rational man from carrying his slaves; why, then, were emigrant-aid societies gotten up in the Southern States, private and public subscriptions raised, large appropriations made by the state Legislatures from their public treasuries to pay the expenses of those from the Slave States, who could be induced, with or without slave property, to settle in Kansas? They never expected nor hoped to make a permanent slave state of Kansas. Why, then, all this management and expenditure? Why, because it was a part of the programme by which the North was to be kept in a violent state of exasperation, and the South in fevered excitement on the subject of "*our rights*" in the territories, and at the opposition that was made to those rights by the people of the North.

In speaking of the controversies between the two sections on the subject of slavery, if I do not arraign the North as often as I do the South, it is not because I hold them guiltless; very far from it, for they have done a great many things by which they not only entitled themselves to severe censure and rebuke, but to the just punishment of the offended laws of the United States — such as their occasional opposition to the execution of the Fugitive Slave Law, the passage of their Personal Liberty Bills, etc.; but I do mean to say that for the repeal of the Missouri Compromise, which was the proximate and immediate cause of all the troubles now upon the country, and for the evils that have grown out of it, the South is not only particularly, but exclusively and solely to blame; and I say, moreover, as far as the leaders were concerned, it was not done through inadvertence, want of judgment, or by accident, but by design, from a studied and flagitious purpose to produce the very results that have followed; and the attempt since made to shift the responsibility from their own shoulders to those of the Abolitionists, as much belies the truth of history as does the attempt *now* every where, and by almost every body, made to shift the responsibility of making this war from the shoulders of South Carolina and the other Southern States to those of Abraham Lincoln, which he had no more agency in making than I had; for he not only found war actually existing when he came into power, but it had been actively carried on for several months during the administration of his predecessor, Mr. Buchanan, without an effort on his part to arrest it, if it was not secretly winked at and encouraged, especially in its earlier stages. Another reason for not having said more of the Northern Abolitionists was, because whatever might have been their personal inclinations and their local action in the states, they were impotent for mischievous legislation, and never originated, or had the power to carry out any of the ruinous measures that culminated in the great catastrophe; all this was the work of Southern agitators and Southern Democracy; and, therefore, I have had less to say of the Abolition party than I otherwise should, believing it to have been created, nursed, and encouraged by designing politicians South for a purpose little suspected by the deluded people upon whom the *cheat* was put.

But while the South was thus actively engaged in sending off their own people to Kansas that they might adopt a Constitution recognizing slavery, the North was far from being inactive spectators of what was going on; they were also at work, and with every advantage in their favor. In my first letter on the Nebraska Bill in 1854, I said, " The next question is, by which section of the country could this territory be filled up with the greatest facility? The slaveholder of the South is generally a landholder on a larger or smaller scale; he would necessarily require time to sell out his lands, stock, and chattels, while the free laborer of the North packs his carpet-bag at night, buckles his belt around his body, and is off at the first whistle of the locomotive. Thus will he settle the territory and declare it free while the Southern man is getting ready to start." (For a farther plagiarism of this idea, see General Wise's letter above.) And so it proved to be. It was settled by the surplus population of the North while the South was making haste to get ready.

Finding themselves overpowered by numbers in Kansas, the South—I say the South, because it was done by Southern men, and the Southern members of Congress without exception, as far as I know, unless Mr. Millson, of the Norfolk district, formed an exception, all approved and encouraged it; and the Southern people, with very rare exceptions, participated in the excitement growing out of it; the Southern Democracy, their aiders and abettors, I say resorted to stratagem and trickery to effect what by open and undisguised means they had failed in, and that by a most open, bold, unprincipled, and nefarious swindle, to force upon the people of Kansas a Constitution framed by the representatives of about two thousand persons out of a population of twenty thousand, by which slavery was not only declared to be a perpetual institution, but that no man should be permitted to question it, and affixing high penalties, either of death or imprisonment in the penitentiary, for any who should write, print, or publish or circulate in the territory any book, paper, magazine, pamphlet, or circular containing a denial of the right of persons to hold slaves, etc., etc., with other equally offensive provisions, upon which the people were not permitted to vote, because, as it was openly avowed, it was known they would reject it, but were to have it crammed down their throats as you would cram dough down the throat of a calf to fatten it for market.

I have not the time or space to write out the history of this piece of Democratic handicraft, which excited the disgust and contempt of every man who had any regard for the freedom of his own race, or any respect for honesty and fair dealing. Now that the excitement of the occasion has passed off, I know that there are thousands and tens of thousands who, if they would examine this subject and its history fairly, could scarcely be made to believe they had ever permitted themselves to be made participators in, or had lent their active aid to the perpetration of such an iniquity. Yet such was the fact; this was a part and parcel, and but one of the scenes in the great drama that had been put upon the stage by Southern Democracy, the boasted friends and champions of the rights of the people and the rights of the states; and then the people of the South, in the wild excitement of their passions, were made to believe that the resistance offered to this scheme of tyranny, despotism, and fraud by men who had the right to establish their organic law that we claimed for ourselves, was an unconstitutional and unholy war made upon the rights of the South. I quote what I said of it at the time in my Academy of Music speech in 1859.

MR. BOTTS'S SPEECH IN NEW YORK IN 1859.

"They claim to be a State-rights party, and utterly deny that any man can be a friend to the rights of the states who does not attach himself to their Democratic organization.

"Well, in the course of my reading and my experience I have known of but few instances in which there has been any attempt on the part of the general government to interfere with or encroach upon the rights of the states; and those few are very striking and very remarkable instances, as well as of transcendant importance, and of very recent date, and have all originated and been sustained by the Democratic party.

"The first case was that of the Lecompton Constitution, in which the doctrine was asserted by a State-rights Republican Democratic President (for that is the title they have assumed to themselves), and strenuously attempted to be carried out in Congress, that it was in the power of the Federal authorities to legislate one of the territories of this government as a state into the Union, with a Constitution which had never been submitted to the people for ratification, on the avowed ground that, if submitted, it would be rejected, and against which seven tenths of the people of that territory were then remonstrating and protesting—a doctrine that struck a death-blow at the basis and foundation of our Revolution — a doctrine that denied both the right and the capacity of the people for self-government—a doctrine, the advocacy of which, in the absence of party machinery and party demands, there was not one of its advocates within the broad limits of this nation whose standing and popularity could have withstood the storm of popular indignation and wrath with which he would have been overwhelmed—a doctrine that was the most anti-Democratic, anti-Republican, anti-state-rights, anti-constitutional, anti-common-sense, and anti-common-honesty doctrine that was ever propounded to the American people; and yet there was not one Southern Democrat in either house of Congress that had the consistency, the principle, or the independence to vote against it. And it is a historical fact never to be forgotten or overlooked, that the only party in this country that could be found to give it their support was the Democratic Republican State-rights party, and that *that* fraction of the party claiming, "par excellence," to be the true and genuine Simon-pure State-rights wing of the party, gave it the most earnest and active support.

"For my own part, having just returned from abroad

when this question was raging with its greatest violence in Congress, I stood by an inactive but not an unconcerned spectator, feeling that if the final result should show that the power and influence of the President had become so omnipotent and overwhelming, or that the people had become so debased and indifferent to their own rights and the enjoyment of free government, as to have submitted patiently to such outrageous and intolerable oppression and wrong, that then there was no despotism in the Old World under which I would not as soon have lived as under the tyrannical and iron despotism of Democracy.

"Thanks to God, the doctrine did not prevail; and, thanks to God, the people are resolved to be left free to choose their own form of government, in defiance of bribes on the one hand, and the threats on the other of the Democratic Republican State-rights party that now holds the reins of government in its hands, I trust for a limited period only; for if after this they shall be retained in power, the moral effect and virtue of the action of the people will have been thrown away.

"Does this action of the party indeed constitute Democracy? If a case parallel to this *could* occur in England, it would drive any ministry into everlasting disgrace, if no more. In France it would produce a revolution that no power of government could resist. In Russia it would be regarded as an act of detestable tyranny, against which the serfs themselves would rebel. Yet here it is claimed as evidence of Democratic consistency, and adherence to the principles of true Democracy.

"Look again at the question of the admission of Kansas under a new Constitution. Every Southern Democrat has already voted for its admission under a Constitution that the people of Kansas have disavowed, rejected, and spurned. They were offered admission, with their thirty-five thousand population, if they would ignore all that had passed, stultify themselves, and yield obedience to the dictation of the Federal Executive and Congress; and now, since they have indignantly rejected the bribe, and spurned the threats which accompanied it, it is recommended by the representative of the Democratic State-rights party, that one rule shall be adopted for the admission of Kansas, and another for Oregon, and all the other territories of the United States.

"May we not ask, in the name of Heaven, what has this government come to? In what direction are we drifting? What haven are we to reach? Is this Democracy? Is this justice? Is this honesty? Is this constitutional liberty? Is this what our fathers fought for? Is this state rights? Is one territory to be left free to form a government to suit itself, and another to be required to frame one to suit the President or the Democratic party? Is this the way the President hopes to put down agitation, and restore harmony to our already distracted country? Yet where is that party which looms up in bold relief for the equality and sovereignty of all the states? Where is that Democracy that is always loud-mouthed in proclaiming the equality and sovereignty of the people?"

I also append a sketch of the proceedings of the Kansas Convention, as taken from the *National Intelligencer* of that day, that a fair conception may be formed of what an outrage the South had been led to take an active part in perpetrating, while, as I have said, they were made to believe they were only contending for their plain legal rights in the territories, of which they were about to be unceremoniously robbed. Here is the sketch:

"The Douglas wing of the Convention wanted to submit

the slave clause to the people, but not the body of the Constitution. The plan is to force the people to vote for the instrument itself, whether they are for it or against it. This Constitution legalizes all the laws past by the spurious Legislature, including the Black Code, which punishes with death those who oppose slavery.

" We have space only for a condensed sketch of the proceedings :

"Mr. John Randolph, a blunt, outspoken pro-slavery delegate representing Atchison County, in the course of debate on Friday said that he was in favor of the minority report, because he considered the plan of the majority (Calhoun's) a swindle. The idea of submitting one clause of the Constitution, and not allowing the people to vote on the whole, was mean, cowardly, and infamous; it was worse than a swindle, it was scoundrelism! He ridiculed the idea that the love of Democracy and the principles of free suffrage actuated the 'Nationals' in the Convention. Else why did they deny to the people the right to vote upon the whole instrument? He was in favor of submitting the whole or none; he was down on all sneaking, half-way dodges. For himself, he believed the Convention to be a sovereign body, and therefore possessing the right to send up to Congress its Constitution without submitting it to the people at large. He was opposed from principle to letting the Abolitionists and Black Republicans vote down their Constitution, as they would do if they had a chance. What he did he wanted to do openly; he was opposed to stabbing in the dark. He hated Judases, who kissed only to betray. The majority report was a cheat and a fraud.

"Mr. Morley, of Riley County, pitched into both reports. He denounced the proposition of the majority as a base attempt to swindle the people, and the minority report as a high-handed outrage. He said that the 'Nationals' wanted to slip poison into the Free-soilers' cup, while the Atchison-ites were for blowing out their brains openly, and that was all the difference between them on the slavery question. He then offered a substitute proposing to submit the whole Constitution to all the legal voters, with a proviso requir-ing every voter to swear to support this Constitution if it should be ratified, the Nebraska Bill, and the Fugitive Slave Law. His substitute was tabled by a large majority.

"Colonel Jenkins, fugleman of the ultraists, next spoke. He took the broad Southern Democratic ground, and claim-ed that the Convention held the sovereignty, and should decide not to submit the Constitution, or any part of it, to the people. He said the public good and the proper equi-librium between the Free and Slave States required that Kansas should come into the Union as a slave state. He knew it would be received if a slave Constitution was sent up to Washington. He said that he had read a letter from President Buchanan to a prominent member of the Pro-slavery party in Kansas, to the effect that the 'Constitution· would be received in the form as sent up by this Conven-tion.

"Mr. Wells, of Douglas County, was opposed to both re-ports. He denounced in bitter terms those who were des-ignated as Abolitionists in the Convention. They were all National Democrats; there was not a Black Republican among them. Although he considered Republicans as en-emies to the Constitution and country, yet they were citi-zens, and entitled to a voice in the institutions under which they must live. We can not get over this, and we should not, said he, make a Constitution in which the people were prevented from expressing themselves on the institutions under which they wish to live. This Convention represents

only two thousand voters, and there are twenty thousand in
Kansas.   It was repugnant to all his ideas of right for two
thousand men to attempt to dictate to ten times their number, and force upon them institutions which they hated and
abhorred.   He did not believe that Congress would accept
a Constitution so framed; he thought the Northern Democrats would not dare to vote for admitting a state under
such circumstances; and, if they did, the Black Republicans
would destroy the party in every free state.   The destruction of the Democratic party in the North would be a calamity which the admission of a dozen slave states would
not counterbalance.

   "General Calhoun, of Springfield, Illinois, made a long
speech in favor of the majority report, and of only submitting the slavery clause to the people.   He was opposed to
giving the 'Topekaites' a chance to 'vote down our Democratic Constitution.'   The majority report would *compel*
the Abolitionists to vote *for* the Constitution while they
were voting down the slave clause, no matter how repugnant it might be to them.   'In this way we have got them
tight,' said he, 'and they can't help themselves.'   There are
several provisions in the body of the instrument which sufficiently protect slave property, which, with the Dred Scott
decision, is all that Southern gentlemen should ask.   By
this means Kansas will come into the Union as a Democratic state like Illinois.

   "A dozen other speeches were made, which we have not
room to sketch.

   "As the matter stood at adjournment, the Fire-eaters had
achieved a signal triumph.   A clause had been adopted in
the Constitution making Kansas forever a slave state; and
this Constitution was ordered to be sent to Congress without submission to the people in any shape, not even in the

swindling form proposed by the Douglasites. The people of Kansas are in a ferment. An explosion may take place at any moment. An extra session of the Legislature is talked of, and also a general convention of the Free-state party, to decide upon the best policy to pursue in reference to the spurious pro-slavery Constitution. The affairs of Kansas are yet far from settled. The Nebraska Bill is working most beautifully!"

The pro-slavery report was adopted by a vote of twenty-six to twenty-three.

This was the measure that, in a copy of the Richmond *Whig* now before me, is declared to be the " test-question between the North and the South," by which the orthodoxy and fidelity of every man was to be tried; and because, with a knowledge of the facts here recited, I could not lend my support to this shameless fraud and disgraceful piece of trickery and despotism, I was not only proscribed by my enemies, but looked upon with distrust by a large number of my own party. Could any thing better serve to show the state of ignorance or utter depravity in which parties in the South had been kept by their excitement or reduced by the iron heel of Democracy?

THE JOHN BROWN RAID.

Then, too, was rebellion again threatened if they elected Banks Speaker of the House; but he *was* elected, and, so far from rebelling, many of the rebels united at the close of the session in a vote of thanks for the ability and impartiality he had displayed. The same scenes were re-enacted at the time that Sherman was a candidate; and then at last, as if the devil himself had engaged in their service, came the John Brown raid, which many of the leaders in Richmond declared to be a "godsend" for the party; and then, again, the Helper book, brought to light by the New York *Herald* to help them along with their most unrighteous work of manufacturing excitement which now amounted to frenzy.

The wild freak of this crazy fanatic, John Brown, aided and helped on by the scarcely less crazy fanatic who then exercised the functions of chief magistrate of this state, afforded a convenient opportunity for the blood-and-thunder scenes that are usually gotten up behind the curtains, but on this occasion were not only performed in the midst of the audience, but they, the audience, were, as if by a magic wand, converted into managers and actors of the play. The city of Richmond was thrown into a ferment that has rarely had its parallel even in Paris, which soon extended to and was spread all over the state. When we look back, at this distance of time, calmly and dispassionately at the scenes of that day, it would be *amusing*, except that they were too ridiculous, and yet too serious to excite a laugh over the follies that ruled the hour. I have seen nothing like it since the war commenced, unless it might have been on that memorable Sunday when the city was startled with the appalling cry that the Pawnee was coming up James River, when every pocket-pistol for miles around was brought into requisition for her total annihilation. But the John Brown affair answered the purposes of the party; it not only excited the universal apprehension for the safety of the slave property of the South, but it furnished an occasion for the display of military ardor rarely witnessed by any people, the cost of which to the state bordered on half a million of dollars. The eighteen or nineteen followers of old Brown, free negroes and whites, were nearly all caught and executed; bushels of letters that have never seen the light were said to have been received by "his excellency," implicating a large number of the most prominent men of the Republican party; and when the Republican members of the Investigating Committee of the Senate demanded that the governor should be summoned to testify and exhibit the letters in his possession, Mr. Mason, the chairman of the committee, backed by the members of his own party, peremptorily declined to furnish the proof of what they had charged, although that proof was claimed to be in the possession of the governor. But even this did not block the game that was being played. The Legislature demanded, and ultimately dragooned the unsuspecting or timid Whigs, if there were any then that could be so called, to grant without serious opposition large appropriations of money for arming the citizen soldiers, erecting armories, manufacturing and purchasing arms, etc.—all preparatory to this very war, which they knew was at hand, and which I was most bitterly denounced for exposing at the time in my letter addressed to certain members of the Legislature, in which I set forth the folly of what they were contributing to bring about. I think there has scarcely been any period of time during this war when the public mind was more excited than it was from the time of the discovery of John Brown's entrance into Virginia up to his execution (some thirty days), all of which was manufactured for a purpose by "his excellency, the governor," who was always ready "to fight in the Union," but has done precious little fighting since he left it, although he contributed largely toward taking himself and the state out together, as far as the state could be carried out.

THE NOMINATIONS FOR PRESIDENT IN 1860.

But at length the time arrived for the nomination of candidates for the Presidency in 1860 by the three parties then existing—to wit, the Democratic party, the "Opposition" party, and the Republican. The Opposition party nominated first, and nominated "honest John Bell" as an honest Union man, and so he was as long as it promised to be profitable to be so. The Democrats met at Charleston, and the secessionists and conservatives, not being able to agree, broke up in a row. The former wing afterward met in Richmond and nominated John C. Breckinridge, of Kentucky, who is now in arms against both governments, state and federal; and yet he is held in these Confederate States as a brilliant type of a true patriot. The other wing met in Baltimore and nominated Stephen A. Douglas. The Republicans nominated Abraham Lincoln, and, as a part of their platform, adopted the following resolution:

"That the maintenance inviolate of the rights of the states, and especially the right of each state to order and control its own domestic institutions according to its own judgment exclusively, is essential to that balance of power on which the perfection and endurance of our political fabric depends; and we denounce the lawless invasion by armed force of the soil of any state or territory, no matter under what party, as among the gravest of crimes."

This was a part of the platform on which Lincoln was elected, while he himself, when a candidate for the Senate of the United States against Judge Douglas, and when he sought the vote of the Abolition party, never then dreaming perhaps of being a candidate for the Presidency, was known to have said, "I have no purpose, directly or indirectly, to interfere with the institution of slavery where it exists. I believe I have no right to do so, and I have no inclination to do so." Upon which, together with other similar declarations during his canvass in the State of Illinois, Judah P. Benjamin—the St. Domingo Jew, since Secretary of State for the Confederacy (God help us!)—said in the Senate that Lincoln was a safer and sounder man on the slavery question than Douglas, who by this time had become particularly obnoxious to the Southern Democracy, because Douglas, who found himself cheated by the South in the nomination he had expected, desired now to make favor with the North by adhering to the doctrine of "non-intervention," or hands off, which constituted the main feature of the Nebraska Bill, on the ground that it *would* pay to the North, while the South now sternly repudiated this doctrine, which at first constituted with them the chief and almost only recommendation for the passage of the bill, because they found it would not pay to the South.

THE CONSPIRACY DEVELOPED.

Yet no sooner was this "safer and sounder man"—in the language of the Jew—nominated, than the tocsin of war was sounded. The platform on which he was presented to the country, together with all that he had said as quoted above, was not only ignored, but resolutely and perseveringly denied; and it was every where proclaimed that his election would inevitably inaugurate a war against the institutions of the South, until thousands and tens of thousands of well-meaning and patriotic men were led to believe that their welfare, safety, and honor all depended upon the destruction of such a government as the world will never perhaps look upon again.

In the mean time four at least of the Democratic Cabinet of Mr. Buchanan were lending every energy toward the overthrow of the government they were sworn to support, while he was too *Democratic*, if not too *treacherous* to resist.

Up to this time the highest aspirations of the leaders had been to break up the Union and establish a Southern Confederacy; to this they hoped at a future day to annex Cuba and a considerable portion of Mexico, under which the power of the Democracy would remain undisturbed. But when they found nearly the whole power of the government enlisted in behalf of the contemplated rebellion, when they found the heads of so many of the departments, embracing the Secretaries of the *Treasury, War, Navy,* and *Interior,* viz., Messrs. Howell Cobb, John B. Floyd, Isaac M. Toucey, and Jacob Thompson, all lending an active co-operation to their treasonable purposes, and the President himself, either from imbecility, cowardice, or want of patriotism, if not decidedly encouraging the movement, at least indisposed to take any steps to check its progress, then " vaulting ambition o'erleaped itself," and, with treason *doubly damned*, they struck for nothing less than the absolute control of the entire country, and consequent seizure of the Capitol at Washington, which has already been explained in the preceding pages of this outline of traitors; but the day of retribution will assuredly arrive, and the poisoned chalice will be returned to their own lips.   Oh!

> "Is there not some chosen curse,
>   Some hidden thunder in the stores of Heaven,
>   Red with uncommon wrath, to blast the man
>   Who owes his greatness to his country's ruin?"

During the canvass the public mind was filled with the most frightful apprehensions, from the studied misrepresentations of the press and public speakers.   Yet the Union spirit of this state remained firm and unshaken, and Virginia was carried by a plurality vote for the man who stood upon the platform of " the Union, the Constitution, and the Enforcement of the Laws."

THE ELECTION OF LINCOLN.

Lincoln was elected by a plurality vote only, falling very far short of a majority. South Carolina went into ecstasies over the event; the city of Charleston was illuminated, bonfires blazed in every direction; the pretext was offered, the time for open rebellion had at last arrived; a convention was called, and an ordinance of secession was passed. The property of the United States of every description was seized, consisting of arsenals, arms, ammunition, revenue cutters, mints, custom-houses, post-offices, with all their contents; in short, whatever of government property they could reach was appropriated. After a severe struggle, and a great deal of chicanery and false play, the Gulf or Cotton States followed suit to South Carolina, while it is extremely doubtful whether there was not a clear majority in every state, possibly with the exception of South Carolina, against disunion, if a full, fair, and *free* vote could have been taken; but every where the more desperate, the reckless, the idle, the thoughtless, the depraved, and the youthful portions of the community, who had every thing to gain and nothing to lose by commotion, as they imagined, were easily enlisted in such a cause, while by coarse denunciation and threats of violence the sounder and more respectable portions of society were deterred from an honest expression of opinion.

During the administration of Mr. Buchanan, who had at length been stirred up by General Scott to a sense of duty to the country, and long before Lincoln was inaugurated, the steamer "Star of the West," sailing under the United States flag, with re-enforcements for Fort Sumter, was fired upon as she attempted to enter into the harbor of Charleston, and was forced to put back, she being an unarmed commercial steamer, selected specially that no suspicion

might attach to the object of her entrance, and that no offense might be given to this rebellious state, which was a
great and inexcusable error: re-enforcements should have
been sent openly, and with a force that would have landed
there in spite of all opposition.

Shortly after South Carolina had assumed her position of
hostility to the government, Governor Letcher issued his
proclamation calling the Legislature together in extraordinary session, which was composed of a body of men that
had been elected nearly two years before, and did not, therefore, come fresh from the people, and consisted of a large
majority of Breckinridge men, or of the disunion party.
They made hot haste, without consulting the people, and
without the slightest authority to call a convention, for the
invariable habit heretofore in Virginia had been first to submit to the people whether they would have a convention
or not, which was determined by the vote *for* or *against* it.
But no such course was pursued here; all precedent was
set aside, and the convention called. The people acquiesced in what they seemed to think they had no power to
control; but still the state held fast to her moorings, and
elected something more than two thirds *professed Union
men.* But even then, distrustful either of their wisdom or
virtue, they voted by an overwhelming majority that nothing they might do should have a binding operation until it
was submitted to them for ratification or rejection.

THE "SO-CALLED" PEACE CONGRESS.

While this Convention was in session, various *pretended*
efforts were made to gull the people with the belief that
they sought for compromise and peace, but could not obtain it. I say *pretended efforts,* because, I repeat, the Democracy never intended to accept any compromise that did

not secure to them the power of the government. This is a broad and bold assertion, and ought to be established by proof. Well, here it is:

1st. A Peace Congress had been proposed to be held in Washington, to come, if possible, to some terms of understanding; five gentlemen were appointed as delegates from this state, to wit, Messrs. William C. Rives, James A. Seddon, George W. Summers, John Tyler, and John W. Brockenbrough. The Congress met; certain terms of arrangement were agreed upon, which were satisfactory to a majority of those delegates or commissioners, to wit, Mr. Rives, Mr. Summers, and Judge Brockenbrough, one a Whig, one a Democrat, and the third supposed to stand in about as close proximity to the one party as to the other; but they did not prove satisfactory to Messrs. Tyler and Seddon, of the secession party, nor did they prove acceptable to any one secessionist in the Convention, as far as I have ever learned; and it surely may be supposed that any proposition that could have been acceptable to all others than the secessionists would have been far better than a resort to civil war, even if they had not gotten all they had asked for.

But as very few of the Southern people have had the opportunity of knowing what terms were offered by this Peace Congress, I incorporate them here, as indispensable to a correct understanding of this question.

"ARTICLE 13, *Section* 1. In all the present territory of the United States north of the parallel of 36° 30' of north latitude, involuntary servitude, except on punishment of crime, is prohibited. In all the present territory south of that line, the status of persons held to involuntary service or labor as it now exists shall not be changed; nor shall any law be passed by Congress or the Territorial Legisla-

ture to hinder or prevent the taking of such persons from
any of the states of this Union to said territory, nor to impair the rights arising from said relation, but the same shall
be subject to judicial cognizance in the Federal courts according to the course of the common law. Whenever any
territory north or south of said line, within such boundary
as Congress may subscribe, shall contain a population equal
to that required for a member of Congress, it shall, if its
form of government be republican, be admitted into the
Union on an equal footing with the original states, with or
without involuntary servitude, as the Constitution of such
state may provide.

"*Sec.* 2. No territory shall be acquired by the United
States, except by discovery and for naval and commercial
stations, dépôts, and transit routes, without the concurrence
of a majority of all the senators from states which allow
involuntary servitude, and a majority of all the senators
from states which prohibit that relation ;. nor shall territory
be acquired by treaty unless the votes of a majority of the
senators from each class of states herein before mentioned
be cast as a part of the two thirds majority necessary to
the ratification of such treaty.

"*Sec.* 3. Neither the Constitution, nor any amendment
thereof, shall be construed to give Congress power to regulate, abolish, or control within any state the relation established or recognized by the laws thereof touching persons
held to labor or involuntary service therein, nor to interfere
with or abolish involuntary service in the District of Columbia without the consent of Maryland and without the
consent of the owners, or making the owners who do not
consent just compensation ; nor the power to interfere with
or prohibit representatives and others from bringing with
them to the District of Columbia, retaining and taking

away persons so held to labor or service; nor the power to interfere with or abolish involuntary service in places under the exclusive jurisdiction of the United States within those states and territories where the same is established or recognized; nor the power to prohibit the removal or transportation of persons held to labor or involuntary service in any state or territory of the United States to any other state or territory thereof where it is established or recognized by law or usage, and the right, during transportation by sea or river, of touching at ports, shores, and landings, and of landing in case of distress, shall exist; but not the right of transit in or through any state or territory, or of sale or traffic, against the laws thereof. Nor shall Congress have power to authorize any higher rate of taxation on persons held to labor or service than on land. The bringing into the District of Columbia of persons held to service or labor for sale, or placing them in dépôts to be afterward transferred to other places for sale as merchandise, is prohibited.

" *Sec.* 4. The third paragraph of the second section of the fourth article of the Constitution shall not be construed to prevent any of the states, by appropriate legislation and through the action of their political and ministerial officers, from enforcing the delivery of fugitives from labor to the person to whom such service or labor is due.

" *Sec.* 5. The foreign slave-trade is hereby forever prohibited; and it shall be the duty of Congress to pass laws to prevent the importation of slaves, coolies, or persons held to service or labor, into the United States and territories from places beyond the limits thereof.

" *Sec.* 6. The first, third, and fifth sections, together with this section of these amendments, and the third paragraph of the second section of the first article of the Constitution, and the third paragraph of the second section of the fourth article thereof, shall not be amended or abolished without the consent of all the states.'

" *Sec.* 7. Congress shall provide by law that the United States shall pay to the owner the full value of his fugitive from labor in all cases where the marshal or other officer, whose duty it was to arrest such fugitive, was prevented from so doing by violence or intimidation from mobs or riotous assemblages, or when, after arrest, such fugitive was rescued by like violence or intimidation, and the owner thereby deprived of the same, and the acceptance of such payment shall preclude the owner from farther claim to such fugitive. Congress shall provide by law for securing to the citizens of each state the privileges and immunities of citizens in the several states."

These were the resolutions or recommendations for amendments to the Constitution adopted by the Peace Congress, and that were recommended for adoption to the Virginia Convention by Messrs. Rives, Summers, and Brockenbrough, but which Mr. Tyler and Mr. Seddon in their report denounced as an insult to the South, and upon *their* recommendation they were defeated.

What there was of offense to be found in them I have been utterly unable to comprehend; and what more could have been expected by men who preferred *peace without power* to *war with power* I am unable to conjecture; and to impose upon the people the belief that the Peace Congress "*refused all concessions to the South*" was simply a delusion and a cheat, to call it by no harsher name.

Again, when the question was asked Mr. Hunter in the Senate of the United States, in January, 1861, whether, if the two houses of Congress would adopt by constitutional majorities such amendments to the Constitution as would be acceptable to the South, he would exert his individual influence to maintain the Constitution and government as it was until the states would have time to act upon them, *Mr. Hunter declined to give any such pledge.* If Mr. Hunter was for peace and union, why would he not give such a pledge? and why profess to want amendments to the Constitution for the security of any Southern right, if they were not willing to afford time for their adoption according to the forms and requirements of the Constitution?

THE CRITTENDEN COMPROMISE MEASURES.

But again, Mr. Crittenden had offered certain resolutions of compromise to the House of Representatives, to which Mr. Bigler, a Democratic senator from Pennsylvania, had offered an amendment, and those resolutions, that were proclaimed every where, at least by all but the extreme secessionists, as entirely satisfactory to the South, were referred to a committee of the Senate, of which Mr. Jefferson Davis and Mr. Robert Toombs were members. When the vote was taken, Mr. Davis and Mr. Toombs both voted against them, when their votes would have carried them, and have secured other Northern votes for them also, but which were not given, because Northern members said, naturally enough, it was not worth while for them to make concessions to the South which Southern members rejected; and yet, after they had been thus defeated, before the sun went down on the same day Mr. Toombs telegraphed to the Georgia Convention that the *North* had refused to give this boon to the South, and all that was left for the state to do was to go out of the Union. They took him at his word and went out.

Again, the whole subject of settling this difficulty was referred by the House of Representatives to a committee, of which Hon. Thomas Corwin was chairman; they adopted certain amendments to the Constitution which secured all

the rights of the South forever, and to which no Southern
man could reasonably object; they were brought up for
consideration in the House, and, as far as they were acted
upon, passed that body by a vote of two thirds. Among
those acted on and passed by two thirds was an amendment
forever prohibiting Congress from legislating on the subject
of slavery; but the impetuosity of the secessionists was such
that they would not wait for the final result.

Again: here is the testimony of the Richmond *Whig* as
to the true objects of this resolution; and it must not be
overlooked that that paper and its editor had become thoroughly indoctrinated in the secession school, and claims now,
I believe, to have been an original secessionist; but whether this is so or not, it is certain that no Democratic paper in
the South, from the time the secessionists outbid the Union
men for its support, has been more violent and extreme during the progress of the war, as well as in its efforts to carry the state out of the Union, than this once honored and
honorable organ of the Whig and Union party.

THE RICHMOND WHIG ON RECONSTRUCTION.

This is what the *Whig* said:

"*Reconstruction.*—The plan of ex-Senator Bigler, of Pennsylvania, for ending the war consists of a suggestion that the
Legislatures of the Yankee States shall petition Congress to
call a convention for the purpose of 'reconstructing the Constitution,' with the view of making it satisfactory to the
Confederate States and inducing their return to the Union.
Mr. Bigler mistakes the point of the difficulty. The fault
was not in the Constitution, nor did the Southern States
withdraw on account of dissatisfaction with that instrument. No alteration of it, even if such alteration were left
altogether to themselves, would begin to satisfy the South-

ern States. What they object to, and what they never will cease to object to, is association with the Yankee race on any terms. If Senator Bigler could 'reconstruct' the Yankee from head to heel, *intus et in cute*, in mind, heart, soul, and body, so that there would be no atom or instinct of the original beast left, we might then consider the question of reunion, but even then would probably determine that it is best for us to be alone."

Then, again, hear what Mr. Preston Brooks said in 1856. Now I do not pretend to introduce Mr. Brooks exactly in the light of a representative man of his party *per se ;* but when his political associations and connection with the State of South Carolina and all the secessionists in Washington are considered, it may well be conceived that he imprudently gave utterance to what he well knew to be the general sentiment of the party.

He said, "Mr. Fillmore is, privately, a very respectable gentleman. He made a good President, and I believe sincerely that, if elected, he would desert his own party, and make a better President than we think. But that is the very thing I don't want. I am afraid he would do so well that he would throw back the prospects of disunion."

Mr. Brooks only expressed the sentiment of every man's mind who was connected with the leaders of the Calhoun wing of the Democracy.

WHAT ANDREW JOHNSON SAID.

But once again, read the testimony of Governor Johnson, of Tennessee, once a bright star in the galaxy of Democracy. In a speech delivered by him in Nashville in the spring of 1862, he said,

"Tariff was the pretext for disunion in 1832, and the slavery or negro question is the pretext now. How do the

facts stand when we come to examine them? Let us go
back to the proceedings of the last Congress.

"What was the true phase of the times? A compromise, you remember—the Crittenden proposition—was introduced. The Southern senators, including Toombs, Benjamin, Iverson, and a host of others, pretended that, if the
measure passed, the South would be satisfied; but they desired every thing else but compromise. Senator Clark offered an amendment which we believed would be acceptable to the South. I had critically kept pace with these pre-
tenders. Their protest was only to disguise their real intentions. When the vote was put on Clark's amendment, mark
well, only fifty-five ballots were recorded. The amendment was adopted by two votes, thus defeating the original
compromise. Who is responsible for this work of destruction? Six Southern senators standing and refusing to record
their votes. If the Crittenden Compromise had been adopted, they would have been deprived of a pretext for their
treason. Judah Benjamin, a sneaking thief and perjurer,
and an unconscionable traitor, was seated near me while the
vote was being taken. I told him it was his duty to come
to the relief of the country by voting upon this important
proposition. He sneeringly answered that, 'when he wanted my advice he would make the request.' I said, 'You are
a senator, and I demand that your vote be recorded.' With
six others, he contrived to defeat the measure by slipping
out. They wanted no compromise.

"This, then, has caused the present difficulties. These six
senators destroyed the compromise, upon which they base
revolution. Let us examine ourselves, gentlemen, that we
may arraign the guilty ones at the shrine of public suffering.
Did Lincoln or the Republicans dissolve the Union? No!
Who, then, are to blame? Men who in themselves were ca-

pable of averting the storm, and yet cried there was no help for the South, no escape from separation.

"You know the clamor has been raised that the non-slave-holding states would amend the Constitution so as to legislate upon the subject of slavery. On the 20th of December South Carolina passed an ordinance of secession, took Fort Moultrie, and the revolution commenced. Soon after South Carolina went out, seven other states followed. Their argument was that the Free States would interfere with their peculiar institution by legislation. By the withdrawal of these states the North had over three fourths of the votes in Congress, and, consequently, had the power to legislate. Having the power, did they so amend the Constitution? No, they did not. They came forward with an amendment to the effect that 'Congress, in all future time, shall have no power to legislate upon the subject of slavery.' The amendment was passed by a vote of two thirds. Why did you not accept it instead of being governed by a petty tyrant?"

I could multiply and pile up evidence upon top of evidence to an interminable extent to show that no compromise was desired or would have been accepted; yet the people have been persuaded to believe that every expedient was resorted to to obtain a peaceable settlement of the difficulties existing, and that the overbearing power of the North had doggedly refused to listen to their complaints. And when such opportunities as these were presented for reconciliation and peace, which were not only not accepted, but purposely and pertinaciously smothered over, and, as far as could be, kept concealed from the people, what have they to say for the price they have had to pay for the costly cheat that has been put upon them?

I

THE VIRGINIA CONVENTION OF 1861.

To come back to the Virginia Convention. They had been in session for some two months without making any perceptible progress toward secession, except by a change of some few known aspirants for office, who conceived that the Democratic craft was the safest to take passage in; and, unfortunately, there were too many of that class of small politicians in the body, nearly every one of whom have since received office, or have been candidates for the Confederate Congress or of the State Legislature, major generals, brigadiers, colonels, majors, captains, commissaries, quarter-masters, or something else that would pay well and give them notoriety; still secession was at a great discount, notwithstanding the Convention was surrounded by a reckless and unprincipled public press, all of which not already in the service of the secessionists had become subsidized, and notwithstanding every effort at intimidation was resorted to by an infuriated mob, who assembled daily and offered personal insult to those members who still expressed attachment to their country and its institutions.

MR. BOTTS HAS AN INTERVIEW WITH MR. LINCOLN.

About this time Mr. Lincoln sent a messenger to Richmond, inviting a distinguished member of the Union party to come immediately to Washington, and if he could not come himself, to send some other prominent Union man, as he wanted to see him on business of the first importance. The gentleman thus addressed, Mr. Summers, did not go, but sent another, Mr. J. B. Baldwin, who had distinguished himself by his zeal in the Union cause during the session of the Convention; but this gentleman was slow in getting to Washington, and did not reach there for something like a week after the time he was expected; he reached Washington on Friday the 5th of April, and, on calling on Mr. Lincoln, the following conversation in substance took place, as I learned from Mr. Lincoln himself. After expressing some regret that he had not come sooner, Mr. Lincoln said, "My object in desiring the presence of Mr. Summers, or some other influential and leading member of the Union party in your Convention, was to submit a proposition by which I think the peace of the country can be preserved; but I fear you are almost too late. However, I will make it yet.

"This afternoon," said he, "a fleet is to sail from the harbor of New York for Charleston; your Convention has been in session for nearly two months, and you have done nothing but hold and shake the rod over my head. You have just taken a vote, by which it appears you have a majority of two to one against secession. Now, so great is my desire to preserve the peace of the country, and to save the Border States to the Union, that if you gentlemen of the Union party will adjourn without passing an ordinance of secession, I will telegraph at once to New York, arrest the sailing of the fleet, and take the responsibility of EVACUATING FORT SUMTER." The proposition was declined. On the following Sunday night I was with Mr. Lincoln, and the greater part of the time alone, when Mr. Lincoln related the above facts to me. I inquired, "Well, Mr. Lincoln, what reply did Mr. Baldwin make?" "Oh!" said he, throwing up his hands, "he wouldn't listen to it at all; scarcely treated me with civility; asked me what I meant by an adjournment; was it an adjournment 'sine die?'" "Of course," said Mr. Lincoln, "I don't want you to adjourn, and, after I have evacuated the fort, meet again to adopt an ordinance of secession." I then said, "Mr. Lincoln, will you authorize me to make that proposition? for I will start to-

morrow morning, and have a meeting of the Union men
to-morrow night, who, I have no doubt, will gladly accept
it." To which he replied, "It is too late now; the fleet
sailed on Friday evening." He then said to me, "Botts,
I have always been an Old-line Henry-Clay Whig, and if
your Southern people will let me alone, I will administer
this government as nearly upon the principles that he would
have administered it as it is possible for one man to follow
in the path of another"—all of which I believed then, and
believe now he would have done. He said, moreover, "We
have seventy odd men in Fort Sumter, who are short of provisions. I can not and will not let them suffer for food:
they have so much beef, so much pork, potatoes, etc., but
their *bread* will not last longer than next Wednesday, and I
have sent a special messenger to Governor Pickens to say
that I have dispatched a steamer loaded with '*bread*'"—
that was his expression, though I suppose he meant provisions generally—"and that if he fired upon that vessel he
would fire upon an unarmed vessel, with bread only for the
troops; and that if he would supply them, or let Major Anderson procure his marketing in Charleston, I would stop
the vessel; but that I had also sent a fleet along with this
steamer to protect her if she was fired into. What do I
want with war?" said he. "I am no war man; I want
peace more than any man in this country, and will make
greater sacrifices to preserve it than any other man in the
nation."

This is a part of the history of this war that is not generally known; I think it ought to be made public, and therefore I give it. I have often wondered why Mr. Lincoln had
not himself, in his own justification, made it known to the
country. I suppose it was because he felt that he had assumed a heavy responsibility in thus proposing to surrender

a fort of the United States, and did not want it known in the North; but now a knowledge of the fact that he had gone so far, and was ready to make such a sacrifice of himself to preserve the peace of the nation without avail, would greatly strengthen his position in the North as well as in the South.

When I returned to Richmond I mentioned this conversation to several of my friends in the Convention, among them John F. Lewis, who not only expressed great surprise, but doubt of the reality of any such proposition having been made to the gentleman in question, and expressed the confident opinion that *he* could not have rejected it if made, and it was thought such a proposition would have been most gladly welcomed by the majority of the Convention. Mr. Lewis then asked me if he might mention it to the gentleman to whom the proposition was submitted. I told him *certainly;* that I preferred he *should*, as, if his doubts were well-founded, I should like to know it. He did mention it, and Mr. Lincoln's representation was confirmed by Mr. Baldwin both to Mr. Lewis and myself.*

* *March*, 1866.—By the report of the testimony taken before the Reconstruction Committee, it appears that John F. Lewis, of Rockingham, in the course of his testimony given on the 7th of February, referred to this subject, and states the proposition generally ; but not anticipating a denial on the part of Mr. Baldwin, was not as specific as he would otherwise have been. His language is, "While the Convention was still in session, I went to the house of John Minor Botts in Richmond on the 16th day of April, 1861, and he informed me that he had been to Washington a few days before, and had had an interview with Mr. Lincoln; in which interview Mr. Lincoln informed him that he had sent a special messenger to Richmond for George W. Summers to come to Washington, and, in the event of his not being able to come, to send some reliable Union man to consult with him on important matters. Mr. Summers, from some cause or other, did not go, but sent Colonel John B. Baldwin,

In three weeks from this time Mr. Baldwin had accepted a military commission in the Confederate service, and was

of Augusta County, Virginia.   Mr. Lincoln informed Mr. Botts that he had made this proposition to Colonel Baldwin,. that if that Convention would adjourn without passing an ordinance of secession, he (Mr. Lincoln) would take the responsibility of withdrawing the troops from Fort Sumter.   Colonel Baldwin declined to accede to it, and no such proposition was ever made or communicated to the Convention.   Next morning I took Colonel Baldwin to the house of Mr. Botts, who told him he was informed that such an interview had taken place.   Colonel Baldwin did not deny it.   In answer to Mr. Botts's question of how, in the name of God, he could take the responsibility of withholding the knowledge of such an interview from the Convention, Colonel Baldwin remarked that it was then near the hour for the meeting of the Convention, and that he was compelled to be there, but would see him again."

On the 10th of February Mr. Baldwin was examined and questioned by the committee upon this point, when Mr. Baldwin testified in the most unqualified manner that Mr. Lincoln had never made any such proposition to him ; and upon the question being put,

"*Q.* You received from Mr. Lincoln no letter or memorandum in writing?

"*A.* Nothing whatever.

"*Q.* No pledge?   No understanding?

"*A.* No; *no pledge, no understanding, no offer, no promise of any sort.*"

At a subsequent part of the examination Mr. Baldwin very materially qualified all this, as will be seen by the following questions and answers in continuation.

"*Q.* Do you possess a good memory?

"*A.* My literal memory is not good.   I can not say it is peculiarly bad; but in reference to results as bearing on a line of policy or argument which I have pursued, I think my memory is unusually good.

"*Q.* You are by profession a counselor at law?

"*A.* Yes.

"*Q.* Accustomed to listen to the details of testimony?

"*A.* I am, sir.   My habit is to take no notes of testimony at all; and I habitually conduct cases with forty or fifty witnesses, taking no minute whatever except of the name of the witness.   My memory is sufficiently soon after elected to the Confederate Congress (both of which positions he held to the close of the war), and soon

accurate, and is so recognized by my associates at the bar, that when a bill of exceptions in regard to facts developed on the trial is to be made, they very often call upon me to write the testimony from my memory in preference to writing it from such notes as were taken by the bar.

" Q. You recollect the substance and the result?

" A. Yes; the substance and the result.

" Q. Is it in any degree likely that in this narrative you are mistaken as to any material fact that transpired in the Convention?

" A. I think not. I may have omitted entire branches of what occurred. It may be that entire subjects which I have not mentioned at all might be brought to my mind; but as to the subjects I have touched, I have as much confidence in the recollection which I have of them as I can have in my recollection of any thing transpiring that far off. It was a subject of more interest to me than any thing that ever happened to me; and when I returned, I repeated it over and over again to the gentlemen who had concurred in sending me, and it impressed itself deeply on my mind." (Nothing could be more explicit, unequivocal, and unqualified than this.)

" Q. You think you can not be mistaken when you say that Mr. Lincoln did not assure you in any form that it was his purpose to withdraw the garrisons from Sumter and Pickens at that time?" (Fort Pickens was not embraced in Mr. Lincoln's statement to me, nor was it referred to in the testimony of Mr. Lewis.)

" A. Of course I would not be willing to say, if I heard that Mr. Lincoln had given a different representation of it, that it was impossible he should have done so. I have no reason to believe that Mr. Lincoln was a man capable of intentional misrepresentation in a matter of that sort; therefore I would not, of course, undertake to say that it was impossible he could have intended to convey that impression. If I were certified that Mr. Lincoln had said he intended to give me that impression, I should be bound to concede it, although at the same time I should be bound to say that the idea never occurred to me, and that when I first heard that such an idea had been suggested, I was as much impressed as I ever was in my life."

This portion of the testimony, it seems to me, strangely contrasts with became as violent a disunionist as any to be found in the military or civil service of the Confederacy.

that which just precedes it, but such is the testimony of Mr. Baldwin on this point; and as it might, in the opinion of some, throw a shadow of doubt on the truth of the statement made first by Mr. Lincoln to me, as contained in the text of this volume, and next as to the statement made by me to Mr. Lewis, and subsequently to others, I feel it to be imperatively incumbent upon me now and here to remove every shade of doubt, by supplying such testimony as to the veracity of Mr. Lincoln, and the fidelity of my own representation of the facts, as will arrest all pretext for assault on the part of the most prejudiced and vindictive of *his* assailants or of mine.

On the 15th of February last I was summoned before the committee, and examined on this particular point at some length. My testimony is too voluminous to be copied here. I can only make a general reference to it; but it was positive, emphatic, and unequivocal; no ifs nor ands, no equivocation and no qualification either as to the statement of Mr. Lincoln or the acknowledgment of Mr. Baldwin. As to the truth of that statement, see Reconstruction Report, p. 114–117. What Mr. Lewis and myself have sworn to is either true or false; if not true, then we are both perjured men; and the perjury has been committed willfully and deliberately, and we can no longer claim the countenance or respect of honorable men, while it is equally true that Mr. Baldwin has either committed perjury, or his "unusually good memory" has failed him sadly, and is too treacherous and unreliable ever to be depended upon hereafter. With those who know Mr. Baldwin better than I do, it will be ascribed to a defective memory, and I have no desire to raise an issue on that point, but I can not permit my own testimony to be questioned by any one.

I will not say it was any part of Mr. Baldwin's calculation, in the event of the success of that ill-fated star in the galaxy of nations (the Confederacy), to claim the chief credit for Southern independence, on the ground of his refusal to accept an overture by which it would have been defeated, but it does not require a large amount of penetration to perceive that this would have been a natural sequitur.

I have the best authority for saying that Mr. Lincoln made the same representation to Governor Pierpont, General Millson, of Virginia, Dr. Stone, of Washington, Hon. Garrett Davis, Robert A. Gray, of Rocking-

THE VIRGINIA "STATE-RIGHTS" CONVENTION.

Previous to this, the more extreme and violent portion of
the disorganizers had sent out a *secret* circular to their se-

ham (brother-in-law to Mr. Baldwin), Campbell Tarr of Wheeling (and
Treasurer of West Virginia), and three other gentlemen in company with
Mr. Tarr (TARR), in almost the precise words testified to by me. Letters are before me to sustain this assertion, and, in every instance but one,
voluntarily sent.

But all this having occurred in April, 1861, spoken of as it has been in
social circles among the best friends of Mr. Baldwin at intervals throughout that period, why is it that no denial of its truth has ever reached my
ear during the lifetime of Mr. Lincoln, or during the great struggle for
life by the Southern Confederacy, whose ultimate independence for nearly four years Mr. Baldwin did not doubt, and, as he testifies, "expected
to be hanged if it failed?"

But I have said, when Mr. Lewis gave his testimony he did not believe in the possibility of a denial by authority of Mr. Baldwin, and still
less that *that* denial would be made on oath by Mr. Baldwin himself, and,
therefore, he was less circumspect and minute than he would otherwise
have been. See, however, what he now says in a letter written on the
7th of April, 1866, now before me.

He says, "You and I know that Baldwin did acknowledge that Mr.
Lincoln made the proposition to withdraw the troops from Sumter upon
the condition that the Virginia Convention would adjourn without passing an ordinance of secession. Some of the Secesh have been trying to
persuade me that there was only a mistake between Baldwin and myself.
I have always answered, my statement of the matter is before the public.
I am as certain of its truth as I am of my own existence. I am not mistaken. If my evidence is not correct, I am a perjured man. I can make
no compromise."

Again, in a letter of the 14th, he says, "I have seen the report of your
evidence, and I think it as nearly correct as it could be, unless you had
written it out at the time the interview took place. Baldwin and myself
talked over the matter going to and returning from your house, and it is
almost impossible for me at this date to report what was said in your presence, and what was said in going to and from your house. That Bald-

I 2

cession friends throughout the entire state, urging them *all* to assemble in Richmond on the 16th of April, and not only

win admitted to me before we got to your house, and to you after our getting to your house, that Mr. Lincoln did propose to him that, if the Convention would adjourn without passing an ordinance of secession, he would withdraw the troops from Fort Sumter, is as certain as that the sun rose this morning. I recollect the expression he used. He, Mr. Baldwin, said that Mr. Lincoln made the proposition, and that he asked, 'What! adjourn without a day?' (It was the first time in my life that I had heard the English for *sine die*, and, though I knew the general meaning of the term, I never knew the literal translation, and it made an impression that I have never forgotten. I am not a Latin scholar.) Baldwin said Lincoln replied, 'Certainly.' Baldwin then said the Convention would not entertain such a proposition for a moment. I have talked with Colonel Gray (Algernon S. Gray, a colleague of Mr. Lewis in the Convention, and a warm personal friend of Mr. Baldwin) several times about this during and since the war. He is not anxious to be a witness, etc. Colonel Gray and myself, as you know, boarded and roomed together. The morning after you informed me of the interview between Baldwin and Mr. Lincoln I commenced telling Gray about it, thinking he was as ignorant as myself, when, to my utter astonishment, he sprang up in the bed and asked, in the most excited manner, 'How, in the name of God, did you hear that?' I remarked that it was true such an interview had taken place. He replied, 'I thought there were only three men in Richmond who knew such an interview had taken place.' . . . . . Gray is the only member of the Convention that I have met with who acknowledged that he knew any thing about the matter."

Here, then, is proof conclusive on this head. I need only say that a more scrupulous, conscientious, and truthful Christian gentleman does not live than John F. Lewis, and that there is not a man in this state, friend or foe, who will say otherwise; and if any Copperhead at the North or traitor at the South shall hereafter charge that Abraham Lincoln made unnecessary war upon the South, or that he came into office under a pledge to war upon Southern institutions, his friends may exultingly point to this record for a refutation of the slander, and to show what great personal sacrifices that generous-hearted and patriotic man was prepared to make to avert the heavy calamities of a civil war, and to throw the responsibility where it properly belongs.

to bring every secessionist of their respective, but of neighboring counties, the object of which was to exercise an outside influence by giving it the appearance of a great uprising of the people of the state from every part, demanding, in their sovereign capacity, the immediate passage of an ordinance of secession; and if that could not be obtained by peaceable means, then to inaugurate a revolution, the first step in which was to depose the governor, who was at that time supposed to be as strongly in favor of the Union as he now declares himself to be inveterate in his hostility to it, to turn the legitimate Convention out of doors, and establish a provisional government of their own.

THE REBELLION INAUGURATED.

Of all this, of course, there is no record proof, for the purpose was not divulged until after the passage of the ordinance, when many of the leaky vessels did not hesitate to avow this to have been the design, which before had been suspected, from the time the secret circular first came to light, and from the general tone and feeling manifested by the party.

On Wednesday night, the 10th of April, Mr. Roger A. Pryor, who was supposed to have been deputed by his coadjutors in Richmond, as otherwise he would scarcely have ventured to take such a responsibility upon himself, made a speech in Charleston, in which he gave the most solemn assurance and sacred pledges that if they would *begin the war* by firing upon Fort Sumter, the Virginia Convention would immediately pass an ordinance of secession, notwithstanding the vote that had just been taken, which stood 45 for secession and 90 against it. But upon this assurance from Mr. Pryor the state determined to act; they did not wait for the arrival of Mr. Lincoln's cargo of bread. The next day they commenced the attack on Fort Sumter, and an old gray-haired octogenarian from this state, who had been preaching secession for a number of years, claiming and proclaiming every where that it was *his mission* to break up the government at Washington by dissolving the Union, was permitted the high privilege of firing the first gun, but who was the first to take to his heels when the enemy, at a subsequent period, made their appearance in his own vicinity, and has taken good care never to be near enough to them to fire a gun since.

This attack of the 11th resulted in the lowering of the flag of the United States. News of the capitulation reached Washington on the evening of the 13th; *then*, as I have already said, threats became current and unconcealed of the contemplated attack on Washington by an armed mob collected together from the cities of New York, Philadelphia, Baltimore, Washington, Alexandria, Richmond, Norfolk, etc., which was so confidently looked for, that before I left the city (where I happened to be) on the 15th, many of the windows of the Treasury building had been already barricaded as before mentioned. The Secretary of War at Montgomery, as I have also already said, declared in a speech on the night of the surrender of the fort that in thirty days the Southern flag should float over the Capitol at Washington; and then it was, and these the circumstances under which Mr. Lincoln issued his proclamation on the 15th of April calling for seventy-five thousand men for the protection of the Capitol of the nation, which afforded the *pretext* to the Virginia Convention to pass an ordinance declaring the connection of this state with the government of the United States as dissolved.

PRESIDENT LINCOLN'S PROCLAMATION IN 1861.

I do not question either the *propriety* or the *duty* which devolved on Mr. Lincoln for making a call for troops under the circumstances that existed and that were patent to all men's minds. Whether it was for the protection of the Capitol, or for the enforcement of the laws in the revolted states, or for the recovery of the property, which, if taken by individuals, would have constituted a felony—and yet I consider that proclamation in many respects as the most unfortunate state paper that ever issued from any Executive since the establishment of the government. It was un-- fortunate in this: first, that while it was manifest to any reflecting man that Mr. Lincoln could not have called for so small a body of troops with any calculation of overrunning or subduing the seven states that had already virtually declared war against the government, yet it failed to state what was the object of the call, and thereby it was left in the power of the demagogues with which the land was filled to make any and every misrepresentation of its purpose that was best adapted to excite the apprehensions and resentment of the South. General Jackson under similar circumstances, in the height of his popularity and power, did not venture to take the step he did without an address and an appeal to the patriotism of the people to stand by and sustain him in a determination to save the Union from the hands of traitors who aimed at its destruction. How much more important, then, was it that *Mr. Lincoln*, against whom such a storm of prejudice had been raised as to his purpose of striking a deadly blow at the institutions of the South, should have declared his views on this subject in the most distinct and emphatic form! when he would have kept himself beyond the reach of the demagogues and defamers, and retained the support of the Union party of the South, who seemed to be all paralyzed by this single dash of his pen. It is not saying too much, I think, when I say such was the state of excitement and enthusiasm for war that was aroused among the citizens of Richmond, that I was perhaps the only one who raised his voice above a whisper against the ordinance at that moment. Again, it was unfortunate in this, that, if it only could have been postponed for three days, this commonwealth would have been in a state of revolution from the causes I have just recited, but it came just in the very nick of time to save the disorganizers the task of a revolutionary movement.

Three days later, and Mr. Lincoln might have received a call from the executive of this state for the aid of the general government to sustain the lawful authorities of Virginia, when all the other powers under the sun could not have driven Virginia or the other Border States into a participation with the Cotton States.

When that proclamation reached Richmond on the evening of the 15th, the city was crammed with secessionists from all parts of the state, in obedience to the call of the secret circular. I came down myself on the same day from Washington, and I had scarcely set my foot upon the threshold of my own door before I was visited by friends who admonished me that I had better not go upon the street; that the whole city was in a blaze of excitement, and it would be dangerous for me, with my well-known opinions and devotion to the Union, to be seen in public. I ridiculed the idea and spurned the suggestion, hastened to get my dinner, and walked down to the governor's house, where I found a room crowded with members of the Convention of both parties; they were all in a high state of excitement, governor and all. To reason with them would be like dart-

ing straws against the wind. I soon found that my presence was not agreeable to the gentlemen assembled, and
if they had not left I should; but they did not give me the
opportunity; for soon after my arrival, and upon the utterance of the first sentiment I expressed upon the subject,
they began, *one* by *one*, to leave the room, until the governor and myself were left alone. I found all reason in vain,
and I did not remain long, but extended my walk through
Capitol Square and down Main Street to ascertain the extent of my danger, as predicted by my friends. Many
looked askance, some seemed to avoid me, but none ventured to offer me offense. I never felt more proud or step-
ped more boldly, for I felt the most comfortable and confiding assurance that I was *in the right.* I felt that I was
in the midst of a despicable set of traitors on the one hand,
and of timid, misguided men, who had suffered their fears,
in some instances, their prejudices and their passions, in
others, to get the better of their judgments. I walked
home proudly and defiantly; but when safely pillowed under my own roof, my pride and defiant spirit both forsook
me, and I involuntarily burst into tears over what I too
clearly saw — the calamities that were in store for my
country.

There has been no one act of the administration of Mr.
Lincoln, perhaps, that has been more severely censured and
condemned throughout the South as a high-handed usurpation of power and disregard of all constitutional and legal
authority, than the call of seventy-five thousand troops by
his proclamation of April 15, 1861. It was commented upon
by the press and talked of by the leading secessionists, until
the belief became universal in the South that the war was
by this means designedly made upon the South without the
sanction of law; while in truth there was no one act of his

administration more thoroughly sustained by lawful authority or made more imperative upon him.

The authority is to be found in the first volume of the
"Laws of the United States" of 1795, and date of February
28.   In chapter xxxvi., section ii., page 424, it reads: "And
be it farther enacted, That whenever the laws of the United
States shall be opposed, or the execution thereof obstructed
in any state by combinations too powerful to be suppressed
by the ordinary course of judicial proceedings, or by the
powers vested in the marshals by this act, it shall be lawful
for the President of the United States to call for the militia
of such state, *or any other state or states*, as may be necessary to suppress such combinations, *to cause the laws to be
duly executed.*   And the use of the militia so to be called
forth may be continued, if necessary, until the expiration of
thirty days after the commencement of the next session of
Congress."   And again, by the Act of March 3, 1807, which
declares, "That in all cases of insurrection or obstruction
to the laws, either of the United States or of any individual
state or territory, where it is lawful for the President of the
United States to call forth the militia for the purpose of
suppressing such insurrection or causing the laws to be executed, it shall be lawful for him to employ for the same
purpose such part of the land or naval force of the United
States as shall be judged necessary, having first observed
all the prerequisites of the law in that respect."

THE ORDINANCE OF SECESSION PASSED IN VIRGINIA.

The balance of the story is soon told.   On the next day
(the 16th) the outside Convention of secessionists met in full
force and in secret session, clamorous and riotous for an ordinance of secession.   The legitimate Convention sat with
closed doors, and proceeded to enforce an obligation of the .

strictest secrecy on every member of the body as to their future proceedings—*one* and the *main* object of which was to keep the people in the dark as to the extent of the opposition still existing in this body to a rupture with the general government, and also to enable them to possess themselves of government property before it could be known in Washington what they intended. On the 17th, the ordinance was passed by a vote of 88 to 55, but was, until the injunction of secrecy was removed, generally believed to have been almost, if not quite unanimous. Then followed the seizure of the Custom-house and Post-office in Richmond, the seizure of Gosport Navy-yard and Harper's Ferry, with all the munitions of war they contained, the sinking of vessels in the channel of Elizabeth River to prevent the escape of such war-steamers as were then in the harbor of Norfolk.

Thus was this state not only declared to be out of the Union, but actually plunged into *active hostility* against the United States by a Convention whose powers were expressly *limited* by a vote of the people to a *recommendation only* of what should be done.

THE ILLEGAL STATE ACTION OF THE CONVENTION.

But this was not all. On the 25th of April, without waiting for the ratification of the ordinance, the Convention adopted the constitution of the Confederate government as *their* Constitution, and negotiated a treaty with Mr. Stephens, who had been sent on as commissioner for that purpose, by which the whole power of the state was transferred to the Confederate government at Montgomery, introduced large bodies of troops from other states into Virginia to overawe and control the elections, and having converted the peaceful homes of Eastern Virginia into one grand military encampment, with an effrontery unparalleled, they turned to the people whose confidence they had thus abused and betrayed, and said, "Now you can vote for secession or against it, as you choose, *but we advise you to vote for the Emperor,*" as was said in France when Louis Napoleon was voted an imperial diadem. And such was the system of intimidation resorted to, that in the city of Richmond, which would have cast fifteen hundred to two thousand votes against it if it had been understood that men were free to vote without interruption or annoyance, only two such votes were recorded, one of which was by Mr. John H. Anderson. And here let me inquire what is the status of Virginia at this time? Is she a member of the Southern Confederacy or not? For all present practical purposes she is, but for the future, in *fact* and in *law*, she is not. Be it remembered that the Virginia Convention was one of limited powers, and that a limitation, not by construction, but by the express vote of the people, who declared by a majority of fifty-six thousand that nothing the Convention might do touching the organic law of the land should have the force of law until submitted to them for ratification or rejection. The Ordinance of Secession has been submitted and ratified, but has the annexation of the state and the adoption of the Southern Constitution been submitted? Never; and, without such submission and ratification, the Convention was as powerless to transfer the state to Mr. Jeff. Davis and Company, and to adopt a Confederate Constitution for the people, as any other body of men collected together in the state. So far from having given her consent to this transfer, when the amendments adopted by the same Convention to the State Constitution were submitted, which amendments ignored the Constitution of the United States and recognized the Confederate Constitution, the people rejected them, so that Virginia is now in a condition of revolution, and in *alliance* with the Confederate government so long as the war may·last, but at its termination is entirely free of all connection with them, if their independence shall be established, in which event she will *legally* be standing alone, free to form whatever future associations she may think fit.

THE RATIFICATION OF THE ORDINANCE OF SECESSION.

But to return. My own case will illustrate the condition of things in Richmond. I had resolved to cast my vote against the ordinance if it were the last I should ever be permitted to give. For the first time in my life I had armed myself to repel any rudeness or indecorum that might be exhibited toward me. When a number of my friends appealed to me in the most forcible manner not to go to the polls, that they did not believe it would be safe for me to do so, I replied that, let the danger be what it might, I was resolved to vote, and that I would not hesitate .to shoot down any man who might dare to show me indignity, they said, if I did vote they would stand by me, as my friends generally would, but it would probably involve the whole city in a scene of bloodshed ever to be deplored. I finally suffered myself to be dissuaded from exercising my right as a citizen of Virginia, which I have regretted and been ashamed of to this day. The truth is, the vote throughout the state, with the exception of some few counties bordering on the Potomac and in the northwest, was a perfect farce. Thousands voted for it who were as much opposed to it at heart as I was, through fear of the consequences; tens of thousands did not vote at all, while others, again, very naturally inquired, what is the use of voting against it, when we are in actual war, and can not get out of it by any vote we can give? That there was a large majority of the votes polled in favor of the ordinance, I suppose there can be no doubt, but that is all we have been permitted to know about it; what proportion of the vote of the state was given, and what withheld, is known only to those who have chosen to keep it to themselves.* I do not suspect the authorities here of having done quite as bad as they did in Louisiana, where the vote was actually falsified, and declared to have been in favor of the ordinance, while, in truth, as was afterward ascertained, it was against it; but still, the studied concealment shows there was something wrong about it that the authorities did not care to have

---

* *March*, 1866.—I find, by reference to M'Pherson's History of the Rebellion, the vote is reported as one hundred and twenty-eight thousand eight hundred and eighty-four for secession, and thirty-two thousand one hundred and thirty-four against it, making an aggregate of one hundred and sixty-one thousand and eighteen; but where this vote came from, except from the army that had been introduced into the state, it would be difficult to tell. The largest vote ever given in Virginia was in the Presidential election in 1860, when there were four candidates, and then one hundred and sixty-seven thousand four hundred and three votes were polled, while the vote on secession was very generally looked upon as a farce; and it would not be hazardous to say that there were from seventy-five to one hundred thousand votes in the state not given. I recollect very well that for a few days the vote was published as it came in; and from a small number of counties in the northwestern portion of the state bordering on Maryland and Pennsylvania, where the vote was more numerous than in any other part, the vote fell short from six to ten thousand; while in the city of Richmond, that could have given some fifteen hundred against secession, only two votes were given against the ordinance; and in Norfolk, where large bodies of troops were stationed, one regiment, commanded by the then Colonel Roger A. Pryor, was said to have been dismissed from the service because it was found they were voting against the ordinance. What a contemptible farce on free suffrage it was!

disclosed. If any one outside of the official circles has ever been able to ascertain the vote, I have been so unfortunate as never to have found him.

And now, if another outrage so flagitious has ever been practiced upon a people claiming or professing to be free, if another instance of such gross abuse of power can be presented, or that has been so tamely and weakly submitted to, I would be thankful to have it pointed out, for there is nothing within my knowledge that will stand in comparison with it.

MR. BOTTS'S EFFORTS TO PREVENT CIVIL WAR.

Finding that the labor of my life had been spent in vain, and that the South had been plunged into hopeless and inextricable ruin unless the hostilities between the parties could be speedily checked, and believing it would terminate in one of the most bloody and ferocious contests that history had recorded, I immediately set to work in an earnest endeavor to bring about a peaceful solution of this difficulty. I at once opened a correspondence with the Attorney General of the United States, Mr. Bates, urging him, with all the force and persuasion I could command, to exert his influence with Mr. Lincoln to recommend at once the call of a national convention to *amend the Constitution*, so as to give to those states that did not want to remain in the Union *leave* to withdraw. I would not have had the general government, under any condition of circumstances that could have arisen, to recognize the right of secession, because that would at once have annihilated all hope of ever establishing another permanent, enduring government on this continent again, but to give *them leave to withdraw*, and thereby save all the Border States, Virginia, Kentucky, Tennessee, Arkansas, Missouri, and North Carolina to the old government, and confining the withdrawal to the Cotton States, which states had produced all the mischief; and then, if there was to be a war growing out of the navigation of the Mississippi River or any other cause, it would have been a foreign and not a civil war, in which it would have been impossible for any Border State to have participated with the Gulf or *foreign* States without a confession of treason; and if they did not speedily repent of their folly, and seek admission into the Union, then to administer a little of their favorite medicine in the form of a pill from the "*Ostend Manifesto*" or a bolus taken from the Monroe doctrine.

But this proposition gave satisfaction to neither party; it led to quite an angry correspondence with Mr. Bates; and the Southern *extremists* were *extreme* in their denunciation of the suggestions, because in my first letter (which at the earnest entreaty of some of my friends I permitted to be published) I admitted the superiority of the Federal government in all the appliances of war, which they were by no means prepared to concede; and some of their papers were silly enough to charge me with giving information to the United States government of its own power and strength, as if I was not indebted to the statistics furnished by them for all the information I had on the subject, and under this ridiculous accusation a vast deal of violent excitement was created against me. As a mere sample of the feeling existing, I select one extract from the Richmond *Whig* published about that time; and from this miserable specimen of bad taste and worse judgment, of weak, absurd, and childish braggadocio, may be inferred the general feeling that pervaded all classes at that day, for this bombast was regarded as an unmistakable indication of true manliness and elevated patriotism.

"The vaunts and threats of the Yankees to invade and

subjugate us have been widely proclaimed, and are known to all the world. *They* can not eat their words without adding a new infamy to the Yankee name. They are already justly reputed to be bigoted, Puritanic, hypocritical, penurious, envious, and cross-grained, but we were willing to accord them a vulgar brute courage. They will lose this if they don't fight. But fight they must, for the credit of the American name. They have blustered and bullied too much to be permitted to beat a retreat now. They have a *Virginia* general to plan their campaigns and marshal their forces, and, if they let him alone, he will lead them where they will be peppered; but they must not raise the cry of treachery against him by way of pretext for dodging the fight. We tell them frankly and candidly they *must* fight, they *shall* fight; there is no other escape from unutterable shame."

This was the feeling that existed at the beginning of the war; how sadly this tune will be changed, and how they will sue and pray for peace before it ends, you and I may live to see.

But as another specimen of the madness of the hour, and to show what desperate and despicable means were resorted to for the purpose of enforcing the gag on all men's mouths, I select one from the Richmond *Dispatch* at that time:

" *Tories and Traitors.*—We have heard, though we can scarcely credit the statement, that there are men in some parts of Virginia who are endeavoring to paralyze the war spirit of the state by circulating slanders as infamous as that gotten up at the beginning of the troubles about the $16 tax on Carolina negroes. Among other things, they recklessly assert that there was no fleet sent to Charleston for the purpose of re-enforcing Fort Sumter, and that therefore the attack upon that fort was wholly unnecessary.

This is an infamous lie, known to be such by the immeasurable villains who concoct it. *In the North every man is put in peril of his life who does not sustain their murderous onslaught upon the South.* The South can scarcely afford to be more merciful to tories and traitors in her own borders. Give all such wretches fair warning before executing upon them the justice they deserve; convince them that they are in more peril by being traitors than by being honest men, and, our word for it, they will learn in a short time discretion, the only virtue of which their base nature is capable."

The above is a beautiful illustration of the more enlarged freedom for which this war was professedly inaugurated. But enough of this sickening recital.

MR. BOTTS RETIRES FROM THE CONTEST IN DESPAIR.

Finding that I was powerless to prevent my own state from throwing herself into the arms of her destroyers, I quietly retired to the country, with a firm determination to stand aside and take no part in a war that the people had no agency in making, and which, let it result as it might, was assuredly to end in their absolute ruin, but to leave it altogether to those who had brought it on, or approved it, to conduct it to an issue.

I certainly knew full well that my own prospects in life might have been greatly advanced, at least for the moment, if I had followed the fashion and taken service in the cause of those whom I had all my life opposed; but if I had been capable of adopting for myself, or of recommending to others the adoption of a policy of such unutterable wrong, perfidy, and treason as in my inmost heart I felt this to be, and with such results as I believed and *knew* would follow, it would have been only from motives of selfishness, ambition, or fear, for which I should have scorned and despised myself in all future life.

"HONEST JOHN BELL" AGAIN.

When I voted for "*honest John Bell*," *as they called him*, and the platform of "*The Union, the Constitution, and the Enforcement of the Laws*," which implied *nothing*, unless we who voted for it meant thereby to declare to the world our unalterable devotion to the Union, our veneration for the Constitution, and our firm determination to uphold and sustain the Executive authority of the Federal government in enforcing the laws fully, faithfully, and impartially, every where and upon all alike, upon which pledge *alone* this state was carried for "*John Bell;*" for the people of Virginia cared no more for "*John Bell*," except as the representative of a principle, than they did for "*John Doe*" or "*Richard Roe*," and which platform of principles "*honest John Bell*" not only accepted but sought to stand upon, but which he kicked from under him as soon as he found it would not conduct him to station, power, and emolument, and gave aid and comfort to the extent of his power to those whom he had just previously denounced as traitors and enemies to mankind, and who had also just before denounced him as a most selfish and corrupt Abolitionist, from which charges I had often defended him, I say when I voted for that platform I was too intensely honest and in earnest to permit myself to take a step in the opposite direction, and take up arms against the government for an honest effort to carry out the principles we ourselves had not only laid down for him, but required at the hands of our own candidate only at the dictation of the most reckless and corrupt portion of Democracy. How others brought their minds to do it may not be for me to know, or, know-

K

ing, it may not be for me to say; but for myself I can and do say, that as an honest, conscientious, virtuous man, I could not do it, even if my life had paid the penalty; and I am even free to say that, so far did I feel myself committed to this great and overpowering principle, that if Virginia had not so foolishly thrown herself into the contest, then any service that I could have rendered to the Federal government would have been at its disposal for the enforcement of the law in any state North or South, East or West, that was in open rebellion against its authority, while no position under the government would at any time have been desirable or acceptable for a less patriotic purpose; and I am by no means satisfied, and never have been, that the position Virginia had chosen, or *been compelled* to assume, relieved me of the obligation of a superior duty to the United States government; but in this matter alone have I allowed my feelings to control my judgment.

THE SOUTH NO CAUSE FOR COMPLAINT.

It may well be asked here, what complaint has the South to prefer against the government of the United States? There has not been a moment of time from the 4th of March, 1801, to the 4th of March, 1861, that the legislation or law-making power of the government has not been under the control of the Southern Democracy. During that period there have been but eight out of the sixty years that the Federal Executive has not been of their own selection (except once, *when we elected*, and they seduced or bought our man up, and then refused to pay the stipulated wages); and during those eight years (I mean, of course, during the administrations of Mr. Adams, General Taylor, and Mr. Fillmore) they had the absolute and entire control of one or both of the two houses of Congress. What subject of legislation is it that they have not controlled? Bank, Tariff, Internal Improvement, Distribution has each in turn been put up or pulled down precisely as they have chosen to direct, while the subjects of war, acquisition, and slavery have been under their exclusive control and management, except only as to the late efforts to extend the latter into territory to which neither the climate or the soil was adapted, and from which they themselves had triumphantly excluded it, not only in 1787, through the instrumentality of the great high-priest and apostle of Democracy (Mr. Jefferson), but at a much more recent period, to wit, in 1820, when by solemn compact, *forced* upon the North, it was forever excluded; so that if the South has any cause of complaint, it has only been against Southern Democracy, that they ought, years and years ago, to have driven in shame and confusion from their confidence and service.

They have not only put up a bank in its weakness, but pulled it down in its power; put up and pulled down the tariff at pleasure; put up and pulled down internal improvements at will; put up and pulled down the distribution of the proceeds of the sales of the public lands as they desired; but they have elevated the question of slavery far above and beyond all other questions and subjects, and now they have destroyed the institution in the *Border States, at least*, and materially crippled it in all; and, lastly, to close the scene, they have—as far as they could accomplish it— destroyed a Union and a government the like of which the wisdom of centuries had not been able to achieve, and have left for *the South* a *wreck* from which the mind revolts with horror. What more is left for the Democracy to accomplish? Their task is finished; their mission is ended, and yet the people whom they have ruined are still wedded to Democracy.

But this is not the most, nor yet the worst that has been done by and in the name of the Democracy.

They have turned the fair and sunny fields of the South into one general camp-ground and grave-yard; they have covered the land with mourning; they have laid waste the country, and made desolate the happy homes of thousands upon thousands; they have filled the South with helpless orphans, and mourning widows and mothers; they have arrayed in deadly strife citizens, neighbors, and friends, where nothing but peace, friendship, plenty, and contentment were known before; they have excited father against son, and son against father, and brother against brother; they have sacrificed a million of lives, and made cripples of nearly as many more for life; they have filled the air of Heaven with the groans of the wounded and the lamentations of the dying; they have impoverished and ruined the entire South, and brought nothing but desolation, hunger, and want upon the people; they will have cost the nation more than ten thousand millions of dollars from first to last; they have made promises, predictions, and calculations, not one of which have been or will be fulfilled; they have undertaken to do what they will not be able to accomplish, and what will prove to be a lamentable and disgraceful failure, that will involve all in one common whirlpool of degradation and ruin. And all this for what? Why, that the leading politicians of the Southern Democracy might perpetuate their own power and appropriate the spoils of office to their own exclusive use.

It is no exaggeration to say that, if an army from the lower regions, with Lucifer himself at its head, had been turned loose with the most demoniac passions against the Southern people, they could not have done much more mischief than has been done by these Southern leaders in the name of Democracy, and all for their own exclusive and selfish purposes.*

* 1866.—It would scarcely have been credited, and still less *anticipated* that, in less than one year from the overwhelming discomfiture and defeat of this same Democracy by the absolute subjection and surrender of all their forces in the field, which was followed by the most abject supplications for pardon from the chief Executive of the nation, that they would have had the audacity to set up any claim or pretension to get control of the government again; and still less could it have been anticipated that, by the misapplied clemency of the President in granting indiscriminate pardons to all, they would, on this 30th day of March, 1866, be in the ascendency again in almost every Southern state, looking eagerly and laboring earnestly to get control of the national government. YET SO IT IS.

I have recently cut from a newspaper an article so entirely coinciding with my own views that I take the liberty of appending it here, without knowing to whom I am indebted for so true and faithful a picture of the obligations of the people to the once great and overshadowing Democratic party.

"*Record of the 'Democratic' Party.*—We never read one of the numerous complaints which appear in the so-called Democratic newspapers about the burden of our public debt and the consequent heavy taxation, without being reminded of the fact that the Democratic party is responsible for the rebellion and whatever evils followed in its track. Every dollar of our national debt was expended in suppressing the rebellion inaugurated by the Southern Democrats, and connived at and sympathized with by their Northern allies of the same party. This accounts for their desire to repudiate this debt, interest and principal, and at the same time explains the secret of their constant complaint about 'heavy taxation.' A Western orator tells the truth in his own way in the following extract:

" 'Let Democratic journals and orators howl over the debt and taxes their war has brought. They but magnify their own sins. Every dollar of debt is a Democratic legacy. Every tax is a Democratic gift. Every government stamp is a Democratic sticking-plaster. Every person in the United States drinks in Democracy in his tea, his coffee, and his whisky, and in the sugar wherewith he sweetens them. Each ingredient pays its quota for the cost of Democracy to the country. The smoker inhales Democracy. The sick man is physicked with Democracy. The laboring

A party that has been productive of such unmeasured mischief should not only be forever buried in oblivion, but the word democracy itself should be stricken from the vocabulary, that no more abuses should be committed under a name of such magic influence.

THE RESULT OF THE REBELLION.

You ask me also, what I think will be the result of this rebellion? This question is much more briefly answered.

man gives about one hour's labor every day to pay for Democracy. The capitalist pays one tenth of his income for the cost of the Democratic party. Every transfer of property is saddled with the Democratic burden. Before he is begotten the child·is subject to the Democratic tax. From the cradle to the grave he never is free from it. The funeral mourning must first pay the penalty of Democratic rule, and a portion of that which he leaves behind must go into this Democratic vortex. Generation after generation will carry this Democratic burden from birth to death. But for the Democratic party, our people would hardly have known the nature of taxation. But for the Democratic party, the hundreds of thousands of young men whose bones are strewn over the South would now be productive laborers, and the support and comfort of families now desolate. No one can attempt to deny this indictment. No one can pretend that the Democratic party had any cause for rebellion. Yet it has the effrontery to cry over the burdens of taxation. As the father of the Democratic party, when he had stripped Job of family and possessions, charged it to his own sins, and sought to draw him from his integrity, so his Democratic sons now come forward with equal effrontery and charge their doings upon the loyal people, and hypocritically howl over their afflictions, and seek to seduce them from their integrity, to elect to power the party which has brought all these woes upon the land.' "

Let an enlightened public now determine whether my uniform and persistent hostility to the Democratic party was the result of unworthy and unfounded prejudice, as some have supposed, or of a judicious and intelligent knowledge of its true character, and the danger to be apprehended, from the nature of its organization, to the interests and welfare of the nation. ·

The history of the world in 6000 years has furnished but one instance of a David and Goliath. I do not think this is likely to prove a second. Five millions of people, and they far from being united, with two local governments in operation in three of the principal states, to wit, Virginia, Kentucky, and Missouri, without money, for that can not be called money which has no foundation for its basis, and is made payable six months after the happening of an event which is sure never to take place, without credit, without necessary clothing, without a sufficiency of the necessaries of life, without a navy, and without commerce, to overthrow 22,000,000 of people, with an abundant supply of both money and credit, with a superfluity of clothing, provisions, and other appliances of war, with a most powerful navy, and a commerce unrestricted with all the world, would be a miracle that could be worked out by the hand of the Almighty alone; and if he was on either side, as has been so often claimed, then I feel assured that *that* side would never suffer defeat or privation. I am compelled, therefore, to conclude that the rebellion will prove in the end a most signal and disastrous failure, unless the administration at Washington shall be guilty of some act of most absurd and stupid folly that will serve to *divide* a now *united North*, and *unite* a now divided South. But as long as the Southern authorities can raise the men, and the provisions to sustain them, the war will be prosecuted; and when there is nothing left with which to feed the army, which will be first served, what will be left to feed the people? Unfortunately, 'those' who made the war, those who were looked up to by their more ignorant neighbors and friends for advice and counsel, will *not* be the chief sufferers; for after having induced them to adopt a course that drove the husbands, brothers, and sons into the field, they have themselves, for the most part, dodged behind every conceivable pretext to avoid the danger and privation to which they subjected others. What unfathomable contempt I feel for such creatures, who should have been the first to rush to battle and vindicate a cause of their own creation!

CONCLUSION.

I have thus furnished you with a sketch of the origin and progress of secession, as derived from my own personal knowledge of the events recorded, as I have been an active participator in all the scenes referred to for the last thirty years, and you are supplied with the means by which a mere handful of bad and selfish men, a set of political gamblers and stock-jobbers, have gradually and stealthily advanced step by step in their wicked work, and at each successive point succeeded in seducing into their ranks the too easy and timid dupes from the ranks of their opponents, until at last it has come to be a crime to dispute the orthodoxy of their detestable doctrines, or to raise a voice in favor of the great work of our immortal fathers. Thus you have seen how a reckless and desperate set of politicians, who are now courted, honored, rewarded, and caressed, have, for their own hateful and selfish ends, involved the great body of the confiding and unsuspecting people of the South in all the frightful consequences that must inevitably result from their want of fidelity to a government that never had the power to oppress them, and which they were under the highest obligations of honor and duty to support; and now they impiously implore the Almighty on *this*, the day of humiliation and prayer, to help them out of difficulties of their own seeking, and from which they have no power to extricate themselves except by unconditional submission, while their constant cry is that they are "an outraged and oppressed people, upon whom an unholy war has been waged by a tyrant and a despot," and " all *they ask is 'to be let alone,'*" and who are now exhausting every energy to involve the powers of Europe in their own unprofitable and ruinous strife.

I derive no small degree of satisfaction from the reflection, as all can bear me witness, that at every step of their unhallowed and iniquitous proceedings I have promptly, and without a calculation of the cost, arrayed myself against them, and warned the people in public speeches, and by publications innumerable, in different forms, that the design of the leaders of Democracy was the disruption of the Union, accompanied with the entreaty that they would not follow them. The people knew nothing of my deep-rooted devotion to the Union, and of my utter disregard for all parties and for all men, even for myself, when contrasted with the prosperity and happiness of my country. They did not know that I had made the Union the god of my idolatry on earth, and they set it all down to an excess of party feeling, and would not heed what I had to say. All can bear me witness, too, that on all such occasions I have offered an earlier, more persistent, and determined resistance to their measures of mischief than any other living man, which not only exposed me to the most violent denunciation and abuse of the Democratic press and party for what they were pleased to term a want of fidelity to the South, but also subjected me to the groundless suspicion on the part of many of my own political cotemporaries, who could not be made to believe in the dangers with which we were encompassed; and in this way and for this reason it was that I was so often left to stand alone in the breach, and battle single-handed against all parties in the state, until the most bitter and unrelenting of my foes were *those* who should have been found fighting by my side.

K 2

And now, in conclusion, let me say that, whether the responsibility rests upon the North or the South, whether upon the Abolitionists of the North proper or the Secessionists of the South, for breaking up, even for the time being, such a government as our fathers had formed for us, which was the pride and boast of every true American heart at home and abroad, and the wonder and admiration of an enlightened world, and involving 32,000,000 of people on this continent in all the horrors through which we have and are yet to pass before we see the end, and all mankind in a greater or less degree in its consequences, the party that is responsible for the loss of the dead, the sufferings of the living, the sacrifice of human happiness and general prosperity of the whole country, to say nothing of the infuriate, incarnate feeling that has been engendered between the different sections of the country and between citizens of the same states and neighborhoods, will, as I firmly believe, have to answer hereafter, both in this world and in the world to come, for the most atrocious and stupendous crime that has been committed since the crucifixion of our Lord and Savior Jesus Christ.

APPENDIX.

THE GREAT STRIKE FOR HIGHER WAGES.

In the preceding pages I have given a faithful and succinct history of this "GREAT STRIKE FOR HIGHER WAGES," under the direction of the *Trades' Dis-*UNION ASSOCIATION, and traced the progress of the movement, step by step, for a period of nearly thirty years before it broke out into open and defiant rebellion. I have shown, too, how and under what circumstances the plan of the leaders had been changed from their original purpose of separation to a fixed design to usurp the whole power of the general government—to seize upon the Capitol at Washington, inaugurate *their* chief as the head of the nation, and thus force Democracy upon the nation, and, if they could accomplish it, extend the institution of slavery over the whole country, in which gigantic work the active co-operation of a number of the leaders of the Democratic party North stood pledged to come to their assistance.

I have already explained why that contemplated aid was not rendered at the time; but, since the foregoing history was written, circumstances have occurred, and facts have been developed, which, I think, fully reveal the plot, with a necessary change of actors in some of the parts to suit the shifting scenes of the times. The timely-discovered and, fortunately, defeated Democratic insurrection, which was crushed out just before the late presidential election in 1864, and of which Mr. Vallandigham was at the head, and participated in by that very extensive political organization known as the "KNIGHTS OF THE GOLDEN CIRCLE," with the substitution of General McClellan for Mr. Davis (though I acquit General McClellan of all connection with the ulterior and principal designs of the leaders of the insurrection, who hoped to mould him to their own purposes if elected), was only the *delayed action* of the party, rendered necessary by the circumstances already explained. I think there is little room to doubt that, but for the precipitate and unexpected action of the authorities of South Carolina in their attack on Fort Sumter, instigated by the hot haste of the secession leaders in the Virginia Convention, which did not leave full time for the completion of their organization, Northern Dem-ocratic insurrection would have developed itself in the spring or summer of 1861 instead of the fall of 1864.

Not having had access to Northern newspapers since the war, it was by mere accident that another piece of evidence has fallen under my observ-ation, of which, I dare say, a great deal more has appeared of which I have no knowledge, and of which no doubt much more will hereafter ap-pear. That to which I now refer was the statement made by "*General Gantt*," of Arkansas, who was himself an active secessionist in 1861, and afterward a general in the Confederate service, was taken prisoner, re-lented, and testified against his Northern Democratic friends, who did not "*come to time*," as promised, in '61· I cut the following article from the New York *Tribune*, the date of which I have forgotten:

"PROOF DIRCET.—General Gantt, of Arkansas, has been the subject of fierce abuse in the Copperhead journals, for which we were unable to account until we recently observed that, in speaking for the Union cause some weeks since, he made the following statement. He said that, after his capture by the Union forces (he was a general in the rebel service) at Island No. 10, he was brought North to this state as a prisoner of war, and declared that prominent Democrats of Pennsylvania then conferred with him, and assured him 'that if the rebels would hold out a little lon-ger they would be successful, for the Democrats of the North would arrest the war by defeating the conscription, and otherwise rendering the admin-istration powerless to prosecute it.' And he added, with withering em-phasis, 'I COULD GIVE YOU THE NAMES IF WHAT I SAY IS DISPUTED.' There were a number of Democratic members of the Legislature present, and they did not dare to question the statement or call for names. He said 'the Democrats of the North ADVISED THEM TO WAR, PROMISED TO COME TO THEIR ASSISTANCE, AND THEN LEFT THEM ALONE IN THE STRUG-GLE, and confined themselves to cowardly, perfidious, and stealthy as-saults upon their own government.' He said that, instead of Northern Democrats coming to their assistance, the soldiers of the Union came in overwhelming force and conquered them; 'but,' said he, 'they brought government with them, and rescued us from a tyranny more terrible than death.'"

General McClellan was no politician; had never, as far as I knew, been in public life except as a soldier; had never filled any political office or place; had little idea, perhaps, of the quirks and quibbles, acts and tricks of practical professional politicians, and lent his name unwittingly,

I am prepared to believe, to those adroit managers and skillful manipulators, who, if they could have once had him under their thumb, hoped to mould and fashion him to any shape the Democracy might see fit to demand. Fortunately for himself, he did not fall into the *potters'* hands; fortunately for his country, they had no opportunity to entangle him in their political cobwebs before he was aware of it, from which extrication would have been difficult.

I have called this rebellion A STRIKE FOR HIGHER WAGES, and so it was, nothing more and nothing less. It was a bold and wicked *strike* to hold on, *per fas aut nefas,* to the power and control of the government, which they found was naturally and certainly falling into the hands of the majority of the North. The government had been in operation for seventy-two years; during the greater part of this time the North had had a considerable numerical majority; but, by a *pretty well* united South on the slavery question, the minority had been able to retain sufficient strength in the North, through the patronage of the government, to secure its continuance in power. Accordingly the South had *had* General Washington at the head of the government for eight years, Mr. Jefferson for eight years, Mr. Madison for eight, Mr. Monroe for eight, General Jackson for eight, Mr. Van Buren (who, although a Northern man, was nominated and elected by the South while running against a Southern candidate) for four, Mr. Polk for four, Mr. Tyler (who, though elected by the Whigs, was bought up by the Democracy) for four, Mr. Pierce (who, like Mr. Van Buren, was nominated and elected by the Southern Democracy against a Southern candidate) for four, and Mr. Buchanan for four—making in all sixty years; which was offsetted by twelve only on the part of the opposition to Democracy, to wit, John Adams for four, John Quincy Adams, four, and General Taylor and Mr. Fillmore, four; and, during the whole terms of the two latter, the Democracy had control of one or both of the two houses of Congress; and such had been the success of this minority, by the perfection of their organization and their system of rewards and punishments, that they grew bold, insolent, and insane in their demands, and, throwing off all disguise in an hour of weakness and madness in 1854, they repudiated all compromise, old and new, and planting themselves firmly on the doctrine of "SQUATTER SOVEREIGNTY," which they *had* previously—and *have* again, since they found it did not pay as well as they expected—so indignantly repudiated, declared all compromises evasions or violations of the Constitution not to be tolerated for the future, fairly and squarely tendered the issue to the North, that the powers of the government must be absolutely and entirely in the hands and under the control of the *majority* or the *minority*, and that all efforts at compromise and conciliation would be held as an act of infidelity and hostility to the South. From that hour I saw that the South was doomed, and sacrificed to the unholy ambition of the leaders of Democracy; and the efforts I then made, in numerous appeals to my countrymen, to rise up in their strength and resist this act of insanity and mischief, only served to bring upon me such a storm of indignation, rebuke, and coarse abuse, as was never before or since vented on any public man in this country or elsewhere. Arnold himself was treated with tenderness and kindness in comparison. These epithets emanated from all parties; and my own party, if possible, was more bitter than the rest; I was sustained by none, the fruits of which they have since and are now reaping. I must be excused for this partial repetition of what I have said in the foregoing pages, but I want to impress it strongly on the minds of the South, that they may see to whom they are so deeply indebted for their present terrible and afflicted condition.

Mr. Lincoln was elected in November, 1860. The climax had arrived, the pretext was afforded; and so proud am I of the position I then took, and have ever since maintained, that I hope I may stand excused for thus publicly washing my hands of all responsibility for what has ensued by here producing a portion of my correspondence on that question, beginning with November, 1860, and running down to the present time. The letter which follows was the first after the election. This correspondence was with a gentleman who was at the head of a spirited Democratic secession paper, which was published at the time in some few of the Southern papers.

Staunton, Nov. 20, 1860.

My DEAR MR. BOTTS,—You may perhaps regard me as both vain and intrusive thus to thrust before your notice the inefficient logic of an individual so entirely innocent of weight in the national councils as myself; but you will permit me to plead, as apology, the unusual and sincere interest which I feel in your own personal advancement as well as the public good, to say nothing about a wish to advise you of the error (which posterity will surely point at as the "great blunder" of your life) into which your darling pet and mistress—the Union—has insensibly invited you. A mistress who, when you first embraced her, was comely, and worthy of your love, but has now become hideous and rotten, and only fit to be cast aside for *any* untried novelty.

I am fresh from an attentive perusal of your able, earnest, and patriotic "dream" in the New York *Tribune*, which some friend was thoughtful enough to send me; and, after a very careful review of your mind and character, both well known to me, I can only charge your inveterate and industrious labor in behalf of this *passe leman* to that most potent and tyrannical of despots, habit—a weakness which somebody aptly and pointedly describes as "present action from past motives," or a persevering fondness for a Union whose integrity has been constantly and cruelly violated by the industrious malevolence of the Northern States. But it is not so much concerning the *policy* of disunion that I desire to talk with you; rather do I propose to ask you to sit side by side with me, and suffer a true and earnest friend to entreat you to forego your lofty and patriotic, but suicidal, and consequently insane, efforts to oppose your hand, as weak and powerless as that of old Priam, against the inevitable fall of that great Avalanche which now hangs impending, and only pauses until the devoted band of "dreamers" have dwindled to three hundred, as at Thermopylæ, to blot them from the book of life.

Your own prophetic wisdom, which before has been your bane, but should now become your strength, *must* advise you that a *separation of the states is inevitable.* Then why not, instead of vain Titan efforts to avoid the thunderbolt, why not, I say, rather rack and exhaust every energy of mind and body in search of the policy which may guide it best? For my part, I must say that the sublime martyrdom of those silly people at Thermopylæ has always seemed to me to belong rather to the absurd than the heroic. I want you to live to fight another fight; and, in order to do this to some purpose, you must now snatch the guidance of secession —(the wild horse did not start at your bidding)—and, *with necessity for your apology,* arrest or divert the mad devils that are loose. As far as what is called exalted devotion to the Union is worth, why others, your inferiors in both political and intellectual prominence, have risen a whole head above you by proposing an appeal even from your remote tribunal, the Supreme Court, and tickle the incorruptible sovereigns with the promise of a final reference of any vexed question that may have eluded the wisdom of Congress, and derided the constitutional lore of the Supreme Judges, to *their* distinguished sagacity. So you see that you are nowhere; for with an independent, almost obstinate hostility to popular error, you, of all, will surely not consent to ape these hungry parasites of public favor.

We all know that your mission on earth, like that of Cassandra, has been to foresee and describe, with historical fidelity, the events in the future, only, like that unlucky maiden, to be hissed and scoffed as an impostor, until Time, "the philosopher," had vindicated your claims to the prophetic mantle.   All I now ask of you is that you will for once submit to this irresistible torrent, which not all the patriots of all the South can avert or control, and thus render your voice fit and acceptable to be heard in the new state of things which must soon come upon us; and why not?   Grant that disunion is present and real, and I have you at my feet; for not from you do I listen to hear a song in praise of the dying martyr, who adds the absurdity of suicide, as only more notorious witness to his own despondency, and the weakness of a cause he has upheld and abandoned.   And you too, by such desperate opposition, will render yourself powerless for good, and be guilty of deserting the service in time of greatest need.   Even grant the South is about to perpetrate a great wrong, or call it crime, not *then* should good men fail to tender such counsel as may avoid the evil and secure the right, out of the chaos of conflicting interests that will seek a place in the deliberations of this new confederacy; and shorn of your locks by an uxorious fondness for this skeleton phantom of Delilah, as you surely will be, where, then, will we seek to find the national and intellectual patriotism and power to rebuke the petty schemes of district politicians and rural Machiavellis, whose narrow ambition is racked and content to secure a charitable crumb from the Federal party?

I may have been compelled, my dear sir, in pursuit of my object, to speak of you here in terms which may sound of flattery; but I trust that you will not understand them as such, but only as the common echo of the world, as well as of my own convictions.   With a confidence that you will at least bestow a thought on my suggestions, and with all wishes for your good, I subscribe myself your friend, etc.

Richmond, Nov. 27, 1860.

MY DEAR SIR,—I have been endeavoring to *make* an opportunity for some days past to answer your very friendly and *seductive* letter, but my whole time, day and night, has been so constantly occupied with matters that could not be postponed, that until the present I have been compelled to defer it—and even now I must be brief.

I speak of your letter as being seductive; I refer, of course, to those portions which hold out promises of future greatness, if I will "seize upon the present occasion with a nervous grasp and guide the movement in favor of secession," which you think is fixed and inevitable ; and many a charming woman has sacrificed her honor and her reputation to the insidious tempter under far less imposing circumstances than those you present for my consideration, but it was only because they had not the firmness to say, as I do now to you in the language of our Savior, " *Get thee behind me, Satan.*"

I do not concur with you in the opinion that the dissolution of the Union is inevitable; the sky looks threatening, I grant you; but so it has done before, and yet the clearest sunshine has succeeded without a shower of rain or a peal of thunder—so I trust it will be again. But if it should be otherwise, and the government of the United States is to be overthrown, no part of the *folly*, the *wickedness*, and the crime shall be charged upon me, either by the wise and good men of the present age or by generations yet to come.

True, South Carolina has rushed on with a headlong impetuosity wholly unsuited to the gravity of the occasion, as if she were afraid to trust herself with *time* for calm deliberation, relying more upon the passion than the wisdom of her people, and it may be that, under a ridiculous and false idea of a becoming pride and true greatness, she may plunge the state into very serious difficulty; she may even declare herself out of the Union. She did so by *ordinance* in *convention* in 1833, but still the Union was not rent asunder, nor will it now be, as I think. No other state is likely to go with her, and, what is best and surest of all, Virginia certainly will not, in her present state of mind.

If I could see the least semblance of justification in the attitude South Carolina has assumed, I would sympathize with her, but I do not, for reasons already given in my speech, which you say you have just read. I see nothing in that position but plain, bold, daring, flat-footed *rebellion against*, and *treason* to the rest of the states; and I can not be induced to take sides with her in her disloyalty and treachery. Who can ask it of me when her own most trusted and active leader, Mr. Yancey, in his Montgomery speech, said,

" If I understand my distinguished friend from Virginia (Mr. Pryor), the election of a Black Republican President would be an issue for disunion. I understand my learned colleague (Mr. Hilliard) to say that upon that issue he would be ready to dissolve the Union. I say, with all deference to my colleagues here, that no more inferior issue could be tendered to the South upon which we should dissolve the Union than the loss of an election. . . . . . When I am asked to raise the flag of *revo-*

lution against an election under the forms of law and the Constitution, *I am asked to do an unconstitutional thing*, according to the Constitution as it now exists. I am asked to put myself in the position of *a rebel,*of *a trai-tor*, in a position where, if the government should succeed and put down the *revolution*, I and my friends can be arraigned before the Supreme Court of the United States, and *there be sentenced to be hanged for violating the Constitution and laws of my country.*"

Such is the admission of the leader whom you profess to follow, and you make an earnest appeal to me to unite with you in assuming the position of *a rebel* and *a traitor*, for which I may be sentenced to be hanged for violating the Constitution and laws of my country. Pardon me, my impetuous friend, but *I had rather not!* I am impelled by every consideration of honor and duty to decline your very polite invitation.

Do you doubt, or does any sensible and reflecting man doubt that Mr. Yancey described truly the situation which every man occupies who favors the movement of South Carolina because of the election of Mr. Lincoln? for even *she* does not pretend that she would have occupied her present position if Lincoln had been defeated, and yet are you not surprised to see so many of our own people turning "rebels" and "traitors" at her bidding? are you not, indeed, even surprised at yourself? Rebels and traitors! Very imposing and high-sounding designations truly! But I have no particular desire that they should attach to my name either now or in after time; my aspirations do not run in that direction.

South Carolina, spurning the counsels and co-operation of Virginia and other Southern States, has, of her own accord and upon her own hook, chosen to raise a mighty and a fearful issue with the general government, and upon the general government rests the responsibility of settling the question. Hands off and fair play to both, say I. In its present stage we have nothing to do with it, and, as far as I am concerned, I turn her over to "Uncle Sam;" and if she can maintain her position against that respectable and powerful old gentleman, let her have all the honor, and glory, and benefit of the achievement to herself. I hope she may have a good, pleasant, and merry time of it. She will still be a state of the Union in a state of rebellion, and I have not a shadow of doubt either of the right or the power to control her; the only question would be, *Is it worth while?* Would it not be better to let her go out, and stay out, until she had made the experiment, and, like the prodigal son, returned to her home to eat of the fatted calf?

But that unfortunately would lead to another perplexing difficulty, which is, that it would amount to an acknowledgment that we have no government, and never had one; that our fathers were a set of old fools and fogies, who thought they were making for their posterity a government that would endure forever, while it was nothing more than a mere voluntary association of states, to be *tolerated* only so long as it was *entirely* convenient and agreeable to all parties to remain in, but that the moment it became irksome to any one state it might be broken up as readily as an ordinary whist-party whenever one of the partners might happen to get sleepy. And it requires but little reflection to satisfy any reasoning man that, if the doctrine of the right of secession is once recognized by the government, all its powers cease at once, even though the doctrine may not be carried into practical effect. The government is now supported by loans and treasury notes, and has been, with the exception of short intervals, for the last twenty-five years. What credit would the government be entitled to, and what credit could it obtain, either at home or abroad, if it were acknowledged that any one state might at any moment break up the government and thus cancel the debt, as South Carolina now purposes to cancel hers?

When would we be safe in declaring war for the defense of our honor or rights, or for the protection of our people, if in the midst of the war the Union could be dissolved and the government destroyed, because some one of the states might be disappointed in the election of her favorite candidate for the Presidency, or because her interest would be promoted by doing so, or because it would enhance the price of cotton to open a direct trade with the enemy? What government on earth would thereafter treat with us as one of the *nations* of the world. I do not wish to be disrespectful to any body, and most surely not to you; but I hope you will pardon me for saying that one of the inconceivable and irreconcilable things of this world to mind is, that an idea of such unmixed and unqualified nonsense and absurdity as that of the right of a state to secede at pleasure should ever have obtained a place in the mind of any man who was not an absolute lunatic. Men's minds are differently organized, I know, and we see things through different optics, and I dare say you and others look upon me in the same light as I look upon you and upon them. Well, be it so. *Honors are easy,* and we break even.

It has become a favorite and fashionable mode of expression to say, "this is not a government of force," "the government was not made by force, and can not be kept together by force." It is very true that the government was not made by force, and it is for that very reason that there is no right to break it up, and that it can be kept together by force. Whether that is a desirable mode of doing it is altogether a different question. If it *had been* formed by force, if some tyrannical despot had forced a government upon the people which had never obtained their approval or assent, then any of the parties would be justified in throwing it off whenever they could get rid of it. But it is precisely because it was not made by force, that it was a free and voluntary compact, entered into one with another, and each one with all the rest, that there is a power to enforce the compact.

Debts *are* not, and can not be created by force; but if voluntarily entered into, the payment of the obligation may be enforced by the strong arm of the law. And it is no government at all if it is not one of sufficient force to protect itself against treason and rebellion on the part of its citizens. If it is not a government of force, why was Congress clothed with the power "to provide for the calling forth the militia to execute the laws of the Union, suppress insurrections, and repel invasions," whether they come from within or without? Pshaw! that's all *fal lal*, to tickle the ears of groundlings. It *was* a government of force, and very efficient force in 1833, when the Force Bill passed a Democratic Congress in the House by a vote of 149 to 48, and in the Senate by 32 to 1. When and how has the Constitution been changed since? or is it only because statesmen have grown more wise of late?

Establish their doctrine of secession, and it is at once settled that there is an absolute impossibility of ever establishing a fixed, permanent, and stable government out of two or more states. For if our Constitution does not make this a permanent government, as designed by its founders, then language can not be employed that would make it so, and our institutions are no better than those of Mexico.

But if a new confederacy were to be formed I could not go with you, for I should use whatever influence I might be able to exert against entering into one with South Carolina, who has played the part of a common brawler and disturber of the public peace for the last thirty years, and who could give no security that I would be willing to accept that she would not be as faithless to the next compact as she has been to this, which she is now endeavoring to avoid.

In addition to which, the objects and interests of South Carolina, as she conceives them, are essentially at variance with those of Virginia. This state will never agree to engage in a trade that has been held as piratical by the nations of the world, and if not, South Carolina does not desire our company, and would get rid of us as soon as possible.

What may be the ultimate condition of things I do not pretend to be prophetic enough to foretell, but I do not think there is any likelihood that any other state will go out as South Carolina proposes to do, in a sort of sky-rocket blaze. The rest will be disposed to consider matters more carefully, and will take time for consideration and reflection, during which much *may*, and I think will be done to reconcile existing differences.

The Northern party has succeeded to power ; they are, therefore, deeply interested, in a political sense, in keeping the Union together, and can well afford to do all that we have a right to demand under the Constitution; and if they do not, we may be able to accomplish all that is essential through the action of Congress.

Now, as you say to me, "sit down side by side with me," and let us talk the matter over. Suppose the North should agree to repeal all their obnoxious legislation which has for its object the obstruction of the execution of the Fugitive Slave Law (which they ought not to hestitate to do even if no Union were at stake), and if not, suppose Congress should so modify that law as to relieve it of that obnoxious feature to which I referred in my Lynchburg speech, and thereby *add to* rather than impair its efficiency, and accompany that legislation with a bill declaring it to be a felony of the highest grade, and subject to heavy penalties by fine and imprisonment, to rescue, or attempt to rescue, a slave in custody of the officer, or after he had been restored to his master, and making the general government responsible for the value of the slave that may be rescued, and holding it as a charge against the state that shall permit this law to be thus violated within its territories; then suppose, in reference to the territories, there should be wisdom and patriotism enough in both sections of the country to restore matters to the condition they occupied prior to 1854 by re-establishing the Missouri Compromise line; don't you think, my good friend, you could then be persuaded to agree that all the Southern States, except South Carolina, *would agree*, even without the restoration of the Missouri line, to remain a little longer in the Union, although South Carolina might have assumed that she was too good, and high-toned, and chivalric to remain where Virginia, Kentucky, Tennessee, Maryland, North Carolina, and Missouri would be proud to stay? and if South Carolina should be deaf to all remonstrances, and insist that she would stay out after that, don't you think she ought to be left to share the fate she had invited, and coveted, and provoked?

All this, I have strong hope, may be accomplished if time—*reasonable time*—is allowed, a suitable spirit is adopted, and a proper course is pursued; but I do not think it can be done by the system of bullying and bravado that many of our leading men seem to have a decided passion for. The North and the South are equally brave. A brave people, like a brave man, will always despise and defy a bully, and there has been too much of that game played on both sides.

I believe in the patriotism of reflecting men of all parties and of both sections, and I am confident in the belief that each will, in the spirit that animated our fathers for the sake of the Union, surrender much that has been claimed on both sides before they will pull down this great Temple of Liberty on their own heads.

I will not stop to inquire which section would suffer most from a rupture of the Union, because I do not calculate its value by dollars and cents; it is enough for me to know that both would sustain a calamity that neither time, nor labor, nor money could repair. But to accomplish any thing, reason and persuasion must take the place of threats and taunts, and criminations and recriminations. How all this is to be brought about is another question, which I leave to those who are in power to bring about; but I have an abiding trust and confidence in the same good Spirit that has directed us through every trying difficulty, that the way will be prepared to save the great, glorious, thrice-blessed, and God-like work of our fathers to us, and to our children, and to our children's children.

One thing, my friend, you may be assured of, that when the necessity shall arise for Virginia to take up arms against the government of the United States, she will require no other state to set her an example of what it becomes her honor to do; but she will neither be "*hitched on*" nor "*dragged into*" any rebellious or treasonable movements by the most spoiled child in the whole family. Virginia made the Union: it is chiefly the work of the hands of her children, and she will adhere to, abide in, protect, and preserve it.

One word more. Are we to have a State Convention? I hope not; there is no sufficient reason for a convention; the public mind is not in a condition for a convention; it is in too excited a state for such deliberation as the public interests demand (and artful means have been used to make it so), and the state of your own mind serves as evidence of that fact.

Men are not made wiser or more temperate from being sent into a convention than to any other deliberative body such as Congress or the Legislature, nor have we any reason to suppose, when party spirit runs as high as it does now, that wiser and better men would be selected for such a place and for such a purpose; and would you ordinarily trust, or do you know any body who would be willing to trust the existence or destruction of this national government of ours to the hands of those who fill either of these departments? The world was not made in an hour, it is not likely to be destroyed in a day. There is no occasion for such remarkable haste. Nobody proposes to fire our dwellings or steal our substance away from us; there is plenty of time before us. Let us, then, be patient, be wise, be moderate; give time for the passions excited by the late election and the scenes that now surround us to calm down. Let us act like men, and not like children; and, above all, let us take time to ascertain facts, and not be led away from the path of duty and honor by the ten thousand misrepresentations that are scattered broadcast over the country for the purpose of inflaming popular passion.

It takes a great while to build up a government, and it requires a vast deal of labor, reflection, foresight, knowledge, wisdom, and experience to form a government that will prove a satisfactory substitute for the one you propose to discard. Do you feel sure that the state is prepared at a moment's notice to bring all these various and essential elements to bear upon this subject? If you are, I am not; and as there is less danger to be apprehended from cautious deliberation than from impetuous haste, I beg you to unite with me in urging the people of Virginia not to be in too great a hurry to destroy or hazard the loss of what all the world will never be able to give them again.

I am your obedient servant and friend, JOHN M. BOTTS.

There were very few papers at this time in the South whose columns were open to me; but the above correspondence having been published in the Alexandria *Gazette*, and as that paper accompanied its publication with a desire that the questions involved should be freely discussed, in the month of December I addressed to that paper the following communication:

Letter from Hon. John M. Botts.

To the Editors of the Alexandria *Gazette:*

If I am not mistaken, you have invited a discussion of the questions involved in the present difficulties under which the country is laboring through your columns, and especially what *part* it becomes our own state to take, and I avail myself of the privilege extended by submitting for reflection the following views :

I have observed that in several of the county meetings that have been held, resolutions have been offered and adopted declaring that the interests of Virginia and South Carolina are one and the same, and that we must attach our fortunes to hers, no matter what may occur; that there is no power to coerce a seceding state; and the Clarke County resolutions declare that the government has no right to collect revenues in a state that has withdrawn from the Union.

First, then, let me ask, in what respect are the interests of Virginia identified with those of South Carolina? *Politically* they are identified, because both are intensely Democratic, and intensely tyrannical to the minorities in their respective localities; but *socially* and commercially, it seems to me, we are as far apart as the poles. There is no more social or commercial intercourse between South Carolina and Virginia than there is between Canada and Mexico. We buy nothing from her, and she buys nothing from us. We sell her nothing, and she sells nothing to us, for not even those who trade in slaves deal with South Carolina to any extent, for *their* market is farther south; while in some respects the purposes and interests of South Carolina, as she conceives them, are essentially opposed to those of Virginia. True, South Carolina is a slave state, but so is Maryland, and so is Kentucky, Tennessee, North Carolina, and Missouri; and upon that ground we are far more closely and intimately connected with the conservative Border States than we are with South Carolina, and for all other purposes of commerce *we do not know her.* And let me ask, is it wise on the part of the slaveholding population of Virginia to "*hitch on*" to South Carolina for the sake of the slave-trade, and involve the state in rebellion and civil war, and then call upon the vast preponderance of the non-slaveholding portion of our people to come forward and *do the fighting* with the general government for the exclusive benefit of the holders of and dealers in slaves?

What will be our condition if we secede? For a single item of the account take the following: The debt and liabilities of the state do not fall far short of $45,000,000, most of which has been expended in the cause of internal improvements; our commerce is *now* with the North, but our costly lines of improvement are aiming at commercial intercourse with the great West. If we secede, non-intercourse follows, certainly to a large extent. What then becomes of our improvements—the James River and Kanawha Canal, the Central Railroad, etc.? Trade and travel will all be suspended; the superstructures of your roads all fall into decay; the sills on which the rails themselves wear away with rust from disuse, and then comes the payment of the debt, $45,000,000, an enormous system of taxation without one other source of revenue; and this not only in addition to our ordinary expenses of government, but with the additional necessary expense of keeping up an army and navy for the general defense and protection of our people and property. Happy will that man be who has no property with which he can be *troubled* or *taxed*.

But it is said, *we* should resist any attempt to coerce a seceding state. God forbid there should be necessity for using force, and I am not one of those who believe it will be necessary to resort to force on the part of the general government, unless it be in self-defense; but are you prepared to say that you value so lightly the deeds of our Revolutionary sires that, *if need be*, you would not strike one blow to preserve what they went through a seven years' war of toil and suffering, privation and sacrifice, to establish? May my tongue be blistered, my arm withered, and my name be obliterated from the record, when I take such ground as this for no better reason than now exists for deserting the Union.

How do you propose to resist? If by remonstrance, that is all well enough; but if by force, then you involve yourself in civil war, and bring all its horrors on your own state, and transfer the scene of war from South Carolina, that *has offended*, to the territory of Virginia, that has *not offended*.

We can be engaged in no civil war, unless of our own accord we seek or invite it, or, rather, I should say, *begin it*. For one, I am willing to fight the battles of Virginia in a just cause, but I am not willing to fight the battles of South Carolina in a bad cause; and if others are, then we have reached the point where we must separate and part company.

In this connection, without offense, let me ask a few plain questions, which I hope some of those entertaining extreme opinions will answer if they can.

But let me say in advance that I am one of those who have heretofore opposed the adoption of all platforms in Presidential elections, as being worthless at best, but, in the general, calculated and designed to perpetuate a fraud and a cheat upon the people; nevertheless, I did believe that if one could be adopted which could not be misinterpreted, and respecting which no fraud could be practiced, it was *that* platform adopted by

L

the Convention in Baltimore that nominated Messrs. Bell and Everett, to wit, "*The Union, the Constitution, and the Enforcement of the Laws.*" More especially when, at the time of its adoption, disunion and resistance to the laws were threatened on all sides if a Republican candidate should be elected ; and still more especially, when it was known that each of the candidates selected to be put on that platform had voted in 1833 for the Force Bill, thus recognizing the obligation on the part of the Federal Executive to *enforce* the execution of all laws even in a state that, by ordinance in convention, had declared herself out of the Union. Now, then, for the questions I propose.

Question 1st.—Did they approve the conduct of Mr. Fillmore's administration when it sent Federal troops into Boston to enforce the execution of the Fugitive Slave Law in the case of Anthony Burns?

Question 2d.—Are they now in favor of all the powers of the government being executed for the purpose of enforcing the provisions of that law ?

Question 3d.—Are they in favor of the equality of the states? And if these questions are answered in the affirmative, as I presume they will be, I put as

Question 4th.—How, and upon what principle do they make the distinction between executing one *law by force* in Massachusetts, and at the same time propose to incur the penalty of treason, and introduce civil war into our midst, by resisting the same process for the execution of other laws in South Carolina?

And I will tell them in advance that it will not do for them to put themselves on the ground assumed by some, that there is a difference between using force in a state that has declared herself out of the Union and one that has taken no such ground; because those of *our party* who resist the right of coercion utterly and wholly deny that any state *has the right* to declare herself out of the Union except on the ground of revolution ; and I suppose none will deny the right of *any* and *all governments* to put down revolutions, and that, if not successful, that revolution is treason.

Question 5th.—Did not those who contemplated resistance to the authorities of the general government, if it should find it necessary to resort to force in order to execute the laws, adopt the platform of our party, together with the candidates who planted themselves on that platform, in *good faith,* and with an honest purpose to act in accordance with its professions?

Question 6th.—Did not *they* recommend to the people of this state the support of our candidates upon the ground of their superior nationality, because they were known to be in favor of the *preservation of the Union,* the *vindication of the Constitution,* and the *enforcement of the laws?*

Question 7th.—If they were for six months engaged in urging the people of Virginia to the support of this platform and its candidates, will they inform me now what *Union* it was they were for preserving, what *Constitution* it was they were for vindicating, and what *laws* they were for enforcing?

Question 8th.—According to their understanding, was our platform also a delusion and a cheat; or did we not earnestly and honestly pledge ourselves to each other and to the world that we would contend to the last for the perpetuation of the Union of the thirty-three states composing the confederacy which was formed by our fathers? Was it not the supremacy of the Constitution which authorizes the use of force to execute the laws, suppress *insurrection,* and repel invasion? And was it not the enforcement of all laws upon the statute-book, or was it only certain selected laws in certain localities that they were for enforcing?

Question 9th.—If it was their intention to execute such laws only in the Southern States as Southern interests might demand, do you think it was in accordance with principles of fairness and common honesty that they should have asked our friends at the North to unite with us on the general platform without informing them that they were for using force to execute the laws *among them,* but that they should not be allowed to use force to execute the laws among *ourselves?*

Question 10th.—After having prevailed on seventy-four thousand five hundred and twenty-four voters of Virginia to stand by them in their recommendation to uphold the Union, to protect the Constitution, and to enforce the laws, and since by their votes the state has been carried for John Bell and Edward Everett, do you think they are at liberty now to abandon these seventy-four thousand five hundred and twenty-four men, a very large majority of whom are not slaveholders, and tell them that the Union which our fathers established is not worth contending for; that the Constitution is a toy and a plaything for the sport of folly, and passion, and resentment; and that the laws must not be enforced upon any Southern State that may choose to set itself up in defiance of all laws and all constitutional authority?

Question 11th.—Do you think they have a right now to plunge this state into all the horrors of civil war, and involve the people of Virginia in the crime of treason, by espousing the cause of South Carolina, that is in a state of rebellion against the general government, and thereby transfer the battle-ground from South Carolina to Virginia, and then call upon the non-slaveholding population of the state to do all the fighting for *slaveholding sympathizers only*, when their slave property is not endangered? And do you not think the experiment is a hazardous one to the slaveholding interests of this state?

Question 12th.—Do you not think, as South Carolina is the only state that has taken steps from which war is likely to result, that *hers* is the soil upon which the war (if any comes) should be conducted, and that our women and children should not be subjected to the horrors that will attend it, by transferring the scene from the rice and cotton fields of that state to the hearth-stones of Virginia?

Question 13th.—In this view of the subject, do you not think it would be more becoming and more chivalric on the part of those who think South Carolina is justified in her present position, and who recommend resistance to the general government if the President of the United States should feel that the obligations of his oath required him to "*execute the laws*" and "suppress insurrections," should volunteer their services to South Carolina, *go down there*, and make *that* the scene of their heroism and renown, instead of stirring up the worst passions of our nature, and dragging those into the difficulty who do not believe South Carolina is justified in what she has done, and who have no sympathy with the hot haste with which she has acted, and the insulting manner in which she has treated Virginia?

Question 14th.—As far as South Carolina can make herself so, is she not now as foreign to us as the people of Naples or the people of Rome? And if there are sympathizers here of the Pope on the one hand, or of Victor Emmanuel or Garibaldi on the other, who wish to take a part in the Italian War, ought they not to assume the responsibility, and should they not seek the plains of Italy for a display of their valor, and not strive to involve their own country?

Question 15th.—Finally, do you think they have a right to find fault with and complain of us, who stood by them in the late contest in favor of "the Union, the Constitution, and the Enforcement of the Laws," and still stand faithful to our professions, and because we can not stultify ourselves, as we think we should, by now declaring that we will let the *Union* slide, the *Constitution* be trodden down, and the *laws* be violated with impunity?

It matters not what you think or what I think; it matters not whether it ought or ought not to be so; the man who thinks this Union can be broken up *in peace* knows nothing of the nature of our institutions, and nothing of the power with which this government is clothed by the Constitution. It matters little where your sympathies may lead you, or mine may lead me; it matters not how much we may deprecate and deplore it, whenever you have a President of the United States who feels the weight of his obligation to the country South Carolina will submit to the laws of the United States, or *there will be war; because* the Constitution not only authorizes it, but *demands* it; it does not leave it to the discretion of the President, but *requires* him to take an oath before God that he will, " to the best of his ability, *preserve*, protect, and *defend the Constitution!*" and that Constitution declares that the President "shall take care that the laws be faithfully executed," and for that purpose gives the control of the army and navy, and provides for the calling forth the militia to *enable him to execute he laws;* and, in the name of Heaven, how can he omit this plain paramount duty without having the high and infamous crime of *perjury* resting on his soul? And the same Constitution declares that "treason (which is punishable by death) shall consist in *levying war against the United States, or in adhering to their enemies, or in giving them aid or comfort.*" I beseech the people of Virginia not to be led into error by ignorant demagogues as to the nature of our government, nor yet to judge of its powers by the imbecility of its present rulers.

"One murder makes a villain, millions a hero," says the poet; this may be true in poetry, but it is not true in law, unless they have the power to overcome all opposition that may be made to them. Do not judge of what will be the condition of the public mind when this secession fever, which is now an epidemic, passes off, and when the question comes to be determined by the courts, from the frenzied state in which it is now found. Temper, and passion, and prejudice must sooner or later give way to reason, to common sense, and supremacy of law; and then the day of reckoning will come; and in the mean time, let those who would give *aid and comfort* to South Carolina in her position of hostility to the United States, let those who are solicitous to connect their fate with that of the unfortunate and misguided State of South Carolina go down among them, and take the responsibility on their own shoulders, and leave the Constitution-loving and law-abiding men, women, and children of Virginia in the enjoyment of peace, and in the discharge of their duties to the *Union, the Constitution, and the Enforcement of the Laws.*

I concede that no greater calamity can befall any people than that of a war among themselves; and if I could believe it likely that the Union could be broken into fragments without having constant and interminable forays between the Slave and Free States, I might *possibly* bring my mind to the conclusion that it would be better to give up the Union than have war between the general government and the Southern or Cotton States; but there lies the question, are we not to have the Union *entire*, or is there not to be *war* of some description? It is my belief that one or the other is unavoidable; and if so, which is the better and the wiser course to adopt—to have a war that will be of short duration, or one that is to be perpetual and interminable, until the substance of all parties is wasted away?

But let us estimate, as wise men should and will, all the cost in advance, and calculate the probable result. Suppose the fifteen Slave States should secede, what are our means or our powers of resistance or defense? Can any state live without commerce? Suppose the government of the United States, which will assuredly be in possession of the navy, should station a single frigate at the Capes of Virginia, is not the commerce of Virginia and Maryland effectually blocked up? then one to Charleston, another to Savannah, another to the Bay of Mobile, and still another to the mouth of the Mississippi, leaving the Free States on the Ohio and Mississippi Rivers with the facilities of railroad, lake, and canal communication with New York; I simply inquire, what would be our condition? Where is our navy to drive them off? What would become of all the productions of the South — the cotton, rice, sugar, flour, tobacco, etc.? Would we not be checkmated and conquered without the power to strike a blow? Do the impetuous secessionists of Virginia stop long enough to reflect upon such a condition of things? or do the sober-minded, reflecting men of the state think they are not worthy of consideration? If it is deemed necessary for our honor and safety to leave the Union, let us take time to prepare for what will inevitably follow. If the Cotton States can establish their independence, let them do it, and fix their form of government; then, if we like it better than our own, we can unite with them, but let us not be guilty of the madness of burning down the house in which we live until we are sure of removing to a better one.

As it is, I am clearly of opinion that the true policy of Virginia is to have nothing to do with the controversy that South Carolina has chosen to wage with the general government, but let her attend to her own business and we attend to ours, and remain in the Union as long as it can be done with safety and honor to the state; and when these can no longer be retained *in the Union,* then let us go out like men, and, asserting the broad right of revolution, let us all be united, and shrink from no consequences that may follow.

I am respectfully yours,   JOHN M. BOTTS.

I must confess here to an error in my calculation. As no instance in history could be found in which a gigantic war was carried on for any length of time without a dollar of money, and without credit in any market in the world, so I never dreamed that it could be done here to the extent it has been. I had no conception then that the government was to issue its hundreds of thousands of millions of Treasury-notes, payable six months, and two years after the happening of an event which was sure never to take place, and that any respectable portion of the people could be made to believe it was as good or better than gold, and that the few who had wisdom enough to know that it could never be worth a farthing, and refused to take it in exchange for their labor or produce, would have their property seized by the government for its own use, and the party thrown into prison for disloyalty. But all this I have seen now, and shall be better posted hereafter if another rebellion and civil war shall come in my time, which I hardly expect to see, for I think the present generation and several others~that will follow it will be satisfied with the experience they have had in this; but it may be of some service to future generations to know what may happen under the administration of those who go into rebellion simply for the purpose, as Mr. Jefferson Davis acknowledged in his interview with the two quasi-commissioners of peace, Messrs. Jacques and Kirke, as published in Mr. Davis's organ and other Richmond papers without denial or contradiction, solely to *"get rid of majorities;"* or, in other words, that the minority, or to come exactly at what he meant, that the selfish politicians and greedy office-holders should rule and control the people with the iron hand of a detestable despotism.

My next effort was an appeal to the moderation, forbearance, and magnanimity of the North, made under a conviction of the truth of the old proverb, that "it is better to humor a fool than encounter his wrath;" for I found the whole South getting to be, not simply *foolish,* but *insane* upon this question of secession; and, in reply to an invitation to a dinner at the Astor House, New York, given by the "New England Society" in commemoration of the landing of the New England Pilgrims, I made this appeal; but those to whom it was addressed unfortunately did not look at the question in all its magnitude—they did not attach sufficient importance to the events then in progress. Perhaps they would have thought and acted otherwise if they had been located where I was, and could have foreseen what has followed, as I thought I did at the time.

MR. BOTTS'S NOMINATION FOR THE STATE CONVENTION

A convention was called by the State Legislature, which itself had been convened in extra session by Governor Letcher. Richmond was entitled to three representatives. A number of the Union men called on me in person to become a candidate, to which I gave my assent. They asked who I could recommend to be associated with me. I named Mr. William H. M'Farland, with whom I was not then on speaking terms, and Mr. Marmaduke Johnson, not so much because he was *my* friend as that he and Mr. M'Farland had, at the dinner given to the Presidential Electors a short time before, given, as I thought, the most unmistakable evidence of a steadfast and reliable devotion to the Union and the platform upon which we had carried the state for John Bell. Accordingly a card was addressed to the three gentlemen thus indicated, and I extract the following from my response. The other two gentlemen simply accepted. I was defeated; to accomplish which, very large sums of money were said to have been and, no doubt, were subscribed. Mr. George W. Randolph, late Secretary of War, beat me, I think, some two hundred and odd votes, *his friends* swapping off votes with the peculiar friends of Messrs. M'Farland and Johnson. All this is of no other consequence now than to show how matters were worked to bring about my defeat. Mr. M'Farland and Mr. Johnson were elected, as I have said, and both afterward voted for the Ordinance of Secession.

The following is from my card in the Richmond *Whig* of January 25, 1861:

"The absence of all right on the part of one state to separate herself from the other thirty-two, when no pretense is set up that there is a correlative right on the part of the thirty-two to separate themselves from the one, is, to my mind, an incomprehensible logical absurdity, that I have already argued in your presence during the late canvass, and which need not be repeated here.

"That the time has arrived when the public voice and, indeed, the public welfare, demands that there shall be a satisfactory and final adjustment of all questions of discord between the two sections of the country, in order that we may live in peace hereafter, no one will dispute. The question is, what ought to be satisfactory to us, the Southern section, constituting as we do the complaining party in the case?

"For myself, I am prepared to insist upon every jot or tittle of right that the security or the honor of Virginia will entitle her to claim under the Constitution as it is. I am willing to vote for and take as much more as the North may be disposed to yield. If I have not heretofore claimed as much as others, it was not because I was unwilling they should obtain and enjoy it, but because I did not believe that it would be granted, or that we were entitled to demand it *as of right*, and therefore I never have, and never *will* consent to make the existence or the destruction of this government dependent upon any abstract or impracticable question that may or *may not arise* outside of the Constitution, such as is now proposed, of guaranteeing slavery by constitutional amendment in all territories hereafter to be acquired south of 36° 30', whether in Mexico, South America, or the Sandwich Islands.

"There is nothing that I CAN do that I will not do to avert the utter desolation that will assuredly follow in the train of disunion, rebellion, and civil war. I will go as far as any man alive will or can go to settle, by compromise and conciliation, every question of disturbance in our national councils. I am even free to say that there is no compromise that *has been* or can be proposed that will prove satisfactory to the North and South and restore harmony to the country, that will not meet with my cordial support, and, except as a matter of curiosity, I would agree never to inquire what compromise had been adopted, for I have no interests in this government that are not identified with those around me, and whatever will satisfy them will satisfy me. I do not set myself up as a maker of laws or a maker of constitutions, to which all others must bend and yield; nevertheless, I am not without my own views as to the proper mode of adjustment of all questions of constitutional interpretation, which could be done by *making a case* on each disputed point for the immediate decision of the Supreme Court, which is the tribunal established by the Constitution for that purpose, and then we could see what party it is that is not willing to live under the present form of government fairly and properly administered.

"I do not believe that, since the world was in a state of chaos, there ever was, or that there ever will be again so general and universal an upheaving of society, so ruinous and desolating a disturbance of all the social, moral, political, and industrial elements of a people for such slight and insufficient cause as this country now exhibits to the gaze of the as-founded nations of the earth, every one of which causes, by prudence, discretion, and forbearance, if taken out of the hands of selfish and aspiring or disappointed politicians, and intrusted to the people at the polls, as is now proposed by the Crittenden and Bigler resolutions, may be settled amicably, harmoniously, and satisfactorily in the Union, and under the Constitution, within the next sixty days; while there is not one that will not be a thousand-fold aggravated when we go out of the Union, leaving the Constitution, the laws, the whole organization of the government, the army, the navy, the Treasury, the public lands in all the states as well as all the territories, in the full possession of the Republican party, from whose apprehended designs the secessionists are for running off, and leaving behind them all they claim.

"After the events of the John Brown affair, just one year ago, and the scenes through which we are now passing, let us never again have a word to say about the excitability of the French, who, compared with us, are an immovable and unimpressible race of people.

"Now, I believe I constitute a fair type or specimen of what is the actual condition of every man in the Southern States, in a legal, political, and constitutional sense; and I find myself in the full, free, and perfect exercise of every blessing and of every right of a personal nature that I have enjoyed since I came into the world. I am also in the possession and enjoyment of whatever property I may own, and nobody, as far as I know, proposes to disturb or dispossess me of it; nor can any human being thus dispossess me except by due course of law.· How long this state of things may continue Omniscience only can tell. But is there any one, in these particulars, in a worse condition than I am? If there is—if the instance can be presented of any *one man*, out of the ten millions of the white population in the Southern States, who is laboring under any oppression, wrong, injustice, or grievance, that *can not* be redressed in the Union, and which *can* be redressed out of the Union, then I will pledge myself to vote for disunion whenever the question·comes up; but if no such person can be found, I will never consent to give up this government, the work of men '*whose like we ne'er shall look upon again*,' for any other government which the destroyers of *this* are likely to substitute in its stead. I will not destroy the house in which I live, and which protects me from the blasts and storms of winter, when not one brick is burned nor a stick of timber cut with which to erect another. I will not tear down the works of Washington, of Madison, of Franklin, of Carroll, of Morris, and of Pinckney, to take *upon trust* the clumsy machinery of Yancey, and Rhett, and Pickens, and Toombs, and of Davis. I will not surrender this government until I know that a better one has been provided for me.

"When I see in the distance the frightful and appalling consequences of disunion and civil war, which many will not see until the reality is brought to their own firesides and hearth-stones, where our wives, and our daughters, and all that is cherished on earth is clustered, I can not but persuade myself that both parties will shudder and recoil at its approach, and come to honorable terms of settlement. *For one I shall never despair of the republic.*

"When I see that upon the secession of any or all the Southern States, the President is left no alternative and no discretion, but is solemnly sworn before his God to PRESERVE, *protect*, and *defend* the Constitution, and that *that* Constitution declares the 'laws of the United States to be the supreme law of the land,' which he *'shall take care to see faithfully executed,'* and places the army and navy of the United States under his control, and provides for calling forth the militia to enable him 'to execute the laws and suppress insurrections,' I can not doubt that the declaration of secession, however much it may be deplored, will necessarily impose upon the government the obligation of resorting to such measures as will enable him to see the laws faithfully executed; the right to do which was too firmly established in the days of President Jackson by the legislation of 1832, ever to be overthrown while the government endures. I only speak of this as an existing fact, which is not likely and hardly possible to be changed. If it can be avoided, I shall be rejoiced to see it, and, while I can not doubt the power, would, as your representative in Convention, cheerfully unite in any recommendation or remonstrance against the exercise of the power.

"When I see too, that, without the power to strike a blow in resistance or defense, without the means to vindicate herself, the state may be humbled and subdued (and all the gasconade and bravado of light-headed and flippant would-be patriots can not prevent it); when I see that a single ship of war stationed at the Capes of Virginia will as effectually block up and destroy the entire commerce of Virginia and Maryland as if they were surrounded by icebergs in the Arctic Ocean, while we have no naval force with which to dislodge or remove the blockade; when I see that the commerce of every other Southern state may be cut off in the same way, and by the same means, by sending one or more war-steamers to block up the several ports of Charleston, Cape Fear River;

Savannah, the coasts of Florida, Mobile Bay, and the mouth of the Mississippi, while the commerce of every free state in the valley of the Mississippi is left open by means of railroad, lake, and canal communication with New York; when I see that of three million five hundred thousand militia-men enrolled in the United States, the North has upward of two million five hundred thousand, with no negroes to take care of at home, and the South only about nine hundred and forty-seven thousand, with our wives and daughters to protect and our negroes to watch; when I see that, upon all constitutional obligations being broken down, there must be incessant and exhausting hostilities carried on between the Border Free and the Border Slave States, or else that Maryland, Virginia, Kentucky, Tennessee, and Missouri will speedily become Free States, hitched on to a confederacy of Slave States, from which it is even now proposed they should then be turned adrift; when I see this state groaning under a debt of forty-five millions, to be raised by *direct taxation*, and all her sources of revenue cut off, and without the credit to obtain a dollar in any market in the world on any terms, as will be her condition in a state of rebellion and civil war; when I see nothing but bankruptcy and distress staring every man in the face; when I see all these and other untold calamities to be brought upon our people by the inconsiderate haste of an hour's excitement, or for misapplied sympathy for a state that we were told in advance would '*hitch us on*' and '*precipitate us into revolution whether we would or not;*' when I can see nothing but absolute ruin and desolation for all in common, which neither our safety nor our honor requires us to encounter—I say, if this work is to be done, it must be performed by other hands than mine; for I would not, for all the honors, and offices, and wealth of the world, have such a crime resting on my soul.

"I have said I would take any compromise that would restore peace to the country; but it is not to be disguised that there are those in this state and others in the South who do not mean to be satisfied with any concessions or compromise that can be offered. They are for disunion *per se*, and have been, as Mr. Rhett acknowledges, for thirty years. For them I have nothing to offer but resistance to every proposition and every effort that looks to the secession of this state; and if, upon obtaining all that we have the right under the Constitution to claim, they still persist in their opposition to the execution of the laws, and in stirring up rebellion and treason, I think it manifest that the government *will fall back* on the platform upon which we have just carried this state, to wit, 'The

Union, the Constitution, and the Enforcement of the Laws' equally, fairly, and impartially on all; for then it will be a question between a well-regulated government on the one hand, and anarchy and mob law on the other; for if the government has no power to collect its taxes or duties, to execute its laws, put down rebellion, and punish treason, then it is no longer the government that was formed by our fathers, and the sooner the whole fabric tumbles to pieces the better.

"This Union, as far as my action will go, must and shall be preserved, as long as it can be done with honor. Has Virginia tamely submitted to dishonor for the last ten years, and is she now only stimulated to redeem that honor by the precipitate action of other states? If not, what new cause has arisen within the last two months that makes it necessary to call together the Legislature, or a convention without authority, hold an election almost without notice, meet in convention and declare herself out of the Union in less time than is ordinarily devoted to the passage of a bill for the construction of a mud turnpike in the mountains? If war had actually been declared against us, no more precipitate action could have been taken. This, too, when public sentiment in the North is daily and hourly undergoing modifications, and petitions are pouring in upon Congress to refer the matter to the people for settlement, who say they are ready to yield to all just and reasonable demands for the sake of the Union.

"I will not stop to inquire how long our allies in the Cotton States will be able to hold out, and help *us* after leading us into the difficulty, when their ports are all blockaded and their supplies of actual necessaries of life—of which they purchase one hundred and fifty million dollars' worth a year from the Free States—shall be cut off. I will not stop to inquire whether the world can live as long without their cotton as they can live without bread. I will not stop to show that both England and France have already, by the Chinese War, made arrangements for a supply of cotton from that region of the world, which, together with the supply from the East Indies, will render them in a few years independent of the Cotton States; for all these will be subjects for argument elsewhere; but I simply throw them out as hints for reflection, and as reasons for making haste *slowly*.

"What is to become of that vast multitude of naturalized citizens scattered through the Southern States who owe a *sworn allegiance* to the United States government, which is bound to protect them in every land, whether at home or abroad? Are they to be asked to commit willful perjury by taking up arms against the Constitution and the government they have solemnly sworn to support, or are they to be driven from the South as aliens and enemies to the new-fangled government that is to be erected? It is a question for grave deliberation to determine what is to be their status when we separate from our government and theirs. If you, the natives of Virginia, owe your first allegiance to the state, surely they owe theirs to the general government.

"To be brief, I am ready to sacrifice myself, and live in obscurity and poverty, deserted by friends for whom I would die rather than harm, if by such sacrifice I can save the rich legacy from our fathers, and the rightful inheritance of our children. I am ready to hazard my life, if necessary, in fighting the battles of Virginia in a just cause, but I am not willing to sacrifice the best interests of my state and my country, and the hopes of oppressed mankind throughout the world, in upholding South Carolina in a bad cause, in a wholly unjustifiable and petulant whim, which she avows she has indulged for thirty years. I am not willing to rush upon destruction for a misplaced sympathy for a state that exulted over the election of a Republican President, burned their tar-barrels and illuminated their cities because it afforded them *the pretext* for rebellion, and that has since violently seized upon the forts, arsenals, arms, and ammunition, and money of the United States, and has fired upon and driven from her waters an unarmed vessel bearing that flag of the Union which has borne us triumphantly through every war and every trouble. I am not one of those who profess or feel such sympathy, nor will I uphold her in such conduct. Yet I would afford her every opportunity to retrace her injudicious step.

"My earnest and urgent advice, then, is that Virginia should remain in the Union, demanding all her constitutional rights, the repeal of all unconstitutional laws, or the declaration of their nullity by the Supreme Court, and a just punishment for those who shall resist its decisions. Let her remain in, and act the part of mediator and peace-maker between the extremes of both sections of the country. Recollect that those who now beckon you on to destruction are the same advisers and leaders that lured you on in 1854 to insist upon the repeal of the Missouri Compromise, which has brought you to your present condition. That was a grievous error of which you had timely warning, but to which you would not listen; and those who warned you then were denounced as submissionists and traitors to the South as they are now. Be not deceived by the same men again, who would now lead you into one ten thousand times more fatal; and do not hereafter forget that I tell you now, when you give up your Union, you surrender your liberties and the liberties of all who are to come after you.

"If this brief and hurried exposition of my views should meet with the concurrence of the people of Richmond, and they desire to call me into their service at a moment when all the calmness, deliberation, and philosophy of the most experienced and far-sighted statesmen should be called into requisition, I shall appreciate the honor, and not decline the trust. But if they are bent on committing an act of self-destruction that no time, nor labor, nor money can repair, and involving this state and themselves in everlasting ruin, some other arm than mine must be selected to strike the blow; for I can not and will not commit the parricidal act that would hand my name down in dishonor to posterity as one of the destroyers of my country and of the liberties of the people.

"I am, with great respect, your obedient servant,

"JOHN M. BOTTS.

"P.S.—I have written this letter because I shall have no other opportunity of making my opinions known to the voters of Richmond—which have been greatly misrepresented—as I am called to Washington, and shall most probably not return until about the time of the election. I will be sure to be here in time to give my own vote for Union men.

"JOHN M. BOTTS."

In rapid succession one Cotton or Gulf State after another had passed their ordinances of secession, until they had all thrown themselves headlong into the rebellion. The action of the remaining states, to wit, North Carolina, Kentucky, Tennessee, Arkansas, Missouri, mainly depended upon the course that Virginia might adopt. All eyes were turned upon her Convention. The proclamation of Mr. Lincoln calling for seventy-five thousand men (which I think should have been for three hundred thousand at the least, accompanied with a recital of the wrongs and injuries already perpetrated by South Carolina and her associate states, with a suitable appeal to the patriotism of the people to sustain the integrity of the nation) was issued on the 15th of April, 1861. The representatives of the people in Convention, who had been elected to keep Virginia *in the Union*, betrayed their trust, and in a moment of artfully and ingeniously *contrived excitement*, and in a fit of absolute intimidation, as I have shown, adopted an ordinance of secession on the 17th, which created a wild distraction in the people's mind. The fact was flashed with lightning speed from state to state, from city to city, from village to village, and in less than thirty-six hours the whole South seemed to have been electrified. If there were at that time ten men in the city of Richmond who had not for the instant inhaled the poison, I did not know them; for those who did not, under the reign of terror that was instantaneously inaugurated, thought it most prudent to keep their opinions to themselves.

It was in this condition of things, and under these circumstances, that, apprehending and foreshadowing what has since become a painful and frightful reality, the firm conviction was forced upon my mind that a temporary and partial separation, authorized by an amendment to the Constitution to that effect, could alone prevent the other Southern States from following in the wake of Virginia, which would give to the rebellion such gigantic proportions as would lead to the most disastrous war recorded on the page of history. To save these Border States to the Union, including Virginia—for in that event the people would have repudiated the action of their Convention—to avert the evils that have since resulted, I addressed the following letter to my valued friend, Hon. Edward Bates, Attorney General of the United States.

By the suggestions contained in this correspondence, it was my purpose, if war was inevitable, to make it a *foreign* instead of a *civil* war, in which other states would have no pretext for taking part with the revolted states in the Gulf. I believed then, as I believe now, that such a course, if adopted, would have cut off all co-operation between the Border and Cotton States, which would speedily bring the Cotton States to their senses, and that these people would themselves in a short time ask for readmission into the Union; and that, overwhelming their faithless rulers, they would return to their allegiance with an increased spirit of fidelity to the country; and that if they did not, that then the application of some of their own cherished principles, as contained in the "Monroe Doctrine," or in the celebrated "*Ostend Manifesto*," which was the exclusive work of Southern Democracy, or that the difficulties growing out of the navigation of the Mississippi, or some other of the thousand causes that would necessarily arise, would furnish the occasion of reducing them to subjection and obedience to the authorities of the United States.

I did think if all that has followed could have been foreseen, such a settlement would have been eagerly embraced by nine tenths of the friends of the Union in all quarters, independent of the immense sacrifice of life, and the amount of misery that has been entailed upon the human family. I think the Cotton States would have been dearly paid for at half the amount of money that has been expended, throwing every other consideration out of the question. Here, however, is my letter to Mr. Bates:

THE BATES LETTERS.

Richmond, April 19, 1861.

MY DEAR SIR,—Your letter of yesterday has been received. Before this you will have learned through the press all that has occurred at Norfolk and at this place; but I can not begin to give you a just conception of the excitement created, not only here but throughout the whole Southern country, by the proclamation of the 15th, which in many respects may be regarded as the most unfortunate document that ever issued from the government. In the absence of that paper, this state could not have been carried out of the Union; with it, the Union party and the Union feeling has been almost entirely swept out of existence. You can not meet with one man in a thousand who is not influenced with a *passion for war;* and every one seems to regard the proclamation as a declaration of war for the subjugation of the entire South, and for the extermination of slavery. Reason (with them on this point) would as soon arrest the motion of the Atlantic as it would check the current of their passions.

When I saw you in Washington some ten days since, I had the honor to lay before you and other members of the Cabinet, as well as before Mr. Lincoln himself, a plan for the settlement of our troubles through the medium of a national convention, to give to the seceded states *leave to withdraw.* I thought then, as I do now, that the plan then suggested was the only solution to the dreadful crisis which was upon us. Since that time matters have assumed a far more frightful aspect, and I now venture to make one more effort to save the unnecessary effusion of brothers' blood, and, in the name of liberty, humanity, and Christianity, I implore you to give it your earnest and solemn deliberation.

I need hardly say that no man in this nation has held in higher appreciation the value of our blessed Union. No man has labored more constantly and earnestly for its perpetuation than I; no man's heart can bleed more freely for its loss than mine; no man can mourn more sorrowfully for its overthrow than I will; no man can condemn more severely the immediate causes that have so unnecessarily led us into this awful and terrible catastrophe than I do. Yet, for the first time, after an entire night of sleepless reflection, when I prayed as I never prayed before for wisdom and strength to do my duty, my mind has been brought to the conclusion that a dissolution is an inevitable decree of fate.

I am satisfied that a contest on the part of the general government, with its perfect military organization, powerful naval forces, its command of money, and its credit without limit, backed by eighteen or twenty millions of people, against eight millions, without military organization, without naval forces, and without money or credit, is not likely to be of doubtful result in the end. But after that, what then? Can the Union be preserved on such terms, or would it be worth preserving if it could? After the best blood of the country has been shed in a war which has passion, prejudice, and unnatural but mutual hate for its foundation, intensified by the conflict, could the two sections ever be brought together as one people again? And would it not require large standing armies, in constant, active service, to conquer and maintain a peace? And would not that end at last in a hateful, loathsome military despotism?

If I am right in all this, would not a peaceful separation, not as a military necessity, but as a triumph of reason, order, law, liberty, morality, and religion, over passion, pride, prejudice, hatred, disorder, and the force of the mob, be a far wiser and more desirable solution of the problem than such scenes as will result from a purely sectional warfare (result as it may), and from which the heart sickens and the soul recoils with horror?

You may cut, maim, kill, and destroy; you may sweep down battalions with your artillery; you may block up commerce with your fleets; you may starve out the thousands and tens of thousands of the enemies of the government; you may *overrun*, but you can not *subjugate* the united South. And, if you could do all this, you could not do it without inflicting an equal amount of misery upon those who are its best friends, and who have stood as long as there was a plank to stand upon by the side of the Union, the Constitution, and the laws. Our streets may run red with blood; our dwellings may be leveled with the earth; our fields may be laid waste; our hearth-stones may be made desolate; and then, at the last, what end has been gained? Why, the government has exhibited its power, which has never been questioned but by the idle, the ignorant, and the deluded, and for the display of which there will be abundant opportunities, without an effort now on either side to cut each other's throats!

So far from its being regarded as a betrayal of weakness by the other powers of the globe, will it not be looked upon in the present emergency as an act of magnanimity and heroism on the part of the more powerful party to propose terms of peace? Let me, then, as a strong, devoted, unalterable friend of the Union (*if it could be maintained*), let me, as a conscientious and unchangeable opponent of the fatal heresy of secession, urge upon this administration the policy of issuing another proclamation *proposing a truce to hostilities*, and the immediate assembling of a national convention to recognize the independence of such of the states as desire to withdraw from the Union and make the experiment of separate government, which it will not, as I think, take them long to discover is the most egregious error that man, in his hour of madness, ever committed.

In five years from this time the remaining United States would be stronger and more powerful than the thirty-four states were six months ago, and you will have a government permanent and enduring for all time to come, to which all who seek an asylum from oppression may resort hereafter.

I will not undertake to speculate on the experiment of a Southern republic; my opinions on that subject are well defined, and too well understood to make it necessary that they should be canvassed here. Let it be tried, and let it work out its own salvation.

If this policy can be adopted, all I shall ask for myself will be the privilege of retiring to some secluded spot, where I can live in peace, and mourn over the downfall of the best government, *wisely administered*, with which man was ever blessed.

For God's sake, let me implore you to let wisdom, magnanimity, true courage, and humanity prevail in your councils, and give peace to a distracted and dissevered country.

I write as one who feels that he is standing on the brink of the grave of all he has cherished on earth; my head is bowed down with grief over the madness that rules the hour, and I pray God to give me the wisdom to know and the strength to perform my duty, my whole duty to my country, my state, and my friends.

I am, with great respect, yours, etc., JOHN M. BOTTS.

Hon. EDWARD BATES, Attorney General, etc.

Will you grant me the favor to lay this last effort to serve my country before the Cabinet at its first meeting? I appeal to you, as a native son of Virginia, to do it. J. M. B.

As indicative of the temper and spirit with which this letter was received by the secessionists, I append the following editorial from the Petersburg *Express*, being, perhaps, the most decent and temperate of all the comments made upon it:

"*Hon. John M. Botts.*—This gentleman, it seems, has been recently engaged in efforts to bring about a peaceful solution of the present disturbances in the country by appeals to the wicked authors of these disturbances, the Rump administration in Washington. A letter which he addressed to Edward Bates, the Rump Attorney General, has just been published, and we have read it with vastly more amazement than satisfaction, because sentiments are breathed in it which are unworthy of a high-toned Virginian in a crisis like the present, when his liberty is assailed in a manner utterly disgraceful to the age we live in. Mr. Botts is doubtless very anxious to bring the two sections to a halt in their preparation for war. He is doubtless a friend to peace, and would use all his power and influence to commend it. But he has adopted the very worst course that he could well have done to effect the end he has in view. The letter to Bates betrays a spirit of rank disaffection to the cause of the South which is too obvious to escape notice, and a fear of the Northern *millions* which is conspicuously apparent in a portion of it. Now Mr. Botts is (*no thanks to Lincoln*) a citizen of a free republic, and has a right to his own thoughts. We hope never to see any where in the South an attempt made to muzzle the tongue, pen, or conscience of the citizen.

"Mr. Botts is still an ardent Union man, strange to say; and although he counsels the call of 'a national convention to give the states *leave to withdraw,*' it is evident that their withdrawal is to him a most unpalatable thing to contemplate. The horror which he feels at this picture is only exceeded by that which fills him at the contemplation of the picture of a bloody civil war. Had *we* set about the work that Mr. Botts has undertaken of impressing upon the Rump government a *pacific* policy, the first thing that we would have studiously guarded against would have been the use of any expression which could be tortured into the signification that there was the slightest apprehension at the South of the consequences of war, because it has been a fixed and inflexible principle of the Black Republicans, ever since the secession movement began, to interpret every such expression into a sign of *backing down*, or, in other words, into a disposition to return into the Union upon any terms; and this interpretation has uniformly steeled them against all conciliation and adjustment. We should have spoken in a very different tone to Lincoln from that in which Mr. Botts has thought fit to address him. We would have in a manly way told him that the South had separated from the North because her constitutional rights had been trodden down, and her liberties were threatened; that she demanded the recognition of her separate sovereignty, not as a matter of *favor* but as a matter of *justice*, and that she was fully able and irrevocably determined to protect herself with her own arm. We should have held the proud language of an equal, not that of a cringing, trembling inferior.

"The following passage in Mr. Botts's letter is essentially, totally, and peculiarly revolting to the Southern heart, and we lose no time in declaring that the uncalled-for and craven admission which it contains is the admission of Mr. Botts, and of no Southron. Says he:

"'I am satisfied that a contest on the part of the general government, with its perfect military organization, powerful naval forces, its command of money, and its credit without limit, backed by eighteen or twenty millions of people, against eight millions without military organization, without naval forces, and without money or credit, is not likely to be of doubtful result in the end.'

"We hardly have words to express the surprise and indignation which we feel at this extraordinary assertion by a citizen of the South on such an occasion. John Hickman, the redoubtable hero who had his face slapped by Edmundson, was the first to parade this gasconading nonsense before the world, and his contemptible bravado was only laughed at. Now a native born and bred Virginian, in the face of a people who repudiated and spurned the bullying threat of Hickman, publicly indorses it! Why, even the *North* herself will smile derisively at such a preposterous —such an infinitely ridiculous declaration. The North knows that, of all the stupidly absurd undertakings that she could possibly engage in, that of attempting to subjugate the fourteen states of the Southern Confederacy would be the most stupidly absurd.

"There is not a single particular in Mr. Botts's enumeration of Northern resources that is not grossly exaggerated. The Lincoln government is not near 'perfect in its military organization;' its 'naval forces' are any thing else but a terror; its 'command of money,' and its 'credit,' although great, is not without limit; and as to the eighteen or twenty millions of people, why, if every man of them was to take the field, fully armed and equipped, the ten millions of Southern soldiers arrayed against them would be a full equivalent — a first-rate Roland for the Northern Oliver.

"But why say more on this subject? Mr. Botts may tremble before the monstrous giant his disturbed imagination has conjured up before him, but there is not, we believe, another man in the whole South who will not consider it a bugbear of the first order."

A few days after, without waiting for a reply to my first letter, I wrote a second letter to Mr. Bates, of which the following is a copy:

Richmond, April 22, 1861.

DEAR SIR,—Again I venture to address you, and again in the name of a convulsed nation to sue for peace.

Frantic people on both sides may clamor for war, but the dispassionate and reflecting every where demand a cessation of this horrible and cruel war, and the party that has it chiefly in its power to stop it will sink under the weight of its responsibility, both to God and man, if it is not stopped.

You know as well as I the spirit and fiery zeal of your own Southern race; you know that, no matter what your power may be, you could never reduce them to subjection. As I said in my first letter, "*overrun them you may*," but you can not subjugate; and even to *overrun* them now is becoming more and more doubtful every day. But if you could, what do you hope to accomplish by it? Is it not as clear as the noonday's sun that a dissolution of the Union is a fixed, irrevocable fact? and is it not equally clear that a war between sections, North and South, only makes it a *costly*, *bloody*, desolating dissolution, instead of a peaceful separation of elements that are now as thoroughly and as sternly antagonistic as fire and water?

The disaffection in Maryland to the cause of the government, and especially the scenes enacted in Baltimore, render it certain that the revolution is spreading with immense rapidity. Why not, then, at once come to honorable terms, and let each of the republics, North and South, live after their own fashion and their own fancy? The Southern blood is fired, and you may rest assured that, to the last man, they will resist the powers of the Federal government if their independence is not recognized.

If my counsels could have prevailed when I was in Washington, eight Border States would have been saved to the Union. Now four of them *at least* are gone from you, and probably all. Why, then, make it worse than it is by farther procrastination?

If you knew what it has cost me in mental agony to give up all hope of the government of the United States as it was formed by our fathers, you would listen to my counsels and have respect for what I say.

I pray you, tell me what possible good is expected to be accomplished by a war among ourselves? Which party can possibly be benefited? After 500,000 lives have been lost, and $1,000,000,000 of money has been spent, must it not at last end in a severance of the ties that have hereto-fore held us together as one people?

I never saw the day that I more sternly denied the right of secession under our Constitution than I do now; but the right of REVOLUTION I have always asserted, and no one has ever denied it. This state has not seceded, because the Convention had no power to secede, and the vote, which the people reserved to themselves, has not been taken; yet they are themselves in a state of revolution. It matters not whether you or I think there has or has not been just cause for revolution. We are not made the judges of that; they have decided for themselves, and had a right to do so. I suppose no revolution ever yet arose in which those in-volved in it were entirely unanimous as to the sufficiency of the causes that led to it; therefore I do not conceive that I have a right to set up my individual opinion against what seems to be the almost unanimous voice of the entire South, and I find myself, with the rest, precipitated into a revolution without any agency of my own, and against which I am utterly powerless. So it is with thousands and thousands over the coun-try—some from impulse, some from judgment, and some from necessity, until the sentiment has almost one universal "ay" for revolution.

I can not so far stultify myself as to deny the right of all governments to put down revolution if they can; this is too well recognized a principle to be disputed; and where a successful revolution would overthrow the government itself, I do not question the right of the government to resort to every means for its own preservation.

But would the government of the United States be overthrown by an acknowledgment of the independence of a part of its original proportions? On the contrary, I venture to say your government would be more power-ful, more harmonious, and more happy (when institutions common to all pervaded your entire land, and no jarring interests were brought into contact) than you have been for the last twenty years, and certainly for the last ten or twelve, during which time there has been nothing but one continual stream of discord pouring out from the press, the pulpit, the hustings, and the halls of Congress, on the subject of slavery.

If, after the separation has been accomplished, time shall prove it to have been to the interest of the parties that they should have continued as one, would not a re-union be far more likely to be brought about here-after without, than after such a war as may be looked for, if not checked at once? What would be deemed an act of forbearance and liberality from a father to a son, or from brother to brother, might be esteemed as cowardice and poltroonery to a stranger and a foe, and so it would be here. We are of the same family, and concessions may be made without dishonor.

Look to the country as it was, which I need not describe, then look upon it as it is, and as it is likely to be. Not only is all business suspend- ed, and all prospect of prosperity and happiness banished from the land, but all intercourse is cut off between members of the same household, be- tween partners and traders in business, between man and wife, parent and child, who were temporarily or permanently located in different states, by the destruction of railroads, bridges, and telegraphic communication. How long can this state of things be permitted to continue?

I would give millions this night (if I had them) to have the power of Mr. Lincoln for one moment, that I might say, "Brethren, depart in peace; let there be no more quarrel between us;" and then what a bright sunshine would spread over the land at once!

Upon the restoration of peace, the "plow, the loom, and the anvil" would instantaneously leap to their accustomed work. Commerce would again whiten the ocean with its sails. Prosperity and happiness at home would take the place of death on the battle-field. The affectionate wife, the tender mother, and the fond sister, North and South, would hail as blessed, and a nation's prayers would ascend for benedictions on the head of the man who was brave enough to defy and contemn all injurious im- putations in order to serve the best interests of his country and save it from ruin.

I am, with great respect, very truly yours,　　　Jᴏʜɴ M. Bᴏᴛᴛs.

A few days after this letter was sent, I received the following letter from Mr. Bates, in reply to my first of the 19th, which led to others that follow in order.

Washington City, Monday, April 29, 1861.

Hon. Jᴏʜɴ M. Bᴏᴛᴛs, Richmond, Virginia :

Dᴇᴀʀ Sɪʀ,—Day before yesterday, Saturday, Colonel William Henry Russell, of Kansas (now sojourning in this city), handed me an open note from you to me, bearing date Richmond, April 23, 1861, in which was folded up, but not mentioned in the body of the note, a printed paper (ap- parently clipped from a newspaper) which purported to be a letter from you to me. I say *purported;* for although you *may have written* such a letter, certainly I have received no such letter in your handwriting nor in any form, except the printed slip folded in your note.

You and I, Mr. Botts, know each other's characters very well. Heretofore yours has been marked by bold, frank, and manly traits, which won for you many friends and admirers all over the country, and hence my astonishment on receiving from you such a note with such an inclosure. I do not impute the blame to you, for I can not avoid the conclusion that you are acting under duress—that you have become the victim of a set of desperadoes, who, having wantonly plunged into the guilt of treason and the danger of ruin, would gladly sacrifice you and me, and ten thousand such men, if thereby they can make a way of escape for themselves from the least of the dangers which they have so wickedly incurred.

Here at Washington, perhaps, we know a little more about the machinations of the conspirators at Richmond than they are aware of. But besides that, the documents (your note to Colonel Russell, your note to me, and the printed slip) bear internal evidence of a concerted plan, a scheme invented, not by the bold and patriotic Botts, but by those same conspirators who, failing to intimidate the government by bullying violence, have changed their tactics, and still hope to win the victory and destroy the nation by a less hazardous but more cunning process.

1. Your note to Colonel Russell (which he showed me) imports that you are safe and comfortable at Richmond, while we have melancholy testimony that such men as you are neither safe nor comfortable there.

2. Your note to me of April 23 (covering the printed letter, *but not mentioning it*) contains several phrases which I am persuaded you would not have used if left to your own free action. The note begins by stating its mian object thus: "I write hurriedly *to say* that I have *consented* to the publication of my letter to you, with the hope," etc. Which letter to me? I have received several letters from you, but none of the 19th of April. "Consented to the publication"—at whose instance? The phrase and the context invite the inference that the publication was made at my instance, and that inference was, I believe, generally drawn in this city, and will probably be drawn all over the country; whereas *you do know* that I had nothing to do with its publication.

The note concludes with this very suggestive line, "I am not at liberty to speak of what is going on here." I can earnestly comprehend that humiliating fact; and I do painfully sympathize with you, and with all good and faithful men in my native state, when I behold the capital of the once free and proud Virginia subjected to the tyranny of a lawless mob.

M

3. The printed letter. Alas, that I should live to see such a letter under the hand of the gallant and gifted John M. Botts! I shall not go into any minute criticism of the letter to show how it contradicts all the main facts in your high and honorable political history, and counter-marched the whole line of your active and useful career onward and up-ward for the last thirty years. My personal regard and my great respect for your character forbids me to do that. But I can not forbear to say that the whole scope and tendency of the letter, if not its design, is an ar-gument in favor of dissolving the Union, and blotting from the map of the world the nation of the United States. It is a silent approval (by fail-ing to condemn) of the violent and revolutionary proceedings of the peo-ple of the Southern States (in several of them before the idle form of se-cession was gone through with) in plundering the money and arms and other property of the United States; in seizing upon our ungarrisoned forts; in making open war upon such as refused to surrender; in firing upon, and in some instances actually degrading the flag of our country; and in schemes and projects boastfully announced in the public press, and partially acted out in military preparations, to seize this capital by violence and break up the government.

Your letter does not in terms assert, but by necessary implication as-sumes that this administration can, if it will, restore the peace of the country by the cheap and easy experiment of issuing a proclamation "proposing a truce of hostilities and the *immediate* assembling of a na-tional convention!" It seems to me, my dear sir, that there are some se-rious objections to this cheap plan of peace, and, first, the President has no power to call a national convention. Second, if he did call it, there is not the remotest probability that the insurgent states would obey the call. Third, if they did obey it, there is little hope that they would agree to come in on equal terms with the other states, by recanting their recent assumption of separate and absolute sovereignty, and by restoring all that they have taken by violence from the United States. In short, after all that is past, it seems to me that there are but two alternatives left to this administration: first, to submit implicitly to all the claims of the insur-gent states, and quietly consent to a dismemberment of the nation, or, second, to do its best to restore peace, law, and order by supporting "the Constitution and the Union, and the enforcement of the laws." Let the nation judge which horn of the dilemma the administration ought to take, in view of all its obligations in regard to the permanent interests of the country, and to its own patriotism and constitutional duty.

I am amazed at the course of things in Virginia. Your Convention was not called to dissolve the Union, nor trusted with the power of secession. By the act of its creation that sovereign power was reserved to the *people* of Virginia. Yet as soon as the Convention had secretly acted upon the subject, without any promulgation of the ordinance, and while the people were yet ignorant of its existence, the executive officers of Virginia rushed incontinently into open war against the United States. They endeavored to obstruct the harbor of Norfolk in order to secure the plunder of the navy-yard at Gosport, and sent a military power to complete the work of its spoliation. The enterprise failed, indeed, to clutch the spoil, but it caused the destruction of millions of dollars' worth of public property. The same thing was attempted in reference to Harper's Ferry, and was only frustrated because the vigilant little garrison, knowing its inability to resist such superior numbers, destroyed the property and made good its retreat. They menaced this capital by open threats of military force, by obstructing the roads leading to it, and by active endeavors to command the navigation of the Potomac. And all this was done while the state, according to the letter of its own law, remained a member of the Union.

Think you, my dear sir, that men who do these things in open day, and in contempt of the rights and powers of the people of Virginia, have such a reverence for "reason, order, law, liberty, morality, and religion" as to give much heed to the President's "proclamation proposing a truce?" I lack the faith to believe it.

In conclusion, I assure you in all sincerity that I do deeply sympathize in your present distress. I love the people of my native state, and mourn over the guilt and wretchedness into which they thoughtlessly allow themselves to be plunged by their reckless misleaders.

With long-cherished respect and regard, I remain your obedient servant,
EDWARD BATES.

It was only within the last few days (now March, 1866), to my infinite surprise, I ascertained that the great injustice had been done me by my old and valued friend, Mr. Bates, of publishing all his letters to me during the rebellion, when I had no access to the Northern papers, while two of mine to him, which were indispensable to a full and fair understanding of my position and motives, were, for some cause that I am unable to comprehend, withheld from the public eye. Taking his letters to me, which contained *rather severe* and altogether unjust criticisms on mine to him, which would have explained every thing satisfactorily, I am not at all surprised that some of my Union friends should for the time being have regarded me as occupying a somewhat doubtful position, or as having "backed down" and made concessions to the secession spirit of the South, which no human being south of the Potomac ever, for a transitory moment, was permitted to suspect. Fortunately for me, subsequent events, embracing my free and outspoken denunciation of the rebellion and of all who exercised an agency in bringing it on, together with my arrest and imprisonment for my loyalty to the Union, served to remove the injurious suspicion that had been so unjustifiably created. I am glad the opportunity is now offered to supply the *suppressed letters* from me to Mr. Bates, each in their regular order; and here follows my reply to Mr. Bates's letter of April 29, not heretofore published.

Richmond, May 2, 1861.

To Hon. EDWARD BATES, Attorney General, etc. :

DEAR SIR,—By yesterday's mail I received your letter of the 29th, and I will not trust myself to picture the mortification and pain it gave me to read it, not only for the spirit of war that it breathed toward your own countrymen, among whom the friends and enemies of the government were promiscuously and inseparably identified, but also for the manifest injustice done to my own motives and conduct in an honest and patriotic endeavor to arrest in time the carnage and human suffering that must inevitably follow on both sides in the wake of this unnatural and horrible war that it is now but too clear is to be inaugurated.

. Before I proceed farther, let me make one word of explanation as to the printed copy of my letter being sent you through Colonel Russell, and on which you have commented with some feeling, not warranted, I think, by the circumstances.

My letter of the 19th to you, which it seems was not delivered, was written without consultation with or knowledge of any human being on earth. While I was engaged in writing it, Mr. Whittington, of Alexandria, came in, and I communicated to him the object of the work on which I was then employed, but expressed a doubt whether the letter would reach you by mail, as it was understood that the Post-office had been seized, and that all letters from and to Washington were examined before delivery, and that I believed your letter to me had been opened before I received it. Mr. Whittington then proposed to take charge of the letter himself and see that it was put safely into your hands, and he left here on Sunday morning with the letter and under that pledge, which I had no reason then to doubt would be faithfully redeemed; your letter of last night was the first intimation I had that it had not been.

No secessionist had ever seen my letter until it was published, and the publication was elicited by *my* friends, and *your* friends, gentlemen of the Union party, who believed with me that its publication would encourage the Union men of the state to *hold on* until the last hope for peace had vanished, and that if the letter could produce the *hoped-for* effect, we should still be able to save Virginia to the Union; and then, in writing to Colonel Russell, I inclosed the note to you embracing a printed copy of the letter which I supposed had then been in your possession for several days. The circumstances attending the publication of the letter were explained in an accompanying note published with it, which relieved you of all complicity in its being made public, which you seem so much to apprehend. So much for that.

You pay me a very poor compliment, Mr. Bates, when you avow your conviction that I wrote that letter " under duress, that I had become a victim of a set of desperadoes," and that I had made myself a party *to a concerted plan or scheme, invented not by the brave and patriotic Botts, but by these same conspirators,*" etc., etc., who hoped by such means to win a victory or destroy the nation by a less hazardous but more cunning process than by bullying violence.

You know very little of me, Mr. Bates, if you suppose me capable of writing letters under duress, or of entering into the *conspiracies* of those who I regard as my most embittered enemies; and such a declaration from your pen has struck me with a degree of amazement (I forbear to say indignation) that your own sensibilities as a gentleman upon reflection will enable you to comprehend far better than my pen can describe. I should be sorry to think that a reperusal of my letter and your own will not occasion a pang of regret in your bosom for an injury and injustice to a friend that I have heretofore held you to be altogether incapable of inflicting.

. So far from having written "*under duress,*" or at the instigation of the "conspirators" of whom you speak, the writing and publication of that letter drew from them the most unmeasured denunciation and abuse; it created a wild excitement that many of my friends earnestly thought endangered my personal safety, and advised me to leave the city, which I scorned to do, though my body might be riddled with bullets. They charged me with conspiring against them by the exposure of their weakness and of your strength, and now the charge comes in turn from you that I am the tool of a conspiracy against the government I have so faithfully upheld.

You say my *note* (through Colonel Russell) "concluded with this suggestive line, '*I am not at liberty to speak of what is going on here.*' " Nor was I: first, for the reason that it would have been held to have been in violation of my duty to my state; and secondly, because *it was understood* that the Post-office here was then under the control of an irresponsible body of men, and it would never have reached you or Colonel Russell either; and as Colonel Russell did not receive my letter until last Saturday, the presumption is that it was overhauled before it was sent from here. Again you say, "The printed letter. Alas, that I should live to see such a letter under the hand of the gallant and gifted John M. Botts! I shall not go into any minute criticism of the letter to show that it contradicts all the main facts in your high and honorable political history, and countermarches the whole line of your active and useful career onward and upward for the last thirty years."

What is there, Mr. Bates, in that letter to justify this wholesale condemnation of an effort to stay the hand of war among my own countrymen? What part of my past history does it contradict? In what does it countermarch the whole line of an extremely active if not useful life—*onward* it may have been, but *downward* rather than upward, for the last twelve years, only because throughout that whole period of time I struggled with intense earnestness and anxiety to preserve the peace of my country, and keep down sectional conflicts? When have I been an advocate for civil war? What is it, I ask, that has thus amazed you? In what do the suggestions of that letter differ from those I made to you in Washington, when you not only found no such fault, but voluntarily addressed a note to the President saying I had important suggestions to make to him? And so anxious was Mr. Seward on the subject, that he asked me to lose no time in laying them before the President, who himself received them with much favor, and said they should receive his fullest consideration. What were those suggestions? Why, nothing more nor less than those contained in my letter to you: that a national convention should be called, and *leave be given to the seceded states to withdraw.* The only difference then and now is, that the war had not then commenced, and now it has; that *then* this proposition *might* have been rejected without war, and *now* it can not, which gives the greater strength to the proposition now than then.

When, and under what circumstances, did I become an advocate of disunion ? Only when it became a fixed and irremediable fact ! when, at one dash of the pen, as gallant and devoted a party of Union men throughout this and other Southern States as the land could boast, was sponged out and crushed into the earth as effectually as the pencil-marks upon a slate could have been, and when the simple alternative was presented of separation with war, or separation without it ! Then it was that *I*, who had been for thirty years an object of extreme hatred, and of the most malignant denunciation of the disunion party, seeing that dissolution was inevitable, that the revolution had been permitted to be carried too far to be controlled, sought to bring about a quiet and peaceful solution of the question, rather than witness the scenes of anarchy and distress, of slaughter and of waste, of misery and destitution that must follow, and at last end, *as end it must*, in permanent disruption and eternal hate. And it is for this that I am thus arraigned by you.

Mr. Bates, in perfect frankness and without offense, let me tell you that the man who dreams that this Union can now be reconstructed, and amity restored by the subjugation of those states now in rebellion, is more blind than the mole; for he is not only without sight, but without the instincts of that animal that never works in the light of the sun.

So far, then, from feeling that my efforts to save my country from such a civil strife as we must now encounter have rendered me justly obnoxious to censure, it will be the glory of my future days, as it is now my pride, that I have done all that lay in my power to avert this heavy calamity from the land of my birth, and from the people whom I have loved and looked upon *as one*. Who feels differently is welcome to the honors posterity will award them.

But you add that my letter "is a silent approval (by failing to condemn) of violent and revolutionary proceedings of the people of the Southern States, in plundering the money and arms and other property of the United States; in seizing upon our ungarrisoned forts; in making war upon such as refused to surrender; in firing upon, and in some instances degrading the flag of our country; and in schemes and projects boastfully announced in the public press, and partially acted out in military preparations to seize this capital by violence and break up the government."

Now, Mr. Bates, suppose it were true that I had omitted to express any opinion on these points; in what should it have surprised you or justified the interpretation you have put upon it, that I gave to all this a silent approval ? My letter, as I have shown, was never intended for publication, and was written only for your own eye and for the Cabinet, if you had deigned, as I asked you, to lay it before them for consideration, and you and they were already familiar with my views on that subject, and *you* had them in a *printed form,* in a letter which you asked for, to be preserved, addressed to certain gentlemen who called upon me to become a candidate for the convention, and in which I had already expressed my condemnation, in the most unmistakable terms, of those very acts to which you refer.

But is it true, in point of fact, that in my letter to you I gave them a *silent approval* (by *failing to condemn*) those acts of violence and revolution? Such was not the reading given to that letter by the secession party here. Such is not the construction that will be given by you on a fairer and more dispassionate reading of that letter again. Let me call your attention to the paragraph which contains these words, "*No one can condemn* MORE SEVERELY *the immediate causes that have so unnecessarily led us into this awful and terrible catastrophe than I do,*" and then let me ask you if this can be construed into a silent approval *by a failure to condemn?*

I hope you will pardon me for saying that the enumeration of all these acts of violence might, with far more propriety, have found a place in the proclamation for the benefit of the people, large numbers of whom have never heard of them to this day, than in your letter to me, to whom they were all familiar.

But I will conclude this letter, already perhaps too long, by saying that I knew that the President had no power to demand, but that he could recommend a national convention, which would not be without its influence; and second, that it was no part of my calculation that the seceded states were to compose a part of the convention called to give them leave to withdraw, but that this would be done by all those states that had no desire to withdraw, and lastly, that on the issuing of such a proclamation, both parties would await its action, which could be held as well in a month as in a year; as every state could in that time appoint its delegates except California and Oregon, whose votes would not alter the result if the recommendation was adopted, as I have no doubt it would be, for the country prefers peace to war, and would make any sacrifice to avoid the latter which their honor would permit.

I regret extremely the turn this correspondence has taken; but your letter, which I hope implied more than was designed, leaves me no choice on the subject, and, under the indulgence of this hope, I subscribe myself, as ever, your friend, JOHN M. BOTTS.

Mr. Bates's next letter to me, in reply to the preceding letter to him :

Washington, May 5, 1861.

Hon. JOHN M. BOTTS, Richmond, Va. :

MY DEAR SIR,—In answer to your letter of May 2, I have not and ought not to have much to say. This much, however, both my inclination and my duty require me to say : my personal respect for you remains undiminished. My friendly feelings toward you are not only not diminished, but are made more deep and tender by the distressing circumstances which surround you. And these facts make me regret very much that I should have been compelled by circumstances to write you such a letter as to inflict any pain or mortification, and especially to the degree indicated by your answer, and explained more at large by the friend who bore it. I disclaim all intention to wound your feelings, or to offer you the slightest indignity ; and if there be any thing in my letter from which an intention to insult you can possibly be inferred, I retract it.

This much I say with the intention and hope of preventing any breach, or even weakening of the personal relations between us. Let us be friends still.

But it seems, now that we differ so widely in opinion upon matters of fact, that it is impossible for us to reason upon the same line of argument. You think that the *Union is already* dissolved, the nation already destroyed ! On the contrary, I believe no such thing. You believe that a *peaceful* dissolution of the Union, in the manner and by the means already employed, *is possible.* I believe it impossible. I believe that the insane effort at national destruction, persisted in, will involve a war more terrible than any the world has witnessed since the thirty years' war in Germany. You think that a great nation like this *can consent to die,* and may hope *to die an easy death.* I think that nations, like individuals, are under God's great law of self-defense, and when pressed down by superior force will die in convulsive agonies. You *seem to think* that Virginia can go out of the Union and still preserve her integral statehood. I think that when she dismembers the nation she will herself be dismembered.

But I will not continue the contrast. My heart is sorrowful when I contemplate the present degradation of Virginia. "How are the mighty fallen !" With the loss of her power she has lost all prestige also, and can no longer lead the people and direct the counsels of other states. She remembers her patriots and sages of former times, only to boast of them— not to imitate their talents and virtues, but (by implicit faith) to impute to the present generation the posthumous reputation of the glorious dead.

M 2

Formerly she proudly marched in the van of all the states; now she creeps in the rear of South Carolina, and consents to be detailed as a picket-guard to man an outpost of the Cotton States.

Poor old Virginia! In my heart I pity her. Already they boast in the South that they have transferred the seat of war from their homes to yours. And soon their devouring legions will be upon you, to eat up your substance and do your voting at the disunion election. Now mark my prophecy: unless Virginia, by a rapid revolution, redeem herself from the gulf that lies open just before her, she will be degraded, impoverished, and dismembered. For her, I hope almost against hope. And for you, I remain, as heretofore, your friend, EDWARD BATES.

Next comes my letter to him, also suppressed.

Richmond, May 9th, 1861.

MY DEAR SIR,—I was much gratified last night on receiving your letter of the 5th, as it fully re-establishes our former relations, and I assure you that all unpleasant recollections of our recent correspondence are forever dismissed from my mind.

I have no idea of pressing my views (founded upon deep conviction that *time* will vindicate their soundness and propriety), but I desire to make one or two brief explanations, in justice to myself, on points upon which I have been misunderstood.

1st. When I spoke of the proclamation of the 15th as being, *in many respects*, the most unfortunate document that ever issued from the public press, I did not mean to say that the administration was censurable for making a call for forces to protect the capital of the nation, or for vindicating the honor of its flag; but that it was *unfortunate* in the manner in which it was put before the country, and for the effect it produced by sweeping out of existence at one breath, as it were, the Union party of the South, who might have been rallied to the support of the government by a simple recital of all the wrongs that had been committed, from the first seizure of public property down to the firing upon Fort Sumter, and then by making such an appeal to the loyalty and patriotism of the country as General Jackson, a Southern man, strong in the confidence and affections of the South, found it necessary to make in 1832. The naked call for seventy-five thousand troops, without all this, left it in the power of wicked men to misrepresent the purposes designed, and to create a false impression that dethroned all reason, and substituted criminal passion in its stead.

2d. You mistake me in supposing that I have proposed that "this great nation should consent to die." Not so; as you must have seen by my second letter, which Mr. Lewis was charged to deliver to you. It is true that I think the Union *as it was* is dead, never to be revived, more especially by force, but honestly believing that twenty or more states, with twenty millions of people, *united* and without any jarring elements in their midst, would be stronger than thirty millions divided and distracted, surrounded by the antagonistic elements of free and slave labor, which has led to present troubles, I thought a peaceful separation would perpetuate and strengthen your government, while you know that my judgment has ever been that the Southern Confederacy would prove a failure, and that they would ultimately seek (in the absence of war) a reunion with the old government on such terms as both parties might be willing to accept.

However, a year from this time, or less, will probably bring us together on this subject; experience will prove that I am wrong, in which event I will confess my error, or it will prove that you are laboring under a delusion, when your own manliness will compel you to a similar confession.

But if you are right in your conjecture that "we shall be involved in a war more terrible than the world has witnessed since the thirty years' war in Germany," how can you attach blame to me for an effort to save my country from such horror and misery as it must carry with it?

There are two events in my life of which I can never be made ashamed; first, that I did all in my power to save the Union, and second, that when I felt that that was lost, I did all in my power to prevent the civil war that is to follow.

I am very truly your friend,   JOHN M. BOTTS.

P.S.—I concur in all you say respecting the action of this state.

The object of my proposition was to save Virginia (that had yet to give her popular vote on the ordinance of secession), and through Virginia, the other Border States, to the Union, and thus leave the Cotton or Gulf States to themselves; in which case, if matters had not been otherwise satisfactorily settled, then through the operation of what was understood to be the "Monroe Doctrine," or the principles of the "Ostend Manifesto" as laid down by Southern Democracy, or from difficulties resulting from the navigation of the Mississippi River, we should have had a *foreign* instead of a *civil* war, in which the Border States would have had no pretext for uniting with the rebellion, without even in their own minds, beyond all doubt, incurring the penalties of treason—all of which was subsequently explained to Mr. Bates by the gentleman (Mr. John F. Lewis) who handed him my last letter in person, but which I thought it would be indiscreet to embody in the correspondence, as all letters to and from me were at that time opened and *read.*

That the suggestions here made, and so much objected to by Mr. Bates, were not made, as he supposed, under duress or at the instigation of others, may be clearly and distinctly established, I here give the following extracts from a letter written by me in reply to an invitation to unite in the celebration of the 22d of February in Troy, New York, in 1861, which it will be seen corresponds with the suggestions to Mr. Bates in my first letter to him, and is precisely the same proposition I made in Washington, and that I had every reason to believe met with the approval of Mr. Bates and Mr. Seward, and was treated with marked consideration by Mr. Lincoln. If they were as obnoxious to Mr. Bates at that time as they afterward proved to be, he did not deal with me in that spirit of candor and friendship that at the time he professed. It is very painful to me to labor under the necessity of recurring to this subject, but as I am aiming to vindicate my past course, I think it will be conceded that no alternative is left me.

Extracts from the Troy Letter.

"But the evil is upon us, and the question is, What can be done for our salvation?

"There are two rocks, upon either of which, if we strike, we must be shipwrecked. The ship of state is running with a full head of steam down a rapid current, with secession on the one hand, and civil war in some shape on the other. Can *both* be avoided? Can we pass between the two? The seceding states declare most peremptorily that no compromise will now be accepted; that no proposal for reconstruction, or of their restoration to the Union, will be entertained; that the recognition of independence and of their right to secede must be acknowledged, or that war must ensue; and their *nominal* President declares 'that a union with us is neither practicable nor désirable;' and he threatens 'that all who oppose them shall smell Southern powder and feel Southern steel.'

"I take it for granted that the right of any state to annul the Constitution and separate herself from the rest of the states, when no right is acknowledged on the part of all the others to get rid of that state, however obnoxious she may prove herself to be, never will be recognized by the people or the government of the United States under any circumstances whatever, let the consequences be what they may.

"It is a proposition *not to be entertained for a moment*, because it would not only destroy the whole fabric of our existing institutions, but would utterly annihilate the possibility of ever establishing any other permanent and fixed government on the North American continent than that of an absolute monarchy or despotism.

"On the other hand, if such right is not recognized, how is civil war, in some shape or other, arising from the obligation to execute the laws, suppress insurrections, and punish treason, to be avoided? for if the right of secession does not exist, then the seceded states are in a condition of *insurrection* and *treason*, the first of which must be put down and the latter punished, according to the law and the Constitution, or else all government is at an end.

"I see but one mode by which, as it appears to me, it is possible to steer clear of both of these calamities, and that is to call a convention of all the states, *and so amend the Constitution* as to give to such states as desire to discontinue their connection with the present government *leave. to withdraw*, and make the experiment of separate independence; it will not take twelve months to bring them to their senses, and *if it will be desirable*, they can be admitted again, on condition that they will surrender the absurdity of the right of secession, and behave themselves better for the future. This will save the *constitutional question*, and avert the necessity for civil war at the same time, and likewise save the necessity of hanging traitors by the thousand, or of having the laws of the country trampled with impunity under foot.

"Let them keep the forts, arsenals, arms, ammunition, revenue cutters, etc., that they have violently, and without the semblance of right, unlawfully seized, but require them to pay for them; and if they are not ready to pay for them in cash, let them be trusted, but let them settle fair if they never pay; they will be glad to get rid of the expense of keeping them in less than a year, and will ask leave to restore them to their rightful owners; for these forts are the property of the United States, built by and held for the benefit of the United States in common, in which, as long as they constituted a part of the United States, they had a certain interest, as they had in the army, navy, treasury, public lands, and other property of the United States; but the moment they left the United States their right and interest in this property of every description ceased as effectually as if the same number of its citizens had removed from the

United States and settled themselves in Germany or Russia. As no single state is responsible for any part of the debt of the United States, so no single state is entitled to any part of the property of the United States; while, as a constituent part of the government, they are equally bound for all its debts, and equally interested in all its property; but when the obligation to fulfill its contracts, and provide for the payment of its debts, and defend its indebtedness ceases, *or is withheld*, then they are, to all intents and purposes, aliens to us and to the government, and have forfeited all claims to any share of our honor, our glory, our greatness, our property, and our future destiny.

"The plan, gentlemen, which I have here suggested for the settlement of our difficulties may be objectionable to some, but no plan can be devised that will be acceptable to all; and this appears to me to be the only one by which we can possibly avoid one or the other of two evils, either of which would be calamitous and ruinous in the extreme. If the suggestion should lead to any good results, I shall have reason to thank you for the opportunity you have afforded me of offering it to you, as a feeble contribution on my part for the preservation of the work of our national Father on the commemoration of the day that Providence gave him to America for the benefit of mankind throughout the world; for without the benefit of his great and illustrious works, he will have lived for nothing."

As serving to show in what regard these letters were received in other and higher quarters, I hope I may stand excused for making use of the following extracts from one of very many similar letters received from different sources and sections of the country, but all from the strongest friends of the Union, and most determined opponents to secession.

"May 20, 1861.

"MY DEAR FRIEND,—Though I seem to be forgotten by you, I can not longer withhold from you the expression of my warmest admiration for your letters to Mr. Bates. Your noble and devoted efforts to spare the effusion of fraternal blood may be lost sight of now amid the wild and mad excitement of this carnival of evil passions, but whatever the result of the civil discord which now distracts our bleeding land may be, coming generations will bless your name for the effort and the sacrifices you have made.

"We are a ruined people. The only interest I have taken in politics for several years past, was produced by the hope of promoting, through you, the best interests of the country. Now that the greatest and best government the world has ever known has been destroyed by wicked, reckless, and corrupt demagogues, I can do nothing but mourn over this consummation of human folly, until I may be called on to fight for Virginia in a struggle which I had no hand in bringing on.

"I have read your letters to many persons, and all agree in praising them and honoring you. Old Dr. ——, to whom —— had read them, told me, with tears in his eyes, that you were one of the last of the true patriots and wise men of the great republic that now exists only in history. Sincerely your friend, S. C."

THE PARTICULARS OF MR. BOTTS'S ARREST.

· After this last effort had failed, and no hope of a peaceful settlement was left, and with no power to resist the storm that was every where sweeping over the land, when the whole Southern country presented the appearance of one vast lunatic asylum turned loose to ravage and destroy whatever crossed their path, I retired to the country with a determination, as no means were left me by which to serve my country, that no human power, no despotic torture, should ever induce me to take part against it in this most unprovoked, uncalled-for, and wicked war. I *rarely* left my premises; I received a great deal of company under my own roof, but did not seek it elsewhere; yet I never withheld or concealed my opinions from any. These opinions it was supposed were exercising some influence upon the popular mind; and for the purpose of putting a padlock upon every man's mouth, and thus annihilating all freedom of speech, the Confederate Congress, on the 1st of March, 1862, suspended the writ of habeas corpus and declared martial law, ·thus conferring absolute and dictatorial·power on Mr. Jefferson Davis, perhaps the most unscrupulous despot that has appeared since the days of Nero.

· On the morning of the 2d, a little before the break of day, I was aroused from my sleep by the assistant provost-marshal—then Captain, but subsequently·General Godwyn, at the head of one hundred armed men, who had surrounded my home—was arrested and carried off to a filthy negro jail, where I was imprisoned for eight weeks in solitary confinement, with instructions to my jailers not to permit any one to speak to me, nor I to them. Not even a chair nor a table were furnished me by those who had me arrested, but I was graciously allowed to supply my own necessities and comforts, which I did. This arrest was made during the administration of the "*little Jew*, Benjamin," as the head of the War Department, who at once forbid all intercourse with my family and friends.

I was the first victim to loyalty in the state. Franklin Stearns, from his confidence in, his regard for and intimacy with me, was the second; and then came the imprisonment of some hundred and fifty others, to which constant accessions were made, who were all thrown into the same loathsome prison, most of whom were afterward sent to Salisbury, North Carolina, where, from exposure and barbarous cruelty (if possible, surpassing the horrors of Andersonville), some went crazy, many died, and all suffered materially and permanently in health, while their wives and little children were left at home to brood over the wrongs and oppression inflicted, and suffer for the comforts and necessities of life. In the prison where I was confined, these men, far from home, were left with a naked floor for a pallet, a billet of wood for a pillow, and the ceiling for a blanket, while at Salisbury it was even worse, for they were exposed to all the weather, cold rains and burning suns alternately.

But the object was effected by my arrest and imprisonment and that of others: it effectually sealed every man's lips; all were afraid to express their opinions, under the reign of terror and the demands of despotism that had been established in Richmond. Every man felt that his personal liberty and safety required silent submission to the tyranny of the Confederacy.

From this time till near the close of the rebellion, free-born men who had as much interest in the government as Jeff. Davis or any of his satellites, if they spoke at all, talked "*with bated breath and whispering humbleness;*" many dared not let their nearest neighbors—some even of their own families and partners in business—know their honest thoughts. I have myself been often told by gentlemen of the first respectability, after listening to my conversation, when they would say it not to be heard by others, "I concur in every word you said, but you are the only man between the Gulf of Mexico and the Potomac who would dare to express such opinions ; but if it were known that I said this to you, I would be in Castle Thunder before to-morrow night, while another and another would take me out each in turn to tell the same thing, but neither daring to let his friend and neighbor know what the other thought."

During all this time, they were not only conscripting but forcing into the hateful ranks of the Confederacy, men of every state and every country, at the point of the bayonet, " to fight the peoples' war for their own freedom and independence," and all this while every Southern press and every secession mouth indulged in the most intemperate and vindictive denunciation of the tyranny and despotism practiced at Washington.

Such was the humiliation, degradation, and punishment awarded to Union men in the South for their loyalty to the United States, by the very men who are even now permitted, by the misplaced reliance and forbearance on the part of the President, to provide and furnish, to mark and stigmatize, to lord it over the Union men with an iron hand whenever and wherever they can be reached. Of what advantage is it, it may be asked, that the President thinks the loyal men "inherited the estate" as long as he and Congress allow the disinherited to enjoy the income? Why do they not take steps to put the rightful owners in lawful possession? In about three weeks after my arrest, this corrupt and contemptible little vagabond, Benjamin, who was characterized by the President himself as a " *sneaking thief and perjurer*," was transferred to the State Department, and Mr. George W. Randolph assumed the duties of the Department of War, and to him I at once addressed the following communication:

MR. BOTTS'S LETTER TO G. W. RANDOLPH IN 1862.

M'Daniels's Negro Jail, March 22, 1862.

Hon. G. W. RANDOLPH, Secretary of War:

DEAR SIR,—It is well known to you that I have been uniform in my opposition to the doctrine of secession, against which I have argued both by writing and speaking for thirty years, as well upon principle as policy. I did all in my power, with pen and tongue, to prevent this state from taking a step that I thought I foresaw, and foretold would lead to her *dismemberment, discomfiture, and ruin;* but when I found all my efforts fruitless, and the state resolved to secede, I then opened a correspondence with the Attorney General of the United States (Mr. Bates), by which I endeavored to bring about a peaceful solution of the question, urging with all the power and persuasion I could command that Mr. Lincoln should recommend the call of a national convention for the purpose of so amending the Constitution as to give to such states as desired it *leave to withdraw* from the Union, as the only means left of avoiding all the frightful consequences that have since resulted to both parties; but this last effort gave satisfaction to neither party; each seemed confident of its own strength and power, and each determined on a fight. This correspondence led to rather an angry quarrel with Mr. Bates, and for it I was cruelly denounced at home. Finding that I was powerless to accomplish any good, and feeling that I had done my duty, and my whole duty, to my country, I determined to retire from the field, and I said to myself and friends, I will now stand aside and leave the consequences to those who have invoked the war and to those who will control it. This correspondence with Mr. Bates, and one other letter written about the same time—

in April last—to a friend in New York, all of which is now in the hands of General Winder, and to which I ask your attention, was the last correspondence of any kind that I have had with any person outside of the Confederate States.

Finding I could not honestly and conscientiously co-operate with those from whom I so widely differed and had so long opposed, I determined to withdraw myself entirely, not only from the political field, but at the same time to shut myself out from all social intercourse while this war lasted, except with such as should seek me under my own roof, as the only dignified course left for me to pursue. For this purpose I removed to a small farm I had purchased, within less than a mile of the city, in the month of June last, and from that time till I was brought here, I had been to the city but three times, and on each occasion to attend the funeral ceremonies of some valued friend or relative; and the last of these visits was in the month of October or November last.

I have had my own private opinions, it is true, upon questions of public interest, and expect to retain them, and they were just such as I had always entertained, but they were my *private* opinions, which no government on earth, however despotic, claims the right to, or can despoil its citizens or subjects. These opinions were based upon the best judgment I could command, and were not controlled by prejudice or passion, by selfishness, ambition, or fear; but they have not been used to the prejudice of one government nor for the benefit of the other, since the war commenced, for I had no reason to suppose that either party desired farther advice or assistance from me; consequently I have sought no opportunity to impress my views upon others, but, *when asked* for, they have not been withheld from those whom I thought were entitled to know them, whether secessionists or others; but this has always been in the form of *private* letters or private conversations, and I have held none with more freedom than with my personal friend, Howell Cobb, at my house last fall, who then thought the position I had assumed was the only one I could consistently or honorably occupy. From the beginning I have thought I had *no right* to violate any of the laws of the state while I was one of its citizens, and I have been extremely cautious to do nothing that would subject me either to moral or legal censure.

Martial law was declared, it appears, on Saturday, the 1st day of March, to take effect on the next day (Sunday), and it was under these circumstances that, just before or about the break of day on Sunday morning, I was aroused from my sleep, arrested by an officer at the head of one hundred armed men stationed in and around my house, my family and homestead taken possession of by them and held in military possession until some time the next day, and I was hurried off, very much to the distress of my family, of course, and lodged in a dirty, filthy negro jail, where I have been ever since, subjected to close and *solitary* confinement, permitted to see the light of the sun only through the iron bars of my prison-house, and with an armed sentinel constantly at my door. My daughters, friends, and legal advisers have all been refused permission to see me, as if I were an already convicted felon.

Shortly after I had been lodged in jail, I sent to ask an interview with General Winder, which in the afternoon he granted, when I related to him pretty much what I have said to you in this letter. I said to him I had *no favors* to ask of the government, but I had a right to know upon what charge I had been arrested. He replied, You are arrested upon a very serious charge—one perhaps not exactly amounting to treason, but grazing it very closely. And pray, sir, said I, what may that be? He said I was charged with being at the head of a large organization in Richmond, of attending its nightly meetings, the object of which was to break down the Confederate government, and *that I was known to be hostile to the government.* I said, General Winder, if I am amenable to this government for my private opinions upon political subjects—if it is an offense against any law to believe that no state had a right to secede from the Union, then I am liable to the penalties of that law; if to believe there was no sufficient cause for the exercise of the right, if such right existed, *then, too,* have I incurred the penalties of the law; and if, conceding the existence of both right and cause, I still believed that secession and revolution were not the rightful remedies, and that I had never been able to see how it *was at all likely* to come to a successful termination, then, too, was I liable to all the penalties the law prescribed; for all this I had believed, said, and written, in every variety of form, for thirty years before the war, and *nothing had occurred to change them since.* He replied, This government has nothing to do with your private opinions or your private letters. Then, said I, General Winder, this government has nothing to do with me, and I have no business here, and am entitled to and claim to be restored to my liberty and my family; for as to the charge of being at the head of an organization of any description, it is too ridiculous to need refutation; for, in the first place, I have no knowledge of the existence of such an organization, nor have I any reason to believe that such an one exists; except what I have seen in the newspapers and have heard as common rumor, I certainly do not know of any human being who is a member of it; and as for my attending its meetings, I can only repeat what I have already said of my visits to Richmond and the circumstances under which they were made; and I have not been off of my farm after dark since I removed to the country last June (now nine months), except to spend the evening, in company with my daughters, occasionally at the house of an old friend and neighbor (Captain Burton) who lives within two or three hundred yards of my gate.

He then asked me if I knew a man named *Francis Stearns*. I told him I knew *Franklin* Stearns intimately, and had no better friend. ' Well, he said, he is the man that gave the information that you were at the head of this organization, and that he, Stearns, had given $300 to two men to be used in breaking up the Confederate government, and told them that there was such an organization, and that you were at the head of it. Oh, said I, General Winder, the whole story is an infamous *trumped-up lie* from beginning to end. I know that Franklin Stearns never said any such thing of me, for he is a truthful and honorable man, and he not only *did not know* that I did belong to such an organization, but no man knows better than he that *I did not;* for he knows what have been my habits of life, the determination upon which I have acted, etc., and, knowing that part of the story to be an *absolute falsehood*, I feel quite as confident that the balance of the story is equally untrue; for Franklin Stearns is not such a fool as to do business in that way, even if he were so disposed, and especially with strangers; but, said I, Mr. Stearns is a prisoner in this house, and within thirty feet of us, and as he is the witness by whom you expect to establish your charge against me, there can be no reason for delay in the investigation, and I am willing to rest the case entirely on his testimony. General Winder said he was glad to hear it, and if this were so, there could be no difficulty about it. .

Now, then, said I, General Winder, conceding the truth to be as I have represented, I appeal to you as a soldier, a citizen, and a man, if I am not entitled to have the charge against me promptly investigated, and if I have committed any wrong, *morally* or *legally*, enforce the penalty of your law upon me with all its rigor; and if not, let me be restored at once to my liberty and my family. He said I certainly was entitled to a speedy investigation, and he would put the case in the hands of the district attorney the next day.

. On the next morning (the 3d) I sent a note to Mr. Patrick Henry Aylett, the district attorney, asking an interview, to which he politely responded, and in the course of the morning called; and on representing all that had occurred to him, he said he thought, as martial law had been declared, he had nothing to do with the matter, but if he had, and the papers were put in his hands, he would attend to it without delay. Three weeks have elapsed, and I have heard nothing from General Winder or Mr. Aylett; but more than ten days ago, one of the detectives who aided in my arrest told me my papers had all been examined, and they had found nothing against me, and he believed General Winder was ready to return them to me. These are the circumstances connected with my imprisonment.

Hitherto I have not felt disposed to make any appeal to the War Department, because I had good reason to believe I had been made a victim to the petty and unmanly political malignity of a person who holds a subordinate position in your office, and upon whom I have never had the good fortune to cast my eye, and for the additional reason that I had formed the conception that your predecessor (Mr. Benjamin) recognized no responsibility for his official acts to the great body of the people, and especially those of this state, to whom he was unknown, and for whose good or bad opinion he was comparatively indifferent; in other words, the opinion I had formed of him was not of *a very exalted character*, and I did not choose to correspond with him, while, from my slight acquaintance with you, I have supposed *you would* feel a lively responsibility for all your official acts, and that you can not be used as an instrument in the hands of a subordinate for the gratification of a vindictive malice long since expressed, and therefore I have felt it to be a duty that I owed to myself, to my family, to my friends, to truth, and to a sacred regard for popular freedom, that I should address you in your official character, laying all the facts before you, which I am prepared to establish by the most incontrovertible testimony, that they may be placed on file in your department, that no one connected therewith may plead ignorance hereafter if they should be held to a just accountability for the course pursued toward me.

And now, Mr. Secretary, I ask if there is any thing exhibited against me to justify the outrage to which I have been subjected, or to excuse the denial of a public investigation, which I have demanded, into any charge that has been or can be brought against me? And are you not satisfied that if those who instigated my arrest would have found any charge upon which they dared to put me on trial that would in the slightest degree have attached stain or *suspicion* upon my character or position, that they would have been in hot haste to have done it, not only to injure me, but to justify what they had done?

Sir, I have been in St. Petersburg, under the eye of the Czar; I have been in Vienna, subject to the sleepless vigilance of the Austrian police; I have been in Rome, under the government of the Pope; but under neither of these, the most despotic of all European governments, would they have *dared* thus to abuse my personal rights, *with my American passport in my pocket,* upon so flimsy a pretext.

I incline to the opinion that, by the systematic persecution and tyranny that has been practiced toward me, they are building up for me a future strength and popularity that I have never before commanded, but which, as I desire no political preferment, I really do not covet, and for the enjoyment of which I would not exchange one hour of that civil, religious, political, and personal freedom that I inherited from my ancestors, and which for sixty years I have enjoyed until now without interruption, and I vainly hoped had been secured for life—a freedom won by the toil, the sufferings, and the blood of my forefathers; a freedom for which your own illustrious grandsire was an able and efficient champion; a freedom thus inherited no power under the sun has a right to dispossess me of except for some violation of law; and if this *newly-organized government of yours* claims such right, I am both *free* and *proud* to say that *I abjure it now and forever;* in *life* and in the *struggles of death* will I abjure it.

I ask, Mr. Secretary, that you will take such steps in the premises as your own sense of duty and propriety may dictate.

But before I conclude, allow me, in justice to others, to say that there are many other cases under this roof involving as much outrage and wrong as in my own. There is nothing more to be alleged against Franklin Stearns than there is against me, and if there is, he is equally entitled to a trial. Here too is a minister of the Gospel, who, according to the representation of the press, thoroughly incensed against him, was arrested and imprisoned because he did not open his church on thanksgiving-day. Mr. Wardwell too, Mr. Halleck, Mr. Heckler, Mr. Williams, Mr. Higgins, Mr. Davis, Mr. Wigand, and many others, all men of families, of regular business pursuits, torn from their homes and thrown into prison, without a hearing and without the privilege of counsel, under this *detestable, unwritten,* and *unknown* code called "*martial law.*"

Great God! can a Virginian gentleman witness such scenes as these, and not have the blood to curdle in his veins? Can any man born under republican institutions know what is transpiring here, and not shudder at the contemplation of what it promises in the future? Mr. Randolph, come down to this jail and judge for yourself, if you attach any value to human freedom and human rights.

I ask no clemency for myself, or for my fellow-prisoners and fellow-sufferers—I only ask for all; and as a citizen of Virginia, although incarcerated nevertheless as a citizen who has forfeited none of his rights, I claim that they may all be confronted with their accusers, and subjected to a fair and impartial trial for the offenses with which they severally stand charged. Many of these gentlemen are strangers to me, but they are none the less entitled to my sympathy, and to such aid as I may be able to render them, and therefore I venture to express the earnest hope that a regular investigation may be instituted, without farther delay, for the punishment of the guilty and for the discharge of the innocent.

I am, very respectfully, your obedient servant,   JOHN M. BOTTS.

P.S.—The consequences growing out of this communication will serve to show whether or not the Star Chamber, the Inquisition, and the Council of Three have been really transferred from the Old World into the heart and capital of Virginia.   J. M. B.

To this letter Mr. Randolph replied, promising that a court of inquiry should be convened at an early day; and, after more than three weeks' farther confinement, the court was appointed, consisting of one Colonel Tausel, the president of the court, who had openly declared before his appointment that I was not entitled to the benefit of an examination, but ought to be hung on the public square or to a lamp-post, Colonel Porter, who was a respectable gentleman, and an ignorant creature by the name of Brunell as judge advocate or recorder, who was incapable of making up his own record; and before this august tribunal I was summoned to appear. I declined the aid of counsel, and conducted this farce of a trial myself. After an investigation of some ten days, the record of which I would publish herewith but for its length and stupidity, this military tribunal submitted to the War Department the result of its conclusions, and thereupon the following orders were issued:

General Orders; No. 28.

War Department, Adj. and Insp. Gen.'s Office, Richmond, April 25, 1862.

A Court of Inquiry having assembled at Richmond pursuant to Special Orders, No. 81, April 9, 1862, from the adjutant and inspector general's office, to examine "into the causes of the arrest of John Minor Botts, and to report the facts in reference thereto, and whether, in the opinion of the Court, it is compatible with the public safety to discharge" the said John Minor Botts; and the Court having made such examination and reported the result, with the evidence taken in the case, to the Secretary of War, the following are his decision and orders thereupon:

"The Secretary of War, having considered the record of the examination in the case of John Minor Botts, and the report of Brigadier General J. H. Winder as to the practicability of confining him to his house and premises in the manner recommended by the Court of Inquiry, directs that he be discharged from confinement on his delivering to General Winder a written parole of honor to the following effect:

"That, until otherwise permitted by the Department, he will sojourn in Lynchburg, Danville, or Raleigh, or in such other place in the interior as may be selected by himself, with the consent of the Department; that he will proceed without unnecessary delay to the place of his sojourn; that he will not depart therefrom, or go more than five miles from his residence; and that, while on parole, he will do nothing to the injury of the Confederate government, nor express any opinion tending to impair the confidence of the people in the capacity of the Confederate States to achieve their independence.

"Mr. Botts's family will receive passports to join him, if desired."
By command of the Secretary of War,
S. COOPER, Adj. and Insp. Gen.

While I was imprisoned, Captain Alexander, who was then the jailer, came into my room and commenced a conversation by saying, It is a great shame that a man like you should be confined in such a hole as this; this is no place for a man of your character, talents, and standing before the world. To which I replied, Well, sir, I am very much inclined to concur with you in that opinion. Why, then, am I kept here? He said, There is no reason why you should be, and, if you will be reasonable, you need not be. What do you mean by being reasonable? I asked. Why, if you will only say you will accept it, I will bring you a commission of brigadier general in the Confederate Army in half an hour, and by to-morrow morning at this time you shall be placed at the head of ten thousand men.

I looked him sternly in the face and said, Do you know the nature of the proposition you make to me, and to whom you make it? He said he did. If, then, I were placed in command of ten thousand men to-morrow, do you know what would be the first thing I would do?. He said, No; what would you do? I said, with much vehemence of manner, Before the sun went down, I would hang every scoundrel of you from Jeff. Davis down to you. He laughed, and said, If you would accept the commission, you would think better of that. I then said, By what authority do you tender me this commission? He replied, No matter about that. If you will accept it, I'll pledge myself to bring it to you in half an hour. A moment's reflection satisfied me that I had been imprudent in rejecting the proposition in the manner I had, and I said, *I am not in the vein to-day*, and the conversation turned on other subjects.

On bis leaving the room I committed the conversation to paper, and conveyed it by our "under-ground railroad," as we called it, to the room below, occupied by Mr. Stearns, telling him if the subject was broached again, I should endeavor, without committing myself, to manage to get the commission placed in my hands.

A few days after, Captain Alexander again came to my room,. and again tendered the commission. I asked him who sent him to me with this offer. He said, Never mind; will you accept it? I said, You can not expect me to accept your proposition without knowing it will be carried out. Go and bring me the commission, and then I will give you an answer. He replied, You can not expect me to bring you the commission without knowing it will be accepted. Say you will accept it, and I will swear to you to bring the commission in half an hour. I said, No, you can not catch me in that way; bring the commission first, and you shall have a prompt and final answer. He left me, saying, whenever I chose to take it, and could let him know, it was at my command.

But a few days had elapsed, when I was lying on my bed reading, about eight o'clock at night, when the captain came in and took a seat on the bedside, and said, You do not know how much it concerns me to see a man like you occupying this position. Why will you not accept that commission? and by ten o'clock you can be at home under your own roof with your family. I said, You have not yet brought me the commission; and I told you I would not give you an answer until I had seen the commission itself. Why do you not bring it to me? He replied, Only pledge yourself to accept it, and it shall be in your hands in half an hour. In that case, I said, you must have it with you or in your possession, otherwise it could not be obtained to-night. Never mind about that, said he, I will swear to do what I tell you if you say you will accept it. But he would not commit any body else unless I would first agree to accept. All of this was regularly communicated, as was the first conversation, to my friend Stearns as it occurred.

On the 28th of April I received the following note from General Winder:

"Head-quarters, Department Henrico, Richmond, April 28, 1862.
"JOHN MINOR BOTTS, Esq:

"SIR,—With this letter will be presented a parole for your signature. When signed by you you will be released; and I am instructed by the Secretary of War to say that on Wednesday next, before twelve o'clock, it is expected that you will inform me what locality you have selected, and when you will be ready to take your departure.

"Respectfully, your obedient servant,

"JOHN H. WINDER, Brigadier General."

"Richmond, Virginia, April 28, 1862.

"I, John Minor Botts, do hereby accept the conditions proposed in General Orders, No. 26, April 22, 1862, from the adjutant and inspector general's office; and do pledge my sacred word and honor, until otherwise permitted by the Department, to sojourn in Lynchburg, Danville, or Raleigh, or in such other place in the interior as may be selected by myself with the consent of the Department; that I will proceed without unnecessary delay to the place of my sojourn; that I will not depart therefrom, or go more than five miles from my residence; and that while on parole I will do nothing to the injury of the Confederate government, nor express my opinion tending to impair the confidence of the people in the capacity of the Confederate States to achieve their independence.

"JOHN M. BOTTS."

The above parole I accepted and signed, and, instead of appearing at the office of General Winder at or before twelve o'clock, I asked for an interview with the Secretary of War, which was appointed for eight o'clock on the next morning. After a somewhat protracted conversation and strong remonstrance against the injustice of sending me from home, which proved unavailing, I announced my readiness to comply with the terms of my parole, but expressed a preference for some retired place in the country rather than for a city residence, where I should be an object of curiosity and remark whenever I put my head out of the door, and asked that the following protest, which I read to the Secretary, should be made a part of the record.

MR. BOTTS'S OFFICIAL PROTEST.

McDaniels's Negro Jail, April 24, 1862.

Hon. GEORGE W. RANDOLPH, Secretary of War:

SIR,—The undersigned asks leave to file the following protest against the reasoning of the Court of Inquiry which sat in his case, as also the decision of the Department thereupon, and that it may be made a part of the record.

1. Upon the allegation that there can be no such thing as neutrality in a war like this now in progress, the undersigned concedes, as a general principle, in time of war between *foreign states,* that no *individual owing* military service can be permitted to occupy a position of neutrality, for every one indisposed to take up arms might avail themselves of that plea, and thus deprive the state of the means of carrying on the war; but he submits that this is not so in the case of a rebellion, where no such military service can of right be demanded, and especially of a party who is exempt by law, as is the case of the undersigned on account of age, being now upon the border of sixty years.

2. He protests that the neutrality he exercised was in no violation of any law, state or Confederate, which subjected him to the injuries, wrongs, and injustice that have been dealt out to him with an unsparing hand.

3. He protests against the causes of his arrest and imprisonment, with the finding of the Court, and the approval of the Department, as being wholly inconsistent and contradictory in this—that he was arrested and confined as alleged upon the suspicion of *having taken part* in the war, whereas he is detained in confinement for the reason that he had *not taken* part in the war; and, finally, he is subjected to a punishment which imposes upon him as an absolute necessity the very neutrality for which he is confined and punished.

4. He protests that among the thousands in this state, and hundreds in this city, who have taken no more part in this war than the undersigned, that he alone should be selected as an object worthy of the attention and power of the Confederate government. It may be a compliment, but one in which he takes neither pride nor satisfaction.

5. He protests that this government has no right to require him to do any thing that, according to his life-long opinions, a thousand times expressed in the last thirty years, founded upon the best convictions of his judgment, would involve him in the *crime* of *treason,* and the forfeiture of his life to the government of the United States, *if ever* and *whenever.*

they should re-establish their authority in Virginia, three fourths of which is now in their possession.

All of which is respectfully submitted.　　　JOHN M. BOTTS.

Upon the reading of this protest, the Secretary agreed that I might stay at home, if I would confine myself to my own house and behave myself like a good boy, and make no effort to impress upon the public mind that the Confederacy was incapable of establishing its independence; to which I replied, "I had no disposition to do so, for, if I was not greatly mistaken, they would not be long in finding that out for themselves." I then expected "*Little Mac*" in Richmond before the end of the week, *knowing he could come* in any day that he thought proper to make the effort, as the authorities were then prepared for an evacuation rather than meet his *greatly superior* force, which they were by no means prepared to encounter —M'Clellan's force at that time being certainly not less than from eighty to a hundred thousand, and Johnson's not exceeding forty-five thousand, and his intrenchments at that time *far* less formidable than they were subsequently made. So well satisfied did every body seem to be that M'Clellan must come to Richmond that every preparation was made for the evacuation of the city. Every valuable document and paper of the government was removed to Columbia, South Carolina; the banks were all closed, their books, specie, etc., sent off; the printing-presses were all likewise sent away; the yellow flag was hoisted over all the hospitals in the city; tar, pitch, turpentine, and other combustible materials were collected around the tobacco warehouses; the locomotives kept for several weeks in readiness for the immediate departure of the government officials; when, finding "Little Mac" would listen neither to the persuasion nor peremptory orders of his superiors (see his Report), their alarm abated, and on the 17th of April they passed the first conscript act, under which the young conscripts poured into Virginia from all parts of the Confederacy by thousands, tens of thousands, and fifties of thousands, until the command of General Lee (who had succeeded General Johnson after he was wounded in the battle of the "Seven Pines") was variously estimated by their own presses at from one hundred and eighty-eight to two hundred and eight thousand men (though I suppose this was rather exaggerated), when, taking advantage of a midnight march on the night of the 25th of June, Lee hurried off some thirty or forty thousand men from his right wing, that confronted the main body of M'Clellan's left on the opposite side of the Chickahominy, marched them up to Mechanicsville Turnpike, which they reached about daybreak, and threw them with great and sudden impetuosity upon M'Clellan's left and weakest point, and by overwhelming superiority of numbers drove him for seven days, from point to point, down the Chickahominy, until he reached and *made a stand* at Malvern Hills, where the tables were most effectually turned, and the most *decisive* of all the battles during the seven days' fight was made, in all of which the Confederate losses were immense, and far greater than those on the Federal side; but all the prestige of victory inured to the Southern cause by forcing a retreat of the Federal army, and the occupation of the various positions they had held.

The day after the battle of "Malvern Hill" M'Clellan could have marched into Richmond without serious impediment, for the Southern army, worn out with fatigue and discouraged by this last unexpected disaster, was in a state of extreme disorganization; but instead of pushing his way then into Richmond, the extraordinary spectacle was presented of both armies *in full retreat*, one from defeat, and the other from one of the most *decisive*, and, if taken advantage of, might have been the most important victories of the war. Nothing occurred during the whole war so much to give new life, spirit, energy, and courage to the Confederate army and people as this untoward retreat of M'Clellan from the Peninsula, and they at once conceived the idea of marching upon the capital at Washington, which movement was deserted, and resulted in a movement on Maryland, and the battle of Antietam.

The Secretary of War, at the close of the interview heretofore referred to, handed me the following order:

. "Richmond, April 29, 1862.

"Mr. John Minor Botts is permitted to remain at his own house on parole until notified by the War Department that he must withdraw in compliance with the order already given.

"(Signed)   GEORGE W. RANDOLPH, Secretary of War."

Under this order I was confined to my own premises for the next four months, when one of my friends, a Confederate officer, remonstrated with the Secretary against this continued imprisonment, and he was authorized to say to me that, continuing under my parole, I need no longer consider myself circumscribed in my walks.

My situation was most unpleasant and painful. I was looked upon by the government and general community with suspicion and distrust, while I looked upon them with any thing but confidence or respect. They hated me, I despised them, as a political body. They regarded me as treacherous to the South, I held them as madmen, false to the nation, false to the Constitution, false to their obligations of duty, and especially false and faithless (*in fact*, whatever might have been their purpose) to every interest most cherished by the Southern people; and whether they did me or I did them the greater injustice, a more unprejudiced judgment may now be formed than then.

Under these circumstances I applied for permission to leave the state, which was refused.

MR. BOTTS MOVES TO CULPEPPER.

After this, I obtained *a pass* from the Secretary of War to visit the county of Culpepper to purchase the farm on which I am now residing, which I was urged to by the then owner to come up and examine. I purchased in the fall of 1862, and moved to the county on the 8th of January, 1863; but I had hardly gotten comfortably warm in the house before General J. E. B. Stuart came in with his whole cavalry force, took possession of every part of my premises (of 2200 acres), except my house, yard, and garden, turned his horses loose to graze in every field, to the exclusion of my own stock, which was left at the mercy of his highly-incensed command, without any effort or desire on his part to restrain them. They killed my hogs, drove off portions of my cattle with their own whenever they moved, and stole from me $50,000 worth of horses, at Confederate prices, and in Confederate money. Daily and hourly I was subjected to all sorts of vexatious annoyances. I had neither peace nor rest, day nor night, from the time this cavalry force came upon me until the arrival of the Federal army under General Meade in the month of September, except during the battles of Chancellorsville and Gettysburg, from both of which they came immediately back *to take care of me.*

General Meade moved into Culpepper on the 12th of September, 1863, and General Stuart moved back at double-quick across the Rapidan.

On the 12th of October, just one month after, General Lee took a circuitous route from the south side of the Rapidan, and endeavored to throw himself somewhere in the neighborhood of the old battle-ground of Manassas between Meade and Washington, and thus cut off his supplies, which was frustrated by a rapid movement of the Federal army by railroad in the direction of Washington. General Lee was not only disappointed in his contemplated advantage, but being severely handled at Bristoe, fell back to the south side of the Rappahannock, tearing up the rails from Bristoe to the Rappahannock, and quartered his whole army around Brandy Station, where he remained until General Meade could relay the road, which he completed about the 5th, and on the 7th of November he recrossed the Rappahannock, killing quite a number, and capturing many prisoners, both at Rappahannock Bridge and at Kelly's Ford, some few miles below; and taking *Lee entirely by surprise*, he commenced a rapid and confused retreat at twelve o'clock at night.

The rout of the Federal army at the first battle of Manassas could not have occasioned a much greater panic or greater state of confusion than this sudden and unexpected midnight retreat. Lee's head-quarters were within two miles of the Rappahannock bridge, where Meade was crossing, and when the news came that "*the Philistines be upon you*," and the orders were issued for an instantaneous retreat, the wildest terror was spread over the various camps extending over the country; and from the time the retreat commenced, cavalry, infantry, artillery, baggage-wagons, ordnance stores, commissaries, cattle, and all, in one general confused mass, were pushing across the fields and through the woods, all striking for the *one* and only great road through Culpepper Court-house, on their way to the south side of the Rapidan; and if General Meade had known the actual condition, and instead of halting at Brandy had kept up a vigorous pursuit, he must have captured or destroyed Lee's whole army before they reached the Rapidan.

Having safely reached the right bank of the Rapidan, Lee went into winter-quarters in one of the strongest positions that could be found in Eastern Virginia, and Meade took up his winter-quarters around and about Brandy; and in this position, with the exception of the Mine Run affair, which occupied about a week, both armies rested until the 3d of May, 1864, when General Grant had assumed the immediate command of the army, and moved off on his brilliant and successful campaign against Richmond, an account of which I leave to others more conversant with the minute particulars. In reference to the incidents of the war, I propose to give such only as came under my own personal observation or knowledge, and are not likely to be given by others.

When General Meade fell back from Culpepper on the 12th of October to prevent the flank movement of General Lee, by which his communication with Washington and his base of supplies would have been cut off, Stuart, with his whole cavalry force, came in to follow up and harass Meade's rear, and he followed them to the Rappahannock, skirmishing as they went. Immediately before my door they had a very brisk little fight about four in the afternoon, which left five-and-twenty killed and wounded men of both sides almost within a stone's throw of my house, all of whom I had brought in—the dead to be buried and the wounded to be nursed; and while I was engaged in this work of mercy General Stuart's command returned from the Rappahannock just after night-fall, when the work of destruction began, which continued through the night, and until ten or eleven o'clock the next morning. When I reached my house with the last load of wounded men, I found the inclosure to my yard, garden, and corn-field all torn down, camp-fires burning in each, near enough, with a good wind, to endanger my buildings, four or five hundred horses turned loose into my orchard and corn-field, fence-rails blazing in every direction, and the men in a state of frenzied excitement; and if my family and myself escaped personal violence, I was more indebted for it to Providence than I was to General Stuart, who passed immediately by on his way to his quarters a mile off, and witnessed this general havoc, or to Captain Randolph, who was in immediate command of the regiment occupying my yard, garden, etc.; except that none of my household were tomahawked or scalped, the scene reminded me more of what I had read of in Indian or savage warfare than any thing that had occurred among a Christian and civilized people. What corn they could not feed away to three or four thousand horses that night and next morning or carry away with them, they piled up with the rails and burned in the field; and if they left me one ear of corn on the farm, I have never seen it. With the whole premises closely grazed (consequently with no hay), the situation in which I was left may be understood when I say that two of my best work-horses died before my eyes *from actual starvation;* and this was the situation in which General Meade's arrival found me, and from him and General Ingalls I obtained permission to supply myself with provisions for man and beast, otherwise my stock would all have perished.

All this may appear to be personal matter, in which the public have little interest, and for which they have less care; but I mention it for a purpose, and that is, when people who brought all their troubles on themselves shall hereafter prate about the vandalism of the Union armies, they may take this as an offset. Of all these facts I made a minute written report to General Lee. He replied civilly, and sent one of his staff-officers to see me, but if he took any official action upon it, I have not heard of it. The open account left standing between General Stuart, Captain Randolph, and myself was all settled by the early death of each in the spring of 1865 near Richmond.

The morning after these outrages were committed upon my premises, General Stuart and staff passed by immediately along the line of depredation, and within thirty or forty yards of where I stood, and, if he did not exult over the destruction that fell under his eye, he certainly had no word of censure or reproof for his men. About two hours after he passed, I was arrested by his provost marshal and carried to Culpepper Courthouse; all of which will be explained by the following letter, which I addressed to the Richmond *Examiner* at the time, but which they declined to publish; and my friends in Richmond would not press it, from an apprehension of the consequences that might result to me, an apprehension in which I have never participated.

MR. BOTTS'S LETTER TO THE RICHMOND EXAMINER IN 1863.

The following letter was written and sent to the Richmond *Examiner* in November, 1863, but, greatly to my regret, it was not published. When the Federal army occupied Brandy in 1864, a reporter of the New York *Herald*, hearing of the fact, solicited a copy for that paper, in which it appeared. The copy below is from the Richmond *Republic* of June 28, 1865.

"Head-quarters Army of the Potomac, near Brandy Station,
Saturday, November 21, 1863.

"Hon. JOHN MINOR BOTTS: .

"SIR,—I have been informed that, previous to the recrossing of the Rappahannock by General Meade, you had prepared a letter for publication in the Richmond press; and knowing that any thing from your pen, particularly at this time, has a deep interest for the country, I would respectfully solicit a copy of the letter, on behalf of the Associated Press, for publication. Respectfully,

"T. BARNARD, Correspondent Associated Press."

"Auburn, Culpepper County, Va., November 21, 1863.

"DEAR SIR,—Your note of to-day has been received. You have not been misinformed as to my having written a letter for publication in one of the Richmond papers prior to the arrival of the Union army in this vicinity, which I have reason to suppose has before this reached the public eye through the channel for which it was intended. I therefore inclose you a copy of the letter for the purpose indicated in your note.

"I am, very respectfully, "JOHN M. BOTTS.

"T. BARNARD, Esq., Correspondent Associated Press."

"Auburn, Culpepper County, October 13, 1863.

"To the Editor of the *Examiner :*

"Sir,—Yours is the only paper published in Richmond to which I could make an application with any likelihood of success, in order to set myself right before the public, and you will pardon me for saying that I am by no means confident of obtaining such a privilege at your hands; but I think I have a right to expect it, inasmuch as you have chosen to publish an extract from a letter written by a correspondent *for*, and pub-lished *in*, the New York *Herald*, accompanied with some uncalled-for and ill-natured comments of your own. But I do not ask you to publish it for me without making a suitable charge, which I am more than willing to pay. I hope, therefore, you will allow me to say that, while I have long since forborne to make corrections of any misrepresentations of me by the public press, yet there are some of such a nature, and calculated to beget so much prejudice in the public mind, that I do not feel I would be act-ing wisely or properly to let them pass unnoticed.

"I am willing at all times to be held to a proper responsibility for any thing I may say or do, but I am not willing to be so held for what oth-ers, who may draw upon their fancies for their facts, may choose to say for me or of me. I have seen several statements in the Richmond papers lately, copied from Northern papers, calculated to excite popular feeling against me, which had no foundation in fact.

"1st. That I had been accosted by some Indiana major, then engaged in a skirmish with some of the rebel cavalry, and, on being asked which way they had gone (which, by the way, if he was skirmishing with them, he ought to have known for himself without asking me), I replied, 'I was not at liberty to tell him, as I was on my parole,' and then very gratuitous-ly added that 'I was a Union man without any ifs or buts.' Now, what-ever my opinions and position on this subject may be, it is not true that I have had any such interview. I have seen no such major, and had no such question put to me, and have given no such answer.

"2d. In the letter, a portion of which you have copied, I am represented by the writer as having said, 'I wish the Federal generals knew half that I know of the rebels, and their resources and intentions.' I have only to say that I said no such thing, and nothing that would bear a resemblance to it; and when I read the *Herald* containing it, I mentioned the error to other correspondents of that paper and asked them to have it corrected, which they promised should be done. I see nothing in it, if I had said it, to be complained of by other parties, as it matters not what I knew of their

intentions and resources, provided I did not disclose them to others.
I complained of it, because it made me appear in the ridiculous attitude of
pretending to know what every man of intelligence and reflection was
obliged to know was preposterous in the extreme. For all know that I
am not in the confidence of the government or the commander of its
forces, and therefore could know nothing of their intentions; and as to
their resources I profess to be profoundly ignorant, either as to what they
are or where they are. What he says about my purchases in Richmond
is true. For what would have cost before the war, at regular market
prices, $64 15, I did pay $1368 03. But this was disclosing no important state secret, inasmuch as you furnish them with the prices current
once or twice a week, and these current prices are as well known in New
York as they are to me. But I did not tell it with any expectation that
it was to get into the newspapers, for when I mentioned it I did not know
to whom I was addressing myself. The gentleman came, as many others
did, to pay his respects, and it was not until he was going away that he
handed me his card, by which I ascertained that he was an army correspondent of the New York *Herald*. I incidentally mentioned the fact in
speaking of the great scarcity of and high prices for every thing. To
this part of his letter, therefore, I made no objection. But, in your comments on this letter, you say 'Mr. Botts came to Richmond on quite a
different errand than on a marketing expedition. He came to draw some
twelve or fifteen thousand dollars of the government which he delights to
abuse, and affects so much to despise. He abhors the government, but
loves its money.' In the first place, let me say that, whatever I may
think of the government, I have never felt myself entirely at liberty in this
land of freedom to say half as much against its administration as I have
read in your own editorial columns. But I have never made professions
of devotion to the government. I have never ceased to feel a warm interest in the welfare of the people of Virginia, with whose prosperity and
freedom my own are entirely identified ; and I will take occasion to say
here what I said to General Meade, and have said to all, that my earnest
prayer is that this revolution may result in whatever may contribute most
to the permanent peace, happiness, prosperity, and freedom of the people
of Virginia. These are the blessings of a good government. This is
what I suppose is desired and aimed at by all, unless the selfish politicians and the corrupt speculators in and out of the army may constitute an
exception. They care not under what sort of government they live, provided they fill the high places and have their pockets well lined. We

may differ possibly, and perhaps honestly, as to the best means of attaining these desirable ends. If it is by the success of the revolution, then I pray God the revolution may succeed; but if by a restoration of the Union, then I hope the Union may be restored. What I want is a government that has the will and the power to protect my person and my property against all abuses, and that I would prefer living as I did before the war to living as I have done since the war, is beyond all question; and I would be a madman or a fool if I did not, and a knave and hypocrite if I were to pretend otherwise.

"3d. I hope I committed no unpardonable offense if I did go to Richmond to collect, or try to collect some $12,000 or $15,000, for which I furnished supplies, or, rather, for which supplies were taken from me for the use of the Confederate army, all of which were certified to as being due by the commanders of regiments or by quarter-masters, but which were not paid because the accounts were not made out in the precise form authorized at what you have called the "red tape and circumlocution offices," which accounts are still due, and unpaid, and, I fear, are likely to remain so.

"Finally, it has been announced that I have been arrested and sent to Richmond; but those who made the arrest and those who made the announcement have taken good care not to mention the cause of the arrest, thereby leaving the public to infer that I had committed some grave offense against the government which you say I do much abhor. God knows it, and its agents have given me no great reason to worship it.

"Let us see how the account stands. On my part I have done nothing, from first to last, of which this government can complain, unless it be that I have not become Democratized, and have made no concessions to Democracy, and have none to make hereafter, and because I have not chosen to follow blindly wherever Democracy might choose to lead.

"On the other hand, of what have I to complain? First, the legislative power of the government has been especially directed against me while I was leading the most retired and secluded life, as was clearly admitted by the Hon. Henry S. Foote at the following session of Congress, when he said he had been induced to vote for the declaration of martial law and suspension of the writ of habeas corpus upon a representation of the condition of things supposed to exist in the neighborhood of the city of Richmond, but which turned out to be entirely groundless. Second, the power of the Executive branch of the government has been exerted against me, when, under this detestable, unwritten, unknown code called martial law, upon no charge preferred before the Court of Inquiry, they had me arrested in my bed between the hours of midnight and daybreak, hurried me off to a dirty, filthy negro jail, where I was kept in solitary confinement for eight weeks, when, with all the vigilance and research of their numerous detectives, they could find nothing upon which to hinge a charge; and now comes the second arrest, without a charge, while the army itself has been turned loose upon me to destroy my property by design, and by order of officers in high command, which I can establish if I cán procure their arrest and trial by court-martial; under which order my yard, garden, and corn-fields have been ruthlessly invaded, the fencing of each torn down to the ground, and all converted into a general camp-ground, camp-fires built, and horses turned into each by the 4th Virginia Cavalry, under command of Captain Randolph; and when Dr. Kidwell (with whom I had been until ten o'clock picking up and nursing the wounded men of both parties, more than twenty of whom were brought to my house) remonstrated with them, they said it was wrong, and should not have done it, but they were ordered to destroy 'whatever they damn pleased.' And upon this being repeated by Dr. Kidwell to Captain Randolph, he neither affirmed nor denied that such orders had been given. From which cases of violence, together with the effects produced by my arrest on the next day, one of my daughters has been ill of nervous typhoid fever ever since. And not only has my fencing been torn down and destroyed in every direction, but some twenty-five or thirty of my best hogs have been shot down, and I have not been left one ear of my entire crop of corn, all of which that could not be used was carried off or burnt in the field. And I now challenge any and every man of the Southern Confederacy to come forward with any charge that can be made against me for any thing said or done for which their government or its army can justly complain. And but for the protection now afforded me by a guard from the head-quarters of General R. E. Lee, none can tell to what condition I should have been reduced. Have I then, Mr. Editor, think you, had much reason for attachment or devotion to a government by which I have been thus treated? You complain of the treatment Mr. Vallandigham has received at the hands of his government. He made many violent speeches, in which he took active and strong grounds against his government, and for this he was sent among his friends, as they supposed.

"But I have done nothing, taken no part, but maintained firmly and consistently, as I shall continue to do, my own private opinions and the convictions of my best judgment, which have not been controlled by any considerations of selfishness, ambition, or fear, as I wrote the Secretary of War while I was confined in M'Daniels's negro jail in the spring of 1862; and because I can not surrender these convictions, am I thus to be oppressed and persecuted by the government and army? I want no better vindication for having withheld my approval of the war than is to be found in the fact that there is not one of those who aided in bringing it on that would do it, if, with their present experience, it had to be done over again, or if they could have foreseen what has followed, all of which I did foresee and foretell; and if any man with brains in his head and a heart in his bosom says he would, then I say flatly I don't believe he tells the truth.

"But to come back to my second arrest by General J. E. B. Stuart. On Monday morning, the 12th inst., following the night of the ruthless and heartless destruction of my property, General Stuart's provost marshal rode up with a guard to my house with a warrant, of which the following is a copy:

"'Head-quarters Cavalry Corps, October 12, 1863.

"'Lieutenant RYALLS:

"'You will arrest John Minor Botts and send him to Richmond. Charges will be forwarded from these head-quarters as soon as practicable. Don't allow him to annoy General Lee, but keep him as a prisoner of state. Let me know how many prisoners.

"'By command of Major General J. E. B. Stuart,

"'A. R. VENABLE, Major and Adjutant.'

"Upon this warrant, containing no charge, I was arrested about half past ten o'clock on Monday morning, carried under guard to Culpepper Court-house, kept there until five o'clock, and then discharged on the ground that there was no charge against me; but I have been semi-officially informed from two sources, either of which would be regarded as authentic, that the sole ground of my arrest was that I had entertained General Meade and other general officers at my table; and if it was not that, it was some other pretext equally frivolous and contemptible, which I hereby challenge General Stuart to lay before the public; and if it be any offense against the peace and dignity of General Stuart or of the Confederate government that I should have entertained Federal officers at my table, which would justify my arrest, then Major General Stuart has signally failed in the discharge of his duty to the peace and dignity of the aforesaid Major General Stuart by not bringing me to trial for this high crime and misdemeanor; for although it is not true that General Meade took his dinner at my table, I hereby make it known to all whom it may concern that I invited him to do so, and deeply regretted that his constant engagements prevented his acceptance of the invitation. I moreover proclaim that, if he should return to this vicinity (which I do not at all anticipate), I shall, in all probability, subject myself to another arrest by a repetition of the offense, without consulting General Stuart's pleasure on the subject.

"The truth is, I have entertained freely and hospitably the officers and gentlemen of both armies whose acquaintance I have enjoyed, and shall continue to do so so long as I am master of my own house, and so long as they treat me with kindness and civility, let it offend whom it may, provided the means are left me with which to entertain them, and unless, in the mean time, I shall be prohibited by law or by some higher authority than that of General Stuart.

"In fact, I have met with no officer in the Confederate army, and with few privates, with whom I was acquainted, from General Robert E. Lee down, with the exception of General Stuart, that I have not invited to my house—nearly all of whom have partaken of my hospitality—while hundreds of half-famished soldiers have been furnished with meals, for which I have never charged the first dime, while they were in the habit of paying, as they said themselves, to brawling secessionists from two to three dollars a meal; but this furnished no ground of complaint with any *gentleman* of the Northern army, many of whom expressed their surprise and gratification on hearing that they had visited me thus freely and familiarly.

"But no sooner was I arrested, than the whole atmosphere was filled with rumors to my disadvantage and prejudice; among the rest, that I had been caught in the Federal lines on the day of the fight with arms in my hands, to be used against the Confederate government.

"The circumstances which gave rise to this rumor are as follows: As a portion of the Federal cavalry passed my house about two o'clock on Sunday, my neighbor, Mr. Bradford, sent me a note, saying he had been arrested, and was then in the custody of the Federal officers, and asked me to ride over to Brandy Station to meet him, which I did.

"On my return, I passed General Lamar's brigade; and when half their column had passed me, and was between me and the Unionists, and in the presence of the other half, I met young Slaughter, the son of Dr. Slaughter, of Culpepper Court-house, who had a gun and knapsack in his hand, with which encumbrance he could not control his horse, and he asked me to take it with me to my house, and to keep it until he called for it. At great inconvenience I took it, and this act of kindness and accommodation to Mr. Slaughter was tortured into my bearing arms against the South, though General Stuart himself knew what had carried me to Brandy; for he had seen a letter from me to Mrs. Bradford telling her of the arrest of her husband, and of my having been sent for to meet him at Brandy Station.

"However, these rumors, publications, and arrests have had their desired effect, as they have led to the most wanton, wicked, and savage destruction of my property such as I have already mentioned, and excited the prejudice of the army, and, possibly, of misled citizens, against me. But I hope to outlive it all, while the authors of such vandalism will be held to a just accountability at the hands of a military commander whose moral, intellectual, and military qualities are justly esteemed by the whole country; and if not by him, then by a still higher military authority, to wit, the War Department; and if not there, then by the civil tribunals of the country; and if not there, then by a just, discriminating, and indignant public judgment.

And now let me inquire, has martial law been declared again? and if not, when, where, how, and from whom did General Stuart derive the authority to arrest me or any other citizen for any offense whatever, and retain me as a prisoner of state? If any charge was to be preferred against me for a civil offense, where were the civil authorities? and why was not complaint lodged with them upon affidavit, as the law requires? How came I, a private, peaceable, and quiet citizen, subject to the military authority of General Stuart, and why was I not to be allowed, if I thought proper, to appeal to his superior in command, General Lee, against his flagrant usurpation of power and most inexcusable instance of false imprisonment?

"If I mistake not, Congress, by an express vote, refused to grant these high prerogatives of dictatorial power to Mr. Davis. How is it, then, that General Stuart undertakes first to establish a martial law for himself, and then virtually to suspend the writ of habeas corpus by a denial of my right to appeal to his superior in command?

"If such power can be exercised by General Stuart with impunity, with whom and where does the power stop? To how low a grade of military authority does it descend? And I may farther ask, why, of all the gentlemen in and around the court-house who entertained Federal officers, was I alone to be selected for the exercise of this military power—for this indignity and outrage? These are all questions of grave interest to the liberty of every citizen that can not and shall not be slurred over, if there is any justice in the military department of this government or independence in the judiciary of this state.

"Hitherto I have been silent as to the wrongs, injuries, and indignities that have been heaped upon me; but I am not a spaniel to lie down and crouch at the bidding of any master, nor to lick the hand that smites me, nor am I Christian enough when one cheek is slapped to turn the other; and if I am thus to be selected as a particular object of persecution, and can find no protection from the law, then will I protect myself. This I can not do against the government or the army, but I can and will do it when the law, military and civil, both fails me, against any one man that this Confederacy can boast.

"When I purchased my present home, it was to seek retirement and obscurity, to get out of the way of the world, and to follow for the balance of my life the peaceful pursuits of agriculture. There was then no army here, nor did I suppose there would be one. I disturbed nobody, went nowhere except among kind and friendly neighbors, with whom it has been my good fortune to secure as large a share of respect and esteem as any one who has ever lived in the county; and in this condition of things it was that, in imitation of the Confederate government, 'All I asked was to be let alone.'

"But what is the liberty of any citizen worth if a military commander can, in the exercise of a despotic power, or a weak and imbecile discretion, or in a fit of spleen toward one who has offended, by reporting him for official misconduct, in which eight other gentlemen united, drag that citizen from the bosom of his family, heap upon him the indignity and wrong of having him arrested and conducted through the streets of a crowded village under guard, keep him in that condition long enough for all sorts of idle and malicious rumors to be circulated and sent over the telegraphic wires respecting him, and order his discharge upon the ground that there is nothing to be alleged against him?

"And now, Mr. Editor, in conclusion, let me say that the press may continue to misrepresent and abuse me; I may be arrested and thrown into a dungeon; my fencing may be torn down and destroyed; my crops may be laid waste and carried off; my stock may be stolen or shot down under my own eyes; my house may be burned down over my own head, as has been threatened, but I can not, for all that, be induced to swerve a hair's breadth from the line of conduct that my own judgment and conscience may dictate, which is to take no lot, part, or share in the responsibility that rests upon those who have brought this whirlpool of desolation and ruin upon my unfortunate country. Nor shall I depart from the position I have taken of doing nothing that can justly subject me to outrage, animadversion, or rebuke. But if to adhere firmly and consistently to the opinions and principles that I have maintained for thirty years, and if to prefer living as I did before the war to living as I have done since the war makes me a traitor, then a traitor's life let me live, or a traitor's death let me die. I am respectfully yours, JOHN M. BOTTS.

"P.S.—Since the above was written, a copy of the *Examiner* has reached me, containing the following announcement:

"'The battle took place on the farm of John Minor Botts. * * * We may here remark that the property on the farm of this extraordinary individual, of whom the Confederate States stand in such fear, had been religiously respected by the Yankees; whereas the country around was little better than a wilderness, his fences and crops were untouched. But that night made a change in its condition. Three thousand Confederate cavalry bivouacked there after the battle, and fed their horses in his corn-field. The next morning there were very few fence-rails and very little corn left. The men could be heard to say, while building high their fires, "Pile on, boys; they are nothing but d—d old Union rails."'

"I am glad to avail myself of the testimony of this 'leaky vessel,' who fully confirms what I have said above; but although he does not state what is true in regard to the general destruction of property in the neighborhood, for it gives me great pleasure to say that a guard was furnished to every family that asked for it, all of whose property was amply protected, as every one in the neighborhood will testify, yet he certainly states what is true in regard to the general destruction of my property; and I must say that the achievement of three thousand cavalry conquering one man and a corn-field is one of which, in the future, they can take no great pride when their prejudices and passions have subsided.

"Another article has also appeared in the *Dispatch* recommending my imprisonment or banishment, which is altogether unworthy of notice. I will only say that, whatever other difficulties I may labor under, I do not esteem it a misfortune that I have no soldiers at my command to turn loose upon any citizen, nor aids at my elbow to bring them into discredit with the people. Thank God, when there is a necessity for it, I can do my own writing and my own fighting. J. M. B."

What would have been the effect, if this letter had been published in Richmond at the time, surrounded as I was at the moment by General Lee's whole army, with Stuart and his cavalry on my immediate premises, I know not. Whether it would have produced a reactionary feeling, or have led, as my friends apprehended, to still more serious consequences, can not now be told; but let the consequences have been what they might, I resolved to keep silent no longer. I was actuated far more by a pride of manhood than by the timidity of a contemptible *sneak*, or a submissive slave to military power. When I first heard that Mr. Daniel, the then editor of the *Examiner*, had declined to publish the letter because of its "*hard hits*" at the Confederacy, I wrote to my friends, insisting that it should be published in some paper, and be paid for at advertising prices, but they had become alarmed for my personal safety under its publication and withheld it. This I had not ascertained when the Federal army came in, which cut off all mail intercourse with Richmond. When I did learn it, I was sorely vexed; but as I knew it proceeded from the warmest feelings of kindness and friendship for me, I could not complain; but I could not help feeling that while the government, army, and people were all pommeling me in the face, that it was hard to have my hands tied by my friends, to keep me from striking back at my assailants. It is proper I should here say, that from a scrupulous regard to the obligations of my parole, which I believed carried no moral obligation with it after I ceased to be within the Confederate lines, yet preferring to err, if at all, on the safe side, I was far more circumspect and reticent in my conversations with Federal officers than I was with the officers of the Confederate army, to whom I expressed my hostility to the government and the rebellion in the most unreserved and unmistakable manner.

A CLEAR RECORD DESIRED.

Here my task might be closed, but that I desire to present a clear record, and furnish a full vindication of my whole line of policy from first to last upon all the questions connected with or growing out of the rebellion, and of all that I have said or done of a public nature, which, for want of access to the Southern "reconstructed press," is known only to a limited circle, by which I hope, if I can not secure the confidence of the deluded and cheated South, I may at least command their respect by my consistency and duty to my country, and by my faithful and self-sacrificing devotion to their *true interests*, which have been so wantonly, cruelly, and wickedly sacrificed by the EMPIRICS, PYROTECHNISTS, TINKERS,

QUACKS, *traders and stock-jobbers* in politics, who are again at their old work of educating the people to a feeling of disaffection and hostility to their government, which they have no choice but to obey, and who have, by their exhibitions of disloyalty, retarded for an indefinite period the regular and formal participation of the South in the affairs of their national government, and to whose control I do not mean again to submit my fortunes, or my personal liberties or rights, without raising a voice of remonstrance or making an effort to throw it off.

In the winter of 1863, '4, I received a letter from an officer of the "restored government" of Virginia, whose Legislature was then sitting in Alexandria, and while I was in the Federal lines, urging me to accept at the hands of that Legislature a seat in the Senate of the United States, to which I made the following reply:

"Auburn, Culpepper County, Va., January 7, 1864.

"DEAR SIR,—I have received the letter of Mr. S——, in which he urges in very earnest terms that I should accept a seat in the Senate of the United States at the hands of the Legislature now in session in Alexandria, an election which he seems to think I have no right to decline, as the friends of the Union every where desire it.

"Permit me to say, my good sir, that I duly appreciate the honor designed, which is far beyond any thing that I have reason to expect, now or hereafter, from any other source; but high and dignified as is the position of United States senator, which in ordinary times is one that might reasonably satisfy the ambition of any moderate man, yet in the present condition of the country, and of the state of which I am 'native here and to *the manner* born,' I could not with propriety, and with my convictions of duty, accept any appointment at the hands of either of the *numerous governments* now exercising legislative powers over any of the dismembered fragments of what once constituted the proud and revered old commonwealth of Virginia.

"In taking the position I have done in reference to the rebellion, I have been actuated by no sordid considerations, and by no selfish desire to advance my political or personal fortunes; but it has been forced upon me by the *clear, unclouded, conscientious,* and *overwhelming* convictions of my best judgment, free from all passion, prejudice, or ambition.

"From the present aspect of affairs, as they appear from the standpoint I occupy, it looks as if the day was not very far distant when (if ever) I may be of some service in healing those dissensions and distractions, growing out of the grossest misrepresentations and frauds, that now divide the nation, the state, and almost every locality, and of developing, to some extent, that sentiment of loyalty and nationality which, though smothered for the time, has never yet been extinguished; but this can only be done, *if at all,* by adhering firmly and consistently to the opinions and principles of a long life, which have 'grown with my growth and strengthened with my strength,' until they have become a part of my second nature.   In other words, I must permit no shadow of suspicion *from any quarter* to attach to my unselfish patriotism or the disinterested integrity of my purpose, which the acceptance of office might subject me to.

"The extent of my aspirations for the present is to return 'good for evil' to this once venerable and venerated, but now poor, down-trodden, shattered, heartlessly sacrificed, and dilapidated old 'Mother of States,' that has been reduced to her present miserable condition by her leading and trusted statesmen, who, with miscalculation upon miscalculation, and blunder upon blunder, with every prophecy and promise unfulfilled, have been groping their way in Siberian darkness, and with the most inexcusable ignorance, after a phantom engendered by a corroded and diseased imagination, which was excited by a heartless selfishness and insane ambition to perpetuate their own power, that has been without a parallel in the history of the world.

"I am aware that my counsels, for the last three years, have been spurned and derided, and my person even threatened with violence by many who once looked with a more charitable and friendly eye upon my suggestions and advice.

"I have reason to think this hallucination is passing away, and is being rapidly dissipated by the terrible ordeal to which the fortunes of the South have been subjected; and it may be, at least I am not without such hope, that at some future day I may, in *some way,* stand as a link between the North and the South, by which the chain which once bound them together may again connect them; and to this complexion I must come at last, for neither *passion,* nor *prejudice,* nor *pride,* nor *suffering,* nor *want,* nor *hunger,* nor *strife* can endure forever; and the time must come when men will look at things as they are, and no longer close their eyes at bright midday, and swear that the sun does not shine, because they *desire to shut out the light.*

"For these and many other reasons not necessary to mention here, I must beg to be excused for respectfully declining the high position to which it is proposed to elevate me.

"I am, very respectfully, your obedient servant,   JOHN M. BOTTS."

MR. BOTTS'S LINCOLN LETTER.

About this time I received a letter from a friend in Washington, who expressed an anxious desire to learn what impressions I had formed of Mr. Lincoln and his administration. I answered him at some length. In the discussion of various questions connected with the war, embracing the Emancipation Proclamation, the status of the states, etc., etc., with Federal officers, reverend divines, professors of law in collegiate institutions, and others who called to pay their respects, I had not unfrequent occasion to read this letter. There was a general wish expressed that Mr. Lincoln could see it. I said, while it was a private letter, intended for no eye than that of the friend to whom it was addressed, and while I had no right to obtrude my opinions upon Mr. Lincoln, yet if Mr. Lincoln should express a desire to see it, I could have no objection to his doing so. This, I suppose, was communicated to Mr. Lincoln, for he shortly after did express a wish to see the letter, and the gentleman to whom it was addressed was authorized to place it in his hands, which he did. Some three months after the friend called upon Mr. Lincoln for the letter, and Mr. Lincoln replied, "The letter is your private property, of course, and, if you require it, I must return it to you, but you would greatly oblige me by permitting me to retain it;" to which my friend assented, and Mr. Lincoln died with it in his possession.

There is one incident connected with this letter of which I feel considerable satisfaction, and at the risk of the charge of vanity, I will here mention.

On one occasion, twelve gentlemen, chiefly ministers of the Gospel, headed by Charles Stewart, Esq., of Philadelphia, President of the Christian Association, and the Rev. Dr. Kirk, of Boston, called to see me; we got into a discussion of the Emancipation Proclamation, and I read this letter to them, as expressive of my views on the subject. When I finished the letter, Mr. Stewart rose from his seat, and with some very flattering remarks, said, substantially, " that no such emotions had been created in his bosom since the commencement of the war as had been excited by the reading of that letter, and that he thought it was eminently proper that they should return thanks to God that one such man had been preserved in the South, and that the Divine blessing should be asked upon the head of the 'venerable statesman' who had been capable of entertaining and expressing sentiments of so much patriotism and devotion to his country;" whereupon the Rev. Dr. Kirk offered up a most impressive prayer, which awakened feelings in my bosom which I shall not soon forget.

The following is extracted from the letter dated 22d of January, 1864: "Next you want to know what I think of Mr. Lincoln and his administration, and you express the hope that it has met with my approval." Well, I will be frank with you, and tell you freely but confidentially what I think of both.

I think, then, that Mr. Lincoln is by nature a vigorous, strong-minded, and conscientious man, honest in his purposes, and indefatigable in the exercise of what he conceives to be the duties of his office. In natural endowments, I doubt if he is not quite equal, if not superior to any of those by whom he is surrounded. He is not so cultivated as many, because he had not the same advantages in early life, but he is what I always honor, an original and self-*made man*, and is what I have generally called one of God Almighty's educated men; that is, he gets what he knows chiefly from his Creator. Dogberry says, "Reading and writing comes by nature, but to be a well-favored man is the gift of God;" and in this latter particular I do not think Mr. Lincoln is as munificiently endowed as he has been in the more essential qualities of head and heart; but believing him to be a true and sound patriot, and an honest man, I can make proper allowances for many things of which I might otherwise complain; for you must not infer from what I have said that I approve of all that Mr. Lincoln has done; but then I do not expect any man to do exactly as I would have him to do, for I am not very certain if I were in his place, I would not do many things that my own judgment might not entirely approve. We are all creatures of circumstances to a greater or less extent, and are more or less controlled by the circumstances that surround us.

Take his Emancipation Proclamation, for example. It would be impossible for me to say that I think he had *a right* to issue such a document; he certainly had not, according to his own oft-repeated declarations before the war. And if he had no such power then, I do not see from what source he has derived the power since the war, especially in regard to the property of those citizens who have forfeited none of their rights under the Constitution; the argument is, that it is a military right growing out of the rebellion. If that be so, I must think it a very dangerous right, as I do not perceive any limit to its exercise, which depends solely on the will of the person who may happen to control the military power at the moment; and it is, to say the least of it, a vagrant, rambling, unsettled, and unfixed power, that would be very differently exercised by different persons that might be in a position to execute the power. One might limit it to personal property only; another to slaves that are of a mixed character, being both persons and property; another might extend it to real estate for life; another to real estate in fee; another to imprisonment, or imprisonment and fine; and another, still, to life itself. I confess I do not like these unwritten, unknown, and undefined laws, dependent alone on the arbitrary will of whomsoever might happen to fill the presidential chair for the moment, and who might be either a Washington or a Nero. And it is quite clear to my mind, that this power of confiscation was not intended by the framers of our government to be lodged in the hands of Congress and of the President at the same time, or that the power was to be divided. Now if Congress can confiscate the *real estate* of one in rebellion against his government, of which there can be no doubt, I think it clear they could also confiscate the slave property of the same party; and it seems to me to follow that, if the President can confiscate the slave property, he could, with equal propriety, confiscate the real estate. Yet we see the one power exercised by Congress, which is a denial of the power on the part of the President; while the other power is exercised by the President, which is a denial of the power of Congress; unless we can believe that it was designed to give the same powers and functions to each, which would be an anomaly in government that would reflect very little credit on the authors of our system. In other words, I think if it required an act of Congress to confiscate one species of property, to wit, real estate, it necessarily required the same authority to confiscate any other species of property.

But conceding that there was a military right, and a moral propriety in seizing upon and emancipating by proclamation the slave property of those in rebellion against the government, who had forfeited all claims to the protection of the Constitution, for I am not one of those who think a man may take a sword in his right hand and the Constitution in his left, and, after a vain effort to strike down the Constitution, thrust his left hand forward and claim the protection of the instrument he has renounced and endeavored to destroy; but, I say, conceding that there is a military right on the part of the President by *proclamation* to emancipate or confiscate (for, practically, it means the same thing) the slave property of one in rebellion against the government, and who has thus forfeited all right to the protection of the Constitution, it by no means follows that the right exists to take the slave or other property of the loyal citizen, who had forfeited none of his rights, and who stands exactly where and as he stood before the war. *Congress*, for example, does not claim the right to confiscate the real estate of *loyal citizens*, for confiscation only applies to traitors; how, then, could Congress, or rather the law-making power, which includes the President, confiscate the *personal property* of the loyal citizen? and if this could not be done by the President and Congress combined, how could it be done by the President alone? In one word, if the President had a right to take my slaves from me because Jeff. Davis and Co. had rebelled against the authorities of the United States, while to the full extent of my power and capacity I had resisted such rebellion, I do not see why he might not also take my lands and other property because General Lee and Co. had forfeited theirs. To my mind, therefore, it is clear that the confiscation of slaves should have been confined to those who were in actual rebellion against the government, and to those who, in the language of the Constitution, had given them aid and comfort, and that this confiscation of slave property should have been embraced in the act of confiscation, and not have been effected by a simple proclamation of the President. Nor do I perceive how that clause of the Constitution which forbids the seizure of private property for public uses without just compensation is to be gotten over, as far as loyal persons are concerned.

But waiving the question of right on the part of the President to confiscate by proclamation, I must think *that* a very badly constructed instrument which, by its terms, protected the property of Henry A. Wise, who has been for the last twelve years stirring up rebellion, and for the last three in open arms against the authorities of the United States, because he happened to live in the county of Princess Anne, which at that time was within Federal jurisdiction, and at the same time in terms confiscated the property of John M. Botts, a loyal citizen, because he happened to live in the county of Henrico (or Culpepper, to which I have since removed), which at that time was within the Confederate lines, but which is now within the jurisdiction of the Federal government. I think, therefore, it is quite clear that the question of property should have rested upon the loyalty of the citizen rather than upon his local habitation at the time.

Now I do not want to be misunderstood. Under this proclamation I have lost a good many of my most valuable servants, it is true, but I have never been one of those who estimated the value of the Union and institutions of our fathers (upon the preservation of which I religiously believe the happiness, welfare, and liberties of the people South as well as

O

North depend) by dollars and cents, nor yet by the bondage of the African race. And if the question between the life of the nation and the destruction of slavery has arisen, without one moment's hesitation I say, *Let the Nation live, and let slavery perish;* and if the balance of any *slaves, landed property, and all* should be necessary for the preservation of the institutions of the country in all their integrity, all I have to say is, *In the name of God, let it go;* though I confess I should have preferred a voluntary relinquishment of it myself to its forcible seizure by the government.

Nor am I one of those who confound cause with effect. If Mr. Lincoln had issued this proclamation, and it had been enforced before the war, then I have no hesitation in saying I would probably have been found in the midst of this revolution, because it would have constituted good ground for resistance, but instead of its having been the *cause,* it is simply the *effect* of the war. It is the consequence growing out of the most accursed, the most flagitious, the most stupendous, and the most atrocious crime that in my opinion has been committed since the day that Jesus Christ was crucified; and, being the consequence of secession, I charge the loss of my property to the secessionists, who are *wholly* and *solely* responsible for the war, and who created the necessity, if such necessity existed; and although I can not see the subject in that light, yet at such a crisis as this I will not quarrel about property until my own liberties and the liberties of the people are restored to that condition of security which we enjoyed before the rebellion.

By Divine law we *are all,* the good and the bad alike, made responsible for the original sin of that venerable old lady known as Madame Eve; and I do not know that it is any harder upon me that I should lose my property on account of the original sin of those with whom it has been my fortune to be mixed up geographically, than it is that I should be *damned* unless I make atonement for the original sin of that good woman for eating an apple six thousand years ago that I never saw, and do not know *certainly* if it ever grew, and, therefore, I shall make no factious opposition or quarrel with Mr. Lincoln about it—*at all events, not just now.* The best vindication for Mr. Lincoln's individual law at last may be, that it rests upon precisely the same principle as does the most important of all Divine laws.

As to Garrison, Parker, Beecher, Wendell Philips (who, by the way, is not only a mischievous but dangerous fanatic, as his ravings about dividing the lands of the South among the army and the negroes has no other effect than to furnish the Southern demagogues with material for keep-

ing up a frenzied excitement against the North), and all that class of extreme or radical men, they may properly be termed the *theoretical Abolitionists* of the country; while Jeff. Davis, William L. Yancey, Bob
Toombs, Frank Pickens, Henry A. Wise, James M. Mason, Bob Hunter,
James A. Seddon, John Slidell, and company, the great *architects of mischief and ruin*, have been the *practical Abolitionists*, who have done more in
three years for the abolition of slavery than the *theoretical Abolitionists*
could have done in three thousand; and it is to them, and to their inexcusable and blundering stupidity and folly, against which I have been
warring for thirty years, that I charge whatever I and others may have
lost in slave property. Did Heaven in its wrath ever raise up such a set
to delude, cheat, and destroy a sensible people before in the history of the
world? Has there been one promise or prophecy made to the people before the war that has been fulfilled since the war, or that is likely to be
fulfilled hereafter? Yes, there is one; and that was the prediction of Bob
Toombs, who foretold in the Senate of the United States "that the day
was not distant when he would be able to call the roll of his slaves at the
foot of Bunker Hill Monument." Verily, he blundered upon the truth,
provided he can get Mr. Lincoln to collect them together, and then grant
him permission to go to Bunker Hill Monument for the purpose of calling
the roll; from present indications, it is certain they will be more convenient to that point than they will be to his cotton estates in Georgia.

One word more upon the subject of the Emancipation Proclamation,
and I drop it. The emancipation of the slaves is, as it appears to me,
but the beginning of the end; the solution of the difficulty is yet to come,
and, I confess, it is far beyond my capacity to work out a satisfactory result. What is to become of the four millions of slaves that are to be set
free on this continent after the war is over? Will they be permitted to
spread themselves over the now free states, and bring their labor in competition with the free white labor of the country, and yet live in safety
and peace? I do not believe it. Will they be permitted to remain in
the Southern States in a state of freedom after those states shall have resumed their legislative rights as states in the Union? No man who
knows any thing of the wild spirit and temper of the Southern Democracy can dream of it? Can they be colonized in such numbers and sent
out of the country? It will be a most gigantic undertaking, and one that
is not likely to be realized in any remarkable time; and if it could be
done eventually, what is to be their condition until it is done? Between
you and myself, I venture to predict that the day will come when the lar-

ger portion of them will wish a thousand times over to be restored to their former condition. I do not say this in any political sense. I am not giving expression to my feelings, but to my judgment. As Mr. Willoughby Newton would say, " *These are the reflections and deductions of a retired political philosopher* ;" but as his predictions were so far from fulfillment, so may mine be also ; but I think not. According to his philosophy, Norfolk was at once, upon secession, to become the great emporium of a Southern empire, and Virginia would become the most powerful state in the world, and in twelve months her whole fortunes would be revolutionized. Well, I can not, in justice to Mr. Newton, deny this latter conclusion, but it is somewhat after the manner of Mr. Toombs's prediction about his slaves; this "retired philosopher" also predicted that the idea of a civil war, upon a dissolution of the Union, was a "chimera," but if there should be, that twelve intrepid Virginians would put it down. And it was such puerile nonsense as this that was listened to with admiration by a convention of bearded Democrats, and it was such arguments as these that carried Virginia out of the Union, as far as they could carry it, and brought such untold and unnumbered calamities on her people.

I have seen a great deal too, in the management of the war, that I do not approve, the proper solution of which I am not sure I did not see this very night in a speech delivered by a " *Miss Dickinson*" in the hall of the House of Representatives, in which she stated, in the presence of Mr. Lincoln, that at the beginning of the war, out of some two hundred and twenty odd officers appointed to the army, two hundred and seven of them were from the Democratic party. If this were so, no doubt a large number of them were of the Copperhead school, and that would account for a great deal that has occurred; but before I saw that statement I did not attribute the mismanagement so much to Mr. Lincoln as I did to others. You have had, in my judgment, a mistaken policy controlling the legislation of Congress, especially in retaining that feature in the Enrolment Act which authorizes the substitution of money for men, when it is men and not money that is required for closing up the war, which has already lasted much longer than it should have done.

There is another matter about which I think Mr. Lincoln has made two great mistakes, and those are to be found in his recent Amnesty Proclamation. First, he has set no limit to the time within which one in arms against the government may come in and claim the benefit of its provisions. As it stands now, they may continue in arms for one, two, three, or five years, if the war should last so long, and then, when at last overpowered, they may claim the benefit of the pardon. Secondly, I regret that those desiring to avail themselves of its benefits should have been required to swear to support the Emancipation Proclamation, simply because it can do no good, and will do harm; for whenever a man comes in to claim the benefit of the amnesty, and means to support the Constitution and the laws of the United States, he would mean to take the government as he found it, and would never think of offering resistance to the proclamation, while as it is, it furnishes a weapon in the hands of the leaders to excite the prejudices of the ignorant; and where one will come in under the proclamation as it is, three or, perhaps, five would have come if that portion of the oath had been left out; however, this is mere matter of opinion, but one in which I think I can not be mistaken.

Now, then, you have my opinion upon some of the main features of Mr. Lincoln's character and administration, and, upon the whole, I conclude that, in the language of the Book of Common Prayer, Mr. Lincoln "has done those things that he ought not to have done, and has left undone those things that he ought to have done;" yet that he is honest, patriotic, and indefatigable in what he conceives to be his duties, and in his efforts to bring the war to a speedy and successful issue; that he is entitled to the gratitude of the people of the North, and has established strong claims upon their confidence and support; and I think I hazard nothing in saying that if I had a vote it should be given to Mr. Lincoln in preference to any man that is likely to be brought out against him. And as for a Copperheaded Democrat, I would as soon think of voting for the bones of old John Brown, as they lay mouldering in the grave, as for one of those men whose primary object it is to restore to power that party which is responsible for all our troubles, as a condition for a restoration of the Union; and upon my soul, I religiously believe that if such a thing were probable as that the South could detach herself from the Union, having the North for a hostile neighbor, as they assuredly would, that the South would present a scene of impoverished, helpless misery, for which it would be difficult to find a parallel in any quarter of the globe where civilization exists, and that the country would become depopulated and abandoned. In five years there would be another exodus such as we read of in the Book of Books.

I have prepared for the press a history of this war for thirty years before it broke out, which I think, as the few friends who have seen it all think, is one of the most important and interesting documents that has appeared in our history. There is one thing that attaches peculiar value and interest to it, and that is, that there is no other person in the country that could write it who would write it. No Northern man knows what my political and social intercourse with Southern Democracy, and all the political events of the last thirty-five years in which I have taken an active part enables me to know. No man, I think, has kept a more complete record of events during that period than I have done; and there is no Southern Democrat who knows all that I know of their purposes and designs that would not, if he could, cover up and cancel what it is my desire and purpose to lay before the world. It has been ready since the fall of 1861, at which time it was written, but it can not be published, under the circumstances that surround me. I wait for a more propitious season; but if it ever sees the light, as I hope it will, it will startle those who have been duped and swindled as never were people duped and swindled before in any age or country; for then it will be seen that slavery had nothing to do with this war farther than that from the time of the adoption of the "twenty-first rule," at the instigation of Mr. Calhoun, it has been used as an instrument and a lever for the accomplishment of another purpose, which was the perpetuation of their own power under a Southern Confederacy whenever they found they could not retain it under the Federal government; but neither the extension of slavery, nor rights in the territories, nor fugitive slave laws, nor security of the property nor the interests of slavery were in any other sense involved in this controversy.

2d. It will be seen that at the time of the breaking out of the rebellion it was no part of the purpose of the leaders to dissolve the Union, or to strike for separation and Southern independence. So extensive had been their plan of operations during the administration of Mr. Buchanan, not only with the great body of leading Democrats in the North, who were pledged to come to their assistance, sustained as they were by the Secretaries of the Treasury, War, Navy, and Interior Departments, with a large number of officers of the army and navy, that they struck for higher game; and the purpose was to seize upon the capital of the nation, take possession of the archives of the government, get control of the treasury, army, navy, etc., and, in the language of Mr. President Davis, to "*make the North smell Southern powder and feel Southern steel,*" and in the language of Mr. Secretary Walker, on the night of the fall of Sumter, to "*float the flag of the Confederate government from the Capitol in Washington in thirty days;*" and the watchword was to have been, in the language of Mr. Vice-president Stephens, "*On to Washington!*" "*On to Washington!*" "*On to Washington!*" and of this plan of operations I myself informed Mr. Lincoln about the 8th or 10th of April, 1861 ; and this not only *was to have been*, but would have been the programme, but for the impetuosity of the leaders in the Virginia Convention, who through their agent, Mr. Roger A. Pryor, urged an immediate assault upon Fort Sumter, with the assurance that upon the firing of the first gun Virginia would go out. Before this assurance they acted ; but it so startled and excited the North that the leaders in that locality were paralyzed, and dared not come up to the work to which they were committed ; and thus was the war, which was originally designed to be carried on in the Northern States alone, transferred to the hearth-stones of those who had kindled the conflagration ; and if Mr. Lincoln's proclamation of the 15th of April, 1861, had been postponed for three days, a rebellion against the Virginia Convention and the authorities of the state would have commenced in Richmond ; but then the proclamation came just in the nick of time to afford the Union men in the Convention, who had already become thoroughly intimidated by the outside pressure of the mob—*a pretext* for passing the Ordinance of Secession. Oh, the history of this whole affair is rich and startling from beginning to end !

I see quite a struggle is going on in Washington and through the public press as to the status the states are to occupy after the war is over ; some contending that they must be held as territories, and that by the rebellion of the leaders and public authorities they have lost their character as states, and this it is proposed should be declared by law. We all know how territories may by law be converted into states, but the process of converting by law a state into a territory is a new problem that I confess I do not comprehend. I can understand how it is if John Letcher and Billy Smith (late and present governor), or the members of the Convention, with Congress and the State Legislature, all turn traitors, that *they* incur the forfeiture and penalties of treason, and thus alienate themselves from the government of the United States, but how they can by a violation of the law and the Constitution annihilate the existence of the state, and force the loyal men of the state out of the Union, I do not understand, nor can it, to my comprehension, be established, otherwise than by a recognition of the right of secession in its broadest sense. If Virginia is not now a member of the Union, when and how did she cease to be so ? The answer must be, on the 17th of April, 1861, and by the Ordinance of Secession ; then if it is acknowledged that she was no longer in the Union, it must be conceded that she had a right to go out. And it necessarily follows that there was no right on the part of the Federal government to enforce the laws in a state that did not form a part of the Union, and it would also follow that if the existence of the state was annihilated by an ordinance of secession passed by a convention representing a *minority of the people*, as was the case in this state, then it would not have been competent or legitimate for the people constituting a *majority of the state* to have called another convention, and to have repudiated the action of the first.

But, again, if Virginia ceased on the 17th of April, 1861, to be a state in the Union, then the citizens of the state ceased to owe allegiance to a government of which they did not constitute a part, how, then, could any citizen be convicted of treason that has since taken up arms against the United States? And what becomes of the Act of Confiscation? If the state is no longer in the Union, then this is a *foreign* and not a *civil* war, and there can be no confiscation of property, for confiscation applies only to traitors, and there can be no traitors and no confiscation where there can be no conviction for treason.

I conclude, therefore, that the revolted or rebellious states are still states in the Union, and are only struggling to get out, in accordance with the declaration that they would not remain in, and that they can not be out until they succeed in establishing by *arms* what they have declared upon paper.

Such arguments and deductions as those of Mr. Sumner and others are derived from the passions and not the judgments of those who use them; they involve the most important principles, and cover grounds that should be well and maturely considered before they are adopted.

I am very truly yours, JOHN M. BOTTS.

THE GILMER LETTER.

On the 12th of February, 1865, I received a letter from Hon. John A. Gilmer, then a member of the Confederate Congress from North Carolina, appealing to me in behalf of a number of the members of Congress to repair to Washington and endeavor to effect terms of peace on a basis suggested in his letter, to which I made the following reply:

Culpepper County, February 13, 1865.

Hon. JOHN A. GILMER:

MY DEAR SIR,—Owing to the snow-storm of the 7th, all mail communication with this county has been suspended until within the last two days, consequently your letter of the 6th did not reach me until yesterday.

I have given due attention to your several suggestions touching my going to Washington, your basis of terms for putting an end to the war, etc., and, with all due respect, I proceed to give you my views upon them, and to point out some of the obstacles in the way of their accomplishment that it seems to me must loom up with transparent light to every impartial and unprejudiced eye.

With respect to my going to Washington, it is only necessary to say, first, that I have no means of getting there, and secondly, that I have no authority or *pass* to go. But if I *were* to go, it could accomplish no good; first, because I could not recommend your plan of adjustment, looking to a separation of the South from the North, when there is not and never has been a *shade of doubt* resting on my mind that the very worst condition of things that could befall the South, and more especially the Border States of the South, would be a separation, with the North as a hostile neighbor, as she assuredly would be, which would lead to constant and never-ending warfare, and the necessity for regular standing armies, which, if we are to judge from the experience of the past, would be quite as destructive as the armies of the North. Calamitous and ruinous as this war has been, from my inmost soul I believe a separation from the North, with two peoples so immediately contiguous to each other, and with the bitterness of feeling that would be perpetuated under separate organizations, would prove to be even more ruinous and deplorable than the war itself has been, and *that* has left the Southern country little else than a general grave-yard or a desolate waste.

But if I could entertain other views upon this subject, and adopt those presented in your letter, I have no idea that they would receive a respectful consideration either from the administration of Mr. Lincoln or any portion of the people of the North, the whole mass of whom have become Abolitionized by the events of this war. Rely upon it, Mr. Gilmer, there is no peace party in the North that has ever lent a serious ear to the idea of separation; and all appearance to the contrary during the last year was nothing but a piece of political jugglery, adopted with the hope of restoring the Democracy to power. Whatever else may be done, there are two things that the North *can never afford to do.* The first is, to recognize secession and disunion, under any disguise; and the other is, to repudiate its public debt. No, sir; from the moment that our once glorious old Union Whig party "*refugeed,*" and kicked from under it the platform of its own erection, as a guide for presidential incumbents, to wit, "The *Union,* the *Constitution,* and the ENFORCEMENT OF THE LAWS," it was taken up as something worthy of preservation, and adopted with entire unanimity by all parties in the North, with a determination to maintain it in better faith than did those who first adopted it and then spat upon it at the dictation of the corrupt and profligate Democracy, who gave us timely notice that we *should* be *hitched on and dragged in* to the feast of ruin they were preparing for all in common; and so strong and universal has this sentiment of the *Union* and the *enforcement of the laws* become throughout the North, that you may rest assured that if Mr. Lin. coln were to entertain the proposition for a moment of recognizing a for. eign government that would run up to the banks of the Potomac, and within a mile of their capital, he would run great risk of being torn to pieces alive by men of all parties in the North. I speak of these things *as facts*, as I know them to exist.

I do not know what value may be attached to my opinions now, but certain it is that I have had no desire to obtrude them upon any one since this war broke out; for on more occasions than one, when they would have been of service to those with whom my own interests and happiness were entirely identified, they were repudiated and denounced. But your letter invites it, and I proceed to say :

From the day of the first battle of Manassas, if not from the time of the bombardment of Fort Sumter, I have regarded all compromises at an end; and that when the minority in the South madly broke up old com= promises and repudiated all new ones, and thus brought up the issue, whether the absolute control of the government should be exercised by the minority or majority, that the fate of the South was sealed; and I said so at the time, unless the people would discard their treacherous leaders and return to that spirit of conciliation which had controlled their fathers in the formation of the government. And as this has not been done, I have looked upon all attempts at negotiation as a useless con- sumption of time. I have, therefore, been satisfied from the first that there could be no peace but a *conquered peace;* that there could be no ne- gotiations but at the cannon's mouth; and that the only negotiators that could be recognized were those already appointed by their respective gov- ernments, General Grant and General Lee, and to their ultimate arbitra- ment all would be compelled to submit at last. How it is likely the mat- ter will be adjusted under their negotiations, your means of information are at least as good as mine, though possibly we may draw different con- clusions from the present and the past. Any other peace than such as I have described would be a delusion and a cheat, which would not last much longer than it would take to make it.

My opinions of the result of this war were formed long—very long before it commenced—and have been often laid before the public in a voice
of warning to avoid it, but they were of no avail; but those opinions have
never, under any success or defeat of either party, varied or wavered for
a single moment, and I have never doubted that the terms now offered,
of absolute and unconditional recognition of the authority of the Federal
government, and of the supremacy of its laws, could alone lead to peace;
and it appears to me that the only question to be determined is, whether
they should be accepted at once, or postponed until they are forced upon
you by still farther loss of life, sacrifice of property, and additional humiliation and defeat. As for all this villainous trash in the daily press, and
not unfrequently to be found in the halls of legislation, about *subjugation*,
Northern masters, and *Southern white slaves*, *spoliation* and distribution of
our lands among the foreigners and blacks in the army, which may serve
to keep up a war spirit and a feverish passion among a few who are deluded by it; and as for all the furor that certain officials may get up
among their followers in the city by their public harangues, let me assure
you that it has no effect upon the country, whose substance has been eat-
en up, and whose patriotism has subsided and given way to empty and
hungry stomachs. They are for peace, and will not stop to inquire into
terms whenever it is offered to them. The people have seen and know
that among the leaders of this rebellion there has been, from first to last,
nothing but miscalculation upon miscalculation, and blunder upon blunder, with every promise and prediction falsified, until they have lost all
confidence in their calculations, promises, and predictions, and they see
too many stragglers that are daily leaving the army with a determination
never to be taken back to it alive, not to know something of its absolute
demoralization and disorder.

· Believe me, Mr. Gilmer, when I tell you that the feeling of the people
is that the lives of their sons, brothers, and friends will be uselessly sacrificed by a farther prosecution of this war; and if the Confederate authorities do not believe it, let it be submitted to a fair and untrammeled vote
of the army and the people to decide it.

If the ruling men could see the matter in this light, then, in addition to
the blood that might be saved, they would find a strong incentive to an
early peace in the fact that, by prompt action in the Southern States,
they might yet defeat the Amendment to the Constitution in prohibition
of slavery. By a general vote in all the states, which can not be had
during the war, Virginia, North Carolina, South Carolina, Florida,· Geor-

gia, Alabama, Mississippi, Louisiana, Texas, and Kentucky might be carried against it, and thus defeat the measure; and if it had been made last fall, and the Southern States had been represented in Congress, two thirds of the two houses could not have been obtained in its favor. So far as I am personally concerned, I have become quite indifferent to its defeat. Through the instrumentality of the secessionists I have lost all my most valuable slaves. What remain to me are a great convenience, but dreadfully expensive, and very worthless, as far as their labor is concerned.

As to prolonging the war by arming the negroes to fight against their own race and their own kindred, who come to offer them immediate and unconditional freedom, to my mind it betrays a want of insight into the natural instincts of the human heart, as well as a degree of wild fanaticism and insanity that has had no parallel in modern times; even if they were willing to fight against what they have been taught to believe were their *rights* and interests, how will you manage to feed two hundred thousand negroes, with blockade-running suspended and rail communication with the more Southern States cut off, as it is sure to be, when you can barely make out to feed your present army, and then only by reducing the people to a state of starvation? If ever there was an occasion when the old Latin maxim of "*Quem deus vult,*" etc., could apply, I think it must be this. But did you ever see a *willing* negro worker with a short allowance of bread? If you have, your experience does not accord with mine. They can not and will not stand hunger and privation as the white soldier, who lives half his time on hope, and pride, and love of glory; and as sure as the experiment is made, just as sure will their arms be turned against you at the first opportunity that offers.

Moreover, mark what I tell you. If you put negroes in the field as soldiers, they must be put on equality with your white soldiers, for that is the condition of those they are expected to meet in the ranks of your opponents; and this will demoralize the army ten times more than it is already, and it will afford a pretext to thousands and thousands *who only want one to quit*, to lay down their arms and desert to the enemy, or return to their homes, upon the plea that they did not engage in this war to establish the equality of the negro or for the abolition of slavery, but against both; and if this had become a government of Abolitionists, it could have no claims upon them. Mark this well, I beg you.

And now, Mr. Gilmer, let me ask you to look this question full in the face as it really stands. It has been said that no man ever played the game of "*solitaire*" that did not cheat himself; and it appears to me that this game of war is like the game of "*solitaire*," at which every body has tried to cheat himself first, and then cheat his neighbors; it is time this was done with, and men looked at things as they really are.

Four years ago your Vice-president, Mr. Stephens, said in the Georgia Convention, "When we and our posterity shall see our lovely South desolated by the demon war, which this act of yours will inevitably invite and call forth, when our green fields of waving harvest shall be trodden down by the murderous soldiery and fiery car of war sweeping over our land, our temples of justice laid in ashes, all the horrors and desolation of war upon us, who but this Convention will be held responsible for it? And who but him who shall have given his vote for this unwise and ill-timed measure, as I honestly think and believe, shall be held to strict account for this suicidal act by the present generation, and probably cursed and execrated by posterity for all coming time for the wide and desolating ruin that will inevitably follow this act you now propose to perpetuate? Pause, I entreat you, and consider for a moment what reasons you can give that will even satisfy yourselves in calmer moments. What reasons can you give to your fellow-sufferers in the calamity it will bring upon us? What reasons can you give to the nations of the earth to justify it? They will be the calm and deliberate judges in the case, and what cause or overt act can you name or point to on which to rest the plea of justification? What right has the North assailed? What interest of the South has been invaded? What justice has been denied? And what claim, founded in justice and right, has been withheld? Can either of you to-day name one governmental act of wrong, deliberately and purposely done by the government at Washington, of which the South has a right to complain? I challenge the answer.

"Leaving out of view for the present the countless millions of dollars you must expend in a war with the North; with tens of thousands of your sons and brothers slain in battle, and offered up as sacrifices upon the altar of your ambition—and for what, we ask again? Is it for the overthrow of the American government, established by our common ancestry, cemented and built up by their sweat and blood, and founded on the broad principles of *right, justice,* and *humanity?* And, as such, I must declare here, as I have often done before, and which has been repeated by the greatest and wisest statesmen and patriots of this and other lands, that it is the best and freest government, the most equal in its rights, the most just in its decisions, the most lenient in its measures, and the most aspiring in its principles to elevate the race of men that the sun of Heaven ever shone upon. Now for you to attempt to overthrow such a government as this, under which we have lived for more than three quarters of a century, in which we have gained our wealth, our standing as a nation, our domestic safety, while the elements of peril are around us, with peace and tranquillity, accompanied with unbounded prosperity and rights unassailed, is the height of *madness, folly,* and *wickedness,* to which I can neither lend my sanction nor my vote."

Such was the language, and such the testimony of this high official, who was within three weeks from that time, and now is the Vice-president of the Southern Confederacy; and it was at such a time, and under such circumstances that the South entered upon this war against the United States, *then as now,* and *now as then,* the richest and most powerful nation on the face of the globe, and before which, as your own papers almost daily assure us, both France and England now stand trembling in their shoes.

Four years ago, then, the South commenced this war for the establishment of their independence, and for four years has it been carried on with alternate victory and defeat; but now, at the expiration of these four years, ask yourself the questions, first, What advances have been made toward the accomplishment of the end? *They* have invaded *your* territory, and *you* have invaded *theirs.* How many of their states have you taken, and how many of yours have they taken? What portion of their territory do you hold, and what portion of yours do they hold? How many of their native population have you killed or disabled, and how many of your native population have they killed or disabled? (Some idea of this may be formed from the fact that the vote at the Presidential election last fall was every where larger than it was in 1860 before the war, and that the vote of the entire Army of the Potomac was only some eighteen thousand, showing that an overwhelming proportion of that army is composed of unnaturalized foreigners and negroes.) How near a state of exhaustion are their materials for war, and how near are yours, when you have to rely upon arming the slaves to fight against those who come to set them free?

Draw this contrast, and then ask yourself the one other question, whether the Southern Confederacy is in a condition to prosecute this war to a successful issue with a government whose resources are scarcely half developed, notwithstanding what may have been said to the contrary? There has not been, and will not be a real anxiety for an *immediate peace* at the North until this whole slavery question can be forever settled. Your relations with the government of the United States at one time ought to enable you to know what its resources are when all its energies are put forth for their development, *which I know* (and for reasons that I could give you) have never yet been exercised. Now if, upon review of the actual situation, you can persuade yourselves that there is a reasonable prospect of ultimate success, then there may be some justification for a farther trial at arms; but if no such reasonable hope can be indulged, then, in my opinion, it is both wicked and criminal to prosecute the war any farther at the bidding of those men who would sacrifice what is left of the country to take the chance of saving themselves.

You must have observed one thing—that those men who would adopt a universal system of abolition have no slaves to set free; that those who would set fire to the cities on the approach of the enemy have no houses to burn; that those who would die in the last ditch, and live on roots and berries in the mountains, are the men who do not take their places in the ranks of the army; and those who would take all the cotton, tobacco, and gold in the country for the use of the government, have neither cotton, nor tobacco, nor gold to be taken; these are not the men who have the largest stake in the country, and are not the men who should control it; and, as far as Congress is concerned, they pass their conscript laws, their impressment bills, and levy their taxes, when a majority of that body not only have no constituencies upon whom their laws can operate, but who are not themselves subject to the provisions of their own laws, even to the payment of a tax that they unconstitutionally, fraudulently, and impudently impose upon others.

What conscript officers, what impressment agents, and what tax-gatherers have you in Missouri, Arkansas, Louisiana, Kentucky, Tennessee, Western Virginia, and other portions of the South? And what right have a body of refugees, who have neither constituents nor homes to which they dare go, to assemble in Richmond and keep us in an eternal war to save themselves from harm and find themselves a home at the public expense.

It is supposed that because the people are afraid to speak out that they do not grumble and complain of this, or that it has not weakened their confidence in the authorities by which they are oppressed? If so, let me assure you it is a woeful mistake.

I have written to you freely, and in a spirit of confidence and friendship, and marked it *private*, because I have no opinions for public use, which would only subject me to unmeasured denunciation and abuse by those who have every thing to gain and nothing to lose by a continuation of the war; but if I were a member of the Confederate Congress, these are the views I would enlarge and enforce, because I know they repre-sent the views and feelings of seven tenths of the people of this state, who think the experiment of separate independence is a failure, and has been carried quite far enough, but among whom are those who would be the first to cry out "*treason*" until they knew they were safe in proclaiming their true and honest sentiments—if there is any honesty left in them.

I am very respectfully and truly yours,

JOHN M. BOTTS.

THE CONGRESSIONAL TEST-OATH.

The oath required (by the Act of 1862) to be administered to all officers of the Federal government, but which is more generally known as the congressional test-oath, has given rise to a good deal of feeling in the South, and its constitutionality has been assailed with some bitterness, especially by those against whom it operates, and who are thereby disap-pointed in their confident anticipations of being able to slide *out* of office in one government *into* office under another, and, *like other weak vessels*, be kept "RIGHT SIDE UP WITH CARE" all the time.

In regard to this question a number of gentlemen of intelligence and respectability did me the honor to seek my views, which will be found in the following correspondence:

Charlottesville, September 5, 1865.

Hon. JOHN M. BOTTS:

DEAR SIR,—The undersigned voters of the county of Albemarle, sin-cerely desirous of being represented in the next Congress of the United States, naturally feel much anxiety as to the probable effect upon their chances of representation of the congressional test-oath.

We are not unmindful of the grave questions that may be raised as to the power of one Congress to bind another by the prescription of tests of membership, or the still higher question as to the right of that body to add to the constitutional tests of eligibility; but the crisis is one of too much moment to authorize us to trust our dearest rights and interests to a favorable solution of these problems, and we therefore deem it expedi-ent to seek for some explicit information in regard to them.

Confiding in your judgment of public affairs, and your facilities for a fuller knowledge of the probable course of events than we possess, we respectfully ask your opinion as to the chances of the repeal or relaxation of the existing test-oath in favor of Southern delegates.

We know full well that, in the peculiar circumstances of our case, inability to take the congressional oath may well consist with the most thorough loyalty; but this may not be enough for those who have our destiny in their hands, and we do not want to throw our votes away.

Very respectfully, your obedient servants,

W. H. Southall,	G. Peyton,
James H. Burnley,	Thomas Wood,
J. J. Bowcock,	Ira Garrett,
William T. Early,	C. H. Price,

T. W. Wood.

Auburn, near Brandy Station, September 12, 1865.

Gentlemen,—Your letter of the 5th was not received until the 8th, in which you ask my opinions on the several points therein contained touching the elections and qualifications of members to the next Congress.

The presence of a houseful of visitors, together with a correspondence with which I am literally overwhelmed, and which it would require half a dozen secretaries to keep up with, has, until this moment, put it out of my power to give you an answer. Each of the points presented, and all of which I have seen raised by one or more of the candidates who offer their services to the country, are, I think, not well taken, and are of plain, clear, and easy solution.

1st. As to the power of one Congress to bind another Congress by the prescription of tests of membership.

It is difficult to perceive under what strange delusion the idea could have arisen that one Congress could not bind a succeeding Congress by any law it might choose to pass until that law was either repealed by the succeeding Congress or pronounced unconstitutional by the proper judicial tribunals of the country. If Congress can not bind its successors, then we should have no laws beyond the period for which Congress was elected, and there would be an absence of all law until each was re-enacted by the succeeding Congress. And if this be true, which no man can deny, in what consists the difference between this and any other law? Even if it be admitted to be unconstitutional, still it is the law of the land until repealed or declared null and void by the tribunals constituted for that purpose. And the next question is, Is the act of July 2, 1862, requiring each member of Congress to take the oath therein prescribed before he shall be admitted to participate in the Legislature of the country, in violation of any provision of the Constitution? I think it is clearly, distinctly, and unquestionably within the constitutional power of Congress to require this oath to be administered to every member of the body.

It is not pretended that there is any provision of the Constitution in terms forbidding it; but it is *assumed* that, because the wise men of the last century who made the Constitution deemed it essential to require certain qualifications which should in no wise be overlooked or dispensed with, such as that no one should be permitted to participate in the Legislature of the country who was not of a certain age, and a citizen of the United States for a certain period, and an inhabitant of the state at the time of election, and who should be bound by oath or affirmation to support the Constitution, that therefore it was intended to forbid all who might come after them from availing themselves of the right to impose such other conditions and qualifications as the experience and wisdom of their successors might prove to be judicious and necessary; such is not my reading of the Constitution, such is not my judgment of the purposes of those great and wise men who were framing for us a form of government which they declared to be, and intended *should* be perpetual.

What is the language of the Constitution?

"The senators and representatives before mentioned, and the members of the State Legislatures, and all executive and judicial officers, both of the United States and the several states, shall be bound by oath or affirmation to support this Constitution; but no *religious* test-oath shall be required as a qualification to any public trust under the United States."

Here, then, is to be found the prohibition, and the only prohibition on the action of Congress—that no *religious test-oath* shall be required. If it had been intended that Congress should prescribe no other oath than that to support the Constitution, is it not patent to all men's minds that they would have said so in terms? The true reading of this provision, as it seems to me, is that Congress may prescribe such other qualifications as their wisdom and experience may hereafter suggest; but they shall not omit this one all-important oath to support the Constitution, and they shall not prescribe any *religious* test-oath for members of Congress and others.

Again, if this clause of the Constitution is construed as fixing the only qualification that can be required for members of Congress, it equally applies to the state executive, to all members of the State Legislature, and to all judicial officers in the states, for they are all embraced in the same clause, and the same provision is made for each; and as this is declared to be the supreme law of the land, any thing in the Constitution or laws of any state to the contrary notwithstanding, it would necessarily follow that no other qualification could be attached to any of the state officers enumerated; and if it is to be inferred that this was intended as a limitation on the power of Congress over the qualification of its members, it is equally to be inferred that it was a limitation on the powers of a state, either by law or Constitution, to impose any other qualification upon the legislative, executive, and judicial officers of the states. Where, then, did the framers of the State Constitution of 1830 derive the power to require that a senator or delegate should be of the ages, respectively, of thirty and twenty-five years, and an actual resident and *freeholder* of the district or county, etc., that they represented? And from what source did they derive the right to confer upon the Legislature the power to require any elected member to swear that he had not fought a duel, or sent or accepted a challenge to fight a duel, etc.? Where would the framers of any State Constitution get the power to limit the time of a judge to a certain age, and say he should not be capable of holding such office after he had reached the age of seventy?

But again, in another article of the Constitution, it is declared that " each House of Congress shall be the judge of the elections, returns, and qualifications of its own members"—that is to say, they may prescribe *when* and *how* they shall be elected, and what returns may be required, and what qualifications may be established, *except* that they may not be required to conform to any *religious* test-oath. But the power is also given to Congress to *expel* a member. If, then, the House can expel one that has already been admitted to his seat for accepting a bribe, for the commission of any infamous offense, for perjury, murder, arson, or treason, why may they not also *exclude from taking a seat* any who have been guilty of the same offense? And if certain parties labor under suspicion of having been guilty of bribery, perjury, murder, arson, or treason, why may they not be required to purge themselves of this suspicion before they are allowed to *take* a seat? It is ridiculous and absurd to say that a person having committed one or all of these offenses must first be admitted, and then on the moment, and at the instant, he may be expelled. The very fact that Congress is empowered by the Constitution to expel for cause establishes their right to affix a qualification or qualifications other than those already prescribed by the instrument itself, and it must be clear to all reflecting men that the same qualification for *holding* a seat may be prescribed for *taking* a seat in the first instance.

You next ask my opinion as to the chances of the repeal or relaxation of the test-oath in favor of Southern delegates, to which I respond, that I have seen or heard nothing that would lead me to suppose there was the *least possibility* either of its repeal or relaxation ; on the contrary, I have strong reason to believe that neither will be done, and that the oath is more likely to be made still more stringent than to be relaxed or modified.

1st. Because the next Congress is (as the term goes) more radical than the last.   2d. Because this is the first time that those states that have been in rebellion have sent their representatives to Congress, and a strong suspicion prevails in the North that, although the rebellion has been crushed and the South has been forced to yield to superior power, that the spirit of rebellion has not yet been subdued in the hearts of the leaders of the rebellion ; and again, because this suspicion and distrust will be vastly increased by the fact that so many disqualified persons are presenting themselves as candidates for Congress, who not only have no possible chance of obtaining a seat, but who openly avow upon the hustings that they can not and will not, if elected, comply with the laws of the United States ; and this distrust and suspicion must inevitably extend to the mass of the voters as well as to the leaders, if, after hearing these declarations on the part of the candidates, they shall be so imprudent and unwise as to cast their votes for them at the polls : that it will betray on the part of such voters, as it necessarily does on the part of the candidates, a spirit of resistance to the law, is beyond all question ; and all such votes, I *think*, will be disregarded and thrown away.   But the *election* of such men will necessarily be the means of postponing the restoration of the civil authorities of the state, and consequently of prolonging the military authority (which is now exercised over us) to an indefinite period.

If, then, my judgment and advice is of any weight in this state or elsewhere, I would urgently recommend that no man should be voted for who would hesitate to take the oath in good faith which the laws of his country require him to take.   Better for all in common that you should go unrepresented.   Better far to take the most ignorant men in your respective districts who can comply with the law than the wisest who can not ; and although it may be unpalatable to some that I should say so, yet, when so much is at stake for us all, I will not hesitate to say that it appears to me that nothing but *absolute thoughtlessness*, or an overweening, vaulting, and inordinate ambition, or an utter disregard of the best interests of the state, could induce any one who is conscious of his inability to take that oath to permit the use of his name for stirring up farther discord

and confusion among a people already worn out and ruined by the pernicious counsels of those who led them into the terrible scenes through
which the country has just passed. The South wants not only peace or
cessation of hostilities in the field, but she wants peace, order, harmony,
conciliation, and concord in her public councils. She wants unity of
feeling, unity of purpose, unity of action in her legislative halls, that she
may prepare for the work of complete restoration of the civil authority,
for the suppression of all discord and angry feeling, and for repairing the
heavy losses sustained—the fields laid waste, the dwellings destroyed, the
labor lost, the ruined fortunes, the blasted prospects of an abused, misled,
and misguided people; and surely this is not to be attained by perpetuating controversy, by resisting the laws, by inviting collisions between the
civil and military authorities of the country. I can conceive of nothing
more impolitic and unwise than to elect such persons at a time like this
for *experimenting*, or for the mere purpose of gratifying the vanity of those
who idly imagine that by their unsurpassed and heavenly-gifted eloquence
they can persuade the two houses of Congress that they have made asses
of themselves for the last four years.

Let such experiments be postponed to a more favorable and quiet
season, and let all such candidates be assured that the country can manage to get along without their *Godlike qualities* for the present. And to
suppose that Congress would at this time admit or patiently listen to one
of the signers of the " *second Declaration of Independence*" and declaration
of war against the United States, in the absence of which there could have
been no war, is little short of madness itself.

There is one other point that I desire to say a word upon, as I think
great misapprehension exists in relation to it. In a card of my friend,
Mr. Tim. Rives, of Prince George, now before me, he says :

"I can not take the above oath for the reason that I accepted the office
of captain in the Confederate service, and held a commission as such, and
exercised the functions thereof for a period of six months. You will thus
see, gentlemen, that, appreciating as I do this continued proof of your
confidence in me, I can not comply with your request and 'announce myself a candidate.'

"I will farther add that, if I could take the above oath and swear that
'I had voluntarily given *no aid, counsel, or encouragement* to any persons engaged in armed hostility thereto,' I should be ashamed to show my face
in the Second Congressional District, much less to ask the intelligent voters thereof for their suffrages. With the fact staring me in the face that

every man in the district from seventeen to fifty years of age, by the rigid law of conscription, has been compelled to engage in the carnival of death and blood which has been going on for the past four years—the wounded, the dead, and the dying daily before my eyes; the hungry and almost naked sons of the voters of the district in the trenches or on the march; to see every other man in the district, through the sympathy he has for his race, giving aid of some kind to relieve their sufferings, and I, with the callous heart of a fiend, stand unmoved at the tragedy before me; ·to see the fair mothers and daughters of the district, like good Samaritans, ministering to the wants, not of the 'wayfaring man,' but to the fathers, sons, and brothers of the district; some in the hospitals, wiping the clammy. sweat of death from the brow of the dying soldier, others bathing the ghastly wounds and moistening the parched lips of the suffering conscript, still I stand unmoved, and swear that I gave no 'aid, countenance, counsel, or encouragement' amid all this suffering! To see blankets, shoes, clothing, etc. daily sent to cover the almost naked soldiers in the trenches; to see the benevolent of heart sending daily their pittance of food to help out the short rations which the soldier is put upon; to see Christ's commandment carried out in all its beauty and benevolence, 'clothe the naked and feed the hungry,' still I stand ready to swear that I carried not a drop of water on the tip of my finger to cool their parched lips! And for *this* reason I come and ask you for your suffrages, and you vote for me, not for any merit that is in me, but *because I can take the oath,* and by the grace of somebody else take my seat and hold it!"

As this erroneous or false construction and special pleading of Mr. Rives may mislead others, I may stand excused, I hope, for availing myself of this occasion to answer it. Others, too, have taken very much the same ground—that, having fed Confederate soldiers, or clothed their own sons in the service, they could not conscientiously take the necessary oath. I apprehend it will be found generally that those who take this ground have some other reason for not taking the oath, for if that be a fair construction of its meaning, then I freely admit that the South will have to go without representation in Congress until this oath is modified; but I think it bears no such construction; it is a false construction of what was intended and of what the language of the oath imports.

To clothe or feed a son in the army, which you would have to do if not in the army, to nurse the sick, to feed the hungry, to administer to the suffering of the individual man, is not to aid the rebellion, for if it did in the sense here indicated, there is perhaps no man in the South who is not a traitor; and there were few officers or men in the United States armies who were not also traitors to their country, for they nursed the wounded and the sick, relieved their suffering, and fed their enemies; and who but a brute would not help a fallen foe? And does any one suppose that a civilized and enlightened people would regard it as treason to hold a refreshing glass to the parched lips of a wounded soldier whom he himself has just laid prostrate at his feet? And the government of the United States too, under this interpretation, has been a traitor to itself; for who fed so many as *Mr. Lincoln?* Who nursed so many of the sick and wounded as Mr. Lincoln? Who clothed so many as Mr. Lincoln, and then restored them to the ranks of the Confederate army; and yet, could not he take this oath? If to give food to the hungry or nurse the wounded and sick was an offense, so it was equally a crime ,to give a glass of water to the thirsty; and if this constituted treason, I confess myself as among the most culpable of traitors; for all this have I done. I have probably fed to a greater extent than any one man in the Confederacy (only because they were around me all the time); but God knows as well as I that it was never done with a view to help the rebellion, for which I *never*, for the first moment, had the least particle of sympathy or respect. I did sympathize with my misguided, deluded, cheated, betrayed countrymen, but *never* did I have the least sympathy for the rebellion or its authors.

If this was the only difficulty in the way of my friend, Mr. Rives, I think he would manage to swallow the oath; but, unfortunately, there is the other difficulty of his having accepted the commission of captain in the Confederate service, under which he could not take the oath; and I regret it deeply and sincerely, for I believe he was in his heart all the time a Union man; and although we have always differed in politics, I believe he is an honest, fearless, patriotic man in every sense and in all relations but this, in which he made, as I think, a great mistake; and believing in his entire loyalty *now*, I should be highly gratified to see him in the public councils at this time if it were not that he can not conscientiously comply with the laws of his country; and I commend his example, in withholding the use of his name for the purpose of stirring up more discord and trouble in the land, as one worthy of imitation by others who are in the same situation. .

I am, with great respect, your obedient servant, JOHN M. BOTTS.

To W. H. Southall, James H. Burnley, J. W. Bowcock, William T. Early, G. Peyton, Thomas Wood, Ira Garrett, C. H. Price, and T. W. Woods, Esqs.

Auburn, near Brandy Station, September 26, 1865.

My dear Sir,—Your letter of the 22d instant was received yesterday, and I have given to the views you present that careful consideration which your opinions always command from me, and to my mind it appears that if we do not entirely agree, it is a distinction without a difference.

You claim for Congress all the power that I claim; but you put it on the ground of a "general legislative function" and an "inherent power of Congress to defend itself against disloyalty in the service of the government;" and in doing this, I think, you surrender the whole question, for how can this general legislative function, this inherent right to pass a law which creates an additional qualification for members of Congress be defended, unless it is in pursuance of the provisions of the Constitution? And if its constitutionality is conceded, from what clause can it be more clearly derived than from that to which I have traced it? If the same power can be derived from any other clause, it only serves to strengthen my position.

You first deny the power of Congress to prescribe any additional qualification to those already enumerated in the Constitution, and then you claim for Congress the power to prescribe this particular test-oath, which you admit, and which does, beyond doubt, *create* an additional qualification.

Now I might content myself with asking you "What is the difference between the power of Congress to prescribe an additional qualification and the power to pass a law the effect of which is to create this qualification? *Or*, if you prefer it, what is the difference between a law that is designed to produce a certain effect and one by which the same effect is produced? The first maxim we were taught in mathematics in our school-boy days *was*, that 'things equal to the same are equal to one another.'"

But I want to vindicate my own position with you, and will not be content with your solution of this problem, and therefore I proceed.

You and Mr. Stuart (in his card) both seem to dread the abuse of this power of Congress over the qualification of its members. Undoubtedly this, like all other powers, may be liable to abuse, but less so, perhaps, than almost any other, for the reason that it operates equally upon themselves as upon their successors; but its liability to abuse is no argument against its legitimate exercise. There are but few if any powers conferred upon the executive branch of the government that have not been abused—especially the veto power and the power of appointment *to* and removal *from* office have been grossly abused; but it can not for that reason be argued that the veto power and the power to appoint and remove for cause have not been conferred upon the President, although not a word is said in the Constitution about the power of *removal*. It is a derivative power, and one derived from the power to appoint; as is this a derivative power, derived from the powers to which I have already called attention. Now if the framers of the Constitution meant to say that no other oath should *ever* be required, why didn't they say so? Why did they confine their prohibition to this one specific religious test-oath? In short, all power is liable to abuse, whether lodged with the executive, legislative, or judicial department of the government, and each, in turn, has abused its power.

If the Constitution had said, as our State Constitution reads, "Any person who has attained the age of twenty-five, has been a citizen for seven years," etc., etc., shall be entitled or qualified to serve as a representative in Congress, then I might agree with you that the qualification was fixed and unalterable. But such is not the reading of the Constitution; it deals in the negative, and not the affirmative qualifications. It says: "No person shall be a representative without certain specified qualifications, which are deemed all-important, and shall, under no circumstances, be dispensed with." Then in another part of the Constitution one other indispensable requisite is prescribed, to wit, that the representative shall be sworn to support the Constitution, but *no religious test-oath* shall *ever* be required. Shall ever be required by whom and how? By Congress, and by law, of course. But is not this equivalent to saying that, if hereafter it shall be found necessary and proper, Congress may by law require any other than a religious test-oath, especially, too, when it is provided that Congress shall have power "to make all laws which may be necessary and proper for carrying into execution the foregoing power, and all other powers vested by this Constitution in the government of the United States, or in any department or officer thereof?" And can there be any thing more necessary and proper in conducting the government than that there should be wise, judicious, *patriotic*, and *loyal* legislation, and an honest and faithful execution of the laws?

The only qualification prescribed by the Constitution for a judge of the Supreme Court, and consequently for chief-justice, is that he shall take an oath to support the Constitution. Now suppose some beast of a President, with a demoralized Senate at his heels, should nominate for chief-justice an ignorant tool as a reward for his partisan services, or some political prostitute who had been convicted of bribery, perjury, or other infamous

P

offense, or an alien, ignorant of our laws, customs, and language, or a popular military commander who had no knowledge of law, or in any other way *the necessity had arisen* or was likely to arise, do you think it would violate either the letter or the spirit of the Constitution if Congress were to add to this oath to support the Constitution such other qualifications as that he should be of a certain age, that he should have studied and obtained a license to practice law, that he had never been convicted of an infamous offense, and that he should be a *white man*, and a citizen of the United States; and if they could thus add to the constitutional qualifications of a judge, why not to those of a member of Congress?

"Each house shall be the judge of the elections, returns, and qualifications of its members." I can not concur in your interpretation of this clause, that it was *only* intended to interdict mandamus, etc. That this was one object I do not doubt, but not the only one. Nor does it follow, as you suppose, that by my construction one house might prescribe one set of qualifications, and the other another.

I think this clause was intended to apply to the qualifications as provided by the Constitution, or such as might at a future day be prescribed or required by law, and not that each house might establish qualifications for itself, but that each should judge for itself whether its members possessed the qualifications and came up to the requirements of the Constitution and the law. At the time of the adoption of the Constitution negroes were nowhere and by nobody recognized as citizens of the United States; therefore to require that the President, Vice-president, members of Congress, etc., should be citizens of the United States, was equivalent to requiring that none but *white persons* should be capable of filling these offices. But now this whole matter has been changed. Negroes have been made citizens, and the right to vote and to represent has been claimed for them; and already a colored lawyer has been admitted to practice in the Supreme Court. Now let me ask you if you think it would conflict with the terms of the Constitution, or with the purposes of its framers, if Congress were to provide by law that no one of African descent should be capable of filling these high offices? Or do you think our institutions would be endangered thereby? But can any thing be more absurd than the pretensions set up, that while these men have forfeited their lives to the requirements of the Constitution and law, that, nevertheless, the same Constitution has secured to them an inalienable and indestructible right to legislate for the country they had for four years *labored and fought* to destroy?

You can not infer from my letter to the gentlemen in Albemarle who did me the honor to seek my opinions that I intended to deny the power of each state to fix the qualifications of its own officers, in addition to the one prescribed by the Constitution of the United States. On the contrary, my purpose was to show that they *had such power*, and that it had never been disputed; but my argument was, that as this clause did not operate as a limitation to the power of the state except as to the religious test-oath, so in like manner it did not operate as a limitation to the power of Congress to add to as circumstances might require, but not to depart from the qualifications therein prescribed.

I am sorry there should be any difference between us on this point, but, as I have already said, it is more in the use of terms than in substance, and I care very little for the use of terms provided I get the substance.

May I not, then, ask you to review your own argument, and tell me why more apprehension should be felt for the safety of our institutions because the law-making power is intrusted with the right to add to the qualifications of the members of Congress, and to throw additional safeguards around the legislation of the country, than they are from the power to raise armies, make war, regulate commerce, impose taxes, and enforce the laws by arms if necessary; and, when you have done this, I will take much pleasure in reviewing my own arguments, and recanting my opinions if convinced of my error.

I am ever faithfully and truly yours,   JOHN M. BOTTS.

PRESIDENT JOHNSON'S POLICY OF RECONSTRUCTION.

When Mr. Johnson's policy of reconstruction was first announced, I thought he committed a mistake in not calling Congress together, that the *law-making power* might act harmoniously together, and because I believed that reconstruction could not be valid and complete without the sanction of the Senate, House, and President; nevertheless, it was not for me to cavil about it while all others seemed to acquiesce.

That policy, as I then understood it, was to extend pardon to the least culpable of the rebels, and to make " *treason odious*" by some judicious system of punishment for the more wicked and guilty offenders, and especially that all political power was to be withheld from those who had shown themselves so unfaithful to their obligations of duty, and so unfit and unworthy to be trusted again.

Under these circumstances, and with this understanding, I labored for months in efforts to restore harmony to the distracted South, in procuring release of prisoners, and in obtaining pardons for the least undeserving, but by what I have always believed to be gross deceptions practiced on the President. I found that through the use of money paid to pardon. brokers and feed attorneys, aided by the influence of subordinates in the employment of the administration, pardons were more readily procured for the most vindictive and obnoxious traitors, than for those who had sinned the least but had no money wherewith to purchase a release. I found these same pardoned rebels flaunting their pardons in the faces of those whose generosity or misplaced confidence had recommended them, and assuming a superiority over those to whom they had in humility appealed for aid. I saw men in the State of Virginia, upon whom the Constitution itself had set its seal of condemnation and declared unworthy of holding office, rushing with impetuous haste into the legislative halls in utter disregard of its plainest provisions, trampling under foot the constitutional oath prescribed, and then and there exercising dictatorial and tyrannical power by hurling headlong from office better men than themselves, who had been released by the governor of the commonwealth for their loyalty to the government of the United States, and substituting for them those only who had given evidence of their loyalty to the rebellion. I saw them in the social as well as the political circles availing themselves of their superior numbers, assigning all loyal men and women to a position of absolute inferiority, and demanding for themselves, as if by Divine right, the favor to control and rule with an iron rod. I saw them educating the masses of the people to look upon every demonstration of loyalty, either during or since the war, as degrading and infamous, until the interposition of the national authorities was found necessary to set aside elections of public officers known to have been selected for their services to the rebellious government; to suspend the publication of various papers published through the state for their obnoxious and disloyal sentiments scattered among the people. All this I saw from men who but yesterday were sworn citizens of another government, warring against the government of the United States, and struggling to overthrow the great Republican Empire of the world; and I thought the time had arrived when the *law* should be appealed to, and justice should be enforced upon a people who in the beginning had forsworn their obligations, treacherously and sacrilegiously abandoned their posts of duty, and in the end were insensible to the mercy that had been extended to them, oblivious to all marks of kindness, and were still bent on mischief to the country, and ruin to all who did not tamely submit to their outrageous oppressions and to their despotic demands.

It was under these circumstances that I prepared the following suggestions, in the form of political axioms, for the public press, that the national authorities might be recalled to the great duties they had to perform for the future peace and safety of the republic, and for the permanent security of the rights of loyalty, which I am happy to say have not been without effect.

MR. BOTTS'S AXIOMS.

A few plain political axioms that can not be successfully disputed or denied, and which serve to solve the perplexed problem of the status of the states and the people of the states lately in rebellion against the authority of the United States :

1st. The right of secession is not only not authorized, but is expressly forbidden by the Constitution of the United States.

2d. It follows, that all ordinances of secession adopted by the states lately in rebellion were null and void in law.

3d. That the allegiance of the citizen is due to his state, and that there are thirty-six different allegiances in the United States, and not one man owing allegiance to the great central government, which is supreme over all, is a proposition too absurd to be argued.

4th. From which it results that no state has been out of the Union, and could not be carried out otherwise than by successful revolution ; and to admit that any of the rebellious states are or have been out of the Union, would necessarily amount to an admission that the Union had been dissolved, and that we had been engaged in a foreign and not a civil war ; all of which would materially impair the virtue and efficacy of that instrument, which is recognized and claimed as the supreme law of the land.

5th. But while no body of men, however constituted, could take a state out of the Union except by force of arms, yet any attempt to do so by those owing allegiance to the United States assuredly constituted the great crime of high treason, if any such crime still exists under our institutions.

6th. The right of expatriation or denationalization, however, has never been denied to the people of this country ; and while they could not take a state out of the Union, it can not be denied that the citizens of the rebellious states could take themselves out at pleasure, either individually or collectively.

7th. Nor can it be disputed that the late so-called Confederate States did for four years constitute a government "*de facto;*" and it follows that all those who assisted in creating that *de facto* government, by voting in convention for an ordinance of secession or signing the same, or who voluntarily took the oath of allegiance to or held office, civil or military, under the said "*de facto*" government, which offices could only be held by *citizens* of a government then hostile to and at war with the United States, thereby alienated themselves from the government of the United States, and, by thus renouncing their allegiance, disclaimed all pretensions to its protection, and are therefore *aliens* to this government, and can only be restored to the rights of citizenship through the established laws of naturalization, or by a special act of legislation.

8th. There can be no difference in law or in fact in the political status of those Southern persons who have taken the oath of allegiance to the "*de facto*" government of the so-called Emperor Maximilian, and those who have taken a similar oath, or otherwise made themselves citizens of the "*de facto*" government of the so-called President Davis.

9th. These being the natural, lawful, and unavoidable consequences of secession, alienation, and treason, it follows that the functions of government in those states lately in rebellion have been suspended by the unconstitutional action of those temporarily in authority in those states; and that these state governments can only be restored through the action of the *law-making power* of the United States; and upon the suppression of the rebellion and the restoration of peace, the right to govern and control these states naturally, constitutionally, and inherently devolves on the loyal citizens thereof, who have fallen heirs to the estate, and who can not lawfully be subjected to the power and control of alien enemies to them and to the country; and that these loyal citizens have also a natural, constitutional, and inherent right, under the sanction of said law-making power, to resume their original position in the government and councils of the nation; and, therefore, all representatives to Congress who present themselves with the proper evidence of election, and who are prepared, honestly and in good faith, to comply with the Constitution and laws of the United States, should be admitted without unnecessary delay to a participation in the legislation of the nation; and to withhold this right is to place the *loyal* on the same platform with the *disloyal*—the friends on a footing with the enemies of the country. .

10th. The President is clothed with the power to grant reprieves and pardons to those who have committed offenses against the United States; but as none are *legally* offenders, and as no man in this country can be legally punished for any offense, no matter how atrocious or aggravated the crime, until he has been tried and convicted of the offense with which he stands charged, so no reprieve or pardon (the exercise of which powers commence simultaneously) can be constitutionally granted before the party or parties have been tried and convicted according to law; and, therefore, all pardons heretofore granted to those lately in rebellion have been premature, and are null and void.

11th. It is patent to observing men that all attempts at reconstruction in many of the states, through the misplaced confidence and unappreciated kindness and magnanimity of the President, through the action of those who have occupied the relations of alien enemies to the United States, have not only failed in their anticipated effects, but are in many respects unsafe as a precedent, pernicious in their results, dangerous to our institutions, and should be commenced " *de novo*."

12th. Therefore, in all such states as have not, in the opinion of the law-making power, been finally reconstructed, it will be right and proper that a military or provisional governor of loyal antecedents should be appointed (except for the State of Virginia), with instructions to call a convention, to be composed of loyal men only, to be elected by those who are authorized to vote by their existing State Constitutions.

13th. The State of Virginia, although a large majority of her people were in rebellion, has been continuously and without interruption, through the action of a portion of her loyal citizens, recognized as a state government by every department of the government of the United States; with a governor regularly elected under the Constitution of 1851; with her representatives admitted to seats in each branch of Congress during the rebellion, she therefore stands in a different relation to the government from those States that have disclaimed all right to such representation, and that have had provisional governors since the war appointed by the President.

14th. But inasmuch as the Constitution of Virginia, now in operation, declares that the House of Delegates shall consist of *not less* than eighty, nor more than one hundred and four members, and the Senate shall *never be less* than one fourth that number; and inasmuch as the first Legislature that assembled under that provision of the Constitution consisted of only fourteen in one house and six in the other, and as the present Legislature now in session at Richmond was authorized and convened by the said "*town council*" (as it has been aptly termed in the Senate of the United States), which possessed no such authority; and as the present Legislature is composed, in a large part, of those who were expressly forbidden by the

Constitution under which they profess to act to hold any office whatever; and inasmuch as such Constitution imperatively requires an oath to be administered to each one before he shall be qualified to serve as a member of the Legislature, which oath has never been administered to any one member of the body, but has been totally disregarded and set aside; and inasmuch as they have proceeded without authority to remove all disabilities imposed upon themselves by the Constitution, and have at the same time endeavored, by their legislative action, to make treason a virtue to be rewarded, and loyalty to the United States a crime to be punished, by removing from office every loyal citizen whom they could reach, and substituting in their stead those who have figured conspicuously in the rebel service, and who are disqualified by the Constitution from holding the offices which they have been selected to fill; therefore, it is clear that there has been no constitutionally organized legislative body in Virginia since their present Constitution was adopted in the year 1864, and that, by necessary consequence, all acts, and parts of acts, resolutions, elections, appointments, and other proceedings adopted by either of the bodies styling themselves "The Legislature of Virginia" since the adoption of the Alexandria Constitution, have been in violation of the plainest provisional requirements of that Constitution, and are absolutely null and void, and of no effect.

15th. In this condition of things it is imperatively necessary that the restoration of that state to its national rights should be commenced "*de novo*" by the call of a Legislature by the governor of the state, to be composed of *loyal men only*, under such restrictions upon the eligibility to office as the Constitution provides, and under such enlargement of the qualification of suffrage as the military authorities may prescribe (that state being still under military control), as will render an election practicable.

THE GARNETT LETTERS—THE FIRST LETTER.

The following letter will explain itself. It was addressed to a gentleman that I knew to be a warm personal friend, and I had supposed sympathized in all my political views, but in this it seems I was mistaken. Whether the fault was mine or his, it is not proper here to inquire; but I addressed the letter to him through the public prints—having first asked his permission to do so—in reply to one just received from him.

This letter was intended as an explanation of the above axioms, and as illustrative of my views of the political sentiment and condition of Virginia at the time.

Alexandria, Va., February 16, 1866.

MUSCOE GARNETT, Esq. :

DEAR SIR,—Your letter reached me last night, in which you say, "The report of the proceedings of the Alexandria meeting has been published here, and is doing you serious injury; the committee appointed to wait upon you reported that suffering from neuralgia prevented you addressing the meeting, and that you declined doing so with *thanks*, leaving it to be inferred that, if well, you would have accepted the invitation, and that you approved the object of the meeting. This has inspirited your enemies and dispirited your friends to a degree you can scarcely imagine. Your letter to me says you disapproved of the movement, but I am not authorized to publish it; it is due to yourself and your many warm friends that you should clearly define your position. We can elect you to the Senate before the adjournment, with this difficulty removed; let it rest as it is, and there is no chance."

You will excuse me, my good friend, for saying that no man, in my opinion, ever had a body of as many warm friends as I know, and *gratefully know*, I have, who was so frequently called upon to defend himself *before them* for every idle and ridiculous conjecture that his enemies might whisper to his disadvantage. Let me state the facts of the case: I arrived here on that afternoon without the slightest knowledge that such a meeting was in contemplation; during the evening the committee appointed for that purpose called, and extended the invitation to attend the meeting and address them, to which I replied, "Why, gentlemen, it would be impossible for me to address the meeting without making myself an unacceptable guest, as I do not concur with you in your views. I am inflexibly opposed to your whole scheme. I can not admit that there is any power in Congress to reduce a state to the condition of a territory; the Constitution provides for making a state out of a territory, but it nowhere provides for reducing a state to a territory." They then asked me if they should give *that* as my reply to the meeting. I said, "Oh no; that might be regarded as discourteous to the meeting; make some excuse for me: say I have the neuralgia, and am afraid to venture out," and I might have added, return them my thanks for the compliment. If I *did not*, I *should* have done it; common civility required it, and I am obliged to the committee for supplying the omission if I did not; but it never entered into my mind that this most innocent occurrence would involve me in so much trouble with my friends elsewhere; but that to decline an invitation to address a meeting, with "*thanks*" for

P 2

the compliment extended, would justify the inference that I was neces_
sarily in sympathy with the views and political purposes of the meeting, is
just one inch and a half beyond the extent of my comprehension!

It was but the last month that I declined an invitation from the Tam_
many (Democratic) Society of New York to dine with them, and I expressed to them, in more than ordinarily strong terms, my thanks for
the invitation; but I have never heard of any Democratic enemy whis_
pering the apprehension that I was, therefore, in sympathy with the De_
mocracy, and was about to join that party. Moreover, it was *known* to
at least thirty or forty of my friends in the two houses that I was entirely opposed to the objects and purposes of the Alexandria meeting, for
they had heard me express that opposition only ten days before while I
was on a visit to Richmond, and, without any publication from me, they
could have made that fact known to every man in both houses in thirty
minutes by the watch. The only question connected with territories in
which I felt any interest was that General "*Terry*" should be left to
manage the "*Tories*" in Richmond according to their respective merits.

If the record of my life should hereafter be deemed worthy of a chapter in history, it would contribute a singular paragraph that would read
thus: The Legislature of his state was just about to elect him to a seat in
the Senate of the United States, but it unfortunately happened that just
at that time a meeting of his fellow-citizens invited him to address them,
which he respectfully declined, with his "thanks" to the meeting for the
compliment, which was deemed so offensive to his friends that they abandoned the idea.

But you say, "It is due to myself and my many warm friends that I
should clearly define my position." If I could live to the age of " Me-
thuselah," when would the necessity cease for defining my position? I
see other public men pass through a long life of public service without
ever once being called on by their *friends* to define *their position*, and
when their enemies take them to task, and hold them up to public censure, their friends are never backward in coming to their defense and defining it for them. Not so with me and my friends; they have always
lent a too ready ear to the tales of our common enemies. Is this because
I have been a doubtful man—one who halted and hesitated, waiting to
catch the popular breeze before I took my position, and who, having taken
it, was not to be relied upon for holding and maintaining it? I do not
think the record of my life would justify this lack of confidence on the
part of my friends. I believe my worst enemies entertain no such opinion
of me.

But my views have been quite fully expressed in a publication which I had the honor to inclose to you and other friends, headed, " A Few Plain Political Axioms," etc., upon the present condition of men and things in the South, and in Virginia in particular, and now let me define my positions on the points involved in that document without waiting to be called on for it.

If there was a man in the South, except those who stood in fear of the consequences of their treason, that desired more earnestly than others the restoration of the states, with all their former power and grandeur, to commence the laborious task of reconstructing their dilapidated fortunes, and that the misguided men who had forfeited their lives and their property to the government by the commission of the highest crime known to the laws of the nations of the world should be restored to rights which they had forfeited, and to which before they received their pardons they set up no pretensions to—I say if any one man in the South desired this as much, or more than any other, I might set up a strong claim to being that man ; and I certainly do claim to have spent more time, labor, and money in procuring pardons, and in getting prisoners released, than any other one man who did not receive any compensation for his services, and *that* I never did, even to the payment of my expenses, or any part thereof ; and after I found that the most obnoxious had, through the power of the purse, obtained their pardons, I urged, again and again, a general and universal amnesty.

At the earnest entreaty of his almost broken-hearted wife, I visited Washington three times to procure the release of Mr. Seddon from his confinement; that he might be restored to his family on parole for the recovery of his health ; and what of justice, not to say of thanks, have I received from his party friends ?

Notwithstanding the views set forth, in the political axioms I have introduced were those that my best judgment commended from the first as the only true and lawful mode of the settlement of the various questions involved, yet I held them back from an anxiety to co-operate with Mr. Johnson in good faith in *his* plan of reconstruction; if the pardons were not issued or granted under constitutional authority, I was willing to acquiesce in them ; if those who had been engaged in rebellion, and had become citizens of another government "*de facto*," were to be recognized as citizens of the United States, I was content not to complain ; and if this and the preceding so-called legislative bodies under the Alexandria Constitution were to be regarded by others as lawfully constituted or constitutionally organized, I was willing, with others, to overlook all irregularities and informalities in *non-essentials;* but all this I acquiesced in, because I *hoped* that the pardoned secessionists would display a degree of gratitude and generosity in harmony with their apparent humility, in return for the forbearance and generosity with which they had been received by the men whom they would have driven from the state, or executed in a summary manner, if they had been successful in overthrowing the government; but this hope has been far from realization.

I believe if there was any one thing intended by the people at their last elections to be more emphatically expressed than another, it was that the conduct of the government should be taken out of the hands of those by whom they had been so woefully deceived, and place the state in conservative hands; and I believe, moreover, that you have had all the winter a majority in the two branches, but especially in the lower House, a clear majority of members ready to carry out the will of the people, but, for the want of organization, concert of action, and a bold, intrepid leader, the advantage of that majority has been thrown away. In all political organizations a good leader is just as important as a good general in the field; yet, with this strength in the body, we have seen it led by a few flippant lawyers and practiced Parliamentarians, to the infinite injury of the state and disappointment of the people.

. If there has been the first indication of loyalty, forbearance, or generosity manifested either by the press or by those who have thrust themselves into high places forbidden by the Constitution, beyond what might well be called "*lip service,*" I have failed to perceive it. On the contrary, I have seen Union men who had been appointed to offices by Governor Pierpont, whose power has been reduced, as our friends the Yankees would say, "to the *leetle* end of nothing whittled down to a point," to serve them, and who is now treated with scorn and contempt, not to use harsher terms, by those for whom he has made this sacrifice—I say I have seen the men who filled their offices respectably and responsibly brought out, one by one, day after day, for the keen whetted knife of the secession guillotine, to be decapitated as fast as they could be brought to the block, and their places supplied from the secession ranks in every instance, and generally by men less qualified than those removed, while Mr. Taylor, the auditor, a secessionist, and one of Governor Pierpont's appointees, was unanimously confirmed in his place.

I have seen that so-called legislative body, as if in derision and contempt of the Constitution, and in the absence of all proper respect for public opinion, and for the authorities in whose power the state is still held, and as if to provoke the resentment of that power, and to drive all conservative men in Congress into the ranks of what is called the Radical party, and thus to retard restoration or reconstruction, to the great injury of the whole state and of the South, and as if in derision, contempt, and defiance of the civil and military authorities, that the best interests of all required should be conciliated and harmonized—I have seen that body in the first stage of their organization select a gentleman (well qualified in all other respects, no doubt) as their presiding officer, who was, perhaps, more obnoxious to the requirements of the Constitution than any other member of the body, as he held both a military commission and the office of member of Congress under the Confederate government throughout the war, when it was expressly declared by the Constitution that "No person shall hold any office under this Constitution who shall not have taken and subscribed an oath to the following effect :

" I do solemnly swear that I will support the Constitution of the United States, and the laws made in pursuance thereof, as the supreme law of the land, any thing in the Constitution and laws of the State of Virginia, or in the ordinances of the Convention which assembled at Richmond on the thirteenth day of February, 1861, to the contrary notwithstanding; and that I will uphold and defend the government of Virginia as restored by the Convention which assembled at Wheeling on the eleventh day of June, 1861, and that I have not, since the first day of January, 1864, voluntarily given aid or assistance in any way to those in rebellion against the United States for the purpose of promoting the same," etc.

And which Constitution also provides that "No person shall vote or hold office under this Constitution who has held office under the so-called Confederate government, or who has been a member of the so-called Confederate Congress, or a member of any State Legislature in rebellion against the authority of the United States," yet without he or any member of the body having taken this oath, and in defiance of these provisions of the Constitution, as if to brave public opinion, and challenge the resentment alike of the civil and military authorities of the United States, place this gentleman in the chair as a fit representative of the loyalty of the state. I have seen a nomination made of General Robert E. Lee as Governor of Virginia, which met with the applause of the House as well as the gallery, when the only claim of General Lee upon the state was that he fought for four years for the overthrow of his country. I have seen resolutions adopted by this body, as an exhibition of their loyalty, which *carefully*, perhaps, express no word of loyalty to the Union or the government of the United States, but only to the reconstruction policy of Mr. Johnson, by which they hope soon to be admitted without restriction into the Union, with the nominator of General Lee at the head of this committee, who, in his address to the President, vouched for the loyalty of the people of Virginia in the following language: "In declaring that the people of Virginia accept and abide by the results of the late contest, and that they intend in good faith to meet all the obligations thereby incurred, the General Assembly express a sentiment and a purpose which have been uniformly recognized by our people, individually and in masses, and, in regard to which, there is no hesitation or division in all Virginia;" while General Lee testified, as I learn from other witnesses who had been summoned, and were present, to a very equivocal loyalty of the people, rather, in the fashion of the resolutions of the Virginia Legislature, in the form of devotion to Mr. Johnson's policy of reconstruction than to the Union.

Here, then, is a strange conflict between the representations of the committee and of the statement of their chief, who rather seems to concur in the substance of the resolutions than in the representations of the committee. I should think, from what I learn, that, according to General Lee's opinion, the loyalty of the state is by no means to be depended upon; rather, that it is equivocal and contingent, dependent upon circumstances. Now which version of the loyalty of the people is the country to accept? for myself I adopt neither. They are not all loyal, nor are they all disloyal. I believe the element of disloyalty predominates, but among the masses of the people, those who had least to gain and most to suffer, the men who carried the musket and the sabre, and did the hard fighting (for the benefit of the politicians, who, for the most part, sought "bomb-proof" positions in the army, or safety from the enemy in the legislative halls and editorial chairs, and other soft places), they have had enough of war, and can not be easily dragooned into another; and, if let alone by the press and other leaders, or if protected, as they have a right to be, by the government of the United States, would by thousands and tens of thousands proclaim their loyalty in trumpet tongues to the world.

There are two points upon which Mr. Johnson has expressed himself very pointedly and emphatically. The first point was that "treason was a crime to be punished, and that traitors must be hung." Do gentlemen conceive this to be a part of his policy? If so, I think it is a part *they* will *not insist* upon. The last was that "if there were five thousand, or a smaller number of loyal men in a state, that they were entitled to govern it and fill all the offices." This, I take it, is a part of the policy that *he will insist upon;* and the sooner those who have usurped the powers prohibited by the Constitution prepare for it, the sooner will the balance of Mr. Johnson's policy be carried out.

I have seen it stated in a Richmond paper, and, I suppose, by the authority of the committee, that when one of the gentlemen (Mr. Grattan) was asked by the Reconstruction•Committee whether a jury could be found in Virginia that would convict Jefferson Davis of treason, he promptly answered "No!" which was afterward qualified by saying, "that as Richmond always contained a large number of Union men, such a jury might be found there," but of course nowhere else in the state. This statement was also confirmed by General Lee, as I learn.

I have seen this same Legislature overstepping its legitimate bounds, usurping the functions of the courts, with Argus eyes peering over the state for another victim to satiate their rapacity, and stretching out its Briarian arms to strike at a Union railroad president, in order to put a secession president in his place. I do not mean by this to express any opinion as to the merits of this unfortunate controversy—unfortunate for the interests of the stockholders and the state—but I do mean to say that, in my opinion, the Legislature had no right to interfere in the matter, and that, if Mr. Barbour felt aggrieved, his remedy was to appeal to the proper judicial tribunals for relief; and I mean to say, moreover, that *he* exhibits an extraordinary degree of credulity and simplicity who believes that if Mr. Barbour had been the Union candidate, and Mr. Jamieson the secession candidate for the presidency of the Orange and Alexandria Road, that he would have been able to obtain the same proceedings from this body calling itself the Legislature of Virginia. I have seen that Mr. Alexander Stephens, himself but yesterday steeped up to his eyelids in secession and rebellion (which in April, 1861, in a speech delivered in Richmond, he said had been forced upon the South, and that the South had the right on their side), and who has just been elected to the Senate of the United States because of his participation in the rebellion, declaring in a letter to a friend in Washington that "the condition and persecution of the Union men in Georgia are vastly worse than during the rebellion."

I have seen application after application, and memorial after memorial coming up to Congress from Union men in nearly all the so-called reconstructed states, complaining of the bad treatment and violence done to them by the secession element of their several localities. I myself have been almost daily in receipt of letters for the last two months, saying that they are looking to me to do something to stay the hand of this proscrip_ tive and intolerant party in this state, and praying that I will come to their relief.

I have seen, too, those men whom a becoming modesty, and a com_ mendable diffidence of their capacity and pretensions to govern, after the events of the last four years, would have kept at least for a time in the background, rushing with hot haste to assert their own indestructible and inalienable right, as if by Divine injunction, to govern and control, by thrusting themselves into places they had no constitutional right to fill, and grasping, with greedy hand, at every high and petty office for those whose claims rested alone on the fact of their service in the rebel cause. I have seen men wheedling and cajoling President Johnson in the press, in public meetings, and in the legislative halls, who, when they get him in their power, will measure out to him the same allowance that they have to Governor Pierpont for the *unpardonable* sin of having been a Southern Union man during the rebellion, all of which is set forth and fully avowed by that infamous, mischievous, and treasonable sheet, the New York *Daily News*, which would lead the South to her still deeper ruin and degrada- tion, and which has a larger circulation, is more extensively read, is sought after with greater avidity throughout the South than any other paper in the United States, and which is regarded as the most faithful organ of the disloyal element of the South, when it says of the Hon. Joshua Hill, of Georgia,

"Never can he represent there or elsewhere the brave and gallant men of Georgia. They know better than to intrust the honor of their dead and the interests of the living to such as he. Men do not trust those who have been false to them in the hour of danger and darkness. The South- ern people never will, never can confide in those who, born among them, or living in their midst during the dark and stormy days of their grand struggle, prayed, or sighed at least, for the success of the foe, and for the ruin and devastation of the houses, and temples, and fields of the South, and for that fearful oppression beneath which these people are now stag- gering and groaning."

Here, then, is the edict that has gone forth from the fountain-source, the law-maker and the lawgiver of secession depravity, the fate that awaits all good, true, and loyal men, who stood by their country in the country's peril, and hazarded fortune, liberty, and life in its defense, as did Andrew

Johnson in Tennessee during the great strife and struggle for the life of the nation, and for the liberties of mankind on the one hand, and the perpetuation of the power of Southern Democracy on the other. And all this we are asked to receive as unmistakable evidence of a purpose on the part of the *conquered* to do full justice, and to extend a full measure of mercy and forbearance to their *conquerors* in the great conflict and *strike for higher wages* through which we have just passed. In this is foreshadowed the fate of Mr. Johnson, whom they now smother with caresses, and stuff with professions of loyalty to him, if he should ever have the misfortune to fall into their forgiving and merciful arms.

Now to all this I answer in the vulgar vernacular of the day, "Nary a time," if you please. I have patiently submitted to the control of that Democracy for thirty-five years that at last brought ruin and desolation upon the country, and, for the last four years, whose civil and military power has trampled with an iron heel upon every class of its citizens, until it has turned "the fair and sunny fields of the South" into a general grave-yard or a desolate waste. To all this I have submitted, because I had no remedy, and could not help myself or others. But now I can; I have a remedy. I can help myself and all other good men at the same time; and I'll do it. As there is a God in heaven I'll do it, if the devotion of all my energies, and half that I am worth, will effect it. And as for a seat in the Senate of the United States, I have not cared a pin for one, except that I thought, as others seemed to think, I could serve the best interests of the state by being there. But I would forfeit forty seats in the Senate, ay, the Presidency itself, if it were offered to me to-morrow, sooner than see that element of secession Democracy raised to power again, except that such a position would enable me to crush it the more effectually than by any other means.

And now I have to say that I have not met with the first man, the first lawyer, or the first statesman who does not subscribe to the general propositions as set forth in the axioms I have presented in regard to the true status of those lately in rebellion, with the exception of one point only. I have found some who, without inquiry or investigation, have rather taken it for granted that the power of the President to pardon might be exercised before trial and conviction; but this idea seems to have arisen from the fact that Blackstone and other commentators of the English law recognized the plea of pardon in bar of an indictment, and that such had been the practice under the British government; and it is well known that this power has been claimed as one of the prerogatives of the king; but I fancy it will be found that the prerogatives of the king have little to do with the powers of a president, tied down by constitutional enactments, in this country. With us the case has never arisen that would lead, or rather has led, to an adjudication of the Supreme Court, or of any Federal court. That such powers have been exercised in extreme cases by some of the state governors, I am aware, though I do not know under what particular phraseology of their State Constitutions; but, I am informed, it has never met with the approval of the best legal men in those states where it has occurred.

The best and only authority I have been able to find is contained in the legal opinions of the several law officers of the United States, as, for example: Mr. Attorney General Wirt, March 20, 1820, says, "The King of England grants *conditional pardons* by the common law. We have no common law here. There is nothing in the force of the term pardon which implies a previous condemnation. A pardon presupposes an offense—nothing more. But where a pardon is granted on the *voluntary, confession* of one who has not been indicted, the confession should be in writing, and *the pardon founded on the specific offense confessed;* in other words, it should be a special pardon, so as not to protect the party against a prosecution for any more aggravated offense than he has thought proper to confess. And it would be proper to suggest farther that it would be much safer, as a general rule, to require a previous trial and condemnation, because all previous pardons must be granted on ex parte representations, by which the President may be deceived. The latter course, too, so far as I am informed, is more consonant with the general practice both of the state and federal government."

Upon this opinion of Mr. Wirt I will here remark, that this, as in all the cases to which I shall refer, related to offenses of a minor character, and, farther, that I apprehend in none of the cases in which pardons have been granted by President Johnson has there been a confession of guilt, and especially of the crime of treason; and that if there was, that confession in the case of treason, as required by the Constitution, *must be in open court.* I have had occasion to read a very large number of those applications for pardon, and I have never seen any such confession in any of them; but they usually represent that they are excluded from the benefits of the amnesty oath under such or such a clause of the proclamation of the 29th of May, 1865—generally the $20,000 clause, as it was called —and ask to be pardoned for that; so that Mr. Wirt's opinion would be clearly against the exercise of the power in all such cases as these.

Attorney General Berrian, October 12, says, "A variety of considerations seem to me to render it inexpedient generally to interpose the pardoning power previous to trial. It is not denied, however, *that cases may exist* in which such an interposition would be proper."

Of course, Mr. Berrian must be presumed to refer to minor and unimportant cases, in which the public interest and safety would not suffer, where there were greatly extenuating circumstances or doubt about the guilt of the parties, when he speaks of cases that MAY EXIST.

Attorney General Cushing, April 15, 1853, says, "The President has the power to pardon before conviction. But there must be satisfactory evidence as to the guilt of the party; and it has been held unwise and inexpedient, as a general rule, to interpose the pardoning power in anticipation of trial and condemnation, *although particular circumstances may exist* to justify such an exceptional act on the part of the President."

Recollect that none of these cases had reference to any crime of a very serious nature where it is said *cases may exist*, or particular circumstances may exist, etc., etc.

But I have reserved the most important and authoritative opinion, against which no Southern Democrat can raise his voice, for the last. December 28, 1831, Attorney General Roger B. Taney said, "I do not, however, agree with you in deriving this power (to discontinue judicial proceedings) to the President from that clause in the Constitution which authorizes him to grant pardons and reprieves. This is a specific grant of power which can not be extended beyond the fair import of the words. He can pardon or reprieve *only* when an offense against the law has been established by proof" (legal proof, of course) "or by the admission of the party" (in open court, of course, as in the case of treason), "*and the penalty thereby incurred.*"

I can not find or hear of a case in which in any Federal court the question has been *adjudicated* whether a pardon can properly be granted by the President before trial and conviction, and the *attorneys* quoted above would all seem to think not, as a general rule. Mr. Wirt thinks the confession should be in writing, and the pardon founded on the specific offense confessed; in other words, says Mr. Wirt, it should be a *special* pardon, so as not to protect the party against a prosecution for a more aggravated offense than he has thought proper to confess.

The question may well be asked, What offense have any of these reconstructed gentlemen confessed? That they have been guilty of treason? Surely not, for they deny it; they have only confessed that they were excluded from the benefits of the proclamation of May, 1865, by such or such a clause—and most generally the $20,000 clause—and it will be found that it is *their property* that has been pardoned, which, in the language of Mr. Wirt, can not protect them against a prosecution for the more aggravated crime of treason.

Mr. Berrian and Mr. Cushing both oppose the exercise of the power, but admit that *cases may exist,* or *circumstances may exist* to justify "*such an exceptional act,*" and this I am willing to concede. It would not be difficult to conceive a case in which the public interest, or justice to parties accused, might justify a *stretch of power,* and this is done every day, perhaps, in every department of the government; but this does not establish the law to be exercised in the most flagrant cases and most aggravated offenses.

Attorney General Taney, afterward Chief-justice, utterly denies the power, and says it can ONLY be exercised when an offense against the law has been established by proof or the confession of the party, and the penalty thereby incurred—all of which could be reached only by trial and conviction.

But since the above was written I have found still better authority in an opinion of Chief-justice Marshall, to which all must yield respect, if not obedience.

The opinion I found recorded in the American Encyclopædia, under the head of pardons.

"A pardon," said Mr. Marshall, "is not an act of justice, but of grace. Pardon necessarily implies punishment, and punishment in all well-ordered states, at least, supposes guilt *ascertained in the due course of law,* and justly visited with a penalty. * * * The theory is that the courts have the monopoly of doing justice, that is, if the impartial and exact application of law, which are intended and supposed to dispense justice, does, in fact, accomplish that end ; so, theoretically, it must be assumed that he is guilty whom the courts declare to be so, and that the penalty inflicted is justly inflicted." He farther says, "The ultimate power, the real sovereignty, whether it reside in a king or in the people, as it is the source of the law, so it would be the source of grace to him who breaks the law. In the forms of government which have most prevailed, the crowned prince has been regarded as sovereign. In democratic states the people '*is*' sovereign. The Constitution of the United States gives the power to the President alone. Now a pardon presupposes guilt and *just condemnation, and works a suspension of the sentence,* and defeats and annuls SO FAR the law which pronounced it. But it is the first principle of the best form of government that the law must be supreme.

"Now if the judgment which the law passed upon the offender consisted exclusively in fine and imprisonment (or confiscation), remission of them does, in fact, restore him to full enjoyment of all his civil rights," but of course could neither suspend nor repeal the enactments of law, such as the test-oath, nor override the provisions and requirements of a State Constitution. But Judge Marshall proceeds: "but when infamy attaches, by particular laws, to the conviction, as it does in the case of felonies, forgiveness of the fine, and imprisonment only," as (confiscation of property) by no means makes the pardoned equal with the innocent. In short, the pardon is partial, or, it were perhaps better to say, IT IS NO PARDON AT ALL.

Can any one doubt what would be the decision of the Supreme Court if any one of these cases should be carried up to that court?

Now, then, I may be asked for what good purpose have I opened up, or propose to open up these cases, and I answer, I propose to show to these gentlemen what is held by some of the best lawyers in this country to be sound, incontrovertible law in their cases; that they are not yet far enough out of the woods to put on all these airs of superiority and lordly dictation to those who have rights in this government superior to their own; to show them that they stand on dangerous ground, with a mine beneath; and that they can not and will not be permitted to frown down, or crush down, to trample down, to vote down, to write down, or to put down in any way the Union men of the South, who have it in their power to place them in a far worse condition than they have yet occupied from the beginning of the rebellion, and in a far worse condition than they can place the Union men, either by voting them out of office, or otherwise oppressing or harassing them. As for their social distinctions, let them be kept up to their hearts' content. Nobody cares, I suppose, to associate with any of those who prefer other society. This pretension and arrogance is too ridiculous and contemptible to produce any other feeling than that of pity and derision. If this disposition proceeded from the pride of the conquered, it might be respected; but when it proceeds from bad taste, bad temper, bad feeling, and worse judgment, I should despise the man or woman who would stoop to conciliate it. They have the right to do it, but those who encourage it stand much in the way of their own interests, and the interests of the state, when we should all work together for the common good; but they can be permitted no longer to treat Union men

with indignity, nor to stigmatize them as traitors, for every such Union'
man has his remedy in his own hands. If any man calls me a traitor, or
thinks me one, I challenge him to a trial of the question; let him make
an affidavit against me, and I will return the compliment to him, and
have the question tried. I will promise to plead no pardon in bar that I
have crawled to the footstool of power to solicit.

Do you ask me what this remedy is? I will tell you. Suppose the'
loyal men refuse to pay the taxes imposed by the body now in session—
and I give timely notice now that I will not pay one dollar of tax imposal
upon me—on the ground, first, that the Legislature is not a lawfully and
constitutionally constituted body, and, second, that it is composed in
part of aliens, whose pardons are of no avail, and who have no more
right to tax me than a Mexican Legislature would have. The sheriff
seizes my property, and I apply to the judge for an injunction and appeal
to the law for protection ; he grants the injunction, and he decides that
they did or did not comply with the provisions of the Constitution, that
they were or were not aliens, and that the pardons were or were not granted in accordance with the provisions of the Constitution. The case is
carried up to the Court of Appeals, and from there to the Supreme Court
of the United States. Here is a case made for the Supreme Court, and
suppose they decide that the pardons are good for nothing. Then all any
citizen has to do is to go before a magistrate or district judge of the Fed-'
eral court and make oath that such a party has been guilty of treason,
and demand a warrant for his arrest—and he is bound to issue such war-'
rant—and bring him to trial, when the pardon can be plead in bar, and
thus bring it to the Supreme Court for adjudication.

Now I want to be understood. Not a pardon has been granted that
I desire to see revoked. There is no man that I have cared to see pronounced an alien by the law, provided full justice is done to the Union
men, of whom there are from thirty to fifty thousand in this state, and
who would openly proclaim it if it were not for the terror of public opinion and the fear of denunciation from the public press ; but if there were
but a handful, a baker's dozen, or if I stood alone, I would demand it for
myself. Therefore I call upon every Union man in the state, and in the
South, to stand up for their rights without fear, and say to all who would
withhold them, "stand from under."

Of course I must expect to hear a general howl and volumes of abuse
from the "reconstructed," but I am so used to this that it does not hurt;
and if they knew what contempt I feel for all such trash they would save

their wrath, and bottle it up for somebody else that would feel it more than I do. I once heard it said that if a man throws a stone in the dark, and he heard a dog howl, you might be sure it hit him. This much in anticipation of what is to come.

This thing has to be stopped, or I pledge myself to bring the whole matter to a judicial decision, as I said before, if it costs me half that I am worth in the world if it is not. *"Verbum sat inpresenti."*

I am very respectfully and truly your friend, JOHN M. BOTTS.

THE SECOND LETTER.

On the morning this letter was published in Richmond, "Mr. Garnett," the member of the Legislature, to whom it was addressed, rose to a personal explanation, in the course of which he said,

"The letter being addressed to me, it might be supposed that I coincided in the opinions, or sympathized in any way with the views expressed, neither of which have my approbation; but I repudiate both the one and the other," to which the following reply was made:

Auburn, Culpepper County, March 1, 1866.

To MUSCOE GARNETT, ESQ. :

It was very much the habit of Mr. Clay when he offended his friends, which he not unfrequently did, by way of apology, to say, "Well, if a man can not take liberties with his friends, who the devil can he take them with?" I suppose it was on this principle that, on the 24th ultimo, you took what I must think the most uncalled-for and unwarrantable liberty of dragging me before the legislative (so-called) body to arraign me for opinions expressed in a letter to you in terms that might well have been left to those who set up no pretensions of friendship. It would have been quite time enough for you to refuse to indorse for me when I had asked you to put your name on my paper. You must, therefore, excuse me for acting on the same principle with you, by taking the same liberty you have taken with me. How long has it been since it was understood that a person to whom a letter was addressed was responsible for all that the letter contained? In what school has such a principle been affirmed? God forbid that I should be held responsible for all letters I receive. If I were, I should be for Mr. Johnson and against him; for Congress and against it; for the emancipation proclamation and against it; for negro suffrage and against it; and for every conceivable shade of opinions that can be held by the great number of persons who think proper to address me, and furnish their views of the multitude of vexed questions which agitate the public mind.

I regret very much, *far* more than you say you do, in your last letter to me, that you should have felt yourself under the necessity of doing any thing that I think reflects no credit on your discrimination or moral courage, and that, in the end, will, I am satisfied, operate far more to your disadvantage than it will to mine. For the present, I am perhaps the chief sufferer; for you, as my friend, being the first to put the ball in motion, have, by your repudiation, afforded the opportunity to others lately professing friendship to introduce my name before the same body, in the mere wantonness of offensive insinuation, upon a subject with which I had no connection, as a corporator in a railroad bill of which I had never heard.

For more than thirty years we have been personal and political friends. There have not been a great number in the state from whom I have had more numerous and stronger professions of friendship than yourself, even up to the 27th of February, three days after you had indulged in this wholesale repudiation of my entire views, etc.

You may be my friend; you say you are, and I will not doubt it, though, to be entirely frank with you, I must say you have an extraordinary and somewhat disagreeable way of showing it.

1st. A report is in circulation, or rather *an inference is drawn*, of my connection with the Alexandria movement to reduce the state to a territorial condition—an inference drawn from a circumstance that should have led to exactly the opposite conclusion—which you write me is doing me incalculable injury, and is likely to defeat (what you have often written and told me constituted your chief object in coming to the Legislature), to wit, my election to the United States Senate. Possessing the evidence to remove that inference, and to obviate that injury, you refuse to use it, writing to me at the same time that it is necessary to define my position, which definition you have in your pocket.

2d. When I answer your letter through the press, to do which, as heretofore explained, I thought I had your permission (for had I written to you privately again, I had no assurance you would use it otherwise than you did the first), for *fear* of being held responsible by the dominant party and their press, who are aiming to drive you, and me, and all of our class to the wall, and establish their own *superiority* over us, you feel it incumbent upon you to rise in your place and repudiate what you are not called upon to indorse, and what no man in the world could have held you responsible for; and then, in a private letter, as if in apology for this injustice, you express your regret at the "*painful necessity*" that compelled you to make the explanation, put some half dozen or more far-fetched and unwarrantable conclusions as to the objects and effects of my propositions, such as I had never dreamed of, and such as it would appear to me that no man of your intelligence could by possibility draw from them, and you conclude by saying, "although you can not sanction the ultra views and opinions which I have published, or coincide with me in the denunciation of our state government" (so-called), "you can never, until you forget all of the past, cease to be my true friend and well-wisher." Yet, notwithstanding this, you see published in the *Sentinel*, immediately under your eye, a statement from that fellow "Dick Smith"—I believe that is his name—to the effect, "No wonder Mr. Garnett has *been* quick to get away from his good friend as fast as he could, and to *repudiate both him and his opinions.*" This quotation does attach the responsibility to you of having repudiated *me* as well as my opinions, and does not coincide with your letter to me; yet you do not choose to disclaim it, but leave the world to suppose that you have in truth repudiated your *friendship for me* as well as the views I have presented. You will here permit me to say, that if I had erred in my judgment, inasmuch as my whole object was to prevent *you*, in company with all Union men, from being forever a proscribed class, reduced to a position of inferiority in this state in all future time, and for which I was disposed to make a willing sacrifice of myself, it might have been received with a little more generosity and forbearance than it seems to have been.

You say you are my friend! and I repeat I will not doubt it; but on this score I have the advantage of you. You wanted to secure an office for me for the benefit of the state, but I have yet to see that you made the first movement in that direction before the body of which you are a member. I labored to get two for you—one for yourself and another for your son. I failed, it is true, in both; in the former, either because the appointing or nominating power did not have as much confidence in you as I had, or from a lack of influence with him on my own part; the latter, I think, would have succeeded in Washington, but for the fact that the office sought had been discontinued. Of this I wrote you from Alexandria, in the same letter in which I asked your permission to answer yours through the press to me, which was far more open to you than to me; for while there was but one in Richmond that would publish mine to you, all would gladly have published any repudiation you had to make of me or of my opinions.

Q

Now, *my friend*, let us look this matter straight in the face, and see what it is you thus unqualifiedly repudiate.

You are either a loyal man or you are disloyal. If you are disloyal, you have woefully deceived me, both during the war and since its close. If you are loyal, then, I say, you have gone far beyond what you can sustain yourself in, or be sustained in, either by the loyal or disloyal men of the state or country.

Your language, as reported in the *Republic*, is that "the letter being addressed to you, it might be supposed that you coincided with me in opinion, or sympathized *in any way* with the views I had expressed, neither of which has your approbation, but you repudiate both the one and the other." The construction put upon this by the *Sentinel* is that you repudiate both the opinions and myself. This is flatly contradicted by your letter of the 27th ultimo, to which I have before referred; for to repudiate me before the Legislature and in the public prints, and in a private communication to say that "you would never cease to be my *true friend* and *well-wisher*"—the italics your own—would exhibit a want of candor and sincerity that I can not and will not suspect you of, and, therefore, I must look for some other interpretation, and the only one it bears, as I see it, is that you repudiate, one and all, the opinions I have expressed in my axioms and in my letter to you. Now, what are the opinions you repudiate?

My first proposition is, that the right of secession is not authorized, but forbidden by the Constitution. Differing with me on this, you think secession is not forbidden, but authorized by the Constitution.

My second is, that the ordinances of secession were null and void. You think they were not null and void.

My third is, that there can not be thirty-six different allegiances in the United States, and no one man owing his first allegiance to the central and supreme government. You think there are thirty-six different allegiances to the thirty-six states, and none owing their allegiance to the only power that can make peace or war.

My fourth is, that the states have not been out of the Union, and could not be carried out but by successful revolution. You think the states have been out of the Union, and the Union has been dissolved.

My fifth is, that any attempt to set up a new government within the United States hostile to it, by force of arms, is treason. You think it is not treason.

My sixth is, that the right of expatriation and denationalization has never been denied in this country, and that the citizens thereof had the right to take themselves out, either individually or collectively. You think that such right has not been recognized, and that they can not either expatriate or denationalize themselves. (I guess, then, these colonies that are being prepared for Mexico had better be stopped at once.)

My seventh is, that the late Confederate government did constitute a government *de facto* (the Legislature, I see, questions whether it was not one *de jure*), and that all who assisted in creating that *de facto* government, or who took the oath of allegiance to it, thereby alienated themselves from the government, renounced their allegiance to the United States and their claims to its protection, and can become nationalized again only by the law of naturalization or by some new law. You think it was not a *de facto* government, and that those who took the oath of allegiance to it did not renounce their allegiance, and were entitled to the protection of the United States, and have nothing to do but to walk, without ceremony or permission, out of one government into another.

My eighth is, that there is no difference in the political status of two citizens, one of whom takes the oath of allegiance to one *de facto* government, and the other, who takes the same oath to another *de facto* government. You think there is.

My ninth is, that after the rebellion was put down, the loyal men of the rebellious states had a natural and inherent right to take control of the government, to the exclusion of the disloyal men (which is in accordance with the policy of Mr. Johnson), and that all the representatives, properly elected, and who went to Washington prepared in good faith to comply with the Constitution and the laws of the country, should be admitted to seats without unnecessary delay. You think that they had no such right, and that Mr. Johnson's policy, which you profess to sustain in the resolutions of loyalty unanimously adopted by the Legislature, should be overthrown, and that the states are not entitled to be represented by loyal men.

My tenth is, that as all men are presumed innocent until they are proved guilty, the power of the President to reprieve and pardon commences after the offense and penalty have been ascertained. You think all men are not innocent until they are proved guilty, and that the President can pardon before the offense and penalty are ascertained. (To your dissent to this latter conclusion I would not object, as it may be considered a disputed point, and is not at all necessary to the establishment of my general propositions.)

My eleventh and twelfth are, that the attempts at reconstruction are a failure, and that the shortest and best, if not the only way to get them in, will be for such states as the law-making power does not recognize as having been reconstructed according to law, should be commenced *de novo*, under such conditions as will enable them to get in at the earliest practical moment. You think these efforts have not failed (Query, How many states have gotten into Congress under this policy?), and that they had better stay out as they are now, and are likely to continue (under the concurrent resolution of the two houses, which will surely pass the Senate), rather than begin again and get in at an early day.

My thirteenth is, that Virginia has been continuously a recognized government, and can not now be properly subjected to a military or provisional governor. You think she has not been a continuously recognized government (though she had two senators throughout the war), and that she ought to have a military or provisional governor, and be treated as those states that did not claim to be in the Union during the rebellion.

My fourteenth is, that as the Constitution declares that the House of Delegates shall consist of not less than eighty, and not more than one hundred and four, therefore, fourteen in one house and six in the other did not constitute a lawful Legislature. Again, that as the Constitution declares that no person shall serve as a member of the Legislature without taking an oath therein prescribed, and farther provides that no person shall *vote* or *hold any office whatever* who has held office under the Confederate government, or any state in rebellion, which oath no member of the Legislature has taken; and as many of them did hold office under the Confederate or state government in rebellion, therefore, that the body has not been organized according to the requirements of the Constitution, accordingly all their acts are null and void. You think that fourteen in one house and six in the other is a sufficient compliance with the provisions of the Constitution, and that the oath prescribed as essential to the qualification of each member (which you well know has not been administered) might be disregarded and set aside by those who are otherwise disqualified, and that rebel officers, civil and military, could, under the Constitution, proceed to legislate as if no such provisions had been contained in the Constitution, and that their acts are all legal and binding.

These are the points of difference which would appear to exist between us, by your universal repudiation and condemnation of all my views, while I know, in reality, that you entertain no such opinions, and that there is no such difference between us. The truth is, Mr. Garnett, you found my axioms and letter offensive to the disloyal men with whom you are associated, and you lacked the moral courage to sustain them; and, *for fear of* a suspected acquiescence, you incautiously, inconsiderately, and unnecessarily repudiated one and all in a breath. I say, moreover, that neither you nor any other man in the state, who has a reputation to lose or to make, dare go before the public upon these issues as made with me by your general repudiation.

When I was on a visit to Richmond, in the month of January last, I read my axioms to many of the members of the Legislature, who did me the honor to call upon me, and I said, "It is apparent to all that this Legislature is about to educate the people into the belief that treason to the United States is a virtue to be rewarded, and loyalty a crime to be punished; and if you do not exert yourselves, and make a stand-up fight with your adversaries, this will be the unavoidable consequence of your submission, and, as I do not mean to submit to any such state of things, I shall feel myself not only at liberty, but bound to present these axioms to the public, as containing the true solution of the status of those who are struggling to place us in a position of inferiority and degradation." Not a man made an objection to any one axiom presented except to that which related to the pardons, upon which some few remarks were made, to the effect that "We have got our pardons, and do not want to give them up, and do not mean to do so;" to which I replied, "The loss of your pardons is no consequence if my propositions are adopted, because neither your persons nor your property can be disturbed, under my propositions, without trial and conviction, and certainly no loyal man need stand in fear of that." But they all acquiesced in the necessity of making the fight, and that an issue should be presented. There are many witnesses to all this. I left Richmond, and waited for three weeks, and no issue was presented. The day for adjournment was drawing to a close, and I concluded that if I waited until after the adjournment it might be said that I had taken all the chances of an election to the Senate, and, being disappointed, I had made war upon the organization of the Legislature.

I determined, therefore, that while I was in "receipt of letters assuring me of my election before adjournment," to throw all chance of an election to the dogs, rather than remain passive and see my own inferiority and that of the whole class of loyal men in the state established, as if by law, and I resolved to hold back no longer.

I claim that we are entitled to occupy a position of *superiority*, but I would have been content with *equality;* less than this I will not patiently or willingly submit to, and those who would are not political associates for me, and are welcome to go into the ranks of the other party ; but let them make no farther pretensions to loyalty, or even to *equality with rebels.*

Now, to show you how differently my views are regarded by others of the loyal class, I subjoin one or two extracts from numerous letters re. ceived.

The following is from a consistent and most respectable source, a Union man from first to last, who has not, at any time, been afraid to avow his sentiments. He says, "It is laughable to hear people, whose brains never gave them the headache, talk about the indiscretion of Botts. * * * Your column of truth in the *Republic,* being copied into so many papers, must do some good, and must save us from a Democratic death or secession hell. I am delighted to hear the crack of your whip, and beg you not to spare the lash. The illegality of the Legislature and unconstitutionality of the pardons, and of all their proceedings, touches them on the raw; in fact, they feel deeply every word you have written."

The following is from one of the most intelligent, respectable, and responsible Union men in the Southern States :

"I am greatly indebted to you for your masterly and indignant recital of the contumacious and disloyal conduct and aims of our Southern rulers. I hope it will arouse our friends every where. * * * I would have preferred it should have been done by some other than yourself (so would I, but who was to do it?); by one who, like yourself, had the wisdom and courage of Hampden. * * * I could not feel otherwise than indignant at the supercilious repudiation of your opinions and feelings by your late friend and correspondent, Mr. Garnett. I could not have suspected any one of such meanness. You have had by far too many of such friends, and it is time for you to discard them, and be more wary of your confidence in the future. Such a man as Mr. Garnett should have a Roland for his Oliver," with many more such expressions of indignation.

I quote these passages from letters received, only to show you that all my friends do not concur with you in opinion. I repeat, I have no other object under the sun than to secure fairness and justice to the loyal men of the South generally, and those of this state in particular, and until it is obtained "I will fight it out on this line" to the last resort, for which, if you belong to that class, you should have given me your thanks instead of your rebuke.

I know of no man who has had so much reason as *I* to exclaim, "Save me from my friends!" I am willing to bear, and have borne, a great deal from some of mine, but I am not willing to be sacrificed or slaughtered by them, or that they should make capital for themselves by endeavoring to bring odium upon me. This is asking too much, and a little more than I am willing to yield.

When you have given votes, or made speeches or reports that were offensive to Union men, which you have frequently done during the session, did I make haste to repudiate you or your action? No! I did not approve of what you had said or done, but I offered a defense for you; I did not *justify*, but *palliated*, to reconcile those who distrusted you (as seven tenths of my friends did): and this you know, for you have been present when I did it, and you will recollect the acknowledgment you made, which I will not repeat, but which might apply as well to this case as to the one then under consideration.

And now, Mr. Garnett, I have given you a Roland for your Oliver, and let me assure you I have said nothing here except to defend myself from your most extraordinary, unprovoked, and uncalled-for assault upon me. If I thought it proceeded from treachery or baseness of heart, as others do, I would drop you altogether; but I do not think this. I think you were put up to it, and in a moment of weakness you gave way to the bad counsels of interested men, who would rejoice at my discomfiture. It is for you now to say what shall be our relation in the future. I am willing to break even, let by-gones be by-gones, and let matters stand as before; but of this you must determine for yourself. But I am admonished by the *little Dispatch* that my letters are always long, and that the printers dread me, which I do not think concerns them much, as I am never permitted to trouble them in this way except in the form of a paid advertisement; and, to be frank, I could not be content with short paragraphs like one who has a paper always at his command, and writes for it every day. But for any thing I can now see, I shall be under no necessity of troubling any of them again very soon.

I am respectfully yours,   JOHN M. BOTTS.

THE THIRD LETTER.

In continuation, the two letters below are furnished, as serving to show the real condition of things as they now—spring of 1866—exist in Virginia, under Mr. Johnson's reconstruction policy.

Auburn, Culpepper County, February 26, 1866.

To the Editor of the *Republic:*

No doubt many of my friends will think it strange, and will probably condemn me for the position I have assumed in the "axioms" I have presented, and the letter following upon its heels, addressed to my friend, Muscoe Garnett, Esq.; and sometimes I think it a little strange myself, that in violation of what I thought was an absolute determination on my part, for the last five years of my life, never again to permit myself to take an active part in politics, that I should now have departed from it, and placed myself once more in the foreground, to receive all the abuse that misapprehension, ignorance, stupidity, and malevolence might direct against me; but when I saw the incontestible evidence of disloyalty displayed by the press and Legislature of this state daily exhibited and hourly increasing; when I saw Union men every where, and under all circumstances, overslaughed and turned out of office for those who had served in the rebellion; when I saw the people being rapidly educated to look upon treason as a virtue, and a passport to office, and loyalty a crime to be punished; when I saw, out of all the papers published in the state, only two or three, and those of a limited circulation, remonstrating or protesting against this injustice to those who alone could fill any office in this state according to the provisions of the Constitution, which I at first pronounced a second edition of the "Lecompton Swindle," but which has since been recognized by all, and under which the present Legislature professes to have met, and is now acting; when I saw that the *late rebel Legislature* was virtually and substantially declared a lawful government, when, on motion of a very active participant in the rebellion, in a bill that referred to the late state government, the words "*de facto*" were struck out, on the ground that *many thought it a government* "*de jure*," thereby virtually legalizing the rebellion; when I heard in Washington of the overwhelming testimony that had been given by the most respectable gentlemen from this state, and from almost every other Southern state, of the rapid increase of disaffection and disloyalty among the people; and when officers in command of Southern departments, of the highest respectability, and of the highest grade and distinction, testifying to this disloyalty, and on oath declaring their knowledge of a wide-spread conspiracy on foot among the leaders—not to embark in rebellion again, for of that they have had quite enough—but to involve the country in a foreign war, in order that the discontented and aspiring politicians might have a chance to cut their way to fortune, and wipe out the bitter mortification with which they are devoured, but which for a time was smothered, all of which you will learn when this testimony is laid before the public. It is not in my nature to be quiet until the net was woven and the knot tied by which we were again to be plunged into a sea of calamities as we were in 1861, when it might be too late to resist it. Seeing all this, I hesitated long, I reflected maturely on what my duty required me to do, and I felt I should be no better than a traitor to my country and to my party—I mean to the Union sentiment of the South and of the country, for I belong to no party—if I did not endeavor to nip it in the bud.

So I "pitched in," enlisted once again against the most mischievous, the most reckless, the most untiring and persevering, and the most wicked party, as I religiously believe, that the Almighty, in his infinite wisdom, ever permitted to exist on earth. I speak now of the leaders of that party as a political organization, many of whom seem to think the sun would cease to rise and shine if their infallible counsels were withheld from the nation. Of what materials are our people made, that they do not look more clearly to their own interests? Have they not suffered enough through the agency of this same Democratic party, that they must cling to it and worship it as if it had delivered them from misery and ruin, instead of having brought it upon them? Are my present propositions more obnoxious than were my admonitions against the twenty-first rule (by which the Abolition party was built up) in 1841? or my opposition to the annexation of Texas (the *remote* cause of the late rebellion) in 1844? or my opposition to the Mexican War in 1845, '6, and '7? or my warnings against the repeal of the Missouri Compromise (the *immediate* cause of the rebellion) in 1854? or my urgent entreaties against secession in 1861? Why, then, not listen to me now? I am only a little in the advance now, as I was on the above-named occasions when they respectively occurred. Then all condemned, but afterward, when too late, all approved. I am not silly enough to apprehend another rebellion; but I do fear the ascendency of this party to power, and I do fear that power, if the country should, by any misfortune, become involved in a foreign war, which I have every reason to believe is anxiously prayed for by many who have recently taken the oath of strict fidelity to the United States, as contained in the amnesty oath.

Now suppose, by any misfortune or any indiscrimination on the part of the civil or military authorities either in Washington or on the Rio Grande, we should be involved in difficulty with the French Empire, and these extremely loyal gentlemen were to invite the French authorities to land a considerable force at some southern point—say Charleston, Savannah, Pensacola, or Mobile—and General Grant were to attempt to resist them with the army of the United States, who believes they could reach the point of landing, in the present temper and spirit displayed? They might reach the point, perhaps, but would their supplies and the materials of war be allowed to reach them? Would not the bridges be destroyed, and the rails torn up, etc. ? I believe if the men did not do it the women would, for they are being educated to this feeling every day.

Now if this feeling does not exist, why is it that every Union man is sacrificed, and every one who was in the rebel service taken care of? Why is it that if young ladies, who modestly and instinctively shrink from the appearance of their names in the public prints, and who attend a social party given by United States officers, find their attendance on the occasion referred to in the next day's paper in such terms as to bring odium upon them among their former friends? I know of a young lady who was brought up in a strong secession family, and whose partialities were all in that direction, that, for the sake of an evening's amusement with some warm friends, attended one of these officers' "hops," and the result was, her old friends and companions refused to recognize her when next she met them.

All *profess* to be loyal, and to belong to the Union Church. Is it usual, when one joins a *Christian church*, and kneels at the communion-table to take the Lord's Sacrament, for them to treat with contumely and contempt those who knelt at the same table before them, and, if not, why do those who kneel at the altar of the Union with us give themselves airs, and spurn the association and fellowship of those whom they found at the altar when they came in? Does he who joins a Masonic lodge despise his brother-Masons because they were *Master*-Masons before he joined the lodge?

I know a lady of Virginia birth, but who married in the North, that came to this state, and went to visit her friends and relatives in Richmond (and whose father was an original and life-long secessionist), having no sentiment of resentment toward those who had differed from her in opinion ; not one of her friends called to see her, and one of her near relatives actually gave her to understand that he would not speak to her if she were to visit his house ; and this individual was one of the class who claim to be "loyal men" in the present acceptation of the word, and who had taken the amnesty oath, and who has hitherto passed for a kind-hearted gentleman.

Under all these circumstances, together with those enumerated in my last letter, I determined to remain inactive no longer, and I have enlisted for the war, and "upon this line I propose to fight it out;" not because, as the Charlottesville *Chronicle* elegantly expresses it, "He had rather drive a stage, hectoring and swearing from one tavern-stand to another, than to command a man-of-war and keep his mouth shut," or, as the same paper, with still more refinement, says, "Because he would prefer being the bully among half a dozen followers, to being the leader of a free and independent party." I beg to assure the editor of the paper in question that he does me great injustice when he thinks I could have a taste for stage-driving, hectoring, swearing, or bullying, but I *would rather be dead* and in my grave, honored for my manhood, than patiently to submit to the wrongs and oppressions which are sought to be put upon all of my class, or keep my mouth shut from compulsion or fear; *that* I did not do under the Confederate despotism, and I am still less likely to do it now; and for the "free and independent party" in this state, where is it to be found, for any man of brains to lead, to which I could attach myself as *an humble follower?* If any one will point it out to me, I will promise to fall in the rear rank of that party. My highest aspiration is to see one such arise, Phœnix-like, to claim what they are entitled to demand. "I am not mad, most noble Festus, but speak both the words of truth and soberness."

When I enlisted in this war I knew what odds I should have to encounter; I knew the prejudice I should awaken; I knew the injustice that would be done my motives; I knew the timidity of those I was endeavoring to serve, because I have had to deal with them before. I was also aware of the ignorance and stupidity I should meet with in such papers as the Petersburg *Index*, the leading articles of which have been beneath contempt, not for the abuse of me which has characterized them, but for the absence of all understanding and knowledge of the great questions they undertake to discuss. I knew that the small provincial papers, upon the plea of "want of room," would garble and mutilate my "axioms," and give what they call "a synopsis," but only such a synopsis as suited their purposes, and then reason from *them;* all this I knew, but I determined not to "keep my mouth shut" or my pen idle.

Wait until this "Radical" Legislature shall call a convention to make a new Constitution, which will be composed of the same set or sort of men that now control the Legislature, and then we shall all see where the Union men will be found; and, therefore, I choose now, and just here, to make an issue as to the legality of this body that, by their recent unwise action, has ruined the fairest prospects of Richmond, Petersburg, and Norfolk for the benefit of Baltimore; and I should think every property-holder and business-man in those localities would rejoice to see this Legislature declared an unconstitutional organization by the proper tribunals of the country; and it may be of some interest to them to be informed that this question is likely to be brought before the Federal courts by the Northern stockholders of the Orange and Alexandria Railroad, if the effort should be persisted in to dispossess the present officers of the road under any law that has been passed by the Legislature, and thus relieve me of the necessity of raising the question by withholding the payment of my state taxes, as I have announced it my purpose to do. By the way, I may as well mention here that I have recently been informed by a member of the Board of Public Works, who has been removed from office, "that Mr. Alexander Rives and myself had been appointed directors of this road before the change in the board took place," but, of course, as we were both Union men, we were thought to be very unsuitable persons to serve as directors of a Virginia railroad, and we were both unceremoniously removed by the new board, even before the appointments had been announced, to make place for two gentlemen whose sympathies were in the opposite direction; while the third gentleman who was associated with us (a secessionist) has been retained.

I do not mention this in a spirit of complaint, but to show the extent to which this proscription of all Union men has been and will be carried; and just now comes in a paper from which I cut the following, which furnishes still another instance of secession vindictiveness:

"*The Judges.*—Governor Pierpont's nominations for the Court of Appeals were yesterday confirmed by the Legislature; also the nominations for the first four circuits and the sixth. There was no nomination for the fifth circuit.

"Judge E. K. Snead, the nominee for this district, was almost unanimously rejected, he receiving but nine votes. He was the only original Union man put in nomination by Governor Pierpont, and hence no one should be surprised at his rejection. He was appointed over two years ago by Governor Pierpont as judge of this circuit, and has presided with dignity and ability, giving entire satisfaction to the bar and those having business in his court. But his loyalty killed him. The 'reconstructed' rebels of the Legislature could not consent to allow even *one* loyal man on the bench of the state."

I begin to think that I was mistaken when I said there was no "free and independent party" in this state. But "free" for what? Why, to do just whatever they please, with or without the sanction of law. "Independent" of what? Independent of all legal, constitutional, not to say moral restraint.

Now would it be believed that this Constitution, which is so framed as to exclude all those who participated in the rebellion from holding office under it, has been so abused as to confer the office on those alone who did thus participate; and if they do this under this Constitution, what have we to expect under a new Constitution of their own framing, but that every man loyal to the United States during the rebellion will be perpetually excluded by constitutional enactment? And, by-the-by, I see a proposition has been already submitted to the Senate for the call of a convention to make a new Constitution, which is just what I have expected, and have foreshadowed from the beginning. Is this a time and an occasion when Union men should be asked or expected to keep their mouths shut, with the whole power of the United States government to support them?

I know it has been charged that disappointment at not being elected to the United States Senate has influenced me in this matter. Do the gentlemen who make this charge take me for a fool? I have had assurances all through the winter, *though at no time a candidate for the office*, that I would be elected before the adjournment, and I threw all chances of an election to the dogs when it came in conflict with what I believed to be a duty to my country. And I would inform these gentlemen, also, that I declined a seat in the Senate when Messrs. Underwood and Segur were said to be elected, which, with such "*vaulting ambition*" as is charged withal, I would not have done.

Now, then, the "axioms" I have presented, with the exception of the tenth and fifteenth, I hold to be sound, unquestionable, unanswerable, and uncontrovertible propositions, and upon each of which I am prepared to meet any gentleman, or set of gentlemen, in the United States in fair and friendly argument through the public press, provided I can have equal access to the press which is given to them.

In regard to the tenth proposition, I admit a difference may or does exist, although there has been no doubt in my own mind, especially since I have found my convictions confirmed by the opinions of Chief-justices Marshall and Taney. Still it is a question as yet not adjudicated by the proper tribunals of the country, but is one that it is high time should be settled. But no man *who is truly loyal to his country* need fear the consequences of a revocation of his pardon, as he can not be disturbed, either in his person or his property, without trial and conviction, which will never be resorted to if they conduct themselves with loyalty to the government of the United States, to which they owe their first allegiance, while this revocation will serve as "a hook in the nose of the leviathan" if he should continue to exhibit the same symptoms of disloyalty which now prevail throughout the state.

The fifteenth proposition was the only one that perplexed me for a moment, and that perplexity grew out of the fact that the State Constitution so limits the right of suffrage as to render a fair election under it almost impracticable; and how to enlarge it was the difficulty, as there was no authority given for such enlargement except by the Legislature, which must, of course, be elected before it could act; and as it matters not who votes, provided they vote for those only who are constitutionally eligible, I came to the conclusion that the best, if not only means of arriving at this end (as the state was still subject to military control), was to suggest that the President of the United States, as the head of the military authority, should provide for such enlargement as his judgment and discretion might direct, not doubting that he would extend it with sufficient liberality to answer the purposes of a fair election.

I grant this is an irregularity, but one that I could see no better means of settling. If any one can suggest a better mode, I am willing to adopt it.

I am not afraid to trust Mr. Johnson with this power. I am not one of those who entertain the opinion that Mr. Johnson has intended, or means now, to make any concessions to the Copperheads of the North or the *Coppertails* of the South. To the credit of human nature, be it said, that our history has furnished not even one instance of such revolting turpitude and depravity as would be exhibited by his tergiversation at such a time as this, and under such circumstances as now exist.

His veto of the Freedmen's Bureau Bill may well have been honest and conscientious. Even if he intended it as a rebuke to the extreme men of the North, I do not see that it should lead to the apprehension that he intended thereby to affiliate with the extreme men of the South, who are even more dangerously radical than the Radicals of the North. I do not see, that if I repudiate the teachings of Wendell Phillips and William Lloyd Garrison, that it is at all to be inferred that I intend to affiliate with Jeff. Davis and his party, any more than if I repudiate Davis and his company, that I intend to indorse Garrison and Phillips.

Thank God, the privilege is still left us (since the Confederacy was smashed up) to steer between both extremes; and believing as I do in the honesty of purpose and patriotism of the President, I think the few crumbs of comfort picked up from the shaking of the cloth from the President's table, which the reconstructed have grasped as drowning men cling to straws, will yet turn to ashes on their lips.

Nor do I perceive that any great inconvenience would result from the reorganization of this state, as I proposed. Upon its being decided that all legislative action under this Constitution has been unauthorized, Governor Pierpont would be rehabilitated, and restored to the power with which he was clothed by the Constitution, and he could at once appoint all the present judges and magistrates to hold over until new appointments could be made. But as long as the state is under the control of disloyal men, so long will she be excluded from the councils of the nation, and just so long will her representatives be left "out in the cold."

And now, Mr. Editor, in conclusion, let me urge you to go ahead and fear not. Strike whenever you can strike, and be sure to put in blows that will tell; for be you assured that, when *they* strike, they will strike with all their might, whether you strike or not. Unless we mean to acknowledge our inferiority, we must make a fight; therefore let us go in with all our strength and power, or tamely and shamefully surrender at once. Continue what you have so patriotically undertaken. Stir up the Union element of the state, whether large or small. Richmond is the nucleus for operations. Call a convention of the Union men, and, as a body, make an appeal to the President and to Congress to come to our relief. Of course, all can not come; but call all, and let as many come as are not afraid. Call it at such time as may seem most expedient, and *count me in;* and let those who are afraid, or can not come, stand back while we do the fighting for them, ourselves, and our country; but those who can come and won't come, can, if they prefer it, stay at home and swell the majority against us.

Respectfully yours,   JOHN M. BOTTS.

P.S.—I see by the paper of Monday that a *lamentable case* of timidity and want of moral courage was presented in the House of Delegates. It came from a quarter that I did not expect it; however, although we have no strength to spare, we can get along without this gentleman; but more of this hereafter.

THE FOURTH LETTER.

Mr. Garnett having at a later period made some reply to my second letter to him, only a portion of which I have ever seen, I wrote this, the last letter on this subject:

Auburn, near Brandy Station, April 15, 1866.

During the late suspension of the publication of the Richmond papers, I saw a brief extract in the Alexandria *Gazette* from a communication of Muscoe Garnett, Esq., in reply to my late letter to him, which, in more respects than one, does me great injustice. I have no intention, and still less desire, to quarrel with Mr. Garnett, or to say any thing that can be construed into unkindness, for I have no such feeling toward him.

His inexcusable repudiation of me before the body of which he was a member I thought did me so much wrong, and was calculated to do me so much injury, that I repelled it in self-defense, and in terms that I thought at the time well-merited. I looked upon it as the result of a weakness of nerve rather than a vice on his part, and intended to relieve myself by making this weakness transparent; and I hazard nothing in saying it cost me as much pain to write it, as it did Mr. Garnett or any of his friends to read it. That object accomplished, all feeling of resentment on my part immediately subsided, and in my bosom it shall not be revived. But I wish to correct some of Mr. Garnett's errors in regard to my position, which he strangely appears to have misapprehended. He says, "He (I) proposes to set aside the present state government and all its legislation (repudiates the Legislature from which he was anxious to receive the appointment of United States senator), desires a military or provisional governor to call a convention of Union men *par excellence*, such as could alone take the test-oath, and to be elected by men who could do the same."

In this brief space there are no less than three errors:

1st. So far from desiring a military or provisional governor for this state, I took the ground that this state occupied a different position from the other Southern states—that Governor Pierpont was the regularly elected governor, and must be recognized as such. That I repudiated the action and the constitutional organization of the Legislature, is true; but that was nothing new to Mr. Garnett, for in the month of November last I received a letter from Mr. Garnett, in which he put various questions to me, upon which he asked my opinions and advice. Among them was the following:

"How is the question to be raised as to the members that are elected, who are, by the terms of the Constitution, rendered incapable of holding office?" Here, then, Mr. Garnett broadly admits that there were members of the body who were *prohibited by the Constitution* from holding office, and he wants to know how to get rid of them. And what was the answer I gave him? Here it is: The question must be raised by the oath being administered to each member of the Legislature; but the Constitution does not prescribe by whom the oath shall be administered, while it is evident that it was not contemplated that any should be allowed to "hold" or *take* a seat without first taking the oath; for if he takes the seat to assist in the organization of the House, he certainly *holds it*, even if it should be only for a day, while he is *disqualified* for any legislative duty until he has taken the oath. I see, then, no remedy for a violation of the Constitution both in letter and spirit, unless the governor will require each member to take and subscribe to the oath before him, as the head of the government; and it is his imperative duty to see that the Constitution, which he is here to put in force, is not violated at the outset. * * * "The Constitution authorizes the Legislature to pass an act or acts prescribing means by which persons who have baen disfranchised by this provision shall or may be restored to the rights of VOTERS when, in their opinion, it will be safe to do so." * * * "But no person shall vote or hold office under this Constitution who had held office under the Confederate government, or state in rebellion," etc., etc.; so that the right of suffrage *even* could not be so enlarged as to extend to those who had held office, and I could never consent to countenance so mischievous and pernicious, so disorganizing and revolutionary a precedent, as that of having constitutional provisions amended, annulled, or introduced by an ordinary act of legislation, which must at all times be subordinate to the terms and provisions of the Constitution.

If the example already set by the effort to remove the disabilities for holding office, as fixed by the Constitution, has any merit or virtue in it, then all Constitutions will be worthless in the future; and all that a dominant party may desire to effect may be readily accomplished by submitting the question to the people whether the Legislature may not alter, amend, or abolish any constitutional provision that may stand in the way of their success. In like manner Congress has nothing to do but to submit to the popular vote whether they shall not be empowered at their next session to amend the United States Constitution, so as to make the right of suffrage universal, without distinction of race or color, and the thing is done, without the formality in such cases made and provided.

We of the South should be extremely cautious how we set bad examples, which may be imitated by others to our disadvantage or ruin. With a proper exercise of wisdom and discretion on the part of the South, these disqualifications will, perhaps at no remote day, be greatly modified; and is it not better that these gentlemen who have brought such untold misery on the people should be required to exercise a little patience, and not claim at the start, as if by Divine right, to take the reins of government in their own hands, and so far depart from all the old landmarks, which may lead us into everlasting difficulty and trouble, both in the state and federal governments?

Such were the opinions I entertained at that time, and such was my answer to Mr. G., but which I abstained from pressing until an opportunity was afforded of ascertaining whether the action of this body would be such as to command the confidence and respect, as well of their political opponents as their friends, or of the loyal and disloyal portions of the community alike. The result proved that it was the most disloyal, intolerant, and proscriptive body that had ever assembled in the Capitol of Virginia toward the loyal men of this state, who were alone entitled by the Constitution, as well as by national law, to shape and control the legislation and destiny of this commonwealth; and from the moment I saw this I resolved to raise the very question that I had endeavored to impress upon Mr. Garnett, and through him, and others who accompanied him, upon the mind of Governor Pierpont.

2. He says I was "*anxious*" to receive the appointment of United States senator from the body I am now disposed to repudiate. If Mr. Garnett had substituted the word "*willing*" for anxious, he would have been nearer the mark. I said to him, as to others, from the first, I could not, and would not, under any circumstances, be a candidate for the office, but if the state desired my services they should not be withheld. I had already, before they met, repudiated the Legislature if it should be organized without the administration of the oath prescribed; and if I had been elected before the proscriptive policy which characterized the body was adopted, I would cheerfully have accepted it, and have done all in my power to have gotten the *loyal representatives* of the Southern States admitted to their seats; but from the moment I saw the temper and disposition which controlled the action of the (so-called) Legislature toward all of my class, I resolved, if elected, to decline the position, on the ground that the elective body was not authorized by the Constitution to make an election, and this fact was made known to a number of my intimate

friends, including Alexander Rives, Franklin Stearns, Lewis McKenzie, and many others, both in Richmond and Washington. Nevertheless, I was more anxious for an election than before, because I felt that it would strengthen me in the position I had even then made up my mind to adopt, when I saw that it was the purpose of that body to make loyalty to the Union odious and disloyalty meritorious. I would not have consented to receive honors at the hands of those who would bestow them for the advantages they expected to derive from my services, and leave my friends behind to be sacrificed. This position was distinctly well known to many of those in whom I could confide.

But Mr. Garnett continues, "If I were for a moment to give countenance to this (the call of a convention to be composed of Union men who could take the test-oath), the bodies of my three noble sons, who fought and lost their lives in a cause that they thought to be just, would turn in their graves, and no more could I visit, without shame and confusion, the sacred spot where they rest."

Well, all this may be so, but it only proves that I had been mistaken in Mr. Garnett's position. I thought *he* was one that would take that oath, and was anxious to make all others do so before they could enter the legislative body; or why did he want to know how the question could be raised to get rid of those who could not take a test-oath prescribed by the State Constitution? While I have thus answered all of Mr. Garnett's communication that has fallen under my observation, I hope without offense to him, yet would I not have done so, but that I had something else more important to say, and therefore concluded I would take it all in a lump, and make a finish of the job.

Not long since I received a letter from one of the most quiet, unobtrusive, and intelligent members of the late Legislature, in which he says,

"In this county we have, and had during the war, a majority of straight-out Union men; and I think the same is the case in two of the counties adjacent to this; and, so far as I have been able to ascertain the sentiments of the Union men, they cordially indorse your views. Mr. ———— who is a sound lawyer, says none of your positions can be refuted, yet there is one point on which some would like an explanation; for example, an intelligent friend asked me this question:

"If Jeff. Davis had the right of expatriation, and exercised the right by becoming a citizen of the Confederate States, how can the United States punish him for treason? I would be glad, if you publish any thing farther in explanation of your 'axioms,' that you give your views in regard to the case stated."

It was to explain this view particularly that I was induced to write this article. The explanation is very simple and very plain. The attempt to carry a state out of the Union, and thereby to erect another government within the jurisdiction of the United States, constituted the crime of treason; then to become a citizen of another government, whether "*de facto*" or "*de jure*," was an act of denationalization, or alienation, which in no degree relieved the party of the penalties of the crime of treason.

Benedict Arnold, for example, committed treason, and then made his escape to another country, and became a citizen thereof. Did it ever occur to any human being that if he had subsequently fallen into the hands of the United States, that he would not have been as liable to punishment as if he had never left the country? Similar cases are of *daily occurrence*. A man commits a murder or a forgery, robs a bank or his employer, and makes his escape to Canada or to England; he may or may not become a citizen thereof; he is demanded under an extradition treaty; he is delivered up, brought home, and punished for the offense he committed before he left.

Has it ever entered into the imagination of any one that his having made himself a citizen of another government in any degree impaired his liability to punishment? Yet this is the only point of objection I have yet heard of being made by any truly loyal man to the series of axioms I have had the honor to present as the only means left *us* by the disloyal element of the state to protect ourselves from the position of absolute inferiority to which it is proposed to reduce us.

One other word on this question of alienage. Perhaps it is not generally known what measure of liberality these *howling reconstructed gentlemen*, who complain so bitterly of my want of generosity toward them, proposed for us. Let all men then understand that when they had the power they did not lack the will to make *aliens of us all*, under circumstances far less aggravated than those under which they are now themselves laboring.

In the month of July, 1861, the Convention of Virginia passed an ordinance declaring "that any citizen of Virginia holding office under the government of the United States after the 31st of July, 1861, should be forever banished from the state, and be declared an ALIEN ENEMY; and that any citizen of Virginia hereafter undertaking to represent the State of Virginia in the Congress of the United States should, in addition to the above penalties, be considered guilty of treason, and his property be liable to confiscation."

· Yet those who voted for and those who approved this measure of vindictive harshness toward those who declined to surrender their birthright as citizens of the freest and best government on earth, or to make a voluntary relinquishment of their great inheritance of freedom, are now the most clamorous to represent the people in this same Congress of the United States, and set up a universal howl of indignation, and implore the wrath of God and man on the heads of those who propose to give them a small dose of their own medicine.

Oh, what a difference there is between "*your ox and my bull!*" What a set of knaves and hypocrites are these same leaders of Democracy, and what a set of simpletons are those honest but deluded people of all parties who have not yet learned how to appreciate them!　　·

But if I have made myself so odious to the *partially* "*reconstructed*" by the propositions *they have obliged me to make,* what will they have to say when they find that I am but sustaining the policy of Mr. Johnson, whom (in imitation of the "anaconda") they are covering with their filthy slime before they swallow him *whole,* if he should ever have the misfortune to place himself within the reach of their rapacious jaws, and substitute for him in their affections another Jefferson Davis or General Lee?

If all men were by law aliens to the Confederate government who held office under the United States, why are not all aliens to the United States who held office under the Confederate government? "Answer me that, Master Brooks."

Under this decree of the Virginia Convention, poor old Colonel Payne, a faithful and valued officer of the United States, who carried a Mexican bullet in his hip for the last fifteen years of his life, suffering torture all the time, an honored soldier and a devoted Union man, was *compelled* to resign his commission and half pay, forswear his country (or be stripped of the little property he had saved in a long and laborious life), which in a short time broke his heart, and hurried him to an untimely grave.

Where were these *howling, whining* patriots at that day? ·Where were "Blanche," "Tray," and "Sweetheart" then? Who cried out that this was an outrage against those who had committed neither moral nor legal wrong? Who condemned? Who disapproved? Who stigmatized or denounced the authors of this decree? Or, rather, let me ask which of all those who have hurled their malignant spite at me did not justify and approve?

When the *Examiner* and *Dispatch, et id omne genus,* were, upon my arrest in 1862, calling for my blood and that of other traitors, and daily crying "Crucify them, crucify them!" "Hang them, hang them!" be-cause we would not raise a parricidal hand against the government of our choice, and to which we were born, and to which there was neither moral nor legal right to sever us from, where then were these champions of the great principles of public law? Where these defenders of the rights of the people, and of the doctrine that *all government depends upon the consent of the governed?* When I was ignominiously thrown into a negro jail, and brought to. trial before a military commission by Jefferson Davis, where were then these "*Scribes* and *Pharisees*" who now cry out so lusti-ly against a military commission for him who was the constitutional com-mander-in-chief of the armies in rebellion, and who did not hesitate to use such military commissions for strictly private citizens? What privileges and immunities are guaranteed to this great offender that are not equally secured to every American citizen? Out upon all such hypocrisy. I have heard it thunder before to-day, and I expect to hear it thunder again, and am not to be deterred from the performance of a public duty by such selfish tricksters and hucksters in political trade.

Will it not surprise those who have said so many harsh things of me, in parallel columns with their lavish expenditure of toadyism to Mr. Johnson, to find that upon this question of *alienage* our opinions are pre-cisely alike; that they "run upon all-fours," as is commonly said, and that in his policy (for I take it for granted he does not mean to back down from any pledge he has formally and voluntarily made to the coun-try) he goes far beyond any position I have taken, or am likely to take, especially in regard to *the division and sale of the large plantations into small farms,* and their distribution here? But I hope these gentlemen, before they commit themselves any farther against my policy, will inward-ly digest the policy of Mr. Johnson, and deal fairly with both.

Here is an extract from the speech of Mr. Johnson, made on his nom-ination for Vice-president in 1864. I must, however, say that when I wrote my axioms I had never seen this speech, and did not know that I was indorsed by such distinguished authority. Here is what Mr. Johnson says:

"But in calling a convention to restore the state, who shall restore and re-establish it? Shall the man who gave his influence and his means to destroy the government? Is he to participate in the great work of re-organization? Shall he who brought this misery upon the state be per-mitted to control its destinies? If this be so, then all this precious blood of our brave soldiers and officers so freely poured out will have been wantonly spilled. *All the glorious victories won by our noble armies will go for naught, and all the battle-fields which have been sown with dead heroes during the rebellion will have been made memorable in vain.*

"Why all this carnage and devastation? *It was that treason might be put down and traitors punished. Therefore I say that traitors should take a back seat in the work of restoration.* If there be but five thousand men in Tennessee loyal to the Constitution, loyal to freedom, loyal to justice, these true and faithful men should control the work of reorganization and reformation absolutely. I say that the traitor has ceased to be a citizen, and, in joining the rebellion, has become a public enemy. *He forfeited his right to vote with loyal men when he renounced his citizenship and sought to destroy our government.* We say to the most honest and industrious foreigner who comes from England or Germany to dwell among us, and to add to the wealth of the country, 'Before you can be a citizen you must stay here five years.' If we are so cautious about foreigners, who voluntarily renounce their homes to live with us, what should we say to the traitor, who, although born and reared among us, has raised a parricidal hand against the government which always protected him? My judgment is that he should be subjected to a severe ordeal before he is restored to citizenship. A fellow who takes the oath merely to save his property, and denies the validity of the oath, is a perjured man, and not to be trusted. *Before these repenting rebels can be trusted, let them bring forth the fruits of repentance. He who helped to make all these widows and orphans, who draped the streets of Nashville in mourning, should suffer for his great crime.*

"Treason must be made odious, and the traitors must be punished and impoverished, their great plantations must be seized, and divided into small farms, and sold to honest, industrious men. The day for protecting the lands and negroes of these authors of rebellion is past. It is high time it was. I have been most deeply pained at some things which have come under my observation. We get men in command who, under the influence of flattery, fawning, and caressing, grant protection to the rich traitor, while the poor Union man stands out in the cold, often unable to get a receipt or a voucher for his losses."

These were Mr. Johnson's original, honest views, voluntarily expressed; while the instincts of self-preservation, as well as the preservation of the best interests of the nation, *forced this policy upon me* at the moment I was exerting my utmost efforts to serve those who were the first to repudiate and denounce me, and all who thought as I thought.

Now, then, here we are, Mr. Johnson as the chief, and I as a subordinate helping him to carry out his own policy. Is it not in violation of every principle of law and justice, to reward the principal and punish the agent?

Finally. The Union men of Frederick County have called a convention of all Union men, to be held in Alexandria on the 17th of May. Of course, I suppose it is meant of all *unconditional Union men now* and *all the time*, for with them alone must commence this work of reconstruction; for although there are a great number of truly loyal men now who took the amnesty oath honestly and in good faith, yet there are also a very large number who regard it as a Custom-house oath, taken under compulsion and dictation, as one of the reconstructed and elected candidates for Congress declared during the canvass *he did*, and there will be no ready means of discrimination between the two; therefore, to make the convention effective, it must necessarily be limited in the start to those to whom no objection can be made.

With this limitation, we can have a most imposing convention if we had the means of giving general notice through the state of the purpose. Many, therefore, will be kept away for want of knowledge of the intention, many by poverty, and many more yet by a want of backbone to meet what they hold to be public opinion; but as I am about to leave the state for a while, I will beg leave now to suggest that the day fixed for the meeting is, in my opinion, too early for a successful issue, and would therefore suggest a postponement until some time after the middle of June; but let it be when or where it may, if within the reach of possibility, I will make one of the number. Respectfully, JOHN M. BOTTS.

MR. BOTTS'S PLAN OF RECONSTRUCTION.

The plan of reconstruction as reported by the Joint Committee, and which was in part adopted in the House by such an overwhelming majority, was liable, I thought, to so many grave objections, and calculated to do so much more harm than good, that I took the liberty of offering a plan of my own, based essentially on the axioms I had previously presented, and invited the attention of Congress to it by the card that follows.

The great objects at which I aimed were, first, to place the state governments in the hands of those loyal men who alone are entitled to hold them, and thereby insure loyalty a foothold every where; second, to close the breach as nearly as possible between the President and Congress; third, to relieve the country of that accursed incubus of selfish, corrupt, and abandoned politicians of both the old parties that have always been found ready to sacrifice the country to help themselves, but never to sacrifice themselves to help the country, not so much for *their punishment*, as for the peace, harmony, security, and welfare of the country—although I know the loss of political power is to them the severest infliction that could be imposed, next to the loss of life; for, as to property, few of the most rabid have any thing to lose. If the masses should in the end be treated unkindly, let them thank these leaders for it, and then thank themselves for supporting, instead of rebuking them for their folly and bold defiance.

"Astor House, May 12, 1866.

"To the Members of the Senate and House of Representatives of the United States:

"GENTLEMEN,—I feel that if any one in private life has a right, without presumption, to address the loyal representative men of this nation upon a subject we are all alike interested in, that I might venture to do so without offense, and without rendering myself obnoxious to the charge of vanity.

"I have no personal favors to ask at the hands of any one. I have no 'axe to grind.' I am a candidate or applicant for no office. I desire no preferment. I belong to no political organization. I am entirely free to throw the weight of any little influence I may be able to command in favor of such men and such measures as my judgment my approve, and against such as that judgment may condemn. I can therefore afford to be honest, to be truthful, independent, and patriotic, and I may be excused for saying that I occupy a stand-point I think free from all prejudice and passion, which are too apt to have their influence, and to control the action of those who are surrounded by a constantly overheated political atmosphere. But while I belong to no political organization, my sympathies, affinities, and co-operation are, as they always have been, entirely with the unconditional Union men of the country.

"May I therefore be permitted to ask your calm and deliberate attention to the views presented below. The difficulty of seeing and conversing with each member in private is my reason for adopting this public mode of communication.

"Twelve years ago I addressed myself, as now, from this house to Congress against the repeal of the Missouri Compromise, the bitter fruits of which we are now all tasting. I hope this will not pass unheeded, as did my urgent entreaties then. Very respectfully, your obedient servant,

"JOHN M. BOTTS."

Objections to the Report of the Reconstruction Committee.

1st. It makes no provision for the relief of the Union white men of the South, but leaves them and the state governments in the hands of the un-reconstructed rebels for the next four years, who will improve the opportunity to educate the people without restraint to a more embittered spirit of disaffection and disloyalty to the government of the United States, and in four years we shall hardly have a loyal man left in the South; self-preservation will drive them into the ranks of the other party, and the Southern States will constitute an element of weakness rather than of strength to the government.

2d. The disfranchisement proposed is made to depend upon the grade of office held, instead of the grade of offense committed, and is limited to the higher classes of officers, civil and military, the latter including all over the rank of colonel, leaving all the guerrilla chiefs and their subordinate officers, to say nothing of privates — all of whom would have been generals if they could, many of whom too committed the greatest atrocities of the war—free hereafter to participate in the councils of the nation. It also leaves those who voted in convention for ordinances of secession—which was a declaration of war against the United States, and in the absence of which there would have been no rebellion—likewise free. It imposes no disqualification upon those mischievous politicians who for thirty years have been stirring up disaffection and rebellion among the people. Nor does it in any degree affect the sympathizers with and co-operators in the rebellion in the Northern States, who are, if possible, more guilty and more obnoxious than those in the South.

3d. The bill proposed can not receive the President's sanction, nor is the Constitutional Amendment at all likely to receive the approval of the necessary number of state Legislatures.

4th. It is extremely improbable that any Southern state will adopt the conditions prescribed, and four years hence we shall be as far from reconstruction as we are now.

I suggest, therefore, that all these difficulties may be remedied by a simple legislative enactment, which might probably receive the President's assent, and, if not, might be carried by a two-thirds vote of both houses. I propose, then, in substitution for the report of the committee, that it shall be declared by law,

That no person hereafter shall be capable of holding any office, legislative, executive, or judicial, in the Federal or state governments, for ten years from the passage of the act, who was over the age of twenty-five at the breaking out of the rebellion, without taking the following oath in addition to that now required of all such officers by the Constitution of the United States:

"I, A. B., do solemnly swear that I have not, since the twentieth day of December, 1860 (the date of the Ordinance of Secession of South Carolina), voluntarily taken up arms against the United States, nor have I advised or encouraged others to do so; that I have not sought or held office under the Confederate States government, or of that of any state in rebellion, with a view in any manner to aid the rebellion; that I have not said, written, or done any thing designed, or of a nature calculated to alienate the affections or allegiance of the people from the government of the United States; nor have I otherwise given aid and comfort to the rebellion."

Let this enactment be accompanied with an absolute remission in all cases of the forfeiture of life, liberty, and property, for the crimes committed by and under the authority of those in rebellion; and let it also be declared that if it shall be ascertained that any person has sworn falsely to obtain or hold any office hereby prohibited, such office shall be absolutely vacated, and the party held liable to a prosecution for perjury.

If this plan should be adopted, every loyal citizen would be subjected to the test prescribed before he could hold a legislative, executive, or judicial office, while those of thirty and under who had borne arms against the country would be relieved of such obligations. It would be manifestly proper, therefore, that an oath should be provided for them which would have only a prospective operation, and I suggest the following:

"I, A. B., do solemnly swear that I recognize the Constitution of the United States, and all laws made in pursuance thereof, as the supreme law of the land, and that I am bound thereby, any state law, Constitution, or ordinance, or convention to the contrary notwithstanding; and that I regard all laws of the United States as binding on the citizens thereof, until declared unconstitutional by the Supreme Court of the United States. That I regard the first obligation of allegiance of the citizen as due to the United States, and not to any component part thereof; and I will hereafter observe and obey the laws, and protect the flag of my country when lawfully called upon to do so."

This would be what Mr. Johnson would call an "intelligent treason," not holding to responsibility the boys and young men, who were misled and dragged in by older, more experienced, and more wicked men, nor those who were forced in by conscription, and would leave all now thirty years of age and under to fill the offices, state and Federal, who, with the Union men, would constitute a majority of the whole in most if not all of the states; and the regenerated under thirty-one would naturally at-tach themselves to the government that had thus restored them, and aid in circulating a spirit of loyalty throughout the South, and their numbers would daily increase, while the other party would decline in a still great-er ratio.

Twelve months ago every rebel in the South would have rejoiced at the proffer of such terms. It is due to the nation—due to posterity and man-kind—that some penalty should be visited on those who were wickedly guilty, to prevent a repetition of the offense at a future day. Now is the time to establish a precedent, and so mild a penalty was never before ex-acted for so grave a crime — complete restoration and amnesty, only withholding for ten years political power from those who had voluntarily and treacherously surrendered and abandoned it. Upon the passage of this law reconstruction would be absolute and immediate, upon a basis of unquestioned loyalty; the state governments would be placed in the hands of loyal men; the chief cause of dissension between the President and Congress would be withdrawn; harmony in the public councils would be restored; the more guilty would be mildly punished, and the balance re-lieved of responsibility; and not the least of the advantages of this mode of settlement would be that it withdraws the question of reconstruction from the next election. If the President should sanction it, and Congress reject it, it would indicate that they had some ulterior object in view, and a disposition to delay unreasonably a restoration upon a loyal basis, which would severely damage the Union party; while, on the other hand, if Congress should adopt it, and the President reject it, it would strongly in-dicate on his part a desire to restore to power those elements of disloyalty North and South which have brought such desolation and ruin upon the country, of which many now (but I do not) suspect him.

MR. LINCOLN AND HIS POLICY.

So much injustice has been done to the memory of Mr. Lincoln, and such unfair and unfounded representations made in regard to the respons-ibility for the late rebellion—especially made in a work that has lately, and for the first time, fallen under my observation, called " *The Demo-cratic Almanac,*" published in the city of New York, for the year 1866, I presume for Southern consumption—that I should feel my task incomplete if I did not add a brief synopsis of the course of policy pursued by Mr. Lincoln, chiefly for the benefit of my Southern readers, who, by the events of the war and the necessary interruption of communication between the two sections, were cut off from all knowledge of what was transpiring in Washington, and were limited in their reading to the complexion given to all things as they found it in the Southern press, which, for the most part, studiously suppressed the publication of whatever might contribute to a more favorable feeling toward those whom they had been taught to believe were their persecutors and oppressors, and substituted for it such imaginary pictures as ingenuity could devise to fire the Southern heart, frenzy the Southern mind, and whet the appetite for blood.

In the performance of this task, I begin with what is already to be found in the body of this work, to wit, the platform adopted by the Republican party in 1860 at the Chicago Convention, which nominated Mr. Lincoln. On the question of slavery it reads, "That the maintenance inviolate of the rights of the states, and especially the right of each state to order and control its own domestic institutions according to its own judgment exclusively, is essential to that balance of power on which the perfection and endurance of our political fabric depends; and we denounce the lawless invasion by armed force of the soil of any state or territory, no matter under what pretext, as among the gravest of crimes."

This declaration of principles—so much misrepresented in 1860, '61, throughout the South—of itself effectually disposes of the charge in the aforesaid "*Democratic Almanac*," to be found on p. 17 of said book, which declares that Mr. Lincoln was elected as the representative of a party which had resolved that "slavery must be abolished, if not by the *fear of the sword*, then by the *sword itself*; and again, that the "*Republican party*" had declared, "Against slaveholders as a body we wage an exterminating war." "If the negroes had a chance, they would be delighted to cut their masters' throats." "Slaveholders, it is for you to determine whether we are to have justice (*i. e.*, emancipation) *peaceably or by violence;* for whatever consequences may follow, we are determined to have it, *one way or another.*"

Next, as to Mr. Lincoln himself. This article in the "*Democratic Almanac*" seems to have been written for the purpose of again "*firing the Southern heart,*" of which folly we have had quite enough already, and of keeping a party in alliance with treason, by operating upon the ignorant and uninformed. It contains so much trashy nonsense that is known to its Northern readers to be utterly false and unfounded, that I instinctively shrink from giving it importance by taking any notice of it; but the South, being engaged in war during the whole of Mr. Lincoln's administration, and thus cut off from all intercourse with the North, are liable to be misled; and I have therefore thought it best to give a brief sketch of Mr. Lincoln's policy and action on this subject from first to last, and to show that Southern secessionists imposed upon him the necessity of emancipation, to save, as he thought, the life of the nation; and before he resorted to this extreme measure, he did all in his power to induce Southern slaveholders to accept a fair compensation for slavery, which was indignantly rejected.

I start, then, with Mr. Lincoln's speech on the 4th of March, 1861, in which he said, "Apprehension seems to exist among the people of the Southern States that, by the accession of a Republican administration, their property, peace, and personal security are to be endangered. There has never been any reasonable cause for such apprehension. Indeed, the most ample evidence to the contrary has all the while existed, and been open to their inspection. It is found in nearly all the published speeches of him who now addresses you. I do but quote from one of those speeches when I declare that I have no purpose, directly or indirectly, to interfere with the institution of slavery in the states where it exists. I believe I have no lawful right to do so, and I have no inclination to do so. Those who nominated and elected me did so with the full knowledge that I had made this and many similar declarations, and had never recanted them. And more than this, they placed in the platform for my acceptance, and as a law to themselves and to me, the clear and emphatic resolution which I now read:

"'Resolved, That the maintenance inviolate of the rights of the states, and especially the right of each state to order and control its own domestic institutions according to its own judgment exclusively, is essential to the balance of power on which the perfection and endurance of our political fabric depends; and we denounce the lawless invasion by armed force of the soil of any state or territory, no matter under what pretext, as among the gravest of crimes.'

"I now reiterate these sentiments, and, in doing so, I only press upon the public attention the most conclusive evidence of which the case is susceptible, that the property, peace, and security of no section are to be in any wise endangered by the now incoming administration. I add, too, that all the protection which, consistently with the Constitution and the laws, can be given, will be cheerfully given to the states when lawfully demanded, for whatever cause, as cheerfully to one section as another.

"There is much controversy about the delivering up of fugitives from service or labor. The clause I now read is as plainly written in the Constitution as any other of its provisions :

" 'No person held to service or labor in one state under the laws thereof, escaping into another, shall, in consequence of any law or regulation therein, be discharged from such service or labor, but shall be delivered up on claim of the party to whom such service or labor may be due.'

"It is scarcely questioned that this provision was intended by those who made it for the reclaiming of what we call fugitive slaves; and the intention of the lawgiver is the law. All members of Congress swear their support to the whole Constitution—to this provision as much as any other. To the proposition, then, that slaves whose cases come within the terms of this clause 'shall be delivered up,' their oaths are unanimous. Now if they would make the effort in good temper, could they not, with nearly equal unanimity, frame and pass a law by means of which to keep good that unanimous oath?

* * * * * * * * * * * *

"I take the official oath to-day with no mental reservations, and with no purpose to construe the Constitution or laws by any hypercritical rules. And while I do not choose now to specify particular acts of Congress as proper to be enforced, I do suggest that it will be much safer for all, both in official and private stations, to conform to, and abide by, all those acts which stand unrepealed, than to violate any of them, trusting to find impunity in having them held to be unconstitutional."

On the 13th of April, 1861, a committee, consisting of Wm. Ballard Preston, a quasi-Union man, who soon gave way in the convention—A. H. H. Stuart—a professed Union man, who ultimately voted at the polls for secession, and urged the people to do the same—and George W. Randolph, an original and extreme secessionist, waited upon Mr. Lincoln to inquire "what policy the Federal Executive intended to pursue toward the Confederate States?" to which Mr. Lincoln, with more courtesy and forbearance than they would have received from "Old Hickory," replied as follows:

"In answer, I have to say that, having at the beginning of my official term expressed my intended policy as plainly as I was able, it is with deep regret, and some mortification, I now learn that there is great and injurious uncertainty in the public mind as to what that policy is, and what course I intend to pursue.

"Not having as yet seen occasion to change, it is now my purpose to pursue the course marked out in the Inaugural Address. I commend a careful consideration of the whole document, as the best expression I can give of my purposes. As I then and therein said, I now repeat:

" 'The power confided to me will be used to hold, occupy, and possess the property and places belonging to the government, and to collect the duties and imposts; but beyond what is necessary for these objects there will be no invasion, no using of force against or among the people any where.'

"By the words 'property and places belonging to the government,' I chiefly allude to the military posts and property which were in the possession of the government when it came to my hands.

"But if, as now appears to be true, in pursuit of a purpose to drive the United States authority from these places, an unprovoked assault has been made upon Fort Sumter, I shall hold myself at liberty to repossess, if I can, like places which had been seized before the government was devolved upon me. And in any event I shall, to the best of my ability, repel force by force.

"In case it proves true that Fort Sumter has been assaulted, as it is reported, I shall perhaps cause the United States mails to be withdrawn from all the states which claim to have seceded, believing that the commencement of actual war against the United States justifies and possibly demands it.

" I scarcely need to say that I consider the military posts and property situated within the states which claim to have seceded as yet belonging to the government of the United States as much as they did before the supposed secession.

"Whatever else I may do for the purpose, I shall not attempt to collect the duties and imposts by any armed invasion of any part of the country; not meaning by this, however, that I may not land a force deemed necessary to relieve a fort upon the border of the country.

"From the fact that I have quoted a part of the Inaugural Address, it must not be inferred that I repudiate any other part; the whole of which I reaffirm, except so far as what I now say of the mails may be regarded as a modification."

Unless this committee and the Convention intended to require Mr. Lincoln, like a perjured coward, basely and perfidiously to surrender the forts, arsenals, arms, ammunition, revenue cutters, mints, custom-houses, post-offices, and other property that had by violence, and without shadow of authority, been taken from the government over which he had been elected to preside, what farther guarantee could have been asked for than was here given? But, instead of its being received with satisfaction and gratification by these two pliant and flexible Union men, who were sent in company with another, of superior intellect, and of far more will and courage than either, they united with the secession leader in loud complaints and bitter denunciation of Mr. Lincoln for daring to threaten, in the face of the Virginia Convention, to attempt to get back the stolen property of the United States.

The effect produced by such a report as they made on their return to the body of the Convention upon *facile Union men*, who had been more accustomed to *follow* than to *lead*, may well be conjectured. It was at a time, too, of great excitement. The Convention had given its pledge to South Carolina, through Mr. Pryor, that Virginia would come to her aid on the firing of the first gun; the Confederate batteries were then playing upon the walls of Sumter; Anderson was making a *feeble* or no defense; the fall of the fort was a certainty; for upon a demand from Beauregard upon Anderson to surrender, he had already informed the enemy he could only hold out a few days for the want of bread, and, if he would wait, the fort would be evacuated *by noon on the 15th*, only two days from the date of this interview. On the evening of the 13th Anderson struck his flag to South Carolina, South Carolina having done in three days what the combined military and naval power of the United States could not undo in four years. It might be curious to inquire how many *shell* were thrown from Sumter in this three days' terrific cannonading, which terminated in the lowering of the flag of the United States to "KING COTTON," and nobody hurt on either side.

But to proceed: on the 6th of March, 1862, Mr. Lincoln sent the following message to Congress:

"Fellow-citizens of the Senate and House of Representatives:

"I recommend the adoption of a joint resolution by your honorable bodies, which shall be substantially as follows:

"*Resolved*, That the United States ought to co-operate with any state which may adopt gradual abolishment of slavery, giving to such state pecuniary aid, to be used by such state in its discretion to compensate for the inconveniences, public and private, produced by such change of system."

On the 10th of March, Mr. Conkling, of New York, under a suspension of the rules, introduced this as a joint resolution, and it was carried by yeas and nays: yeas, 97; nays, 36; Southern members principally voting against it.

The same resolution was passed in the Senate on the 2d of April: yeas, 32; nays, 10.

Yeas—Messrs. Morrill and Fessenden, of Maine; Clark and Hale, of New Hampshire; Foot and Collamer, of Vermont; Wilson and Sumner, of Massachusetts; Anthony, of Rhode Island; Dixon and Foster, of Connecticut; Ten Eyck, of New Jersey; Davis, of Kentucky; Sherman and Wade, of Ohio; Lane, of Indiana; Trumbull, of Illinois; Chandler, of Michigan; Harlan and Grimes, of Iowa; Doolittle and Howe, of Wisconsin; Wilkinson, of Minnesota; Pomeroy and Lane, of Kansas; Henderson, of Missouri; Willey, of West Virginia; Wilmot, of Pennsylvania; King, of New York; Thomson, of New Jersey; and Browning, of Illinois.

Nays—Bayard and Saulsbury, of Delaware; Carlisle, of West Virginia; Kennedy, of Maryland; Latham, of California; Nesmith and Stark, of Oregon; Powell, of Kentucky; Wilson, of Missouri; and Wright, of New Jersey.

Upon this proposition Mr. Lincoln invited a conference with some of the more prominent members of the Southern States, the result of which is given below by the Hon. J. W. Crisfield, senator from Maryland.

The following is a memorandum of an interview between the President and some border slave state representatives, March 10, 1862, by the Hon. J. W. Crisfield.

"After the usual salutations, and we were seated, the President said, in substance, that he had invited us to meet him to have some conversation with us in explanation of his Message of the 6th. That since he had sent it in several of the gentlemen then present had visited him, but had avoided any allusion to the Message, and he therefore inferred that the import of the Message had been misunderstood, and was regarded as inimical to the interests we represented; and he had resolved he would talk with us, and disabuse our minds of that erroneous opinion.

"The President then disclaimed any intent to injure the interests or wound the sensibilities of the Slave States. On the contrary, his purpose was to protect the one and respect the other; that we were engaged in a terrible, wasting, and tedious war; immense armies were in the field, and must continue in the field as long as the war lasts; that these armies must of necessity be brought into contact with slaves in the states we represented, and in other states as they advanced; that slaves would come to the camps, and continual irritation be kept up; that he was constantly annoyed by conflicting and antagonistic complaints. On the one side, a certain class complained if the slave was not protected by the army, persons were frequently found who, participating in these views, acted in a way unfriendly to the slaveholder; on the other hand, slaveholders complained that their rights were interfered with, their slaves induced to abscond, and protected within the lines; these complaints were numerous, loud, and deep; were a serious annoyance to him, and embarrassing to the progress of the war; that it kept alive a spirit hostile to the government in the states we represented; strengthened the hopes of the Confederates that at some day the Border States would unite with them, and thus tend to prolong the war; and he was of opinion, if this resolution should be adopted by Congress and accepted by our states, these causes of irritation and these hopes be removed, more would be accomplished toward shortening the war than could be hoped from the greatest victory achieved by Union armies; that he made this proposition in good faith, and desired it to be accepted, if at all, voluntarily, and in the same patriotic spirit in which it was made; that emancipation was a subject exclusively under the control of the states, and must be adopted or rejected by each for itself; that he did not claim, nor had this government any right to coerce them for that purpose; that such was no part of his purpose in making this proposition, and he wished it to be clearly understood; that he did not expect us there to be prepared to give him an answer, but he hoped we would take the subject into serious consideration, confer with one another, and then take such course as we felt our duty and the interests of our constituents required of us.

* * . * . * . * * * * . * * *

"He thought the institution wrong, and ought never to have existed; but yet he recognized the rights of property which had grown out of it, and would respect those rights as fully as similar rights in any other property; that property can exist, and does legally exist. He thought such a law wrong, but the rights of property resulting must be respected; he would get rid of the odious law, not by violating the right, but by encouraging the proposition and offering inducements to give it up."

Here the interview ended by Mr. Crittenden's assuring the President that, whatever might be our final action, we all thought him solely moved by a high patriotism and sincere devotion to the happiness and glory of his country; and with that conviction we should consider respectfully the important suggestions he had made.

The correctness of this report made by Mr. Crisfield is certified to by J. W. Menzies, J. J. Crittenden, and R. Mallory, all of Kentucky.

Did this look like a war upon the institutions of the South, either on the part of Mr. Lincoln or Congress, by the sword, or does it exhibit a desire to remove the chief obstacle to harmony by a fair and just equivalent?

In July, 1862, Mr. Lincoln invited an interview with the members of Congress from the Border Slave States, which was held. During the interview Mr. Lincoln addressed an earnest and patriotic appeal to these gentlemen, in the course of which he said, "You prefer that the constitutional relations of the states to the nation shall be practically restored without disturbance of the institution; and if this were done, my whole duty in this respect, under the Constitution and my oath of office, would be performed. But it is not done, and we are trying to accomplish it by war. The incidents of the war can not be avoided. If the war continues long, as it must if the object be not sooner attained, the institution in your states will be extinguished by mere friction and abrasion—by the mere incidents of the war. It will be gone, and you will have nothing valuable in lieu of it. Much of its value is gone already. How much better for you and for your people to take the step which at once shortens the war and secures substantial compensation for that which is sure to be wholly lost in any other event! How much better to thus save the money which else we sink forever in the war! How much better to do it while we can, lest the war ere long render us pecuniarily unable to do it! How much better for you as seller, and the nation as buyer, to sell out and buy out that without which the war could never have been, than to sink both the thing to be sold and the price of it in cutting one another's throats!

"I do not speak of emancipation *at once*, but of a *decision* at once to emancipate *gradually*. Room in South America for colonization can be obtained cheaply and in abundance, and when numbers shall be large enough to be company and encouragement for one another, the freed people will not be so reluctant to go.

"I am pressed with a difficulty not yet mentioned, one which threatens division among those who, united, are none too strong. An instance of it is known to you. General Hunter is an honest man. He was, and, I hope, still is my friend. I valued him none the less for his agreeing with me in the general wish that all men every where could be freed. He proclaimed all men free within certain states, and I repudiated the proclamation. He expected more good and less harm from the measure than I could believe would follow. Yet, in repudiating it, I gave dissatisfaction if not offense to many whose support the country can not afford to lose. And this is not the end of it. The pressure in this direction is still upon me, and is increasing. By conceding what I now ask, you can relieve me, and much more, can relieve the country in this important point.

"Upon these considerations I have again begged your attention to the Message of March last. Before leaving the Capitol, consider and discuss it among yourselves. You are patriots and statesmen, and as such I pray you consider this proposition, and at the least commend it to the consideration of your states and people. As you would perpetuate popular government for the best people in the world, I beseech you that you do in nowise omit this. Our common country is in great peril, demanding the loftiest views and boldest action to bring a speedy relief. Once relieved, its form of government is saved to the world, its beloved history and cherished memories are vindicated, and its happy future fully assured and rendered inconceivably grand. To you, more than to any others, the privilege is given to assure that happiness and swell that grandeur, and to link your own names therewith forever."

In September, 1861, General Fremont issued a proclamation from St. Louis containing the following paragraph:

"The property, real and personal, of all persons in the State of Missouri, who shall take up arms against the United States, or shall be directly proven to have taken an active part with their enemies in the field, is declared to be confiscated to the public use, *and their slaves, if any they have*, are hereby declared free men," which clause was instantly revoked by Mr. Lincoln.

In like manner General Hunter issued his proclamation from Hilton Head, South Carolina, on the 9th of May, 1862, declaring all persons in the States of Georgia, Florida, and South Carolina, comprising his military department, "*heretofore held as slaves, are forever free.*"

On the 19th of May Mr. Lincoln issued another proclamation, revoking the order of General Hunter, accompanied with a severe rebuke, in which he says,

"On the 6th of March last, by a special Message, I recommended to Congress the adoption of a joint resolution, to be substantially as follows:

"'*Resolved*, That the United States ought to co-operate with any state which may adopt a gradual abolishment of slavery, giving to each state pecuniary aid, to be used by such state in its discretion to compensate for the inconveniences, public and private, produced by such change of system.'"

The resolution, in the language above quoted, was adopted by a large majority in both branches of Congress, and now stands an authentic, definite, and solemn proposal of the nation to the states and people most immediately interested in the subject matter. To the people of those states I now earnestly appeal. I do not argue, I beseech you to make the argument for yourselves. You can not, if you would, be blind to the signs of the times. I beg of you a calm and enlarged consideration of them, ranging, if it may be, far above personal and partisan politics. This proposal makes common cause for a common object, casting no reproaches upon any. It acts not the Pharisee. The changes it contemplates would come gently as the dews of Heaven, not rending or wrecking any thing. Will you not embrace it? So much good has not been done by one effort in all past time as, in the providence of God, it is now your high privilege to do. May the vast future not have to lament that you have neglected it.

Finally, having done every thing in his power for the protection of the property of the Southern slaveholder, though engaged in bloody and flagitious war against himself and the government, his patience and his efforts alike exhausted in appeals to the South to accept a system of remote emancipation based upon fair compensation from the government, he sums up, in a letter to Horace Greeley, in a few energetic sentences, combining extraordinary brevity with masculine strength, the policy by which he will be governed in his ever-to-be-remembered and *revered determination to put down the rebellion, and save the Union and the liberties of his country,* without regard to cost or consequences; and, for one Southern man and Southern slaveholder, I say *God bless him* for his noble and patriotic resolution.

Letter to Horace Greeley.

"Executive Mansion, August 22, 1862.

"Hon. HORACE GREELEY:

"DEAR SIR,—I have just read yours of the 19th instant, addressed to myself through the New York *Tribune.*

"If there be in it any statements or assumptions of facts which I may know to be erroneous, I do not now and here controvert them.

"If there be any inference which I may believe to be falsely drawn, I do not now and here argue against them.

"If there be perceptible in it an impatient and dictatorial tone, I waive it in deference to an old friend whose heart I have always supposed to be right.

"As to the policy 'I seem to be pursuing,' as you say, I have not meant to leave any one in doubt. I would save the Union; I would save it in the shortest way under the Constitution. The sooner the national authority can be restored, the nearer the Union will be the Union as it was.

"If there be those who would not save the Union unless they could at the same time save slavery, I do not agree with them.

"*My paramount object is to save the Union, and not either to save or destroy slavery.*

"If I could save the Union without freeing any slave, I would do it; and if I could save it by freeing all the slaves, I would do it: and if I could save it by freeing some and leaving others alone, I would also do that.

"What I do about slavery or the colored race, I do because I believe it helps to save the Union; and what I forbear, I forbear because I do not believe it would help to save the Union.

"I shall do less whenever I shall believe what I am doing hurts the cause, and shall do more whenever I believe doing more will help the cause.

"I shall try to correct errors when shown to be errors, and I shall adopt new views as fast as they shall appear to be true views.

"I have here stated my purpose according to my views of official duty, and I intend no modification of my oft-expressed personal wish that all men every where could be free.   Yours,   A. LINCOLN."

Such was the course pursued by Mr. Lincoln on the question of slavery, until he found that kindness and clemency then, as it has done since the war, only begat more insolent demands and a more defiant attitude on the part of the political tricksters, knaves. and charlatans who have undertaken to control the public sentiment of the South, and who, I am sorry to add, are in a great degree successful.

Let the impartial, enlightened, unprejudiced people of the South, if there are any such left, ponder over this brief sketch of Mr. Lincoln's desire, so often and so anxiously expressed, to protect the slave property of the South, and then say how much reason there was for the foul calumnies heaped upon him at the time of and after his election by designing and infamous men, who have led them on to destruction, and determine for themselves what reliance is to be placed in the representations of such men in the future.

Will the great body of the people never come to their senses? Will they continue to follow these "bomb-proof" men of war, who talk like heroes, who write like salamanders, until the war comes on, and then do all their fighting on paper, seated on cushioned chairs, by comfortable fires in winter, or sucking ice juleps through glass tubes in summer, and, if called on to go into the trenches to fight the battles of their own creation, effeminately and ingloriously dodge behind the Constitution, and prate about "an invasion of the freedom of the press" to expect an editor to fight, except on his own book and at an advantage. Yet, shame to say, of such are the rulers of the free-born, bearded men of the South.

I will bring this work to a close by giving the following extract from a speech delivered in the Senate of the United States by senator, now President Johnson, as to the responsible parties for this war, at least to a large extent. None of the reconstructed will take issue with Mr. Johnson on this point, I presume.

Respecting the vote of January 16 on the Crittenden propositions in the Senate, Andrew Johnson, senator from Tennessee, in his speech on the expulsion of Jesse D. Bright, senator from Indiana, delivered January 31, 1862, made these remarks. When the six Southern senators refused to vote on Senator Clark's amendment, Senator Johnson said,

"I sat right behind Mr. Benjamin, and I am not sure that my worthy friend (Mr. Latham) was not close by when he refused to vote, and I said to him, Mr. Benjamin, why do you not vote? Why not save this proposition, and see if we can not bring the country to it? He gave me rather an abrupt answer, and said he would control his own action without consulting me or any body else. Said I, Vote, and show yourself an honest man. As soon as the vote was taken, he and others telegraphed South, 'We can not get any compromise.' Here were six Southern men refusing to vote, when the amendment would have been rejected by four majority if they had voted. Who, then, has brought these evils on the country?

"Was it Mr. Clark? He was acting out his own policy; but with the help we had from the other side of the chamber, if all those on this side had been true to the Constitution and faithful to their constituents, and had acted with fidelity to the country, the amendment of the senator from New Hampshire could have been voted down, the defeat of which, the senator from Delaware says, would have saved the country. Whose fault was it? Who is responsible for it? I think it is not only getting the nail through, but clinching it on the other side, and the whole staple commodity is taken out of the speech. Who did it? Southern traitors, as was said in the speech of the senator from California. They did it. They wanted no compromise. They accomplished their object by withholding their votes; and hence the country has been involved in the present difficulty. Let me read another extract from the speech of the senator from California, Mr. Latham:

"'I recollect full well the joy that pervaded the faces of some of those gentlemen at the result, and the sorrow manifested by the venerable senator from Kentucky (Mr. Crittenden). The record shows that Mr. Pugh, from Ohio, despairing of any compromise between the extremes of ultra Republicanism and disunionists, working manifestly for the same end, moved, immediately after the vote was announced, to lay the whole subject on the table. If you will turn to page 433, same volume, you will find, when at a late period Mr. Cameron, from Pennsylvania, moved to reconsider the vote, appeals having been made to sustain those who were struggling to preserve the peace of the country, that vote *was* reconsidered; and when, at last, the Crittenden propositions were submitted on the 2d day of March, these Southern States having nearly all seceded, they were then lost by but one vote.' Here is the vote:

"Yeas—Messrs. Bayard, Bigler, Bright, Crittenden, Douglas, Gwin, Hunter, Johnson, of Tennessee, Kennedy, Lane, Latham, Mason, Nicholson, Polk, Pugh, Rice, Sebastian, Thompson, and Wigfall—19.

"Nays—Messrs. Anthony, Bingham, Chandler, Clark, Dixon, Doolittle, Durkee, Fessenden, Foot, Foster, Grimes, Harlan, King, Morrill, Sumner, Ten Eyck, Trumbull, Wade, Wilkinson, and Wilson—20.

"If these seceded Southern States had remained, there would have passed, by a large vote (as it did without them), an amendment, by a two-third vote, forbidding Congress ever interfering with slavery in the states. The Crittenden proposition would have been indorsed by a majority vote, the subject finally going before the people, who have never yet, after consideration, refused justice for any length of time to any portion of the country.

"I believe more, Mr. President, that these gentlemen were acting in pursuance of a settled and fixed plan to break up and destroy the government.

"When we had it in our power to vote down the amendment of the senator from New Hampshire, and adopt the Crittenden resolutions, certain Southern senators prevented it; and yet, even at a late day of the session, after they had seceded, the Crittenden proposition was only lost by one vote. If rebellion, and bloodshed, and murder have followed, to whose skirts does the responsibility attach? I summed up all these facts myself in a speech during the last session, but I have preferred to read from the speech of the senator from California, he being better authority, and having presented the facts better than I could."

THE END.

Valuable & Interesting Books

Published by HARPER & BROTHERS, New York.

☞ Harper & Brothers *will send their Books by Mail, postage free, to any part of the United States, on receipt of the Price.*

☞ Harper's Catalogue *and new* Trade-List *may be obtained gratuitously on application to the Publishers personally, or by letter, enclosing Five Cents.*

Napoleon's Life of Cæsar. The History of Julius Cæsar. By His Imperial Majesty Napoleon III. A new Elegant Library Edition, with wide Margins, on Superfine Calendered Paper, with Portrait, &c. Vols. I. and II., Cloth, Beveled Edges, price $3 50 each.

Carlyle's Frederick the Great. History of Friedrich II., called Frederick the Great. By Thomas Carlyle. With Portraits and Maps. 6 vols., 12mo. Price per Vol., $2 00.

The Story of the Great March: Diary of General Sherman's Campaign through Georgia and the Carolinas. By Brevet Major George Ward Nichols, Aid-de-Camp to General Sherman. With a Map and Illustrations. 12mo, Cloth, $2 00.

Governor Foote on the War and the Union. War of the Rebellion; or, Scylla and Charybdis. Consisting of Observations upon the Causes, Course, and Consequences of the late Civil War in the United States. By H. S. Foote. 12mo, Cloth, $2 50.

Harper's Pictorial History of the Great Rebellion. By Alfred H. Guernsey and Henry M. Alden. Part I. From the Beginning of the Conspiracy to the Close of the Peninsular Campaign of 1862. With more than Five Hundred Illustrations. 4to, $6 00.

Abbott's Sketches of Prison Life. Sketches of Prison Life, Showing how we lived and were treated at the Libby, Macon, Savannah, Charleston, Columbia, Charlotte, Raleigh, Goldsboro, and Andersonville. By A. O. Abbott, late Lieutenant First New York Dragoons. Illustrated. 12mo, Cloth, $2 00.

Brackett's United States Cavalry. History of the United States Cavalry from the Formation of the Federal Government to the 1st of June, 1863. To which is added a List of all the Cavalry Regiments, with the names of their Commanders, which have been in the United States Service since the breaking out of the Rebellion. By Albert G. Brackett, Major First United States Cavalry, late Chief of Cavalry of the Department of Missouri, Special Inspector of Cavalry, Department of the Cumberland. With Illustrations. 12mo, Cloth, $2 00.

Draper's American Civil Policy. Thoughts on the Future Civil Policy of America. By John William Draper, M.D., LL.D., Author of a "Treatise on Human Physiology," and of a "History of the Intellectual Development of Europe." Crown 8vo, Cloth, $2 50.

Thirty Years of Army Life on the Border. Comprising Descriptions of the Indian Nomads of the Plains; Explorations of New Territory; a Trip across the Rocky Mountains in the Winter; Descriptions of the Habits of different Animals found in the West, and the Methods of Hunting them; with Incidents in the Life of different Frontier Men, &c., &c. By Colonel R. B. Marcy, Author of "The Prairie Traveler." With numerous Illustrations. Post 8vo, Cloth, Beveled, $3 00.

Kinglake's Crimean War. The Invasion of the Crimea: its Origin, and an Account of its Progress down to the Death of Lord Raglan. By ALEX. ANDER WILLIAM KINGLAKE. With Maps and Plans. 2 vols. Vol. I. Maps. 12mo, Cloth, $2 00.

Abbott's Napoleon Bonaparte. The History of Napoleon Bonaparte. By JOHN S. C. ABBOTT. With Maps, Woodcuts, and Portraits on Steel. 2 vols., 8vo, Cloth, $10 00.

Szabad's Modern War. Modern War: its Theory and Practice. Illustrated from Celebrated Campaigns and Battles. With Maps and Diagrams. By EMERIC SZABAD, Captain U.S.A. 12mo, Cloth, $1 50.

Noyes's the Bivouac and Battle-field. The Bivouac and Battle-field; or, Campaign Sketches in Virginia and Maryland. By Captain GEORGE F. NOYES. 12mo, Cloth, $1 50.

Russell's American Diary. My Diary North and South. By WILLIAM HOWARD RUSSELL, LL.D. 8vo, Cloth, $1 00.

General Scott's Infantry Tactics; or, Rules for the Exercise and Manœuvres of the United States Infantry. Published by Authority. 3 vols., 24mo, Cloth, $3 00.

Butterfield's Camp and Outpost Duty. Camp and Outpost Duty for Infantry. With Standing Orders, Extracts from the Revised Regulations for the Army, Rules for Health, Maxims for Soldiers, and Duties of Officers. By Major-Gen. eral DANIEL BUTTERFIELD, U.S.A. 18mo, Cloth, 60 cents. (Suited for the Pocket.)

Alison's Life of Marlborough. Military Life of John, Duke of Marlborough. With Maps. 12mo, Cloth, $1 75.

Story of the Peninsular War. By General CHARLES W. VANE, Marquis of Londonderry, &c. New Edition, revised, with considerable Additions. 12mo, Cloth, $1 50.

Carleton's Buena Vista. The Battle of Buena Vista, with the Operations of the "Army of Occupation" for One Month. By Captain CARLETON. 12mo, Cloth, $1 25.

Alison's History of Europe. First Series.—From the Commencement of the French Revolution, in 1789, to the Restoration of the Bourbons in 1815. [In addition to the Notes on Chapter LXXVI., which correct the errors of the original work concerning the United States, a copious Analytical Index has been appended to this American Edition.] SECOND SERIES.—From the Fall of Napoleon, in 1815, to the Accession of Louis Napoleon, in 1852. A New Series. 8 vols., 8vo, Cloth, $16 00.

Motley's Dutch Republic. The Rise of the Dutch Republic. A History. By JOHN LOTHROP MOTLEY, LL.D., D.C.L. With a Portrait of William of Orange. 3 vols., 8vo, Cloth, $9 00.

Motley's United Netherlands. History of the United Netherlands: from the Death of William the Silent to the Synod of Dort. With a full View of the English-Dutch Struggle against Spain, and of the Origin and Destruction of the Spanish Armada. By JOHN LOTHROP MOTLEY, LL.D., D.C.L., Author of "The Rise of the Dutch Republic." 2 vols., 8vo, Cloth, $6 00.

Hildreth's History of the United States. First Series.—From the First Settlement of the Country to the Adoption of the Federal Constitution. SECOND SERIES.—From the Adoption of the Federal Constitution to the End of the Sixteenth Congress. By RICHARD HILDRETH. 6 vols., 8vo, Cloth, $18 00.

THE RISE OF

THE DUTCH REPUBLIC.

𝔄 𝔥istory.

By JOHN LOTHROP MOTLEY.

New Edition. With a Portrait of WILLIAM OF ORANGE. 3 vols.
8vo, Muslin, $9 00.

We regard this work as the best contribution to modern history that has yet
been made by an American.—*Methodist Quarterly Review.*

The "History of the Dutch Republic" is a great gift to us; but the heart and
earnestness that beat through all its pages are greater, for they give us most
timely inspiration to vindicate the true ideas of our country, and to compose an
able history of our own.—*Christian Examiner* (Boston).

This work bears on its face the evidences of scholarship and research. The
arrangement is clear and effective; the style energetic, lively, and often brilliant.
* * * Mr. Motley's instructive volumes will, we trust, have a circulation commen-
surate with their interest and value.—*Protestant Episcopal Quarterly Review.*

To the illustration of this most interesting period Mr. Motley has brought the
matured powers of a vigorous and brilliant mind, and the abundant fruits of patient and judicious study and deep reflection. The result is, one of the most
important contributions to historical literature that have been made in this country.—*North American Review.*

We would conclude this notice by earnestly recommending our readers to procure for themselves this truly great and admirable work, by the production of
which the author has conferred no less honor upon his country than he has won
praise and fame for himself, and than which, we can assure them, they can find
nothing more attractive or interesting within the compass of modern literature.
—*Evangelical Review.*

It is not often that we have the pleasure of commending to the attention of the
lover of books a work of such extraordinary and unexceptionable excellence as
this one.—*Universalist Quarterly Review.*

There are an elevation and a classic polish in these volumes, and a felicity of
grouping and of portraiture, which invest the subject with the attractions of a
living and stirring episode in the grand historic drama.—*Southern Methodist
Quarterly Review.*

The author writes with a genial glow and love of his subject.—*Presbyterian
Quarterly Review.*

Mr. Motley is a sturdy Republican and a hearty Protestant. His style is lively and picturesque, and his work is an honor and an important accession to our
national literature.—*Church Review.*

Mr. Motley's work is an important one, the result of profound research, sincere
convictions, sound principles, and manly sentiments; and even those who are
most familiar with the history of the period will find in it a fresh and vivid addition to their previous knowledge. · It does honor to American literature, and
would do honor to the literature of any country in the world.—*Edinburgh Review.*

A serious chasm in English historical literature has been (by this book) very
remarkably filled. * * * A history as complete as industry and genius can make
it now lies before us, of the first twenty years of the revolt of the United Prov-
inces. * * * All the essentials of a great writer Mr. Motley eminently possesses.
His mind is broad, his industry unwearied. In power of dramatic description
no modern historian, except, perhaps, Mr. Carlyle, surpasses him, and in analy-
sis of character he is elaborate and distinct.—*Westminster Review.*

It is a work of real historical value, the result of accurate criticism, written in a liberal spirit, and from first to last deeply interesting.—*Athenæum.*

The style is excellent, clear, vivid, eloquent; and the industry with which original sources have been investigated, and through which new light has been shed over perplexed incidents and characters, entitles Mr. Motley to a high rank in the literature of an age peculiarly rich in history.—*North British Review.*

It abounds in new information, and, as a first work, commands a very cordial recognition, not merely of the promise it gives, but of the extent and importance of the labor actually performed on it.—*London Examiner.*

Mr. Motley's "History" is a work of which any country might be proud.— *Press* (London).

Mr. Motley's History will be a standard book of reference in historical literature.—*London Literary Gazette.*

Mr. Motley has searched the whole range of historical documents necessary to the composition of his work.—*London Leader.*

This is really a great work. It belongs to the class of books in which we range our Grotes, Milmans, Merivales, and Macaulays, as the glories of English literature in the department of history. * * * Mr. Motley's gifts as a historical writer are among the highest and rarest.—*Nonconformist* (London).

Mr. Motley's volumes will well repay perusal. * * * For his learning, his liberal tone, and his generous enthusiasm, we heartily commend him, and bid him good speed for the remainer of his interesting and heroic narrative.—*Saturday Review.*

The story is a noble one, and is worthily treated. * * * Mr. Motley has had the patience to unravel, with unfailing perseverance, the thousand intricate plots of the adversaries of the Prince of Orange; but the details and the literal extracts which he has derived from original documents, and transferred to his pages, give a truthful color and a picturesque effect, which are especially charming.— *London Daily News.*

M. Lothrop Motley dans son magnifique tableau de la formation de notre République.—G. GROEN VAN PRINSTERER.

Our accomplished countryman, Mr. J. Lothrop Motley, who, during the last five years, for the better prosecution of his labors, has established his residence in the neighborhood of the scenes of his narrative. No one acquainted with the fine powers of mind possessed by this scholar, and the earnestness with which he has devoted himself to the task, can doubt that he will do full justice to his important but difficult subject.—W. H. PRESCOTT.

The production of such a work as this astonishes, while it gratifies the pride of the American reader.—*N. Y. Observer.*

The "Rise of the Dutch Republic" at once, and by acclamation, takes its place by the "Decline and Fall of the Roman Empire," as a work which, whether for research, substance, or style, will never be superseded.—*N. Y. Albion.*

A work upon which all who read the English language may congratulate themselves.—*New Yorker Handels Zeitung.*

Mr. Motley's place is now (alluding to this book) with Hallam and Lord Mahon, Alison and Macaulay in the Old Country, and with Washington Irving, Prescott, and Bancroft in this.—*N. Y. Times.*

THE authority, in the English tongue, for the history of the period and people to which it refers.—*N. Y. Courier and Enquirer.*

This work at once places the author on the list of American historians which has been so signally illustrated by the names of Irving, Prescott, Bancroft, and Hildreth.—*Boston Times.*

The work is a noble one, and a most desirable acquisition to our historical literature.—*Mobile Advertiser.*

Such a work is an honor to its author, to his country, and to the age in which it was written.—*Ohio Farmer.*

Published by HARPER & BROTHERS,

Franklin Square, New York.

Mr. Motley, the American historian of the United Netherlands—we owe him English homage.—LONDON TIMES.

"As interesting as a romance, and as reliable as a proposition of Euclid."

History of
The United Netherlands.

FROM THE DEATH OF WILLIAM THE SILENT TO THE SYNOD OF DORT. WITH A FULL VIEW OF THE ENGLISH-DUTCH STRUGGLE AGAINST SPAIN, AND OF THE ORIGIN AND DESTRUCTION OF THE SPANISH ARMADA.

By JOHN LOTHROP MOTLEY, LL.D., D.C.L.,

Corresponding Member of the Institute of France, Author of "The Rise of the Dutch Republic."

With Portraits and Map.

2 vols. 8vo, Muslin, $6 00.

Critical Notices.

His living and truthful picture of events.—*Quarterly Review* (London), Jan., 1861.

Fertile as the present age has been in historical works of the highest merit, none of them can be ranked above these volumes in the grand qualities of interest, accuracy, and truth.—*Edinburgh Quarterly Review*, Jan., 1861.

This noble work.—*Westminster Review* (London).

One of the most fascinating as well as important histories of the century.—*Cor. N. Y. Evening Post.*

The careful study of these volumes will infallibly afford a feast both rich and rare.—*Baltimore Republican.*

Already takes a rank among standard works of history.—*London Critic.*

Mr. Motley's prose epic.—*London Spectator.*

Its pages are pregnant with instruction.—*London Literary Gazette.*

We may profit by almost every page of his narrative. All the topics which agitate us now are more or less vividly presented in the History of the United Netherlands.—*New York Times.*

Bears on every page marks of the same vigorous mind that produced "The Rise of the Dutch Republic;" but the new work is riper, mellower, and though equally racy of the soil, softer flavored. The inspiring idea which breathes through Mr. Motley's histories and colors the whole texture of his narrative, is the grandeur of that memorable struggle in the 16th century by which the human mind broke the thraldom of religious intolerance and achieved its independence.—*The World, N. Y.*

The name of Motley now stands in the very front rank of living historians. His *Dutch Republic* took the world by surprise; but the favorable verdict then given is now only the more deliberately confirmed on the publication of the continued story under the title of the *History of the United Netherlands*. All the nerve, and power, and substance of juicy life are there, lending a charm to every page.—*Church Journal, N. Y.*

Motley, indeed, has produced a prose epic, and his fighting scenes are as real, spirited, and life-like as the combats in the Iliad.—*The Press* (Phila.).

His history is as interesting as a romance, and as reliable as a proposition of Euclid. Clio never had a more faithful disciple. We advise every reader whose means will permit to become the owner of these fascinating volumes, assuring him that he will never regret the investment.—*Christian Intelligencer, N. Y.*

Published by HARPER & BROTHERS,
Franklin Square, New York.

☞ HARPER & BROTHERS will send the above Work by Mail, postage pre-paid (for any distance in the United States under 3000 miles), on receipt of the Money.

OF THE

CONSTITUTION.

HISTORY OF THE ORIGIN, FORMATION, AND ADOP-
TION OF THE CONSTITUTION OF THE UNITED
STATES. By GEORGE TICKNOR CURTIS. Complete in 2 vols.
8vo, Muslin, $6 00.

A book so thorough as this in the comprehension of its subject, so impartial
in the summing up of its judgments, so well considered in its method, and so
truthful in its matter, may safely challenge the most exhaustive criticism. The
Constitutional History of our country has not before been made the subject of a
special treatise. We may congratulate ourselves that an author has been found
so capable to do full justice to it; for that the work will take its rank among the
received text-books of our political literature will be questioned by no one who
has given it a careful perusal.—*National Intelligencer.*

We know of no person who is better qualified (now that the late Daniel Webster is no more), to undertake this important history.—*Boston Journal.*

It will take its place among the classics of American literature.—*Boston Courier.*

The author has given years to the preliminary studies, and nothing has escaped him in the patient and conscientious researches to which he has devoted
so ample a portion of time. Indeed, the work has been so thoroughly performed
that it will never need to be done over again; for the sources have been exhausted, and the materials put together with so much judgment and artistic skill that
taste and the sense of completeness are entirely satisfied.—*N. Y. Daily Times.*

A most important and valuable contribution to the historical and political literature of the United States. All publicists and students of public law will be
grateful to Mr. Curtis for the diligence and assiduity with which he has wrought
out the great mine of diplomatic lore in which the foundations of the American
Constitution are laid, and for the light he has thrown on his wide and arduous
subject.—*London Morning Chronicle.*

To trace the history of the formation of the Constitution, and explain the circumstances of the time and country out of which its various provisions grew, is a
task worthy of the highest talent. To have performed that task in a satisfactory manner is an achievement with which an honorable ambition may well be
gratified. We can honestly say that in our opinion Mr. Curtis has fairly won
this distinction.—*N. Y. Courier and Enquirer.*

We have seen no history which surpasses it in the essential qualities of a
standard work destined to hold a permanent place in the impartial judgment of
future generations.—*Boston Traveler.*

Should the second volume sustain the character of the first, we hazard nothing
in claiming for the entire publication the character of a standard work. It will
furnish the only sure guide to the interpretation of the Constitution, by unfolding
historically the wants it was intended to supply, and the evils which it was intended to remedy.—*Boston Daily Advertiser.*

This volume is an important contribution to our constitutional and historical
literature. * * * Every true friend of the Constitution will gladly welcome it.
The author has presented a narrative clear and interesting. It evinces careful
research, skillful handling of material, lucid statement, and a desire to write in
a tone and manner worthy of the great theme.—*Boston Post.*

Published by HARPER & BROTHERS,

Franklin Square, New York.

⁎ HARPER & BROTHERS will send the above Work by Mail, postage paid (for
any distance in the United States under 3000 miles), on receipt of the Money.

Lightning Source UK Ltd.
Milton Keynes UK
UKHW020900050119
334854UK00006B/975/P